Yodel-Ay-Ee-Oooo

"The hills are alive with the ululations of centuries of yodelers, whose echoes persist undyingly. Bart Plantenga shows how yodeling, which may be encoded in our DNA, is humanity's most open secret, linking Swabian and Farsi, mountain and atoll, cowboy and jazzbo. Like an errant cowboy ride, his book is fun, head-spinning, and ontologically profound."
—Luc Sante, author of *Low Life*

"Like yodeling itself, Bart Plantenga's book is wry, humorous, touching, irreverent, vivid, and unforgettable. In addition it is erudite without being stuffy, and is extremely well written. At last, THE book on yodeling!"
—Ranger Doug, Riders in the Sky

"YODEL-AY-EE-OOOO is an amazing, wild, and wonderful book. If there's anything to be known about yodeling since the dawn of recorded time, Bart Plantenga knows it, and he knows how to write about it—wisely, humorously, and stylishly."
—Nolan Porterfield, author of *Jimmie Rodgers: The Life and Times of America's Blue Yodeler*

"Writing a history of the yodel requires qualifications such as a degree in craziness, boundless humour and the capacity to enjoy and understand the entire musical history of the world (or universe, if you include *Mars Attacks*). Happily, Bart Plantenga possesses these in abundance. His enthusiasm for distinctive music and weird facts is capable of curing even the most yodel-phobic reader."
—David Toop, author of *Ocean of Sound*, *Rap Attack*, and *Exotica*

Yodel-Ay-Ee-Oooo

THE SECRET HISTORY OF
YODELING AROUND THE WORLD

BART PLANTENGA

Routledge
New York • London

Published in 2004 by
Routledge
29 West 35th Street
New York, NY 10001

Published in Great Britain by
Routledge
11 New Fetter Lane
London EC4P 4EE

Routledge is an imprint of the Taylor & Francis Group.
Printed in the United States of America on acid-free paper.

10 9 8 7 6 5 4 3 2 1

Library of Congress Cataloging-in-Publication Data

Plantenga, Bart.
  Yodel-ay-ee-oooo : the secret history of yodeling around the world /
Bart Plantenga.
      p. cm.
  Includes bibliographical references and index.
    ISBN 0-415-93989-5 (hardbound : alk. paper) — ISBN 0-415-93990-9
      (pbk. : alk. paper)
      1. Yodel and yodeling. 2. Yodels—History and criticism. I. Title.
  ML1460.P53 2003
  782.4—dc21   2003011578

Contents

THIS BOOK IS DEDICATED TO
MY FATHER, WILLIAM "WILD BILL" PLANTENGA,
WHO DIED DURING THE WRITING OF THIS BOOK,
AND "JUMPIN'" KENNY ROBERTS

Acknowledgments

A book is usually painted as a solo effort. But look at the credits of any solo artist and you see it's pretty much a team effort; there are countless *others* behind the scenes who make a solo performance possible.

This book could have been written without the help of anyone, but then it wouldn't have been any good. So, first, I wish to thank Nina Ascoly, without whom so much could never have happened, including this book and our daughter.

I would also like to thank Richard Carlin, my editor, for being so courageously prescient and for giving me enough room and leash to pursue my subject in my own idiosyncratic manner.

Way beyond the call of duty into the realm of enthusiasm were the efforts of James Leary, Chris Potash, Cyrill Schläpfer, Denis Guiet, Randi Rosenblum, Dagmar Binge, Richard Weize, and Toni Smith.

I would also like to thank Jennifer A. Cutting, Christina Plantenga, Christoph Wagner, Janet McBride, Ethel Delaney, Mason Williams, Wylie Gustafson, Pina Ascoly, John E. Sharp, Black Sifichi, Shane and Graham White, Leonard Gross, Toups Bebey, Ernst Kiehl, "Ole Joe" Ascoly, Paul Bürgi, Jack Collom, Brigitte Bachmann-Geiser, Christine Lauterburg, Werner Pieper, Christian Schmid, Hans Plomp, Laurent Diouf, Annelies Vlasbom, Rob Weisberg, Dave Mandl, Luc Sante, Randy Samuels, Grrrt-Jan, Theo Dorian, Ronald Tol, Pieter Bijker, Ineke Zeldenrust, Jane Harvey, Jim "Jockomo" Harder, Tom Riis, George McWhorter, Jozef van Wissem, Jane Gilday, Eddie Woods, Doug Henkle, Steve Hathaway, Ernst J. Huber, Claudia Carderas, Therese Bruggisser, Claude Aubert, Eva Ludwig, Ron Middlebrook, Nick Tosches, Max Peter Baumann, Daniel and Cornelia

Bertschi-Unternährer, Silvia Delorenzi-Schenkel, Ian S. Horst, Sam Fuqua, Peter Manuel, Werner Deutsch and Franz Födermayr at the Acoustics Research Institute in Vienna, John Lilly, Paul Hazell, Douglas B. Green, Bruce Betler, Sammi Burgwal at the National Pop Instituut in Amsterdam, Bryan Cornell and Jan McKee at the Recorded Sound Division of the Library of Congress, Lukas Heuss at Pro-Helvetia, which funded my research trip to Switzerland, and all the yodelers and vocalists who, in interviews I conducted, provided both illuminating insights and colorful anecdotes, as well as countless others who pointed me in the right direction or led me through obscure back corridors of intelligence and data.

Introduction
Yodel-festo

[Jimmie] Rodger's yodel is the most formidable barrier separating him from unsympathetic modern audiences.

—Nolan Porterfield

If you look at the voiceprint of a yodel, it appears—with a little shove into the imagination—as the graphic representation of how sound imitates topography: The dramatic ascendancy of the voice out of the chest into the head would graphically look a lot like the sketch of a mountain, the kind you find in the Alps. I thought my theory was pretty original until I heard others voice similar notions and then discovered that yodeler-composer A. L. Gassmann had already championed this yodel origin theory fifty years earlier.

Meanwhile, yodeling's essential energy gets a spoofed boost in Tim Burton's 1996 film *Mars Attacks*, which features Martians conquering Earth. An eccentric old lady seems to always be listening to her favorite cowboy singer, yodeler Slim Whitman, on her headphones. When the headphones suddenly slip off her head, the Martians hear Whitman's histrionic yodeling-crooning "When I'm calling you-oo-oo . . . ," which shatters the Martians' helmets and they're "stricken by brain melt," as "yodelologist" Jack Collom describes it, "and they fall into yucky puddles of green and this saves the Earth!" Farfetched? Well, yes *and* no. Manfred Bukofzer, after all, in his 1936 "Magic & Technique in Alpine Music," described the magical powers of various Alpine tones especially when combined with the mystical qualities of certain words.

This magical aspect can be attested to when, in the 17th-century, Swiss mercenaries suffering from *heimweh* (homesickness) deserted, went

Yodeling in Zillertaler: More serious than Bingo!

berserk, or even *died* upon hearing certain Alpine songs. A law was passed that effectively forbade the yodeling of the hysteria-arousing *kuhreihen*.

Hysteria aside, I bet everyone can name a yodel. Most Westerners go right to Julie Andrews in *The Sound of Music* or the Seven Dwarfs. Older readers remember Jimmie Rodgers on the radio, while some may half-remember a yodeling TV commercial—was it for Swiss Miss? Most have some inkling that yodeling is that strange vocal thing you do with your throat; that the Swiss yodel; what it sounds like—someone in the throes of a conniption falsetto; and where yodeling is heard—in the Alps. Picture *biergarten lederhosen*-wearing revelers, beer steins swaying in the fetid, festive air . . .

Despite this exposure, most of us retain vast repositories of misconception regarding yodeling. Myths, half-truths, willful clutching of blatant (if colorful) falsehoods, and worse run rampant. I've experienced the entire spectrum of reactions when I tell people about my yodeling book, although it usually involves a kind of bemused grin or perplexed g(l)aze. If this grin or blank stare is your point of entry into yodeling, I propose we all go in for some basic deprogramming and wipe the slate clean of all cultural prejudice and misunderstanding. Before Paul Gauguin could *really* begin to paint, he insisted on *un*learning everything he had learned about art up until that point. I'm thinking of something similar on a sonic level. Our ears must be cut loose from our cerebral attics full of accumulated cultural clut-

SELECTED DISCO/VIDEOGRAPHY OF INTRODUCTORY YODEL MATERIAL

An introduction into the various worlds of yodeling and related vocal techniques.

- *American Yodeling 1911–1946,* Trikont, 1998.

- *Blue Yodelers 1923–1936,* various artists, Challenge, 2000. From Roy Evans to Emmett Miller. Essential.

- *Cattle Call: Early Cowboy Music and Western Musics, Its Roots Early Golden Era*, various artists, Rounder, 1996.

- *Ethnomusicologie et Représentations de la Musique* organized by Gilbert Rouget, CNRS, 1981. Yodeling around the world.

- *Greatest Yodeling Album of All Time,* various artists, Bear Family, 2000. Priceless.

- *Jodler du Tyrol au Texas*, various artists, ARB, 1995. Interesting linking disc travels back and forth between European and American yodels.

- *Swiss Folk Music, Constantin Brailoiu Collection,* two LPs, VDE, 1986.

- *Voices of Forgotten Worlds*, various artists, Ellipsis Arts, 1993. Good two–CD introductory survey of traditional vocal music of indigenous peoples from around the globe.

- *Voices of the World: An Anthology of Vocal Expression*, various artists, Chant du Monde, 1996. 108 musical samples from fifty-six countries and a broad range of oral traditions.

- *The World's Vocal Arts*, various vocalists, compiled by composer Henry Cowell, Folkways, 1995. Landmark two–CD set includes all styles of world singing, classical and folk.

- *Yodel: Straight from the Heart*, video, producer-director Lori Maass Vidlak, Good Earth Productions, 1996.

DeZurik Sisters ready to tackle a cackle on the cover of *American Yodeling*

ter. Raze the entire housing complex where we've so effectively and staunchly stowed away our petty prejudices and ingeniously dolled-up our biases and misconceptions as personal philosophies.

That no one has ever written a book about yodeling is testimony to the fact that it has seldom been seen as anything but some annoying, kitschy, baroque decorative quirk akin to either white-trash nasal twangs or some pompous Germanic arias punctuated by transvestitic falsettos. And we all know that decorative is surface, and surface is the antithesis of deep, and thus incapable of being taken seriously as something profoundly artistic. In other words, not hip to a hip crowd, not contemporary because it's old fashioned, and not germane because it's mere frivolous veneer. Plus a hint of something that makes people suspicious.

Go to your local bookstore, do an informal survey. Under the signs for any musical style you'll find some books that go some way toward validating it as something of cultural value. Go to a bookstore's music section and you will no doubt find 500 pounds of stock on jazz (*two* books alone on the making of *one* Miles Davis record), 250 on blues or doo-wop. There's certainly a thousand pounds of books on *every* aspect of rock music (no less than twenty books on Bob Dylan alone), including many of questionable, but no doubt profitable, subjects like Boys II Spice Girls on the Block. If Madonna is valid Ph.D. material, and serial killers have their own decks of cards, and the semiotics of backyard barbecuing finds it's way into a few glossy coffee-table books, then why not a book about yodeling—far and wide, deep and shallow, irreverent and respectful, sober and blithe.

Anyone who admits to ever having yodeled, or hollered with the intention of making the yodel's characteristic glottal leap that gives it its uniquely vigorous character, almost always describes his or her early adventures with a repentant apologetic snicker. Yodelers, whether they do it as a hobby, a calling, or as a career-enhancement move, have had to deal with a certain amount of parochial bias and social ostracism. Cowboy singer Wilf Carter recalls his Baptist minister father as being none too pleased by his decision to become a yodeler: "I yodeled upstairs and downstairs, in the parlor and in the apple orchard. Dad couldn't get me to stop though he wore out more than a dozen slippers on the seat of my pants." You can bet your epiglottis that his father would have worn out far fewer slippers had Carter declared his desire to be an Edsel salesman or a junk bond trader.

This contrite attitude toward the affliction called yodeling is impressed upon us at an early age—*very* early! This uneasiness about being involved in something perceived as foolish comes across in some of the negative ways that the yodel has been conveyed to so many of us. All yodelers, it seems, learn to laugh at themselves—before someone else does. And, in an ironic sense, then, this is what gives the yodeler his or her resilience. Under cover of humor and modesty, the yodel can continue to insinuate its presence. This humor at yodeling's expense may actually be somewhat more to its credit than I once thought: Out of self-effacing humor arises a tenacious sense of moxy—perhaps.

Most yodelers admit to rehearsing out of earshot where it won't bother anyone—in the shower, in their automobiles on their way to work, in a studio lined with mattress-thick insulation, or in a spacious piece of nature. Eastside Dave, a yodeler from Central Pennsylvania, practices yodeling "in a dark room so as not to take myself too seriously . . . The kids bust on me . . . when they've had enough yodeling for one day." Patsy Montana, on an old tape, *Learn to Yodel*, suggests that a yodeler "get a ten-acre field and keep all your friends there." Ranger Doug of Riders in the Sky suggests yodeling "in a truck, with the windows rolled up. If you try to do it at home," he warns, "you will alienate friends and family, neighbors, and even pets. Maybe local wildlife . . ."

But the notion that you need to be more apologetic, polite, or diplomatic about your yodeling lessons compared to, say, drum, tuba, or girl-group harmonizing is a cultural prejudice that has been jocularly accepted by one and all. Or, in a Darwinian sense, has it been systematically absorbed into the yodelers' very being to assure survival of their self-esteem? The yodeler offers self-reflexive humor to derail attempts by the audience to frame yodeling in some kind of tongue-in-cheek, denigrating context. You know like, wink-wink, "S/He's a yodeler," raised eyebrows, look of rehearsed horrified befuddlement—as if yodeling is inherently cursed with a high kitsch annoyance factor or is something akin to bestiality. This manifestation of zeitgeist intolerance or call it hip-factor snobbery remains a mystery to me because yodeling is no "worse" than any other type of singing or vocalizing. And so, yodelers begin "life" down a rung or octave on the evolutionary stairway to heaven.

Ultimately, yodeling is something that penetrates your being, gets a hold of all the sinew, cartilage, and connective tissue that links the physical to the metaphysical. Yodeling forces performer, audience, and anyone within earshot to take notice. The yodel will not leave you alone . . . it makes itself heard. But then again, that's not so weird because metal guitars, Caribbean percussion ensembles, screeching laptop electronica, post-punk quartets, avant-noise duos, or the Three Tenors certainly wouldn't let you slip by without making sure you noticed *them*.

And yet—and I'll stake my epiglottis on this—there is no musical genre that has not turned to the yodel now and again. Of course, there's the obvious cowboy and Swiss variety. But did you know that yodeling can be found in rap/hiphop (De La Soul, the Fugees), funk (Parliament), prog rock (Focus), American folk (Pete Seeger), jazz (Leon Thomas), classical (Rossini), avant garde (Shelley Hirsch), trip-hop (We), hick-hop (Kid Rock), dub (Dub Syndicate), alt.rock (Jad Fair), dancehall reggae (Barrington Levy), pop (Vogues), vocal pop (Bing Crosby and the Andrews Sisters), Hawaiian (Ray Kane), political (Fugs), blues (Tampa Red), Cajun (Guidry Brothers), world (Zap Mama), electronica (Roberto Musci and Giovanni Venosta), Australian country (Slim Dusty), African (Francis Bebey), Bollywood (Kishore Kumar), gospel (Buzz Goertzen), children's (Cathy Fink), lullabies (Lefty Frizell), novelty (Dr. Hook), rockabilly (Jerry Lee Lewis), soundtrack (*Raising Arizona*) . . .

In 1996, as a deejay at freeform radio station WFMU (NY/NJ), I decided to tackle this mysterious vocal technique known as yodeling: why it's so haunting and yet so easily written off. I also wanted to know how a Swiss thing became a hillbilly thing. And why I was suddenly finding so many samples of yodeling blended into the ambient, electronic, and post-dub material I was spinning. For my radio special, I'd collected all the usual suspects—Jimmie Rodgers and the like—over a period of five years. I also discovered newer, post-modern *appropriations* of the yodel, mega-sampled yodels swirling around inside atmospheric musics, which welded electronics to the nervous system. Plus all the "new" and tongue-in-cheek yodeling reappreciations, and avant-scat-yodelers like Leon Thomas and Shelley Hirsch, who stretch the yodel's possibilities around new concepts. Midway into the program, things began to click as to why I *liked* yodeling. Like dub music, it involves echo: echo as a rearrangement of our psycho-acoustical apparatus, an entry point into another realm, a way for the modern recording studio to tap into the organic, human voice reverberating through valleys.

Ultimately, I hope this sprawling textual pastiche represents some hodgepodge orchestral maneuver, which will force different types of cultural data to perform together and play a tune, until they create some collective harmony allowing a greater theme to emerge.

Quasi–Mea Culpa #1: The book's title. I would've preferred *Will There Be Yodeling in Heaven?* because of its allusions to loftier climes, a Bob Wills's song, and popular notions of heaven as a place to hear good music. Or *Yodel in Hi-Fi*, as cribbed from an obscure LP, because I liked how it tunes into yodeling as something (like easy listening, lounge, and exotica) about to be rescued from the obscurity of misunderstood history. But I've learned to live with and love this title.

Quasi–Mea Culpa #2: If I come off as some kind of ham-fisted, bad-hair Gandhi who considers it his destiny to represent yodelers as music's untouchables or something, then so be it. I make only vague passes at apologizing for the fact that I'm a dogged generalist who has always known a vague morsel or two about many subjects. In other words, I'm no mechanic although I've fixed a car or two; I'm no poet although I've written a handful of good poems . . .

Least of all, I'm *not*—nor have I ever been—an academic, ethnomusicologist, yodeler, aficionado, cultural preservationist, or any stripe of yodeling fanatic. I'm not even a musician or singer (although my young daughter—bless her three-year-old ears!—might believe differently). I'm a novelist and radio DJ who facilitates various creative audio moments. These instants offer thematic and happenstance (aleatric) situations that might just jostle a few cultural prejudices out of their well-worn grooves and into an instant of pleasant surprise—"I didn't know *he* yodeled"—or even better, a state of Zen-like satori. Populists let everybody in the door, spoiling the party. Purists let nobody in the door, also spoiling the party. I want to be a discerning and yet nice doorman and let in just the right mix to create a proper lively good time.

I'm interested in showing that the dissemination of the yodel is far wider than earlier believed. And that the yodel's effect on popular culture and art culture has been deeper than thus far noted. I'm also interested in finding new paths to how the yodel got from here to there, from Old World(s) to New. I've tried to be inclusive by snooping around in areas not usually considered prime yodeling territory. I've also interviewed lesser-known and younger yodelers to illustrate that the yodel is *not* dying, *not* square, *not* without its spiritual depths, and that it is much more beautiful than people ever imagined.

1

A Jodl Is a Jodel Is a Yodel?

melodic calls, unexpected wordless birds of sound . . .
—Harold Courlander, *Negro Folk Music USA*

We call it yodeling because there is no other word for it.
—Nick Tosches, *Where Dead Voices Gather*

In the 1930s, the McKinney Sisters inquired singingly "Will there be any yodeling in heaven?" Because if there *is* yodeling in heaven, then heaven'll be a rollicking joint and all yodelers can rest assured they'll be at home there. And if all goes well, maybe Bob Wills can front the houseband, God being the manager and all—as long as they packed them in. The question is vaguely presumptuous and rhetorical, bearing a hint of ultimatum: If there's *still* no yodeling in heaven there'd better be—and *soon* . . .

But yodeling, especially the Tyrolean *lederhosen* variety with its frenetic variations in tone and pitch, its esophageal gymnastics, lies within cheap earshot of that potentially annoying Oktoberfest *biergarten* oompah music—jolly, mindless escapism—hoist another stein, stretch another octave. Conviviality found in brew-strained forays into falsetto. As Mark Twain sarcastically noted in *A Tramp Abroad*, "during the remainder of the day [we] hired the rest of the jodlers, at a franc apiece not to jodl anymore. There is somewhat too much of this jodling in the Alps." And yet yodeling, even its crassest Vegas warbles, can aspire to instants of "higher" purpose, because to entertain is a noble distraction from the suffering that seeps into our mundane existences—sometimes the lightest of lyrics might carry the heaviest loads of import.

But maybe yodel heaven will be something closer to a solemn holy place. Because, indeed, there's another side to yodeling (which begins, cartographically and conveniently enough, right in the Swiss Alps), a soulful, incantatory side—steeped in the ancient cowherds' prayer calls to appease valley gods. It's entangled in a vast psychogeographic conflation of yodel, geography, and spirituality whereby one's ability to extract its integral strains are difficult at best.

But aren't yodels just silly ululations that dart furiously back and forth somewhere between regular human voice and falsetto—what Christoph Wagner calls "low-down high-up vocal trickery." Isn't this also the place where chord intervals are created allowing the yodeler to find harmony with him- or herself? Picture yodels bouncing off hillsides (or *any* reflective surface that offers echo effects) until there's any number of versions of your own voice harmonizing in midair. *Voilà*, witness your first instant of "recorded" sound—mountain valley as recording studio; air and memory being replaced by magnetic recording tape only deep into the 20th century.

IN THE BEGINNING THERE WAS THE WORD

Where does the word "yodel" come from? Some *Hauspartiers* claim that *jodel* derives from the Latin word *jubilare*—to shout with joy. If anything, German yodeling fits that description—within a song structure context. Author-singer Ed Sanders has pointed out that "music comes partly out of joy . . . but also out of keening [a wailing lament for the dead], a yodel has a keening quality to it. And so in the Oi-joy spectrum it . . . lurks there with oi but it can be quite exultant and beautiful in the Bavarian and Swiss [context]."

Some have taken great offense with this Latin-roots hypothesis (or rehash of several authoritative-seeming sources). Whoever first merged *jubilare* with *jodel* may have been under the influence of religious studies where, indeed, the meaning of jubilation is defined as an "expression of joy," which is not all that distant from the common definition of yodel as "to shout with joy" or a "type of wordless singing, joyous in nature . . . ," in the words of *Encyclopedia Britannica*. So, the syncretic confusion is understandable. Max Pieter Baumann, writing in the *New Grove Dictionary of Music and Musicians*, notes that the modern German verb *jodeln*, meaning "to yodel," derives from the Middle High German *jôlen* as first seen in George Rhaw's *Bicinia Gallica* meaning "to call" or "to sing."

Denis Guiet, a Canadian yodeler living in Switzerland, in a May 2002 email, notes:

> any awake yodeler will explain the origins of the word, based quite simply on the sounds "vokalisiert" during its practice. Nothing more, nothing less.

Swiss Yodel Choir from St. Gallen. Photo by G. Poschung. Permission by Schweiz Tourismus.

Much the same way that the English word "gurgle" descended from the sound it makes in a person's throat. The word "yodel" shows its origins most clearly in Berner-Deutsch where the word yodel is pronounced very close to "yo-du," the two most common vocalized sounds used in . . . yodeling.

Johlen / jola derives from the interjection *jo,* according to Hans of the Brothers Grimm (1877). It gained a "d" because it was easier to bridge the "jo" and "len/la" with a "d," which Baumann describes as the "vocal-physiological reasons." Each region in Switzerland, for instance, has its own audio/linguistic needs, pronunciations, and psycho-geographical-acoustical profile. There are many spellings that try to represent the many subtle differences in pronunciation. And so from the (presumably) original *jo* in Switzerland we get *joha, jôlen, jodln, jödele;* while from the related *juchui* sound emerged *juchzen, jutzen, yutzen, juuzä, juizä.* Meanwhile, Austrian-German dialects produced *luedeln, dudeln, jorlen, jaudeln, hegitzen;* while from the German and Appenzell *johla* emerged: *jola, zorren, zuaren, ruggussen,* and *länderen.* The *bibihendi* is a yodel that sounds like a hen.

A YODEL IS A JODEL IS A JÜÜTZ?

So, what exactly *is* a yodel? Greeting? Warning? Joyous outburst? Pious ululation? Twain's "Tyrolese warbling"? Flashy pop chorus? Esophageal calisthenics? A cowherd's hootchie-cootchie come-on to the most udder-endowed among his herd? Or is a yodel just some irritating "variation upon the tones of a jackass," as Sir Walter Scott in 1830 opined?

At least three dictionaries offer "warble" as a synonym. The *Wordsmyth* online dictionary offers "quaver." One dictionary claims yodels are mostly performed by men, another insists they're sung by both men and women. Defining a yodel is relatively easy: "Yodeling is understood as singing without text (yodel syllables), with continuous changes from chest to head voice and with frequent wide intervals." It is especially easy if we accept the idea of the human body as musical instrument and as the prototype and shapely precursor for all future instruments. (Doesn't the cello look like a voluptuous woman—i.e., see Man Ray's photo "Violon d'Ingres 1924" with the cello's soundholes on the naked back of Kiki de Montparnasse.) The body also houses a built-in sound system. The difficult part comes later when we move beyond the raw basics and encounter the countless interpreters, each wanting to dress the yodel with his or her own defining characteristics.

The yodel, simply put, is most distinguishable from other types of vocalizations by its characteristic emphasis on the noise, that jolt of air, that occurs as the voice passes from bass or low chest voice to high head voice or falsetto—and vice versa. Yodeling is the decorative wordless passage that is forced across that chasm of spasming muscle and cartilage. The fact that the epiglottal stop (speed bump?) is emphasized gives it its distinct voiceprint. Look at an oscilloscopic representation of a yodeler yodeling and an opera singer singing and you'll notice the difference. Other vocals may tinker with falsetto, trill, and vibrato, but it's that abrupt, almost rude, leap across the cavern of pitch that makes the yodel *yodel*. Simply put: no glottal jolt, no yodel. Everything else is secondary.

Baumann adds that a yodel is "singing without text or words," with emphasis on the "play of timbres and harmonics . . . in the succession of individual, nonsensical vocal-consonant connections." The leaps of pitch are often dramatic and can sometimes (contradictorily?) be characterized by a legato, or a smoothing over, of any interruption between the various notes. Or, more traditionally, the pitch burst is highlighted by the obvious and emblematic glottal leap over the sonic crevice between two notes. A genuine yodel, or *juutz* (various spellings), is wordless and not really "music" per se but an acoustical signal, mostly associated with cowherds communicating with one another and their herds. Ed Sanders calls it "a kind of homemade Morse code for people in the mountains."

A good yodeler effortlessly climbs three octaves between low chest voice and high head voice. Yodelers, according to Baumann, do not exhale "in spurts . . . but rather gradually . . . through abdominal (or diaphragm) breathing, whereby the yodeled tone uses a deeply positioned larynx ('yawning position') and expanded resonance space."

Picture two craftspeople in their respective studios: The yodeler is busy sharpening and accenting that transitional cleft between the two voices like some perverse post-teen trying to preserve the painful audio evidence of that boy-becomes-man rite of passage, the proverbial cracking voice. Meanwhile, the trained professional singer is busy sanding down the voice, polishing *away* that rough seam to the point of imperceptibility. Call it the *portamento* or, more onomatopoeically, *glissando*, which Western singers—regardless of their chosen genre—are taught. So, it's the *Glottals* versus the *Glissandos*. The yodel's glottal leap is emphasized like a valley emphasizes the characteristics that make a mountain a mountain.

This break is found all over the world. According to Oren Brown, a pioneer in the field of voice therapy, "you can hear it in African tribal music, a cowboy 'yip,' or in one person calling another in Tibet." The falsetto is present in most human voices but, for the most part, the glottal pop or break is de-emphasized to the point of obliteration. Western singers consider it a problem like a pothole to a city's road department—something to fill in. Cowgal yodeler Liz Masterson observes: "One thing that makes good yodeling is to have the power in the high register and not have your lower note be a lot more powerful than your high note, where you kind of thin out. . . . It takes a long time just to practice those intervals to where you can train yourself to land right on the button."

This break between chest and head voice constitutes "the release of one set of muscles and the activation of another," according to Brown. The chest voice demands the use of the thyroarytenoid muscles, which are vocal folds commonly employed during conversation. When someone enters the falsetto head voice, he or she is in effect relaxing the thyroatenoids and "a stretch is placed on them by the cricothyroid muscles." This stretch has the effect of thinning and elongating the vocal folds. The desired seamlessness (often described as "silky" or "satiny") is produced by learning how to activate two sets of muscles simultaneously with the larynx resting naturally (unforced) in a low position.

EPIGLOTTIS

> The glottis, orifice of the organic depths, harasses the tongue, until it cries for mercy, full of meanings . . .
>
> —Vincent Barras

The epiglottis is the seat of government in the world of yodeling; it's where the law of yodeling is written. As part of the throat, the epiglottis is a thin,

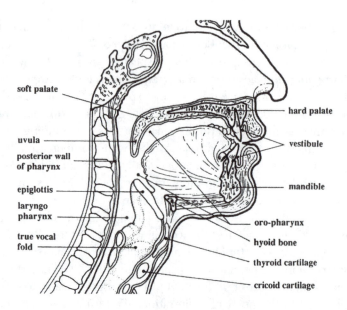

The epiglottis: Anatomical seat of yodeling activity. Illustration from *The Functional Unity of the Singing Voice*. Doscher, Barbara. "Outline of the Resonators and Related Organs." *The Functional Unity of the Singing Voice*, Second Edition, fig. 22. Lanham: Scarecrow Press.

leaf-shaped, flexible flap of cartilage attached to the wall of the pharynx behind the root of the tongue and in front of the entrance to the larynx or voice box. The epiglottis at rest is in the upright position. This allows the breath to pass through the larynx and into the lungs. During swallowing it folds back to cover the entrance to the larynx or glottis, preventing food and drink from entering the windpipe.

The throat consists of an air passage (trachea) and a food passage (esophagus). If both passages are open simultaneously, air could enter the stomach via the esophagus and food could enter the lungs; both are undesirable situations. The epiglottis acts like a cut-off valve to prevent this. At the end of each swallow, the epiglottis returns to its upright position, allowing air to enter the windpipe again. Phonation is the process of generating sound by the air passing through the epiglottis. Sound is not made by vibrating vocal cords but by the recurrent stop-and-go of air flow through the glottis. Loudness of a note comes from the air pressure as air is forced through the glottis. Pitch is determined by thickness of the vocal cords. As the vibrating cords thin, the voice goes higher until reaching the head voice where the amplitude of the vibrations flattens.

The *glottal stop* entails a temporary hesitation of sound with the epiglottis moving up and down to cause that click or audio glitch called a *plosive con-*

sonant. That click is the cultivated instant that "creates" the yodel. It's not a smooth purr or hum; it's dramatic and explosive. As you will notice, "explosive" has as its root "plosive," which comes from the Latin *"plodere"* or "plode" meaning "to clap." The plosive consonant is formed by the complete closure of part of the vocal cords by the epiglottis. This causes the flow of air to stop. This is followed by a dramatic release of air, an explosion, resulting in our pop.

Believe it or not, the conversion of the physiological (throat sound) into the topographical (mountain valley sound) is magical but also poetic, or etymological; after all, the word *gorge* in French means both "throat" and "gorge."

Yodel Soundings

the singular cry that Swiss peasants and some mountaineers employ . . .
Though commonly uttered on quite cheerful occasions, it might be the passionate scream of some wretched animal terrified by the solitude of a desolate place and trying to empty into one impetuous lamentation all its burden of loneliness and desire.

—C. E. Montague

What's a yodel sound like? It all depends on whom you ask. As early as A.D. 397, in *Act of Martyrs*, Roman Emperor Julian complained of the northern mountain people's wild shrieking songs; definitely *not* a yodel fan. Some compare the vocals to those of Tibetan monks. Or somebody taking a cold shower. There's always Sir Walter Scott's earlier "jackass" comment or Mark Twain "melodious 'Lul . . . l . . . l . . . lul-lul-*La*hee-oo!" or a "sort of quaint commingling of baritone and falsetto which . . . we call 'Tyrolese warbling.'" Texas Drifter Goebel Reeves could make it sound like a caffeine-drenched warbler, mixing birdcalls with speed yodeling, insisting that "yuh gotta hum before you can do it." The Ashanti claim the *kokokyinaka* bird as the source of their music with its "kro kro kro kro ko kyini kyini . . . " call. Papua New Guinea's yodelers weave bird and animal voices into their songs as part of religious ceremonies. The Brazilian Bororo Indians don't even distinguish humans from animals and, dressed in parrot costumes, sing "We are parrots."

Others claim yodeling mimics a cow's mooing, or an alphorn, or bagpipes. Tex Morton conflates train whistles and yodeling to produce a very lonesome sound. Christoph Wagner notes that the Excelsior Quartette in a Georgia tent show in 1890 made the yodel sound like a steam engine. Pharoah Sanders described Leon Thomas's yodeling as "the moaning of spirits known and unknown." Liz Masterson thinks it's "where ambulances got their ideas. . . ." Or maybe a bird's plaintive song, the whippoorwill

(Sourdough Slim), or the howling wind. The Three Tobacco Tags make it sound like a "Yodeling Mule," while Kerry Christensen and the DeZurik Sisters both do chicken yodels. Corinna Cordwell, meanwhile, strives to communicate with a mockingbird with her yodeling.

Blues yodelers may be incorporating the vocables of field holler remnants of forgotten mother tongues. Blues artists dealt with everyday experience, so that a guitarist might imitate the sound of a train on a track and a singer might wail like a cat in heat. In the words of Max Haymes, "one of the first sounds to inspire a blues singer was a natural one—the sounds of a bird singing. A story handed down by ex-slaves claims that one evening, a slave was feeling low in spirit and heard a plaintive cry of a night bird. The sound inspired the slave to get a piece of cane from a canebrake and cut some holes in it. He then commenced to play a 'blues' on his whistle."

The Alpine yodeler often sings about the cuckoo, a bird more famous in its laminated wooden form than in its living feathered form. The cuckoo, in any case, is the subject of many yodel songs including Franzl Lang's "Kuckucksjodler," Sepp Mollinger's "Der Kuckuck," Philippe Zani's "Der Kuckucksjodler" "Kuckucklied," and Alfons Zitz's "Kuckucksjodler." It's part of the standard repertoire of professional Alpine yodelers, is found on many records, and is inspired by the cuckoo's call, which some ("cuckoo?") musicologists claim is the ultimate source of the yodel. Hmmm! England's "Whistling Yodeler," Ronnie Ronalde, often combined his expert birdcalls with yodeling. Some ethnomusicologists suggest that the loon, with its characteristic territorial announcement "yodel," serves as a model for some popular American yodels. The Bavarian name for *kulning*, or Scandinavian yodel-like calling, is *gallen*, or the onomatopoeic name for the call of the rooster, or *gallna*, the call of the cuckoo. The Spanish yodel is called *papagayo*, with *papagayo* meaning "parrot."

If you're ever out in the American Far West, under moonlight, in Joshua Tree, California, and you hear the lugubrious "querulous, high-tenor yammering yodel of a coyote," you will hear some of the yodel's complexity in this most psychologically complex howl. The coyote is interesting because it's so interwoven into the cowboy myth—wily, and duly anthropomorphized, the coyote is called the singing dog because he's got more song in his lean body than his three nearest relatives, the dog, fox, and wolf. Coyotes cry to warn off invaders but also to acknowledge friends and family. They howl when they've caught their prey and when they sense a change in the weather. Each emotion and situation changes the nuance and sound of their cries.

The yodel as a distinctive amplified vocalization basically consists of warbled melodies of between two to six sections that use sudden alterations of vocal register from a low-pitched chest voice to high falsetto tones sung

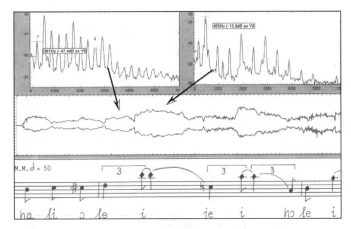

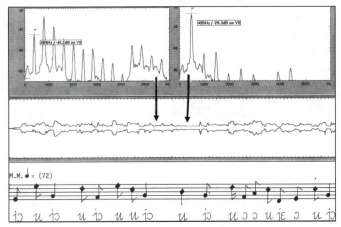

Visualizing the yodel: Spectrograms of two typical yodels—A Jimmie Rodger's Blue Yodel and a Swiss yodel from Muotathal—show the basic composition of their distinct overtones from falsetto (stronger) to chest voice (weaker) in a period of 3 to 5 seconds.

on vowel sounds: AH, OH, OO for chest notes, AY EE for the falsetto. Erich M. von Hornbostel thought the *naturjodel* used consonants as a "lever" to make the leap from low to high and that the singing on syllables gives yodeling its unique aural penetrating ability that led Goethe to groan and cover his ears. Abrupt changes in pitch gives yodeling its ability to project over great distances. Voice therapist Richard Luchsinger (1949) was the first to investigate the relationship between sound and phonetics with regard to the yodel. He noted that the yodel's unique employment of vowels and consonants gives it its high frequency and sonic intensity. The use of vowels allows for a better and easier voice formation that reinforces its strength and power. Alpine yodeling employs Western major scales. Each nonlexical syllable ends with a distinct glottal break at the moment of transition between these two registers, giving yodels their particular character: the dramatic cleave that separates low from high.

... ha-la-i-di.

Harz Mountains, 1912

... hul-la hu-hu.

Lüneburger Heide, north-western Germany, 1916

... ho-li-ja-hu-di.

Thüringer Wald, cowherder's call

... a-la-la - u,

Erzgebirge, Czech-German border, herder's call

Ha-la-re-i-ti ...

Tyrolean yodel

Jo-lo-lo-lo ho-u-hu.

Swiss yodel

Jä-u-hu.

Folksong of Carpathian Mountain lumberjacks in the Ukraine, 1934

jo-u-di, jo-i-di,

Odenwald, western Germany

hei-du-li, e-i-ri,

Steiermark, Austria, woods-man song, 1893

ä-ä-de-lu ...

Norwegian folksong

e-i-ä ja-i-e-i-e-i

Pygmy yodel of southeastern Cameroon

Notated excerpts of various yodel-related motifs. By permission of Ernst Kiehl, "Comparative Research in Yodeling," in *Auf den Spuren der musikalischen Volkskultur in Harz*, Munich: Bezirk Oberbayern, 2002, 245.

Alpine *jodlers* often contain phrase repetitions like AA-BB or as a two-part yodel AB-AB. Other melodic phrase repetitions like AABA or BAA are also common. Alpine versions can go from solo to five-voice yodels.

Official, traditional Swiss yodeling does not make use of the "eee" (as in yodel-ay-EEE-ooo):

The Swiss use the 'oo' (as in Yahoo!) and 'u' (as in the French 'rue de Lulu') sounds instead, especially over the past 50 years, and almost exclusively the 'L' sound as opposed to 'D' vocalizations. The basic rule is fairly straightforward and [according to composer Ruedi Renggli] goes like this: In chest voice, 'a, o, la, lo, ya, yo,' and in head voice, 'oo, u, loo, lu,' and sometimes a 'du' as a help-vocalization, more or less a bridge to handle a difficult rhythmic passage.

This might involve the more esoteric and ancestral links between sound and transcendence.

The "O" sound is round, bellowing, womblike, defining spaces, drawing the contours of our qualms. Some consider it to be the most resonant vowel, the original utterance, the "o" of "OM," the sound that escorts us beyond meaning, beyond the concrete, into the profound ineffable.

Or, as Cathy Fink explains in her charming "Yodeling Lesson," "F for low, E for high, two vowel sounds with a break and that's where the yodel takes place. . . . AY EE AY EE." Fink is not far off from the refrain of "A Young Hunter Went A-Hunting," an 18th-century Swiss song sung in Pennsylvania: "Hei lie, Hei loo." Or the 16th-century German folk song "Dadd Driwe" brought to North America by 18th-century immigrants which contained the refrain: "ei die ei, ei di O." It takes only a small leap of imagination to hear the Seven Dwarfs yodeling "Ho-la-la-ee-ay, Ho-la-la-ee-ay." Like jazz, however, yodels are difficult to describe and certainly much easier to listen to.

THE HUMAN STOOD UP TO BE "HERD"

Yodeling goes back to some hazy early stone age (3000 to 1300 B.C.). It may very well predate language and go hand-in-herd with the development of domesticated animals. *Kuhreihen* were notated as early as 1545, with similar calls arising in similar times in other pastoral cultures from northern Sweden to the Caucasus, down into Romania. The Appenzell yodel has been famous since the 1600s.

Estimates of when man broke away from the rest of the apes vary from 20 to 5 million years ago. Humans stood up erect, became prehensile, and then began using sticks and stones as tools. As Louis Berman notes: "As man's manipulative dexterity grew he developed a larynx and vocal organs that aided in the production of speech. An explanation of why apes can't talk is that they haven't used their hands in the variety of ways humans do, and this could be one of the reasons their brain capacity does not match ours." With manual dexterity came confidence and curiosity and the utilization of the vocal cords for prelingual communiqués. Socially agreed-upon vocalizations laid the foundation of language.

Meanwhile, humans began domesticating animals. This "organized control and selective breeding of prey" began more than 10,000 years ago. Somewhere in that vague broad timespan, humans began using sounds more systematically, functioning as consensual logic and control signals—sounds in the service of human endeavor. Early herding efforts required a communication system that allowed the herder to communicate with his or her herd and other herders over greater distances. Need led to function, and later, to aesthetic applications. Folklorist Alan Lomax noted: "Mankind has used voices to work animals for thousands of years. The singing milk-

THE YODEL'S SPELL

Jo lo lo lo ho–u u–lü ho–u u–lü ho–ju hu–lü ju!

Ur-Ruf: Yodel roots.

"di jo del jo—di jo le - dle i hi—di jo - del ihi"
- "Yodeling Cowboy"

"Coma-cow-cow, coma-cow-cow, yicky-yicky-yea"
- "When I Was a Cowboy," Leadbelly

"Whoop-i-e-e-ee"
- "Cowboy Boasting Chant"

"eeoho—eeoho—weeioho–i"
- "Negro" laborers in the cotton fields

"Oahoiohieu"
- "Negro" boat hand song

"Yodel Lay Ee Tee O / Odel Lo OO Tee AY / Lull Lo OO EE / O Delo OO EE"
- "The Girl I Left Behind"

"Lo OO DEE, Lo OO DEE / Lo OO DEE O Lo Odel OO DEE O Lo OO"
- "Home on the Range"

"ha ha u— iu— u— mai"
- Romanian *hora lunga*

"di–jo de li di jo di jo le–dl e ihi———di jo–dl e i hi–di jo dl e i—"
- "A Drunkard's Child"

"Yo dee oh dee oh"
- "Britches," Elvis Presley

"tri–hol– ri–ti–jo, di–ri–ja tralalala dijo"
- "Zwischen Berg und Tal" (Between Mountain and Valley)

"Whoopie ti yi yo, git along . . . Hoo Hoo-Hoo-Hoo, He-oo-He-oo-oo-He-oo-oo-
oo-oo, Hoo—Hoo-Hoo-Hoo"
- "Git Along Little Dogies"

"Ka la eh (ah) ee yn na le le oh–ho ho"
- "Makala," BaAka Pygmies

"à— ú à— ú à— ú / gèla ú gèla ú gèla / ke ke ke / ke ke ke / ú— ú— ú— / à
ú— ú— ú— / gè-la gè-la gè-la / í í í / pú-lu pú-lu / pé-ge pé-ge pé-ge"
- The Huli from Papua New Guinea

continued on the next page

The Yodel's Spell, continued

"Ho-la-la-ee-ay / Ho-la-la-ee-ay / Ho-la-la-ee-ay-ee-ay-ee-lee-ay"
- "The Dwarf's Yodel Song," The Seven Dwarfs

"Coma ti yi youpy, youpy yea, youpy yea / Coma ti yi youpy, youpy, youpy yea"
- "The Old Chisholm Trail," perhaps the oldest cowboy song

"O de yo de lodi O de lo di"
- "The Yodel Blues," sung by Kenny Delmar and Mary Hatcher

"Yada yada yada voo doo papa / Yodely doo / Da voody doo doo doo . . . "
- "Jellyman Kelly," James and Sally Taylor

"Yodel-a-ee-he-he / He-he-he-he-he-he"
- "Mule Skinner Blues," sung by Dolly Parton

"Du o la la u du o la la he di o la la hu du o la la u"
- "Cow Song," as sung by the Swiss Amish of Indiana

"Tra- la-la la-la la- la- la-la hål- di å- i- ri du- i ri- di- hå."
- "O Du Schiane, Süasse Nachtigall" (Oh, You Beautiful Nightingale), Tyrolean yodel

"lu—lo lu- lo lu—lo lu—lo lo. Lu—lu- lu—lo."
- Norwegian *kulokk*, a melody with a yodel-like refrain, sung by Hanne Kjersti Buen

"ah de lee de lo de lay ee prrr del ee doo de lee doo de del ee dee"
- "The Yodeling Bagman," Tex Morton

"Coo-ee-oo-ee oo (de) lay ee o oo dee"
- "The Australian Bushman's Yodel," Buddy Williams

"Yippy-I-o-ki-ay, Yippy-I-o-ki-ay . . ."
- "I'm an Old Cowhand"

"Ho-li-o-li-o o ho-li-eh, ho-li-o-li-o-li-eh . . ."
- "Du Bist die Rose vom Wörthersee"

"Oh-le, oh-le, oh-le, oh-le-lay / Oh-le, oh-le, oh-le-lay . . ."
- "Rose of the Mountain," Rosemary Clooney, English version of "Du Bist . . . "

"Woh hoo—oo, woh hoo! / Woh hoo—oo, woh hoo! / Yeh-ee-ee, yeh-hee!"
- "Negro" field holler from the early 1900s

"di ri-o-u ri-o-di ri-o-u di-e / ha de-i o-u ri-o u di-e-di ri-o-di-ri"
- "Der Küahsuacher," old Austrian herder's call from Steiermark, Austria

Man, mountain, and yodel in Muotathal.
Photo by Cyrill Schläpfer.

maids of the Hebrides, the shepherd piping to his flock, the Kansas dairy farmer piping Muzak into his milking barn."

The herder's close proximity led to his "relating" to his herd, anthropomorphizing or even hallucinating sheep as Rubensesque women. Many peoples—the Saami and Pygmies, for instance—have had an intimate organic and ritualistic relationship with their habitat's flora and fauna. The Swiss gave personal names to their cows, and this name calling acquired incantatory traits. These calls often employ virtuosic elongations of their vocal range in order to puncture the silence and distance. However, it was playfulness in idle moments—much of a herder's day was no doubt spent waiting, counting clouds, and dreaming—that may have led to imaginative vocal tricks. Music provided amusement, and passed the time, and killed the boredom—converting idleness into creativity, which developed into the sophisticated ornamentation of voice that led to song.

The Alpine *naturjodel*, sung without words, is most closely associated with the herder's need, and sometimes longing, to communicate with other herders and his—and often *her*—herd over long distances. It is often cited as the origin of yodeling because it is characterized by an alphorn-fa sound: a "natural F" characteristic of the alphorn that became a standard in Swiss singing in the 18th century and was commonly sung in the regions of Muotathal and Appenzell. This yodel, as a utilitarian melismatic cry, is aided by its characteristic enunciation of open and closed vowels on the low and high notes of wide intervals, commonly a fourth, fifth, or sixth. Larger leaps depend on register changes. A particular phrasing choice links the glottal leap and the beauty of a melody together. The basic yodel is nonnarrative, wordless, sung to vocables or syllables: onomatopoeic, abstract, and meaningless.

SONG WITH VERSE

While pagan songs were adapted as far as possible to Christian(ity) . . . the convert's ears and throat became accustomed to the chants prescribed by Rome.

—John Horton

The genesis of the yodel goes something like this:

1. Basic call, prelingual yeowl
2. Call develops musical qualities, is now a *naturjodel*
3. Yodel is incorporated into wordless songs, pre-Gregorian scat
4. Yodel is applied to a basic song structure where the yodel serves as refrain
5. Yodel song becomes its own entity, the *jodellied*
6. Commercialization through professional performances and recordings leads to yodel pop songs

In the period between way back then and now, people, being who they were and may always have been—if one believes the Dutch philosopher Johan Huizinga, who thought the *homo ludens*, humans at play, the suppressed participants of social history, should be regarded as every bit as important as reasoning or productive people—began fooling with the basics, hanging ornaments and personal characteristics from the basic branch, and—voila!—unadorned yodel-cries began performing melodically within a song context.

Yodels as something more sophisticated than calls, as actual components of songs with verses, are a more recent invention. One might venture to guess that they arose about four or five hundred years ago, when cowherds purportedly began spending more time in villages. The yodel may have become more like a song as yodels began expressing the townspeople's longing for the idyllic lifestyle they'd left behind when they chose new nonagrarian employment opportunities. They may have taken the yodel, the expression of the lonely cowherd from their pastoral past, and tinkered with it, adding artistic embellishments, narrative verses with yodel refrains, inviting others to sing along, leading to the development of more sophisticated har-

SUMMARY OF ORIGIN THEORIES AND CULTURAL STRATEGIES

The genesis of the yodel has been the subject of many theories. How did the yodel start? Here are eleven basic theories, along with counterarguments.

1. The *echo theory* assumes yodeling's natural origins lie in the phenomenon of echo. But as yodel composer Heinrich Leuthold points out, the yodel is also indigenous to regions that have no "natural" yodel conditions, or echo such as open plains. Leuthold notes that a yodel caught in mountain valley echoes *does* lead to more melodies. Echo can be a formative factor in the yodel's genesis, but it's not a smoking gun.

2. The author of the *affect theory*, philosopher and yodel theorist, George Simmel, believes that when someone yodels, s/he falls under its influence. During the call, the voice crosses over, changes pitch from low to high. But yodeling doesn't *originate* here: a passionate scream can—but doesn't necessarily have to—change pitch.

3. No more formidable musicologist than E. M. von Hornbostel developed one of the most common origin theories: the yodel as human attempt to imitate the "natural F" of the alphorn and other natural instruments such as the shawm (double-reeded wind instrument invented around 1500). Hornbostel was convinced the yodel was an emotional-imitative reaction to the alphorn's sound and that yodeling only began to serve its communication function imitating the alphorn.

Respectfully, however, this theory is easily debunked. First, the parallels between these instruments and the human voice do not necessarily lead to the origin of one or the other. One day, an ethnomusicologist heard Pygmy women yodeling; no mountains, no alphorn. Which is exactly ethnomusicologist, Constantin Brailoiu's point: the yodel proliferated among people with few if any musical instruments.

4. Robert Lach's *phonation theory* states that the primal scream has its basis in the sexual impulse, which is expressed through an "ecstatic phonation." However, in the end, as Leuthold points out, Lach's theory pretty much leads us back to number 2.

5. Alfred Leonz Gassmann (1876–1962), famed yodel composer and one of the most important Swiss folksong researchers, presented the *"Silhouette of Horizons" theory*. He was convinced the yodel's vocal pattern, from extreme low and rapid movement to extreme high note, matched and imitated the natural (Alpine) surroundings of the yodeler: low note = valley, rapid movement (climbing the steep mountainside) to the high note = mountain peak. In a sense, one could say he created a kind of spiritual oscilloscope where the visualization of soundwaves—their amplitude—could be quite easily superimposed over a photo of a representative range of Alps on the horizon. In effect, the human yodel becomes an audio mirror of the yodeler's surroundings. But as Leuthold correctly

continued on the next page

Summary of Origin Theories, continued

points out, this theory may be part of the story of how the yodel came to be, but it's not *the* story of its origin. Because all we need do is note such flatland yodelers as the Pygmies.

Once we admit that the yodel did not emerge from one location (the Alps) as regional nationalists have claimed, but that it emerged simultaneously in any number of locations, we're already a long way toward defanging the various nationalistically tinged theories that have attached themselves to yodeling. In a 1998 email, Utah yodeler, Kerry Christensen, observed: "It seems perfectly possible that people just developed certain skills and talents at similar times in different places."

The music of the yodel *does* however, speak to the yodeler's surroundings: there is praise, thanks, joy, humility, a pre-Christian pagan celebration of place and our position in it whereby the inner meets the outer. Beauty (however regressive this may chime) still inspires. Beautiful musical expressions need not be one's compromise with hipness, nor seal one's pact with boring angels. In the Alpine context, yodeling is believable as a genuine expression of the drama inherent to the mountainscape, both it's frightening, dangerous side, and its glorious, boundless aspect.

However, as Christian Schmid, in a personal correspondence, notes, Gassmann "gives the example of a *schottisch* and declares that it has the typical form of an Alpine melody. Unfortunately, he didn't know back then that this melody was first published in Erfurt in 1860, a region not at all Alpine..."

6. Wolfgang Sichardt, formidable author of numerous yodel studies, in his book *Der Alpenländische Jodler* proposes his *race theory*: "the original folk emissaries, the original couriers of yodeling belonged to the darker peoples (*melanide*), Mediterraneans, and other related races." They were the primary developers of a maternalistic agriculture-based society. However, modern research into yodeling peoples has proven the opposite.

7. The *shout theory* proposed by the Eidgenössischer Jodlerverband (EJV, Swiss Federal Yodeler Organization) is both ideological and idyllic: "Our yodel was born in the mountains through the shouting of one person to another. It was employed both in times of joy and danger, both nearby (deeply) '*jo-ho*,' and at longer distances (high) '*juhu*.' Echo and Alphorn may have also played their parts. And so central to the birth of yodeling are love and distance. Valleys and ravines separated the homes and workplaces of those living in the Alps. It would have been necessary to walk for hours just to meet. The simple shout or 'Yutz' just wasn't enough; they had so much more to talk about."

8. The interesting *magic theory* of Manfred Bukofzer, proposes that the "basic premise of all Alpine music is the belief in the magical power of the tone." In the "Loba" of the *Kuhreihen* he senses a magical word, which casts off evil spirits and illness. The magic of melody is connected with the magic of the

continued on the next page

Summary of Origin Theories, continued

word. Bukofzer laments that the contemporary yodel has shed its original significance as a magical spell, and is now nothing more than a certain singing technique.
The origin of yodeling is nevertheless found somewhere in the magical
Weltanschauung (world outlook) of the ancient people. I agree to a certain extent
with Bukofzer and so does Leuthold. There is a hidden incomprehensibility in both
sound and word vocalization. Magic still serves a major function in most societies:
mantras, *betruf,* charismatic speakers, mesmerizing music, chants as protection.

9. The basic need to communicate over great distances. Necessity is the
milkmaid of invention.

10. The basic human need to be musical. As soon as a shout or cry is issued
humans want to make it musical.

11. Leuthold's own theory synthesizes elements from what came before. It is
a reasonable, holistic look at the origins of the yodel; there is no single explanation and is instead comprised of a number of cobbled-together theories.
Yodeling is among the first musical activities mankind engaged in. This
occurred when mankind discovered its humanity and became self-conscious
several hundred thousand years ago. Man as a self-reflexive being has been
using his mouth, the first musical instrument, which he carries with him
everywhere to play and communicate via language and song.

Yodeling's development can be likened to the development of early language
awareness in small children, Leuthold points out: from the first cry at birth,
the child begins to develop his vocal cords to hit a full register of sounds
from the lowest to the highest. Crying leads to yelling leads to babbling leads
to early attempts at speech and song. A child plainly enjoys hearing its own
voice. With the accomplishment of speech begins the formation of song.
    A child's speech development is not unlike an adult's yodeling develop-
ment. Childlike curiosity led the yodeler to become fascinated with one's own
echo while learning to play with it. Yodelers yelled without fear of consequences and this yell began to attain function as this call was answered by a
neighbor or friend. It's in this natural state of human curiosity where we find
the roots of language, song and especially yodeling. Leuthold has indeed
developed an appealing origin theory.

monies. This style of yodeling, the more established yodel song, is often sung
in Europe by choirs, usually with musical accompaniment like accordions or
string instruments. One yodeler usually took the lead and others followed,
singing a subtle harmony, with improvised melodies.

The yodel became popular entertainment at the end of the 18th century
with the emergence of troupes of intrepid "Alpine" singers or "natural"
yodelers. National choral groups took up the yodel, as did the legendary

Tyrolean (style) singing families from various mountain areas in Switzerland and Austria's Carinthia, Styria, and Zillertal regions. They became the Johnny Appleseeds of pop yodeling, a strange mélange of earthy folk yodels and art songs cribbed from plays popular in places like Vienna.

In Switzerland's Appenzell, yodelers still sing *zäuerli*, a cappella or accompanied by musicians, swinging giant cowbells. Although some pure yodel songs, unadulterated by meaning or message, still exist, most yodel songs are structured and documented either as sheet music or as recordings. They feature the yodel as refrain. It remains its distinguishing mark from regular songs. Pop songs, however, further relegate yodels to the role of ornament. And in a worst case scenario, they become bastardized as punch lines to musical jokes or showoffy riffs—the guitar solo of vocals, if you will—that showcase vocal gymnastics. Professional Alpine musicians often sing snazzy mod yodels called *coloratura,* which consist of trilly decorative veneers and abstract scat-yodels that are provided for tourists. As the Sex Pistols used to ironically snarl, "pretty, pretty va-cant."

YODEL WHO ARE YOU

The Queen of Yodeling is Mary Schneider

The Yodeling Queen is Janet McBride

The Yodeler King is Franzl Lang

The Jodlerkönig is Peter Hinnen

The King of the Yodelers is Kenny Roberts

Hawaii's Falsetto King is George Kainapau

Queen of the Yodelers is Rosalie Allen

The Epiglottis Goddess is Terri Taylor

The King of the Cowboys is Roy Rogers

The King of Country Music is Roy Acuff

The Prince of the Yodelers is Ward J. Burton

The Father of Bluegrass is Bill Monroe

America's Blue Yodeler is Jimmie Rodgers

The Yodeling Ranger is also Jimmie Rodgers

The Singing Messenger Boy is Bill Bruner

The Ramblin' Yodeler is Bill Haley

The Yodeling Jackaroo is Buddy Williams

The Famous Yodeling Blues Singer is Emmett Miller

The Caruso of the Mountains is Riley Puckett

The Caruso of the Mountains is also Sepp Viellechner

The Pavarotti of the Plains is Don Walser

Yodeling Slim Dallas is Dallas "Nevada Slim" Turner

The Original Texas Ranger is Tex Owens

The Oklahoma Yodeling Cowboy is Gene Autry

The Original Singin' Cowboy is Jules Verne Allen

The Cowboy Yodeler is Wylie Gustafson

The Singing Ranger is Hank Snow

The Alabama Yodeler is Monroe Tabor

The Tennessee Plowboy is Eddy Arnold

continued on the next page

Yodel Who Are You, continued

The Texas Troubadour is Ernest Tubb

The Yodeling Minstrel is Al Tint

The World Champion Yodeler is Kenny Roberts

The World's Champion Yodeler is Yodelin' Slim Clark

The Yodel Champion is Paul Gerber

The National Champion Girl Yodeler is May Miccolis

Iowa's Yodeling Cowboy is Jerry Smith

The Texas Drifter is Goebel Reeves

The Yodeling Rustler is also Goebel Reeves

The Yodeling Wrangler is also Goebel Reeves

The Official Cowboy Band For Texas is the Spirit of Texas

Canada's Champion Female Yodeler is Shirley Field

The Gospel Yodeler is Buzz Goertzen

The World Class Yodeler is Margo Smith

The Yodeling Ranger is Donn Reynolds

The Canadian Yodeling Cowboy is also Donn Reynolds

The Golden-Throated Cowboy is Eddie Dean

The Orange Yodeler is Jim Dautry

The Cowboy from Vienna is Werner Zotter

The Neanderthal Yodeler is Michael Welch

The Highest Yodeler in the World is Elton Britt

The Yodeling Cowboy is also Elton Britt

The Swiss Cowboy is Kerry Christensen

The Victor Borge of Yodeling is also Kerry Christensen

The Yodeling Cowboy is Sourdough Slim

The Conquering Lion is Thomas Mapfumo

Hawaii's Songbird is Lena Machado

The Swiss Miss Yodeler is Ethel Delaney

The Pemaquid Cowboy is Rusty Rogers

The Original Singing Cowboy is Carl T. Sprague

The Yodeling Cowboy from Chesterfield is Harry Torrani

The Lonesome Cowboy is John I. White

Montana's Yodeling Cowgirl is Patsy Montana

The Yodeling Cowgirl is Lee Jones

The Yodeling Bushman is Gordon Parsons

America's Only Colored Lady Yodeler is Beulah Henderson

The Well-Known Yodeler of the Police Petrol Company is Eddie Giguere

The Fastest Yodel in Western Music is Curly West

The Tennessee Yodeler is Margo Smith

The Dixie Yodeler is Zeke Clements

The Canadian Sweethearts are Lucille Star and Bob Regan

The Yodeling Cowboy is Yodeling Alberta Slim

The Wandering Cowboy is Buddy Bishop

Australia's Yodeling Sweetheart is Shirley Thoms

The Disneyland Yodeler is Fred Burri

The Voice Of Variety is Ron Ronalde

The Yodeling Cowgirl is June Holm

The Yodeling Boundary Rider is Tex Morton

The Cowboy Troubadour is Tim McNamara

The International Champion Swiss Yodeler is Robbie Schneider

The Singing Puzzle is Harry Torrani

The Yodeler with the Velvet Voice is Alfons Zitz

The Kansas City Butter-Ball is Lottie Kimbrough

The Jimmy Rodgers of Sierra Leone is S. E. Rogie

and last but not least:

The Yodeling Woodcarver is Adi

2

Who Duh Lay Hee Who
Swiss Yodeling

The Tyroleans are here again: I will have them perform those songs for me, even though I can only tolerate the popular yodeling outdoors or in big rooms.

—Goethe, 1829

The yodel probably developed simultaneously in different areas of the world, but most people usually associate yodeling with the Alps that "curve in an arc from southern France in the west to northern Yugoslavia in the east"—and particularly with Switzerland. In a game of word association, if I said "Switzerland," a sizeable chorus would surely pipe in with "YODEL!" Say the word "yodel," and most would no doubt bellow "Switzerland!" The Swiss just can't get away from it. Chapters 2 and 3 focus on the three Alpine nations where people converse, sing, and, for the most part, yodel in some form of the German language: Switzerland, Germany, and Austria. And even though their histories are often tossed together, the three nations have distinct yodel histories and sounds; within each nation, various regions, cantons, and localities maintain unique yodeling traditions. Despite common belief, Switzerland is anything but homogenous when it comes to music or cheese. Switzerland's mountains offer protection and isolation, which incubated an insular (negative) yet distinctive (positive) culture, not pure maybe but at least somewhat intact.

As mentioned in Chapter 1, the official Swiss yodel does not make use of the "eee." And, to the surprise of most neophytes, it has a decidedly melancholy feeling—slow, soulful, forlorn—*heimweh*, blues, and largo with a beat you can count on two hands. In other words, soul music suspended

All dressed up with something to yodel about.

in thin air. The yodel choirs with their formal art-song-like repertoires are typical of formal Swiss yodeling and are more common in the German-speaking region. Women are often yodelers but seem less involved in the choirs (many choirs until recently were male-only clubs, although the official club rules have been amended to allow up to three women in a male club) than in solo or duet yodeling. A duo is commonly composed of a wo/man yodeler accompanied by an accordionist. Swiss yodeling is indeed more choral than German yodeling.

German yodeling is often associated with Bavaria and the German Alps. Here "triadic melodies . . . were . . . characteristic of the Alpine yodel, a nearly textless singing, which even today influences the melodies of Bavaria's secular and religious music." The Harz Mountain region of Central Germany between Halle and Hannover also has its share of unique yodeling. The "Harzer Roller" is characterized by a fast scampering exchange between head and chest voices mostly in the interval of a major sixth. The "rollers" have become staples of *jodelfests* and *Heimatabenden* (folk culture evenings). Despite cultural awareness efforts, however, the German yodel often serves as a folk doily on the furniture of the *schlager* (popular song) and can best be characterized as—or shoved too easily into—the genre of party music: boisterous, goofy, and commercial. In other words, the typical clichéd image we have of yodeling is more German than Swiss.

SELECTED SWISS YODEL DISCOGRAPHY

There are literally thousands of Swiss yodeling recordings. Many are generic in repertoire—songs are composed by the usual demigods like Stähli and Renggli—and they don't go in for off-beat cover versions. There are also hundreds of ethnomusicological surveys and Alpine folk music collections packaged for touristic ears. I had to make a very selective selection, then.

- *Alpine Festival: Songs, Ländler and Yodeling from the Swiss, Austrian and German Alps*, Therese Wirth von Känel and Karli Oswald, Columbia, 1959.

- *Alpine Härte 1 von 2,* Edelschwarz, Lawine/Virgin, 2002. Alpine power-metal quartet produces an uneasy alloy of joyously brutal yodeling. Recommended.

- *The Alps*, various artists including the Appenzeller Space Schötel, WDR, 1994. Includes alphorn, *zäuerli*, *länderli*, *schottisher*, waltzes, and yodels.

- *Belle Romandie*, various performers, EMI/Columbia, 1970s. Collection of traditional French-Swiss yodeling and alphorn tunes.

- *Edelweiss*, various performers, Allegro, 2000. Includes many usual Alpine yodeling antics including "Ski Party Yodel."

- *Caruso der Berge*, Sepp Viellechner, Koch, 1990s.

- *Eidgenössisches Jodlerfest: Thun 23rd Swiss National Yodelling Festival*, various artists, Swiss Radio International (SRI), Musica Helvetica series, 1996.

- *Die Fischerin vom Bodensee,* various performers, Koch Präsent, 1991. Includes "goldene volksmusik" from the Bodensee area, along the German-Swiss border.

- *Die Schönsten Jodler der Berge: 22 neue Jodel-hits*, Hansl Krönauer, Koch, 1990s.

- *Inland*, Stimmhorn, RecRec, 2001. Includes extrapolatory treks into the abstract hinterlands of yodeling.

- *Jodeln is' Mei Freud*, Sepp Viellechner, Telstar, 1970s.

- *Jüüzli of the Muotatal*, Hugo Zemp, Peter Betschart, Charlotte Boigeol, Chant du Monde, 1990. Compiled from 1979 field recordings.

- *Jodler in Gold: Die Schönsten Jodler der Berge*, various performers, Koch International, 1993. Genuine hardcore folk yodeling!

- *Jodlers Freud*, Albert Vitali, PCD, 1990s. Vitali's solo yodels cover many Jakob Ummel "hits."

- *The Kindli Presents Swiss Folklore Music,* Schmid Brothers Show Band, Kindli Records, 1970s. Famed Zurich restaurant's band plays an eclectic mix of yodel music.

continued on the next page

Selected Swiss Yodel Discography, continued

- ***Königen der schweizerischen Jodel**, Vreni Kneubühl and Jakob Ummel, Denon, 1986 (recorded in Japan, 1969). Interesting recording by two of the big throats of yodeling.

- ***Mountain Songs & Yodeling of the Alps**, Fritz Liechti & Family, Folkways Records, 1958. Liechti, from Thun, was considered a top Swiss yodeler and a world-class professional climber and skier; the Liechtis moved to Canada in 1952. Sung in Switzer-Deutsch with rudimentary accordion accompaniment. Highly emotional yodels are sung solo.

- ***Musica Helvetica: Swiss Folk Music—Yodeling**, various performers, SBC/SRI, 1978. Great introduction to yodeling with intelligent narration.

- ***Rossini: William Tell**, Conductor: Riccardo Muti, Opera D'Oro 3-CD, 2001.

- ***Schnee**, Stimmhorn, Röhr/RecRec, 1997. Christian Zehnder: voice and instruments, and Balthasar Streiff: alphorn, trumpet, and other instruments. Eccentric dialogue between voices and alphorn. Recommended.

- ***Schweizer Alpin Klange**, various artists, Request Records, 1977.

- ***Sing and Dance with the Gasthaus Trio**, Gasthaus Trio, WRC, 1980s. A schnitzel of *ländler*, pop songs, opera, and a few yodel standards.

- ***Songs and Dances of Switzerland**, Folkways, 1953.

- ***Songs from Switzerland**, Philippe Zani, EPM, 2000.

- ***Suisses Alemaniques,** compiled by Constantin Brailoiu, 78rm 10–inch, UNESCO Conseil International de la Musique, 1958 (1942).

- ***Swiss Folk Music I: Yodeling,** Swiss Radio International, 1972.

New Year's yodeling and revelry in costumes and masks drives out evil spirits in Switzerland's Urnäsch Valley. Photo by Cyrill Schläpfer.

continued on the next page

Selected Swiss Yodel Discography, continued

- ***Swiss Folk Music V: Great Names in Swiss Folk Music I***, Gottfried Stucki, SBC, 1973.

- ***Wenn Ich auf Hohen Bergen Steh***, Europa vinyl, 1950s. Alfons Zitz was one of 14 children in a very musical family. He was so entranced by music that he went to music school to study sacred music where he also picked up the organ, guitar, zither, and piano. Accompanied by the Inntaler Musikanten.

- ***Yodel in Hi-Fi***, Marieluise Tichy & the 2 Rudis, Fiesta Records, 1958.

In Austria, the yodel has been influenced by Viennese high culture and, consequently, is located somewhere between the Swiss and German varieties: more polished, sweeter, and lighter than the Swiss, and often "more suave [and] heart-rending" than the German yodel.

Despite these generalizations, I know some among you will have long lists of yodelers who contradict this rudimentary attempt at distinction. And yet, despite contradictions and hazy frontiers, each nation (and region) *does* have a unique yodel sound. (Other European regions with a yodeling past such as the Lowlands—OK, *don't* believe me!—Scandinavia, and many Eastern European nations will be covered in greater depth in Chapter 4.)

NOT UNTIL HELVETIA FREEZES OVER

Yodeling for me is pretty much the most Swiss thing there is. I love yodeling, but only in its natural, unadulterated form, which means when a person is yodeling outdoors, in nature.

—Bernhard Thurnheer, popular Swiss sportscaster

To an outsider, Switzerland is like a precision timepiece: trains run on time, everything has its function, and everyone has his or her place. This is no more evident than at the National Yodeler Festival, where preserving yodeling is done with all the fervor of a proud citizenry and all the meticulous concern for detail of a watchmaker. Switzerland offers a highly burnished edge of where tradition meets modern technology, where anachronism and tradition have to find their place in a rich country whose

CSR RECORDS: IMMERSION IN MYSTICAL ESOTERICA

birds and whales sing, lions roar, humans yodel.

—Cyrill Schläpfer

Cyrill Schläpfer is a classic obsessed-genius nerd who has produced discs of exquisite obscurity for his own CSR label: how about sixty-five minutes of cowbells jingling? He's very present in his sound productions as a guiding force but just as absent as an ego. Schläpfer did a long stint as a rock drummer, busily denying his traditions. Accepting tradition meant betraying art, while denying tradition meant being cast adrift culturally—or does it?

During our conversations, I felt Schläpfer's irritation at Switzerland's inability to come to a happier détente between creativity and tradition. This makes Schläpfer's mission and CSR's music catalog all the more important and controversial. Because, in his growing dissatisfaction with the solipsistic pop world, Schläpfer discovered himself turning ever more inventively back to tradition. Defining the traditional is a politicized process. In his pursuits of the "true" traditional, Schläpfer went so deep that he found ur-music that was both mystical and improvisational—*and* "ignored" by Switzerland's traditionalists.

That's what makes CSR's diverse array of Swiss music and yodeling CDs plus its folk-music documentary, *Ur Musig* (video plus three-CD-audio companion), so compelling. Schläpfer prefers to let the images, the locals, yodelers, and farmers speak for themselves, do their own dances, play their own tunes in their own environment. His nonnarrative minimal-academic-musicological documentary style manages to capture a scene, a preserved instant that is rendered with such loving care that one is blown away not only by the music but also by the mystical quality of the various yodels of the Appenzellers and Innerschweizer mountain dwellers.

Am Alte Silveschter Z'Urnäsch effectively captures an Appenzell version of Carnaval complete with costumes of beautiful and ugly demigods. There is much ambient snowy revelry in Urnäsch every January 13th. The chantlike yodels issued through the elaborate masks gives them a strange resonance and eerie timbre.

The two collections of traditional yodels *Rio 6 Stärke Tubak Älpler-Liedli und Jüüzli* and *Rössli 7 Stärke Tubak Älpler-Liedli und Jüüzli* are musts if you want real roots-style yodeling and Swiss-style accordion (a small, nonchromatic thing made of wood). *Rio 6* is a fairly complete collection of the recent repertoire of the Pragelchärlis from Muotathal, interpreted by Toni Büehler and others. *Rössli 7* compiles yodels from the Luzern and Brünig region and from the archives of the Zihlmanns. The overall effect is like the best of Folkways' ethnomusicological material.

CSR esoteric soundscape CDs are intoxicatingly representative sonic portraits of various aspects of Swiss pastoral culture. *True Tone* volumes 1–5 are pure ambiences of, yes, Swiss pastures. What do the Alps, the pastures, and the rolling hills sound like? They are alive and filled with the atmospherically pregnant sounds of

continued on the next page

CSR Records, continued

cowbells and grazing herds. *(Morgeluft)* captures the sound between 6 and 7:30 A.M., May 6, 1990, of Lake Vierwaldstättersee, the lake near Schläpfer's home and along which Luzern stretches. You can picture Schläpfer tromping around the Alps, sneaking up on the herds with his microphone.

- *True Tone ('s Glüüt vols. 1–2), ('s Fahr Glüüt), (Les Sonailles),* and *(Morgeluft), 1993–2000.*

- *UR-Musig* (and *UR-Musig* vol. 2), 1999.

- *Am Alte Silveschter Z'Urnäsch,* 1991.

- *Rio 6 & 7 Stärke Tubak Älpler-Liedli und Jüüzli,* 2000.

- *Echo der Zeit,* Christine Lauterburg, 1994.

Photo by CSR Records. Courtesy of Cyrill Schläpfer.

architecture (modern) is clean and stark. The Swiss are at once open and closed, global and nationalistic, provincial and curious; hi-tech vs. hi-kitsch, hi-season access vs. hi-mountain inaccessibility; from sampler/laptop musicians to the tinkling peals of cowbells and the sound of the yodel as a shout to pagan spirits.

The cliché of Switzerland as a land of farmers is an enduring one, annoying to some, lucrative to others. The majority of Swiss are tourists in their own rural land. The native Swiss are leaving more and more of the herding functions to foreign labor, so one is less and less likely to encounter *naturjodeling en plein air.* The migrant or temporary laborers are usually not of the yodeling sort. Yodeling endures in part because of a nation's denial steeped in romanticized nostalgia of a simpler time, a time when people were down to earth, honest, part of nature, practical, and pious. In any case, the farmer as ur-Swiss is deeply rooted in their souls, and pastoral scenes remind us that the farm is never far away, almost always in sight.

Bucolic farmland Switzerland forms the early backdrop for the development of songs related to farming and herding, including cow-milking

Siegfried Zihlmann: Crying a *betruf* through wooden *folle*. Courtesy of Cyrill Schläpfer.

songs, milkmaid songs, cattle blessings, songs sung while feeding livestock, "calls, yells, recitatives, a three-tone yodel, and melodic vocalizing used to control herds in the pastures and for other farm-related functions." From the 17th to 19th centuries these farmers and herders believed what science continues to suggest, that animals—like people—can be entranced, hypnotized, controlled, and can even be coaxed into giving more milk when sung to.

Although four major languages create distinctive regions in Switzerland, the Romansch (1% of the population) and Italian (8%) areas are relatively small and don't represent a significant yodeling influence. The French-speaking part is significant, but their contribution to yodeling is also small—however exquisite or charming their vocals may be. German (and its many dialects) is Switzerland's dominant language (64%), culture, and yodeling influence.

The Genesis

The herders' calls, at first basic and monosyllabic, eventually developed into a highly sophisticated wordless melody: the *naturjodel*. We can distinguish five distinct strata of development:

1. The pre-yodel call, a *ruf*.
2. The yodel as solo call: *zäuerli; kuhreihen*, and *löckler*.
3. The yodel as folk tune, in the sense that it's improvised and passed down orally. The *naturjodel* is a melody without words, without lyrical content: "Thousands of Swiss folksongs have a jodel refrain in which the singer's voice shoots up from a good, rich bass to an A in alt."

THE EIDGENÖSSICHER JODLER VERBAND

The [EJV] treats Switzerland like some open-air museum and itself as the authorizing museum guard.

—Christian Seiler

The problem is a political one. . . . The EJV is not part of Swiss yodeling history but it is part of our political mentality. And it's a mistake of not only the yodelers but the general population as well. . . . You will see that it is quite interesting and beautiful and you will see many very nice faces and beautiful costumes. Ja, it's a kind of sect, you know.

—Barbara Bachmann Geiser

In Switzerland . . . the Schweizerische Volkspartei's . . . exponents . . . lets others feel that they are the better Swiss. When this party has an assembly, there are usually yodelers or folk musicians there to show that they are maintaining Swiss traditions.

—Christian Schmid

The Eidgenössicher Jodler Verband, or EJV, was established in 1910 in Bern to address the concern of yodelers that the native tradition was vanishing because Tyrolean styles were replacing indigenous Swiss styles. Oskar Schmalz (1881–1960) was the EJV's cofounder. Other important EJV names include Max Lienert (1903–1964), A. L. Gassmann (1876–1962), Jakob Ummel (1895–1992), Robert Fellmann (1885–1951), Paul Müller-Egger (1885–1979), and Adolf Stähli; all were composers and belong among the pantheon of Swiss yodel gods. The EJV has ever since been committed to preserving and promoting "traditional" yodeling and, to a lesser degree, the traditions of alphorn blowing and flag swinging—imagine a color guard with much larger flags and poles. EJV clubs emerged in farming communities in the early 1900s. Some businesses and factories had yodeling clubs, as did some dairy factory unions. The clubs flourished after World War II.

Less than 20 percent of the EJV's members are employed in agricultural occupations. Yodeling is no longer just for herders and farmers. It also means that the yodel song lyrics are not about those who sing them but about an idealized Swiss past. The bylaws dictate that they must be about pastoral concerns because the EJV believes an authentic yodel must be pastoral in theme. There are currently more than 800 yodel groups representing 13,000 of its members, plus 12,500 individual members, for a total of 25,500 members. Every town has a yodel club, and many have more than one. The clubs meet regularly. EJV is composed of five regional associations (four or so cantons per region). Each region has cantonal and local clubs. The general membership includes yodel groups; individual and smaller groups (duos and trios); the composers, directors, alphornists, and flagwavers; the patrons and friends of the EJV; and some "Swiss-immigrant yodel groups" in North America, New Zealand, Australia, South Africa, and elsewhere who cultivate the Swiss yodel heritage.

continued on the next page

The Eidgenössicher Jodler Verband, continued

The main EJV activity is the annual yodel festivals (twice in three years regionally and every third year nationally). Planning these festivals consumes most of the local and regional yodelers' time and money. The first national festival occurred in 1927. It represented the first bureaucratic gestures toward a more formal approach to achieving a more homogenized, logical, and ultimately a more manageable repertoire that could justifiably represent and inspire the nation's self-respect. Nonetheless, the EJV charter plainly states that its activities are all fun and games and that it remains politically unaffiliated and religiously neutral.

The EJV mandate of standardized song structures and male-oriented vocalizations has produced what Baumann and others refer to as "folkloristic music" or raw primitive music reworked into an aesthetically "pleasing" sound. (Nashville works on a similar principle.) It encourages conformity and threatens improvisation and the very existence of the natural yodel, according to Leuthold. Each yodel song in the competition must include accompanying sheet music so that judges can follow along to determine accuracy of interpretation. "The notating of these songs," opines composer and EJV member Leuthold, "has had a sterilizing effect, and at the very least, improvisation and open arrangements are now endangered species."

EJV competition guidelines address every aspect of the yodeler and yodel club, including behavior, costume, vocal range, and parameters of improvisation. Paul Bürgi put it this way: "If you want you can sing and yodel in whatever outfit, you can sing what you want, but to be taken seriously you must conform to the *Verband*'s rules." In this way, the competitions aren't that different from dog shows or tango competitions. You don't enter your pet monkey in a

continued on the next page

Fribourg Jodlerfest: Sitting around drinking and yodeling.

The Eidgenössicher Jodler Verband, continued

dog show and you don't enter a tango competition doing the boogaloo or bump. The organized competitions have led to further standardization of the general perception of what a yodel is. Tunings have been standardized, with minor keys giving way to majors, "descending melodic patterns fell into disuse, functional harmony and modulations were introduced, and yodels were incorporated as choruses into verse songs."

The clubs maintain a lively (inbred and specialized) cottage recording industry. Any club with any clout pretty much can put up the Swiss Francs to produce a CD of their standard repertoire, packaged with the standard group portrait in traditional costume framed by Edelweiss with a church on a hillside in the distance. The official EJV jodel courses are popular, but recruitment problems remain, due in part to the amount of practice and discipline EJV-style yodeling entails. The training involves hard work and time. It is aimed at long-term goals, with no immediate gratification—everything that would seemingly make a young teen groan.

4. The yodel as formal song (*jodellied*) within classic song structures: notation, lyrics, yodel refrain. Alfred Tobler distinguished them as songs where vocables replace words.
5. The pop yodel is commercially available on record or sung for profit and is characterized by its flexiblity; it can compliment a number of diverse musical genres.

Pop Developments

Some sounds commonly associated with Switzerland include cowbells, accordion, and Jew's harp (*trümpi*), which arrived in the Alpine region during the Middle Ages. Playing the spoons remains fairly common in central Switzerland. One *very* Swiss instrument, the hackbrett, most resembles a hammer dulcimer or a Gypsy *cymbalon*. And then there's the yodel.

Just prior to the Swiss Confederation's expansion (15th century), troubadours and *trouvéres* were already roaming the European countrysides, enchanting people with their songs. The less peripatetic Swiss *Minnesingers* sang in cities, not unlike today's buskers. But with the Reformation came stern interpreters of the Bible like Calvin and Zwingli with followers prohibiting musical expression because it distracted them from their faith.

Distinctly Swiss yodels, more than mere herder's calls or other proto-non-pop genres of functional vocalizations, including lullabies, shouts, and prayers, have been around since the 1600s. History suggests that only a few melodies have earlier roots, including a few rudimentary *juchzer*, yodels *betrufs*, and lullabyes. Compared to *zäuerli*, these yodels involved taut vocal chords and faster tempos. Yodelers were often accompanied by background vocalists singing drones.

As 17th-century Europe emerged out of its solemn age, music began reappearing in churches, universities, and elsewhere but consisted mostly of church-sanctioned music, which would lead one toward, rather than away from, God. In 1688, Johannes Hofer wrote his medical treatise about the homesickness experienced by shepherds in farflung pastures, whenever they heard the "Cantilena Helvetica." In 1724, Johan J. Bodmer and Laurenz Zellweger "searched for the famous *Küh-Reyhen* . . . to prove that 'human nature is alike in all reasonable people.'" This in turn encouraged those who espoused a genuine (provable) love for one's surroundings. This sentiment was inspired by Haller's poem "Die Alpen" (1729). Haller heralded a complex 18th-century back-to-nature movement and helped idealize the herdsman's life for the urban dweller, the way cowboy songs did for Americans. Jean-Jacques Rousseau best elaborated the Romantic "return to nature." This was further advanced by the collecting activities of various self-appointed folklorists like G. S. Studer who began folding folk music into the emotional relationship humans had with mountains and an emerging "national folk identity." Meanwhile, those with vested interests began formulating the inklings of a national music. The *ranz des vaches* was a natural nominee as "real" Swiss music.

By the 19th century, classical music concerts flourished with popular performances of Mendelssohn, Handel, and Beethoven, heralding an increasingly heavy influence of German culture. Swiss awareness of its own music, musicians, and history flourished. Gioacchino Rossini's famous *William Tell* (1828) interprets several *ranz des vaches* that open Schiller's play about the heroic leader of the 16th-century Swiss independence movement, creating an appropriate Swiss leitmotif: "The *Ranz des Vaches*," Schiller noted, "and the tinkling of cattle bells, continue for some time after the rising of the curtain."

The first folksong collection, published in 1805, included eight *Kuhreihen*. By 1826, yodels were popping up in sophisticated song structures to satisfy urban-oriented audiences. As yodels began to be documented they also grew more standardized, using stereotypes that transformed folk into folkloristic music or popular music designed to be performed formally or professionally. The yodel may have been popularized through the early efforts of composer F. F. Huber (1791–1863), who gave shape to the calls and had trained singers perform them so that they

KORNHAUS-BURGDORF
(BURGDORF GRANARY FOLK MUSEUM)

My rendezvous with Paul Bürgi at the Burgdorf train station was perfect: blue July skies and the scent of flowers, in the middle of somewhere I'd never been before. Bürgi had hobbled past me and I him since neither knew what the other looked like. As we drove through town, he explained the hobble and cane: childhood polio. "It's not a disability," he was quick to add, finger pointing to the sky, "because I have never known anything else."

Paul Bürgi, the happy yodeler of Burgdorf.

Burgdorf, forty minutes out of Bern, birthplace of Vreni Kneubühl, is a small town with the typical 1970s-unattractive-concrete-bunker-style shopping district built around the train station. But the rest of the town is a glorious scrubbed example of preserved mountain town elegance. Old town to my right perched on a hilltop encircled by its intact castle walls offered a strategic panoramic view of the region.

Our destination: the Burgdorfer, an ex-army building converted to higher purposes—microbrewery-restaurant. We sit outside surrounded by cliffs. "An old rifle range," Bürgi points out, "here they could shoot and not worry. All the bullets go into the cliffs." We spoke over a nice lunch and a couple of substantial Burgdorfer beers. When he ordered a second round in Switzer-Deutsch, I asked, "A second?"

To which he responded, "You have two legs don't you?"

Bürgi (b. 1943) is proud of what he does: oversee the Cantonal archives for folk culture and yodeling. Bürgi likes Burgdorf, his archive, and his *jodelclub*. Swiss yodel clubs are like English pubs or American bowling alleys. He's been in *jodelclubs* since the 1960s and took years of courses to perfect breathing, articulation, and theory. His club plays the usual festivals, weddings, New Years parties, and civic functions to raise money to cover expenses for travel to the various *jodlerfests*, buy studio time, and cover CD production costs. To organize the annual cantonal/regional *jodlerfest* requires coordinating some 900 people who work the entire year toward the festival's success.

After lunch, I stood up and quickly reached for something anchored to the ground; those beers were strong but went down like lemonade. We took the short ride to the Kornhaus, a converted granary that has housed the *Schweiz Zentrum für Volkskultur* for the Emmental region since 1991. It's an important

continued on the next page

Kornhaus-Burgdorf, continued

regional/national nonprofit cultural center created for the promotion of folk music, traditional costumes, old phonograph players, records—stacks of unfiled 78s!—and musical instruments. It was instituted under the direction of Barbara Bachmann-Geiser, renowned folk music and folk instrument expert. The museum is modest but thorough, displaying musical instruments, dramatic alphorns, folk costumes, and audio-visual material in English to explain the folk traditions, including yodeling. The Kornhaus also hosts concerts and, more important, serves as repository for the region's yodel-related archival material including songbooks, catalogs, fading photos of stiffly posed turn-of-the-century yodel groups, dusty academic discourses on yodeling, and lots of bookkeeping.

Upstairs in a wood-paneled conference room that looks more like a spa than a place of serious discussion, the *Verband* holds its regular meetings. Decorating the entrance are some giant ceremonial cowbells, and decorative craftwork and needlepoint dedications to the *Verband*. The room's windows are of stained glass and "narrate" the story of the EJV. The portrait gallery featured dignified headshots of yodeling giants. Downstairs, the shop is a good place to stock up on traditional *jodlerverband* CDs. Among the stuff I bought was a CD of Bürgi's yodel club, *Ds Schützechörli Kirchbärg sing u jutzt*, TBM Productions, 1998. Its cover has stock details of all Swiss *jodlerverband* CDs: traditional local costume—black slacks, blue smock-shirts—with members posed with regulation hands in pockets. *Schützechörli* celebrates the group's 60th-anniversary. The all-male group includes 30 members divided into first and second tenors and first and second bass among whom six (tenors) do all of the yodeling. The rest sing the choral parts and create the framework for the yodeling solos and duets. Wonderful yodeling, typical of *jodlerverband* yodeling: melancholy.

Afterward, Bürgi chauffeured me through the Emmental valley of classic Swiss scenery: pastures, farms, large farmhouses with huge acute-angled roofs (to cope with heavy snow). We stopped on a hillside to visit a touristic cheese factory-restaurant and yodel venue to sample 10 types of cheese. I stabbed a piece of Emmentaler with my Swiss-flag toothpick, while the waitress delivered a beer: the end of a perfect day.

resembled early 19th-century art songs (classic *lieder*) with the addition of topical and contemporary political, romantic, or familial subject matter.

In the early 1900s, men's choirs dominated most aspects of popular music. "And the yodel song had no luck at all," notes Barbara Bachmann-Geiser, "because it was accompanied by the piano and it [yodeling] was cut down right from the start. Yodeling was only reinvented in 1920 by Oskar Schmalz (1881–1960). Schmalz is a holy name" and noted composer ("Föhnnacht") who engineered a yodel renaissance with his collection *Bi üs im Bärnerland.*

The EJV was founded to rectify this situation. Along with other organizations—for some better and some worse—the EJV coordinated the shift from collecting to producing folk music. The late-19th-century yodel clubs were mostly city based although the themes of the songs remained rural: a virtual, consumable, and idealized rural setting. The interesting process of making folk culture part of the official national culture came with the introduction of public alphorn playing, yodeling, and other folk activities by country folk. This process allowed them to reappropriate their own traditions and folk activities—via governmental mediation—and glorify themselves. But the songs they sang were written in a folk style and composed like art/pop songs.

SWITZERLAND'S REGIONS AND CANTONS

The EJV has grouped twenty-four Swiss cantons into five yodel regions; they are overwhelmingly German speaking except for the Western cantons.

Bernisch-Kantonaler Jodlerverband (Bern Canton Region Yodel Organization) covers the central Swiss region governed by the vibrant city of Bern. It is here that the notion of a nationally/regionally organized yodeler organization was first concocted. It is also where the *naturjodel* was commonly found with its characteristic smooth leisurely pace. The great composers Oscar Schmaltz, Jakob Ummel ("Gwattschtützler" and "Alter Flösser-Jodel"), Ernst Sommer ("Rüschegger-Lied"), and Adolf Stähli are all from the Bern region, home to a variation of the Appenzell *naturjodel* with cowbell or coin-rolling accompaniment.

Westschweizerischer Jodlerverband (Western Switzerland Yodel Organization, Neuchatel, Vaud, Fribourg, Geneva, Valais/Wallis) is not known for its yodeling uniqueness other than the French/Romance influence that presents the relatively scarce and generally mellifluous French-language yodel. The region doesn't have an original yodel repertoire except for a few by Fribourg composer Albert Jacquet. The main proponents of yodeling are transplanted Germans who, in three generations of living in the Francophone region, have begun to include some French songs with yodeling in their repertoires.

The Moléson is the dominant mountain in the area northeast of Lausanne and the home of the *Ranz des Vaches*, which is sung in Gruyère dialect. The piece was formalized and preserved by Joseph Bovet, a musically inclined priest, who composed a version based on the folk song "Ranz des Vaches Fribourgeois." It became an unofficial national anthem for Swiss Francophones. Most of their songs however were imported from France. Their vocal songs are performed in 4/4 time rather than the German 3/4 and are characterized by alternating choruses and soloists.

Jodlerclub "Alpenrösli" hails from the Lausanne region of the Vaud canton—rolling hills, vineyards and honey-colored chateaus with roofs of red clay shingle. Lausanne-Ouchy sits on the croissant-like bend of Lac Lehman: to the south is Geneva; go east and you end up in Montreaux. Although the Vaud is no yodeling hotbed, yodeling is also not *that* uncommon. Alpenrösli's founders were Swiss-Germans who came to Lausanne in the early twentieth century looking for work. They eventually settled here. One of their main objectives was to keep their *jodel* tradition alive in their adopted Vaud. This was accomplished through the efforts of members of clubs like Jodlerclub Alpenrösli who sing exclusively Swiss-German *jodellieden* under the leadership of *dirigent* Annelise Cavin (she also conducts three other area *jodelclubs*).

I was lucky enough to meet them shortly after their performance in Fribourg's Eidgenössischer Jodelerfest 2002. They'd just given their best three minutes in a humid hall in the College Saint-Michel. Afterward Denis Guiet, my festival guide, and I followed the troupe to a parking lot overlooking Fribourg. We clumped around the camping trailer of one of the members who opened up his doors and brought out snacks, beer, and wine. And the serenade began—as predicted—with countless impromptu yodel songs. I spoke in a trilingual jumble as the members loosened their ties and warmed up to my naive enthusiasms. What I learned was that some club members are singers who can yodel but within this group do not; some cannot yodel, they just sing; while others perform as the featured solo or duet yodelers. This surprised me.

Alpenrösli has two female virtuoso yodelers, Marianne Graf and Vreni Da Costa. I spoke with yodeler-husband Albert Graf, an ebullient talker and serious farmer with rosy cheeks full of blustery dusks and dawns . . . and wine. Most club members live in cities and have never worked on a farm. So, Graf is an exception. He told me he learned to yodel when he was very young from his father who composed original *jutzes* and *jodels*. These were irretrievably lost—except for bits Graf remembers—when his father died because he never wrote them down. Graf was determined to put his years of yodel training toward keeping the memory of his father alive. Some of the others noted that they rehearse their yodeling at home—alone. Some can read music, some cannot; some are composers, some are not. Then suddenly somebody signaled, they put their drinks down, moved into a semi-circle, hands in pockets, and burst into stirring yodeling somewhere between liturgical and *naturjodel*, like gospel without the *message*.

I should be recording this, I thought. I fumble for my recorder and . . . the performance is over! Beer and wine continue to flow, my enthusiasm mounts in inverse proportion to my journalistic skills to note all of this. At some point it comes out that I'm writing a book and that I would love to record one of their yodels, having missed twice earlier—a beer in each hand, hard to hit the record button with my toe. Half of the group gathered around me. I'm down on my knees with modest tapedeck rolling as they serenaded me with something so lovely I thought I was going through some initiation rite. I gazed up at their gesticulating mouths—open relaxed throats—and beyond into the humid rosy sky. I

continued on the next page

continued

realized that I was witnessing something precious—and typical, as both Barbara Bachmann-Geiser and Christine Lauterburg had mentioned. After the formal contest, yodelers wander around from beerstand to wine tent serenading passersby with whatever comes to mind. That this impromptu aspect was much more resonant, soulful, and enjoyable made the formal aspects of the festival all the more ironic. But they can live with it. They do the contest and then hit the streets. Guiet doesn't see it as a contradiction. He believes they live earnest lives and are guided by the discipline and openings that yodeling affords. With wine and yodel song intoxicating my spirit, I nodded absolutely.

Alpenrösli celebrated its 75th anniversary in 1996 with the release of a CD of typical *jodels*, *Nimme dir Zyt* (Take Your Time), Suisa, 1997.

Nordwestschweizerischer Jodlerverband (Northwestern Switzerland Yodel Organization, includes Jura, Basel, Aargau, Solothurn). Most of their local yodeling derives from other influences. Birthplace of Alois Glutz von Blotzheim and Paul Müller-Egger, the area doesn't have a unique style. Here they're not "*naturjuuz* or *zäuerli*-heads." They generally prefer yodel *songs* and cultivate composition and value composers. Solothurn has some yodeling accompanied by hand clapping, thigh slapping, and table drumming.

Nordostschweizerischerischer Jodlerverband (Northeastern Switzerland Yodel Organization, includes Thurgau, Zurich, Glarus, Sinkt Gallen, Appenzell, Graubunden). "This tiny canton is divided in two," notes Bachmann-Geiser, "the inner [Catholic] and upper [Protestant] regions. 50 years ago, it was still impossible to inter-marry. It is traditional but you'd be surprised at how much industry there is." The region does not have one distinct yodel practice, but there are many fundamental yodels that have different nuances, depending on the locality, that are so fine that only a yodel expert could distinguish them. The area is most renowned for its *zäuerli*, *ruggusserli*, and *zungenschlagjödeli* (tongue stroke/blow yodel). "Sloping" harmonics in their *zäuerli* and *ruggusserli* are very typical for the region. Toggenburg *zungenschlagjödeli* is mostly influenced by Appenzeller-style yodeling but unique because of its livelier snappier composition and its extremely high notes and employment of alphorn-fa.

Appenzell is home to a major Swiss repository of living folk traditions. An early break-away canton in 1513, it's known for its small breweries and Alpenbitter (Jägermeister equivalent). Although major-chord yodeling is the norm, Appenzell's traditional minor-chord yodeling can still be heard.

There are numerous styles including the wordless and nonnotated spontaneous *zäuerli* (also called a *ruggusserli*), which is here characterized by low, slow, melancholic, and relaxed vocals with an open rhythm and a gradually rising intonation and the alphorn-fa. "You can still listen to the *zäuerli*. Go to a village like Urnäsch (Toggenburg region)," advises Bachmann-Geiser, "sit down on a Sunday afternoon in an inn and you will hear it. Which is really astonishing. Something else that's very important in Appenzell is the bell-shaking *(schelleschötte)* accompanying the *naturjodel*." The *naturjodel*, an improvised *jutz* with one yodeler leading and the remaining yodelers following, is native to Appenzell and Toggenburg, where the hackbrett or strings often accompanied yodeling. *Gradhäba* is a form of homophonic psalm–influenced singing characterized by a solo yodel sung with an improvised "sustained block harmony," which has a function similar to that of the drone voice in the Balkans.

Although there may be an Appenzell sound—melancholy, slow, and resonant—many villages in the region have their own dialects, celebrations, and vocal traditions. For instance, the yodels in and around Heiden and Walzenhausen are characterized by a particular liveliness and gaiety — more in the Austrian tradition than a typical Appenzeller yodel. Others involve accompanying drones in large chords or elaborate ornamentation such as grace notes and trills. The hinterland yodel of Herisau and Urnäsch are more Appenzeller-style melancholy.

SELECTED SWISS YODEL ENVOYS

Josef Felder (1835–1914) was a famous Swiss composer of yodel songs. Most of the songs concern the Luzern area where he grew up. His work was influenced by Tyrolean, Steierische, and Kärntner melodies and yodels he heard during his years of wandering. Felder lost both his parents when he was still young. He and his siblings grew up in various foster situations, and by age 12 he'd had enough, setting out on his own. He found work as a *schafbueb* (shepherd). But this was unsteady work, so he wandered from job to job. As this was the golden era of folksong, he was probably exposed to great varieties of music along his journeys. He absorbed everything and got his education where he could. By 1860, he was a master cheesemaker, for which he gained a reputation and amassed enough money to buy a house in Salzburg, Austria. During this amazing peripatetic life, he also emerged as an amateur yodeler who had perfected his high falsetto while he worked.

In the 1890s, Felder lost both his wife and home and returned to Switzerland. In 1899, he began touring with a zither player. A music director

continued on the next page

Selected Swiss Yodel Envoys, continued

helped promote him, and he won notice in Germany where he toured extensively. His talents earned him an invitation to yodel in the Swiss pavilion at the 1900 Paris World's Fair.

In 1901, he met Professor Joseph Pommer in Vienna. Pommer notated some of Felder's *jodellieden* to appear in his *Deutsches Volkslied*, the journal he established to promote Germanic folksongs. Felder toured Switzerland and, in 1902, Germany and the Netherlands to glowing reviews. In 1903, during his Austrian tour, he began being called "Jodlerkönig Felder." He won a number of honors in subsequent years, with increasing fanfare and ever-larger audiences. His voice was distinct because he could sing in the alphorn-fa and often held notes for dramatically long durations. His compositions are refreshingly free and often ended in *appogios* or nonharmonic tones that skew the prevalent harmony just enough to create a more intricate dynamic. He authored three famous yodel songs, "Der Alte Rigijodel," "Rigilied," and "Der Berner Oberländer," about the region he grew up in.

- *The Demonstration Collection of E.M. von Hornbostel and the Berlin Phonogramm-Archiv*, Folkways, 1963. Includes Felder's "Old Rigi Yodel with Inserted Song."

Hugo Zemp (b. 1937), Swiss ethnological filmmaker/jazz musician, has made numerous luminous films about yodeling, vocals, and related subjects in the Solomon Islands, Ivory Coast, and Switzerland.

- *Glattalp*, 35min., video/film, CNRS, 1984? Documents a moment in time in the Appenzell.

- *Yootzing and Yodelling*, CNRS/Ateliers d'Ethnomusicologie, Geneva, 1986.

- *Head Voice, Chest Voice*, CNRS/Ateliers d'Ethnomusicologie, 1987. Demonstrates the mechanics/technique involved in producing a yodel.

- *The Song of Harmonics*, CNRS/Socièté Française d'Ethnomusicologie, 1989.

- *Jüüzli of the Muotatal*, Hugo Zemp, Peter Betschart, Chant du Monde CNRS, 1990. Charming film focuses on Muotatal, where people perform *Jüüzli* sung in Muotatal dialect.

Adolf Stähli (b. 1925), born in the small Swiss town of Oberhofe, in Bern Oberland, is one of the most recognizable and influential of *jodellieder* composer-lyricists. He's a legend in that part of the official Swiss cultural world where the composers are the superstars and what they write is self-contradictorily referred to as "folk music" but is *volkstümlich* (folklike), music composed by professionals in a folk-music style. "He composed *naturjodels*," notes Bachmann-Geiser, "which is of course ridiculous, a contradiction. But they are beautiful." Stähli is very recognizable because his frizzly Swiss-version afro and

continued on the next page

sideburns do not behave. But his mythic status has less to do with his coif than the fact that he's a unique Swiss yodel composer.

Although he's one of many great yodel composers, he's more of a classical composer because he's in total control of every note *and* at the same time someone who has a special affection for the authentic Swiss folk song. Yearning for the folk authenticity he has left far behind, he incorporates its themes and sounds into his compositions. He personifies the tautology that marks the official Swiss yodel world: a classical composer who looks back to his childhood in the mountains and seeks to find folklike sounds that mark the folksinger's vocalizations during a *naturjodel.* And so, the more that composers like Stähli hearken back to their simpler pasts, the more virtuosic and complex their compositions become. Garage rock it ain't. But impressive it is, even if it has nothing much to do with "authentic." His talents were honored in 1978 at the Eidgenössisches Jodlerfest in Schwyz, when Stähli himself conducted a choir of 6,000 who yodeled his springtime composition "Meyetag" to open the festival. Everyone seems to know who he is. He's treated like a pop star, and I guess in a way he is, albeit in the rarefied Swiss-yodeling style. His compositions appear on many *jodelers'* repertoires and yodel choirs' CDs; it's like covering a Cole Porter or Beatles song. Some of his other famous compositions include: "Justistal-Lied," 1966; "Oberländere Kuhreihen," 1970s; "Am Thunersee," 1977; "Bärgchilbi-Jutz," 1988; and "My schöni Heimat," 1985.

Älpler-Jodlergruppe Zihlmann is an extended family of many generations and some neighboring families who gathered to form their yodel group in 1909 in the region around Entlebuch, halfway between Luzern and Bern. What the Carter Family is to Appalachian country—pure and isolated—the Zihlmanns are to Entlebuch yodeling. They perform incredibly good material—sober yet incredibly inner directed and clear and rooted in the surrounding countryside. Yodeling has been passed along for some four generations among the Wigger, Vogel, and Zihlmann families. It began informally, people coming by with instruments, some yodels, and old tunes. They began jamming, dancing, hanging out, and finally, under the direction of Franz vom Klosterbühl, made a name for themselves. They gathered folksongs and yodels from the entire region for their repertoire. Some of the songs folklorists had never heard before. And so the Zihlmanns became a treasure trove of undiscovered folk songs and *naturjutzen, kuhreihen,* and yodels, some of which Siegfried Zihlmann had the foresight to write down. The yodels are mostly for larger groups and involve intricate harmonies and multipart yodeling, slow and solemn but not all that melancholy, as the songs are more about glory than cataclysm.

- *De Schratteschäfer,* CSR, 1999. Radio recordings from the late 1950s and studio recordings from 1964, 1968, and 1975.

Appenzeller *Talerschwinge*—three people rolling coins on the inside of large, wide earthenware bowls by moving the bowls in a steady circular motion in front of them while singers mimic the sounds of the herd's bells—usually accompanies a *zäuerli*. *Zäuerli* are amongst the most treasured of Swiss traditions but, paradoxically, non-Appenzellers are only familiar with them via the sophisticated professional performances of yodel choirs in yodel festivals.

Zentralschweizerischer Jodlerverband (Central Swiss Yodel Organization, includes Luzern, Zug, Schweiz, Unterwalden, Oberwalden) is a rich area for heartland yodeling. Unterwalden has its own less melodic but more sophisticated version of the *naturjodel*, the *Niddem-Wald*, distinct from the Oberwalden version, for instance. But it's still practiced in its purest form in Muotathal with its amazing *büchel* hornlike melodies, which leave the uninitiated awestruck. But this *jüüz* from the area's valley has a rhythm and melodic individuality that actually sounds modern. It's characterized by a dynamic tense-vocal chord *naturjodel* with descending glissandos and melodies that zigzag their way along. Polyphonic forms of *jüüzli* also exist and consist of three voices: bass, second, and lead, where the second voice sometimes sings *überjüüiza* over the lead. Muotathal is known for its duo and trio yodeling with "independent part-movement."

The Innerschweiz has experienced many recent developments and styles of *naturjodels* and *jodellieden*, creating a renaissance of sorts. This is because the area is home to some of the best composers: Renggli, Rymann, Gassmann, Marty, and Lienert. The yodel has even been used for sacred music in church services thanks to the efforts of music teacher and composer Jost Marty. He wrote the first yodel mass with Swiss accordion/alphorn accompaniment, which immediately became *the* most sung religious music in Switzerland. The mass is composed of duos singing alternate verses with choirs.

Berner Oberland and the Luzern area are rich in yodeling and yodel clubs. It's also home to its own version of the *naturjodel*. Here yodeling is more complex and ornamented than the Innerschwyz yodel. In Luzern, singers gather in a circle and surround the yodeler while singing triadic drones, while the songs are characterized by flexible rhythms and slow yodels. The Bern area is the birthplace of many yodel composer greats including Fritz Leuthold, Oskar Schmalz, Ernst Sommer, and Jacob Ummel.

In Interlaken, the annual leading of the herd into the mountain pasture in spring and back down in late summer still occurs. It's characterized by an early morning worship on the day of *Kuhreihen* or taking-the-cattle-up-into-the-mountain-pastures day in spring. It is a festive day of singing and

CHRISTINE LAUTERBURG

The yodel is a strong longing and something deeply archaic and in the computer world I wanted to bring this forth and give it enough room to breathe.

—Christine Lauterburg

Christine Lauterburg is refreshing: creative eyes burning, her English desperately trying to keep up with her thoughts. She's Switzerland's yodeling "*enfante terrible,*" a title earned without an ounce of conscious provocation or malicious intent. But uncompromising artistry often runs afoul with the guardians of official good taste. She once appeared at a traditional *jodlerfest* crossdressed in a man's traditional velvet jacket. She also coproduced Switzerland's best pop disc of the past fifteen years by intertwining traditional yodeling with electro-dance beats. These activities certainly didn't help ingratiate her to the Swiss yodeling establishment—or hurt her popularity.

In 1994, she was on top of her own mountain, garnering excellent reviews, enjoying sold-out gigs, and lots of name recognition. *Echo der Zeit*, her groundbreaking CD that went to #9 in the Swiss album charts, intimately combined yodeling, techno, and ethno-ambient as siphoned through her desire to come to terms with home and roots, and her dynamic inclination to spread those roots into unlikely places. *Echo* is defined by a strange collaboration: Lauterburg, improv vocalist; Cyrill Schläpfer, modern producer at CSR interested in *genuine* traditional music; and dance-hip-hop producer, Pascal De Sapio. They produced an exciting, avant-traditional, local-world music, dance-floor *jutzing* disc that spoke to both tradition and technology—stretching and bending the former, while warming up the latter. *Echo* is considered by many to be a milestone in Swiss pop music, like Yello's progressive-disco-world music fusion on *Solid Pleasure* in 1980. *Echo* spent more than 10 weeks in the Swiss Top-10—not bad for a yodel disc. However, the "pope" and taste-enforcer of traditional yodeling (the Roy Acuff of Swiss yodeling?), Adolf Stähli, reacted like an enraged bull to red lingerie, calling *Echo* "a mess, a pigsty, an ugly intrusion into our Swiss tradition."

Lauterburg has only recently fully recovered from a car accident in the mid-1990s that seriously injured the father of her daughter and put her career on hold. Her comeback has, however, begun. In June 2002, she performed with Hubert von Goisern, the Austrian world music pop yodeler, in a Bern-area music festival. Lauterburg and others, like Von Goisern, are part of the spirited Alpine comeback of yodeling—one characterized by respect and improv, depth of purpose, and a decided sense of humor.

- *Echo der Zeit*, CSR, 1994.

- *Paradiesvogel*, with Zsolt Marffy & Pascal de Sapio, BMG, 1996. Includes the hit yodel single "S'Vreneli vom Guggisberg."

- *Schynige Platte*, with Res Margot, Zyt, 1991.

- *'S Hät Deheim en Vogel Xunge*, with various performers, Narrenschiff, 2001.

Kuhreihen ("line of cows") is the herding call associated with magical rites. Courtesy of Cyrill Schläpfer.

dancing. The men fatten, wash, and even shine their herds, and the women supply embroidery for the men's costumes as well as elaborate beautiful wreaths of flowers for the lead cows.

In Romansch-speaking southeastern Switzerland (canton Grisons) there is a vocal music that is often said to be similar to Eastern European vocal groups. The metallic, tinny, piercing nature of their ululations was characterized in the 1700s as "generally an ugly yelling and screaming." Many of these vocalizations form part of religious rites or other ceremonies.

The music traditions of the Italian-speaking canton of Ticino, wedged between the Slavonic and French Alps, are often neglected. Yodeling is purportedly found in the Italian-Swiss Alps and in the Italian Dolomites along the Austrian border. Ticino is also home to some ancient remnants of part-singing, and its sound is heavily influenced by guitar and accordion. Some organized choirs sing a poly-vocal type of song influenced by other areas and Italy.

SELECTED FESTIVALS AND RITUALS

Most important festivals mark the end of the year or the changing of the seasons. The enduring festivals are based on ancient beliefs and are steeped in the notion that noise and music are magical, capable of affecting events and nature via their ulterior and psychic effects. Many of the festivals, then, involve noisemakers, cowbells, musical instruments, and loud yodeling.

SPRING

Herders guide their herds from the villages in the valleys up into the high-altitude summer pastures of the Alpine hillsides. The ambience includes songbirds (robins and finches), a breeze through tall grasses, and the tinkle of cowbells. During the ascent, the cattle are often heavily decorated with huge wreaths and decorations. There is much revelry, music, drink, and yodeling. In Appenzell (and elsewhere, too), the *zäuerli* forms part of the *ranz des vaches*, the leading of the herd into mountain pastures.

Three lead cows wear large bells that are tuned to one another. Meanwhile, smaller bells worn by the rest of the herd are kept silent until they reach the pastures high above. During the climb, the herdsmen and other locals will break out into *zäuerli* that are accompanied by spontaneous calls and other festive yodel cries.

SUMMER

Schäferfest in Leukerbad occurs on the last Sunday in July and provides a full experience of pastoral Swiss life with alphorn and yodel performances, cowbell swingers, local costume, prayer calls, raclette, local wine and Alpenbitter, *wurst*, and shepherding. And, oh, thousands of bleating sheep.

Escholzmatt Jodlerfest in Escholzmatt is Central Switzerland's (*Zentralschweiz*) oldest yodel festival and happens twice in three years. Like the national event, it's a three-day affair that attracts thousands of yodeling fans and showcases 1,500 of the world's best yodelers presenting a formidable array of solo acts, duos, quartets, and choirs plus the usual flag-waving and alphorn competitions. But the focus is on yodelers in traditional regional costumes.

Schutzengel occurs on the second Sunday in July at Wildkirchli, Appenzell, located near a significant prehistoric cave in the Appenzeller Alpstein mountain range. The celebrations include a church choir performance, hikes up the Ebenalp, as well as some yodeling by various local yodel clubs. The festival was the brainstorm of a Capucin monk in 1621 and became official in 1679.

August 1 is Swiss National Day, a day of celebrating independence throughout the country. This usually involves lots of fireworks, food, drink, singing, and yodeling deep into the night.

AUTUMN

In late summer, herds descend from their mountain pastures, led by the herder and lead cows along precarious paths. The herd's return is also cause for celebration. Special *ranz des vaches* tunes are blown by cowherds on the alphorn and "are based on a simple chord so they will not be out of harmony with the mountain echo." Plus the usual festivities and the roll call of cow's names, as well as lots of yodeling.

The area around Les Mosses in late August celebrates the annual Alpine descent of the herds. It includes yodeling, alphorn players, and flag throwers. Fête des Vignerons in Vevey, Vaud, celebrates the wine harvest, and every twenty-five(!) years they celebrate the annual return of the herds. There is wine and music—traditional folk music is played and sung alongside classical compositions in the 19th-century German tradition of *festspiel*, folk theater.

WINTER

Throughout Switzerland, December 6 (St. Nicholas Day), Christmas Eve, and New Year's Eve are celebrated by the men and boys who wear *chlause* (a large ceremonial clapper cowbell) around their waists, while others wear strings of smaller bells. The bells have a variety of names depending on whether you are in Sinkt, Gallen, the Valais, Glarus, Wald, Bern, or Baselland. The celebration might include other noisemakers such as drummers, trumpeters, yodelers, satirical songs, or even lighted homemade lanterns, again depending on local custom.

Silverklause (*Silvesterchläuse*, New Year's Eve) in Urnasch and other regions occurs on December 31 or January 13 (New Years in the old Julian calendar) all over Switzerland. The celebrations are steeped in pre-Christian pagan rites. Men dressed as good beautiful spirits/Santas wear elaborate headdresses (requiring hundreds of hours to make) that show scenes of everyday life. Ugly Santas are covered in pine cones, twigs, and branches.

Appenzell's Urnäsch features men (almost exclusively) appearing in incredibly elaborate (Halloween-like) masks made of bark and wood "and behind the masks they are yodeling creating a completely unique sound," Bachmann-Geiser notes. The men are divided into good (beautiful or *kläuse*) and bad (ugly) masked men. They begin before dawn, tromping through the snow in their elaborate costumes and masks. They travel in a *schuppel* (group) of four guys dressed as masculine figures and two guys dressed as feminine figures. Three of the "masculines" wear large ceremonial cowbells on their backs while the fourth wears two absolutely unbelievably large bells (fertility symbolism anyone?). The two "femmes" wear thirteen little bells each, with the lead feminine character wearing the higher pitched bells. When the *schuppel* reaches a farm, the two "femmes" (*rolli*) prance around the yard, while the *kläuse* break out in *zäuerli* (usually three are sung, although no one tells them they can't sing a couple more). The farmer comes out to join in the yodeling and singing and offers them a glass of wine (drunk through a straw) and some money before they move on to the next home.

AND THE SWISS YODEL ON . . .

Fame and renown usually involve one part talent and two parts publicity. North American (country/cowboy) yodelers are much more famous than their Euro-versions, not because they're better but because publicity pushes their image. Swiss yodelers are sometimes famous, but only as a result of reputation. This is the way they seem to like it. It points out a different relationship between singer and song, yodeler and yodel. The American star machine emphasizes the (yodel) song as a vehicle to one's success (however marginal that may be!), yodel as ticket to the (small) bank. In other cultures (Pygmy and Swiss, for instance), the yodeler is sometimes a conduit through which the spirit of the yodel passes, anonymously. The yodel—its beauty and vigor—subsumes individual ego, in effect echoing the topographical and psycho-acoustical effects of a yodel echoing through a valley. This is not to imply that love of song is not a motivating force in North American yodeling, just that commerce mediates and dilutes the direct relationship between song and singer. Most Swiss yodelers do not earn or ever hope to earn a living yodeling. They yodel like others collect butterflies—for the love of it.

Contemporary Swiss music tries to have it all ways (and why not) by distancing itself from official traditional music while simultaneously incorporating traditional elements in its music—Swiss pop is Swiss because it sounds Swiss—and it focuses on a broader world market. Yodeling remains a strange genre here: it's essentially a Swiss tradition that a good portion of the Swiss population is unfamiliar with. Swiss yodelers are sometimes alien in their own land. And yet, one can hear yodeling throughout Switzerland to varying degrees. There are radio shows on Radio Eviva and DRS1 devoted to traditional music and yodeling.

There's currently a small yodeling renaissance underway: in avant-garde and religious music "what we call spiritual yodeling dates from the 1970s when we see the first yodeling mass. This is a new direction." Bachman-Geiser observes,

PETER HINNEN, *JODELKÖNIG #2*

Peter Hinnen is that strange audio hybrid, a yodeling popstar, a *volkstümlicher Schlagersänger*. Hinnen is special because he produced hits that featured yodeling—the only one in Switzerland to do so until June 1996, when Christine Lauterburg's "S'Vreneli vom Guggisberg," a modern interpretation of an old Swiss folk song, hit the Swiss Top 40. However, before Switzerland even had an official Hit Parade, Peter Hinnen was producing #1 singles, at least four of them between 1962 and 1966. "Auf meiner Ranch bin ich König" (I'm King of My Ranch; Ariola), based on the 1934 "El Rancho Grande," reached #4 in October 1962. "Siebentausend Rinder" (7000 Head of Cattle) was his biggest hit and reached #1 in August 1963; it also hit big in Germany. These remain his signature tunes, his "My Way." "König der Blauen Berge" (King of the Blue Mountains) was his last real hit, reaching #12 in January 1966. Most of his yodel hits, however, temper the yodels to casual refrains and thus don't fully highlight his epiglottis-twisting talents. Hinnen listened to American country yodeling when he was a young Swiss boy, and his song themes reflect an American iconography (cattle ranches and dusty plains). He mixes country music—exuberant like Bobby Rydell, smooth like Jim Reeves—with his distinctive Alpine yodeling to interesting pop-novelty effect.

His career as an international yodel star began at the pre-shaving age of 11 in the famous Restaurant Kindli in Zurich, where the Schmid Sisters helped promote his ambitions. Hinnen sang the hit "Ro-Ro-Ro-Ro-Robinson" with Cornelia Froboess for the film *Liebessender X* at age 11, which instantly brought him to the attention of a broader public, paving the way for his "*Jodel- und Country-Star*" career. By age 19 (early 1960s), Hinnen had yodeled on NBC's Jack Paar Show for an estimated audience of 40 million Americans. He toured Germany, Austria, Switzerland, Eastern Europe, and even Japan. He had a total of 15 Top Ten hits between 1962 and 1965. But Hinnen was young and sensitive, and the grueling and lonesome lifestyle of constant touring got to him. In 1970, he turned his back on touring and superstardom, and led a band devoted to local Swiss dance music closer to home.

Hinnen became a Red Cross nurse, which gave his life new purpose and perspective, but he also realized that at heart he was still a singer. He returned to performing in 1991 with a Nashville band to great fanfare. That same year, Hinnen entered the pages of the *Guinness Book of World Records* by yodeling twenty tones in one second on TV. In 1992, he bettered that by yodeling twenty-two tones (more than seven triads—seven chords consisting of three notes each, one "yo-lo-di" equaling three tones). I didn't believe it until I actually heard it. These days, the native Zuricher lives in a renovated farmhouse in the middle of Switzerland's glory: pastures of grazing cattle, snow-covered Alpine peaks in the background. From here, he periodically emerges to perform or record something new. Over all, he seems to be living out the words of his first hit: "On my ranch I'm king / The outside world doesn't much appeal to me / All I need is my ranch and my horses . . . (yodeling)."

continued on the next page

Peter Hinnen, continued

- *Volksmusik und Country-Music,* Koch, 1991.
- *Jodel-Echo: 20 Jahre Peter Hinnen*, 1984. Traditional Swiss folk songs.
- *Jodel Feeling,* Schnoutz, 1976.

For instance, [Marty] produced a very nice [yodel] version of Pater Nostre. It's quite important because it has changed our religious services. Instead of the organ now they often have yodeling. That's new. And then there's the experimental side. . . . Swiss people don't realize that what they listen to on the radio and television is not our traditional music. Not our only [music]. That I think is bad and sad.

Yodeling remains essentially *the* audio backdrop of Switzerland, the one sound (well, maybe those cowbells too) that almost anyone can identify as Swiss.

3

Germany and Austria
Velvet Throats & Leather Pants

SETTING THE GERMAN STAGE

Germany's musical history abounds with yodeling. But it cannot be said that Germany's music is *defined* by yodeling the way it is in Switzerland, for instance; Germany is just too large and varied. The word *jodeln* was first used in a German song in 1796 in "Der Tyroler Wastl" by E. Schikaneder. In 1799, the *Mildheimisches Lieder Buch* was published by Rudolf Becker in Götha, Thüringen, south of the Harz Mountains. The songbook included many Goethe-era authored art-folksongs, like the more famous *Des Knaben Wunderhorn*. There was as yet no tradition for publishing *anonymous* folk songs like *naturjodels*. During this evolution, yodeling remained basically a folk activity and sometime inspiration for the Romantics and composers like Beethoven and Berlioz. With the rise of *lieder* came the inclusion of yodels and yodel-like embellishments as refrains, with its folkloric echoes.

Ludwig von Beethoven (1770–1827) used *ländler* melodies and wrote five Tyrolean *lieder* (1815). In the fifth movement of his *Symphonie Pastorale* (1809) there is a "triple pedal at the opening with its horn yodel" where the *ranz* becomes a leitmotif represented by a horn replying to an oboe's calls.

Hector Berlioz's (1803–1869) *Symphonie Fantastique* includes a *ranz des vaches*—in the third movement, "Scène aux Champs." *Fantastique* uses Beethoven as a starting point. Berlioz wrote extensive notes to accompany *Fantastique*: "One summer evening in the country, he hears two shepherds piping a *ranz des vaches* in dialogue."

MANHANDLING ROMANTICISM

Romanticism is neither precisely the choice of subject matter nor the exact truth, but rather a way of sensing things . . .

—Charles Baudelaire, *Les Curiosités Esthétiques*

The early 19th-century Romantic Movement marked a significant time for yodeling as it began to be incorporated into structured popular songs. Romanticism spotlighted the yodel as a pure expression of earlier folk culture, making it a key to the Alpine-Germanic identity. It's somewhat ironic that Romanticism led to an increased awareness of folk culture, which led to the cataloguing of folk music and to the compiling of songbooks. These songbooks came to represent certain peoples' identities, which ultimately led to their being used to fuel nationalistic ire—instead of an Us culture, it cultivated an Us-vs-Them culture. This was most evident in the rise of the German(ic) youth movement known as the *Wandervogels* whose enthusiasm for Romanticism led to some dramatic abuses of folk culture.

Romanticism was largely an artistic-intellectual movement, whose early glimmers appeared in the mid-18th century writings of French philosopher Jean-Jacques Rousseau (1712–1778). Rousseau, seeking evidence of the inherently pure and natural in nature, sought out the simple yodel, the *ranz des vaches*. In his *Dictionnaire* under "*Musique*," he presents the notation for a *ranz*. Albrecht von Haller (1708–1777), a Bernese doctor and naturalist, collected folksongs, but more significantly he authored the influential proto-Romantic poem "Die Alpen" (The Alps; 1732), written during his travels through the Swiss Alps in 1728.

Romanticism's notion of the dissolution of the individual in the collective ambience of culture had its roots in the ideas of the philosopher Johann Gottfried von Herder. Herder saw the individual as valuable only in so much as he or she could integrate into the greater collective *volk* (folk). Herder helped transform *volk* from a provincial or parochial concept into something national with his interesting collection of folksongs, *Alte*

Le Ranz des Vaches   Jean-Jacques Rousseau, 1768

The Ranz des Vaches that started it all.

The idealized yodeler in romanticized nature. A. L. Gassmann book cover detail, 1930s.

Volklieder (1779), not only because it was one of the first of its kind (notated folksongs organized by song style) but also because he included songs from other cultures alongside the German ones. It influenced generations of folklorists, patriots, and musicians. It included sections devoted to *Betruf* (*Alpsegen*), *Juchzer, Jodel, Kuhreihen, Viehläckler, Hirtenrufe, Heimatlieder,* and *Jodellieder* and it encouraged Germans to feel unique.

Des Knaben Wunderhorn: Alle Deutschlieder (Youths' Magic Horn) was collected by the Romantics L. Achim von Arnim and Clemens von Brentano (1806). It's a collection of German poems and songs that further helped give shape to the notion of a collective (and stable) folk culture that would eventually be given further shape in regional and national terms. It includes *"Des Hirten Einsamheit"* ("Shepherds' Loneliness") and some *"Emmentaler Kuhreihen."* Thomas Bornhauser's poem *"Der Herdenreihen,"* published in 1832, was one of many German literary works that used folk culture to produce an idyllic portrait of the herder's life.

The first national songbooks (in Switzerland, Austria, and Germany) served as effective editing tools for removing blemishes from the national character. The yodel was deemed "real" Swiss (and German) music. The *ranz des vaches* was Switzerland's natural first choice because it so indigenously portrayed the idyllic herder's lifestyle. It found its way into the 18th- and early 19th-century travel literature; there's no shortage of mentions of this distinctive herder's song. The *kuhreihen* served a similar function in Germany and Austria.

Classical composers like Beethoven, Mozart, and Schubert tuned into the people's music. They listened attentively, incorporating folk themes and sampling (borrowing in those days) from folk songs. They fused their individual visions and concerns with those of folk culture until their own music with pride of place. Bedřich Smetana and Antonin Dvořák celebrated the landscape and folk rhythms of their native Bohemia. In Austria, the Strausses exploited the waltz and infused it with yodel leaps and phrasing (*Fledermaus*). Meanwhile, in Act II of Richard Strauss's *Arabella* (1932), an opera about two Viennese sisters, Arabella and Zdenka, Hugo von Hofmannsthal's libretto has Fiakermilli, the pretty hostess of the Coachmen's Ball, yodel as she hands a bouquet to Arabella and names her queen of the ball. Fiakermilli's song concludes with exuberant yodeling.

As the 19th century droned on, the fusion of music with nationalism became not just seamless but natural and obligatory. Composers could no longer afford to remain aloof from their social environment or immune to the political zeitgeist. But in the early 20th century, nationalists were faced with a new nemesis, a seemingly innocuous brand of globalization in the form of the phonograph and radio. Their emergence put a dent in nationalism's ambitions while simultaneously "spell[ing] the death of folk traditions, because the record ironed out regional characteristics and killed off all the forms that did not have widespread popularity," according to blues scholar Tony Russell.

The promotion of folk culture was one way "to stabilise the cohesive identity of the population by non-coercive means." German achievements "were functionalised in the nineteenth century and much of the twentieth for the purposes of triumphalist nationalism." To what extent, however, was yodeling used for nefarious national interests in Europe? Let's close the 19th century and welcome in the Wandervogels and see.

WANDERING BIRDS IN SEARCH OF THE NATURE OF NATURE

> I'm a Wandervogel too
> I'm breathing life's fresh air
> And to sing my song
> Is my greatest desire
> —Otto Roquette (1824–1896), "Das Lied der Wandervogel"

The Wandervogels: cowlicks and dimples; rosy cheeks and ideals; bare legs and guitars. How did this Romantic youth protest movement devolve from its lofty goals to something so conformist, obedient, phalangist, and viciously enthusiastic as the *Hitlerjugend*? The movement was founded in

1896 in a suburban high school outside Berlin. They were a back-to-nature, search-for-value movement in a materialistic society. They revived "past traditions that they believed had been abandoned, they sang folksongs, mainly those collected earlier in the century . . . [in] *Des Knaben Wunderhorn . . .* they discovered new folklore and folksongs." Hans Breuer compiled these folksongs, composing new tunes where necessary, and published them in 1908 under the title *Zupgeigenhansl.* Helmut König notes that Breuer included some "soldier songs" but no "hooray-patriotism."

On October 11, 1913, the Wandervogels gathered at *Hohe* (high) Meissner. Here, on this "mountain south of Kassel, on which, according to German folklore, Frau Holle, the maker of snow, has her home" they discussed their future—and declared their independence from the adults who had gotten them into this mess. It was termed a "Festival of Youth," a Woodstock of its day. They came out against "unfruitful patriotism" and for truth, beauty, individualism, and responsibility—principle over nation.

World War I destroyed an entire generation of German youth and cast a shadow over Romantic idealism. The Wandervogels began to change character. After World War I, the number of youth groups in Germany exploded; some Wandervogels continued their Romantic pursuits of nature, naturism, and mysticism, while others turned to extremism on both the Left and the Right. The *Hitlerjugend* was offically founded on July 4, 1926 and would emerge as the sole German youth organization after the Nazis came to power in 1933. It represented the last festering remnant of the many early-20th-century German youth groups; the Nazis managed to rally many of them under a central intoxication.

Various yodels could be found in the standardized songbooks of the day that were used by the Wandervogels. These songbooks helped rouse the Germanic people beyond pride, to an enthusiastic defense of their heritage (as defined by the state, of course). The Association of Authors, Composers and Publishers, founded in 1922 in Germany, began publishing folkloristic texts extolling the virtues of the peasantry within a nationalistic framework. According to Baumann, many yodel songs—"Buurebluet," "Alpaufzug," and so forth—were considered "echoes of the homeland" in a way that helped reflect positively upon the people.

My curiosity led me to pursue the notion that some altered notion of folksongs (including yodels) was used to beguile the people toward the cause of Nazism. According to author Pamela Potter, "The growth of the *Jugendmusikbewegung* [youth music movement] along with a widespread singing movement (*Singbewegung*) in the 1920s and 1930s fueled the interest in folk melodies." These melodies contained "certain national traits which, although difficult to describe, are clearly felt to represent the general character of the people."

"German folk music," notes Potter, "was a research area that held great promise for musicologists to meet the needs of the Nazi state." They emphasized the importance of including folk music as part of the Nazi identity-building strategy. The songbooks did not contain verbatim versions as sung or remembered by the folksingers themselves but by how others *thought* they may have sounded back before they were "perverted" by oral transmission. These songbook yodels could then be taught to further instill pride in the German state. I believe there were many occasions when folk-songs and yodels could be used for political ends. In a 2001 email, musician Jozef van Wissem echoed my suspicions:

> the back-to-nature . . . Wandervogel[s] which started out as an innocent parallel to the hippie movement but later was appropriated by the Nazis were really into herders, folklore, nature and folk and early music as opposed to jazz and modern classical music. Also probably into yodeling. The fact that the Nazis misused this youth movement which later became known as the Hitlerjugend is your Nazi link to yodeling.

With the Nazi victories in the 1933 elections came increased pressures for the youth groups to join the *Hitlerjugend*; call it a hostile takeover of the spirit. And what followed was a full Nazi appropriation of traditional themes, symbols, sentiments, and folk music styles, which were honed into something predictable to be used in the employ of extreme nationalism. As author Barre Toelken noted, "Several people told me that yodeling was especially encouraged during the Hitler years because it was considered so centrally Germanic." The Nazis just steered it down a more dubious and steeper slope of ideological perversion.

4. Jahr · Hefte · Dezember/Januar 1936/37

Bärenreiter-Verlag Kassel-Wilhelmshöhe

Georg Kallmeyer-Verlag Wolfenbüttel-Berlin

Was the yodel abused by the Nazis? Cover of Nazi music journal.

Musik und Volk, a 1930s Third Reich Youth Leadership publication devoted to music, published a lengthy article by Fritz Metzler in 1935 on the racial aspects of yodeling, which concluded: "the *jodler* is without a doubt one of the most authentic musical phenomena in the folk music of the German tribe. And we can assume that the habit of German yodeling harks back to times immemorial. That's why it was often thought that the musical expression of the early Germans was similar to it." The fact that the Nazis used certain yodels for the casual acculturation of the folk to their national pride is borne out in publications like *Kleine Tanz Musiken*, a 1930s collection of folk songs collected by Margarete Derlien. This booklet was included as an insert in an issue of *Musik und Volk*. It includes several *jodlers* as examples of folksongs, including "Zo Luzern uf Wäggis zue." So, even though there were no yodels that became a kind of rousing call to arms, no "Deutschland Über Jodels," yodels *were* included in the songbooks, and they were analyzed and discussed in Nazi journals in terms of how they defined German character.

YODEL VERIFICATIONS

The 1920s saw the rise of the first *heimat* and folk costume clubs in the Harz Mountain region. These yodel and folk-culture clubs performed for visitors to the region in the 1930s. In 1933, the Harz *heimatbund* (homeland association) instituted various singing and yodeling competitions. Its folk-costume clubs actually marched in a Nazi parade called *"kraft durch freude"* ("strength through peace") in 1936. "Mein Harzerland, Wie Bist du Schön" (1931) was a Harz yodel song with typical "I'm proud to be a [fill-in-the-blank] because I live in the most beautiful countryside in the world" lyrics. This *naturjodel*—"hol-dria-ü–dü, trü-a-u-a-u-a-u-a-u-dü, hol-dri-a-u-dü"—was yodeled by Carl von Hoff, accompanying himself on guitar and recorded on a phonograph record.

In 1938, Harz Mountain natives Louis Wille and Helmut Ludwig wrote a song that they hoped would become a new national anthem. It appeared as "Das Neue Volkslied: Hoch oben im Harz" ("High in the Harz"). Its sentimental yodeling and lyrics were aimed at quashing the *heimweh* that soldiers so often felt. It remains popular even today: "The echo sails through the forest, hol-diö-ü-dü, hol-diö-ü-dü, hol-diö-ü-dü—dü—do . . ." They also published a book, *Die Harzer Jodelkunst,* in 1973. Many songbooks including *jodellieden* appeared in the Harz Mountains region in the first half of the 20th century.

SELECTED GERMAN YODEL REGIONS

The most famous yodeling area remains Bavaria. But despite having its own character, a somewhat devil-may-care, beer-battered mixed drink of Alpine and feel-good, it remains closer in character to Alpine than, say, Harz Mountain yodeling. Here is a survey of some of the more prominent yodeling areas, which, by the way, go as far north and east as the outskirts of Berlin.

The Harz Mountains, heartland dead-center Germany, fairly equidistant from Berlin, Hamburg, Frankfurt, and Munich, remain an open-air

FRANZL LANG: THE ORIGINAL *JODLERKÖNIG*

When I hear people talking about Alpine voices that turned their cochlea toward the enchanting aspects of yodeling, they often mention Munich's own Franzl Lang, world famous, known far and wide—India, Japan, Hawaii, and North America—as "a yodeling wonder," and yet, still a well-kept secret except among the epiglottal cognoscenti. Lang has been singing since the 1940s and recording since 1954. He was discovered by a record producer in Munich's Café Platzl where he often helped tend bar by pouring beers while he yodeled. The producer asked him that very evening to make a test record. It turned out to be a hit, and the rest is yodel history.

Franzl Lang is the original king. By permission of Richard Weize.

Lang's songs focus mostly on his beloved Bavaria. The Alps remain an exotic other for most of us urban dwellers, so Lang's songs actually sound like some glacial version of exotica. You've got to experience this place with all five senses to really understand it—or listen to Lang: How the clean, brisk, thin air makes bells, voices, and echoes reverberate with a pristine clarity. Now I know why people on the mend have for centuries come here for "the cure"—just read *Heidi* to understand this therapeutic religion whose only medicine is clean air. Sure you can learn to yodel, to approximate Alpine or hillbilly yodeling (many have), but for true Alpine soul—how place influences one's vocal character— you need look no further than Franzl Lang. Although he has serenaded much of the world with his yodeling, including the United States, he has never forsaken his roots and memories of growing up in the mountains outside Munich. A regular face on German TV, at festivals and concerts in Bavaria and around the world, Lang has recorded some forty albums that mostly focus on that intimate connection between wo/man, place, and voice. The glories of nature lilt through his songs and ooze from his yodels. His songs are in a Bavarian dialect, but his virtuosic yet soulful yodeling make them worth the listening effort even if the lyrics escape you. His biggest hit is "Der Jodlerkönig" (The Yodel King).

continued on the next page

Franzl Lang, continued

- *Stimmung und Jodlerwirt*, Philips, 1960s. With Toni Sulzböck und Seine Waxlsteiner Musikanten and the Fröhlichen Bergvagabunden.

- *Jubilaeum Beim Jodlerwirt: 10 Jahre Franzl Lang*, Fiesta, 1960s.

- *Die Schoensten Jodler der Welt*, with various instrumental and vocal groups, Fiesta, 1970.

- *Zünftig, pfundig, kreuzfidel*, Philips, 1978.

- *Der Konigsjodler*, 2 CD, Universal/Polygram, 1997.

archive of unique yodeling styles, different from its Alpine species to the south. Surviving milking-song yodels accent the basic melody but not at the expense of clear movements between head and chest voices in a minor or major sixth. One such example is "Maidla, mach's Ladele Züa," with its insinuatingly erotic text about a Musketeer who will considerably widen the heroine's "hole."

In the Harz, the yodel is a *ledauzen, ladaunen, trudeln,* or *dudeln.* They're distinguished by how they commence, especially when compared to yodels from Thüringen (south), Egerland (southeast), and Tyrol. Harz yodels are seldom bound to a song's rhythms. They're freeform, a *freien jodel,* ripe for individual interpretation, improv. They often skip an interval note, creating a dramatic jolt. But even this is not necessarily observed. Every yodeler is free to interpret the yodel part in his own manner. Unlike the EJV in Switzerland, the Harz region's many *jodelfests* encourage improvisational yodeling. The *naturjodel* remains popular here, with room for unwritten improv, unlike their Swiss counterparts who must notate each yodel and then be sure to yodel each note correctly.

Harz yodels cover the spectrum from the most primitive call to its most sophisticated pop form. Many surviving indigenous yodels are solo yodels. Duo, trio, and quartet yodels are a newer thing and probably came from Austria's Schneeberg area or Oberbayern. *Freien jodelen* are usually untitled or simply titled after their place of origin. *Juchzer* are less common but do exist.

The Schwäbisch Mountains, north of Bavaria in western Germany, hold an annual "Allgäuer Lieder und Jodlertag" (Allgau Song and Yodel Fest) in September. But true competitions occur only in Switzerland and the Harz. The subject matter of Schwäbisch yodel songs is of the usual pastoral variety.

The Middle Mountain region between the Harz and Bavarian Alps has a history of interesting yodels. Among the herders and woodsmen, one finds original yodels not influenced by the Alps or elsewhere, although records exist that document how the Swiss in the 1860s sent emissaries to establish *Schweizereien* or cultural embassies where Swiss yodelers and traditional folk would live and show off their folk culture. The area also hosted the performances of the *Tiroler* yodeling-singing families.

The Black Forest in southwestern Germany near Stuttgart is a mythical place of fairy tales. It's where herders and woodsmen used to commonly sing and yodel. In the 1840s, the area was alive with yodelers, singers, and flutists who serenaded townspeople and taught locals new songs. There are documents of surviving milking songs with yodel embellishments and various *kuhreihen*. Head south in Germany and you will notice a stronger appreciation for harmony, especially when it comes to yodeling. The southern provinces are host to many more polyvocal yodel harmonies similar to those in Tyrol and Switzerland.

Odenwald is a forested low-mountain region just east of the Rhine to the north of Stuttgart, near Heidelberg. Documents and sheet music of yodels survive. Yodels are usually freeform yodels (*naturjodels*) plus some Harz-like yodels with rapid chest to head pitch changes. There's also a unique example of a lullaby *wiegenlied* that employs yodeling.

A writer's journals (1804) from eastern Germany's Riesen Mountains, near the Czech border, note the able yodeling of herder boys with their noticeable trills and gurgling (chest and head voice). The author also noticed elaborate long distance call-and-response vocables where two herders yodeled back and forth to one another.

Frankenwald, near the Czech border, offers evidence of past yodel bands and a yodel called the "Schnellgerber Galopp," evidently a fast galloping yodel. There are also several unique yodels that combine the Bayern dialect with that of the Thüringer. Although herding occupations were already dying out by the early 20th century, many area hikers continued to yodel on their leisurely hikes through the woods.

Bavaria, home of the cuckoo clock, Nazism, an incredible countryside, and Munich, is also home to contemporary yodeling's strongest strains— commercial *Schläger* (pop torch songs) that add a Bavarian yodel or two not unlike a sprig of parsley on a dinner plate. Some traditions survive, but most are subsumed in either Swissness or popness. The Bavarians also don't have much infrastructural enthusiasm for *jodelfests*.

Watzmann Mountain, located in the eastern corner of the Bavarian Alps, along the Austrian border, is a unique rock-face cliff on the Königsee commonly called the "black mirror." It's a place renowned for its natural

Waiting for the call in Austria.

echo. When your ferry passes this cliff, you are expected to test not only the natural echo but your yodeling technique as well. The natural echo supposedly has an amazing hang time, so be patient and be amazed.

LÄNDLER-LOCKED AUSTRIA

The Austrians are known as the friendliest race on earth. . . . They like to listen to the music of Mozart and Beethoven. And anytime they are happy they start to yodel.

—Auch Wenn Es Seltsam Klingen Mag, "The Austrians"

What Austria lacks in coastline and seaports, it makes up for in picture-postcard lakes. Austria shares borders with Germany, the Czech Republic, Slovakia, Slovenia, Hungary, Lichtenstein, and Italy. So, a peaceful coexistence with its neighbors is essential to its survival. There are 8 million Austrians: mostly Catholic (78%), mostly German speaking (99%), but often preferring local dialects. The main artery is the famous Danube, although not always so blue these days, unless you sense its sadness due to its contaminated condition. Nearly half the country is made up of mountains and forests. Alpine flowers stipple the meadows and hillsides from May through September and have long roots to resist the harsh winds. The bright flowers are a result of extra exposure to ultraviolet light due to the mountain altitudes. Austria is often portrayed in song as the natural home to hearty but beautiful edelweiss.

Austria has experienced many glorious and dubious political periods. Austrians (like just about everyone else, for that matter) have a few dark shadows to walk out from under, such as its Austro-Hungarian empire and its fuzzy relationship to Nazism. Austria is more enduringly and fondly seen as the place where one finds Vienna, birthplace of Hitler yes, but also the music capital of the world for two centuries. In the late 1800s, Austria was arguably the world's most influential nation both culturally and politically. People in the 12th century were already noting that Vienna was host and home to many *minnesängers* and wandering street musicians. Much later, opera was to make its home in Vienna. Mozart, like so many other composer-musicians, moved to Vienna because of the Hapsburg family's generous patronage. Mozart helped establish Vienna's cultural prestige in the late 18th century. Joseph Haydn served as Mozart's mentor. Beethoven was there, as were Schubert, the Strauss family, Anton Bruckner, Gustav Mahler, and Johannes Brahms, plus modern composers Schönberg, Berg, and Webern. Mahler's *Resurrection Symphony* interprets a song from *Des Knaben Wunderhorn*, whose folk poems he translated, while his Symphonies Nos. 5 and 6 create an allusive atmosphere that invokes yodeling via the beckoning, echoing horns across a valley.

But all that's long ago, although one could certainly make a case for the current Vienna scene—the Seattle of the Millennium?—a post-lounge, trip-hop, and cool dubby sound that is engineered most famously by Peter Kruder and Richard Dorfmeister and includes, among others, the Sofa Surfers, Tosca, and Curd Duca. But for Americans, Austria mostly means two World War II–related films: *The Third Man* and *The Sound of Music*.

Musically there remains an uneasy Swiss-like cleave between traditionalists (those nostalgic for a former glory) and sonic adventurists who hope to loosen the past's lockjaw grip on the present. However, Austria, to its credit, fosters a diversity of musical styles and has a general openness to newer musics. Respect for Austria's musical past is based somewhat on aesthetic considerations but more on an essential touristic hunger for faded grandeur, marketable pomp; the past as treasure trove of cultural currency for the future. Austria remains something because it once was something.

The split between Austria's contemporary reality and an idealized (pastoral) past is at its most profound in today's folk music. There exists an uneasy dialectic between tradition and improvisational invention. The mood is best summed up by Viennese industrialist-folklorist Konrad Mautner: "Improvisation is rare and remains within the good framework

defined by tradition." So-called folk music is really something circum-
scribed by cultural bureaucracy, academic acclimation, and people hungry
for a nostalgic fuzzy farmer past: "The bygone folk were rural dwellers,
whose agriculture-based lives gave rise to the functional—and, not inci-
dentally, lovely—music today considered real *Volksmusik*, a set of repertoires with no more than a tenuous hold on oral tradition today, but dear to
academics, the cultural elite, and some tourists." Much of this folksy or
folklike music (*Volkstümlichemusik*) is still recycled as versions and renditions "played by brass- or accordion-based ensembles and rendered relent-
lessly cheerful—the sort of music to which one might swing a stein of
beer." This is precisely—and ironically—the very music that one begins to
associate with Austria and the Tyrol.

Agriculture, however, continues, and Austrian farmers still get up at 4
A.M. In late spring, herders still accompany their herds up to higher summer pastures and pass their time in summer huts and *auberges*, producing
dairy products. The herds slowly descend during the season, as they masti-
cate their way down the hillsides. The departure of the herd and its return
in the early autumn are still celebrated with various festivities—essentially
centuries-old rites of spring and autumn. Villages explode with music, food,
and fanfare, and the cattle get to wear their heavy cowbells and elaborate
headdresses. Folk yodeling is prominent at these celebrations and is, of
course, defined by informal oral transmission. This doesn't mean they've
escaped documentation. Austrians have been producing folk songbooks
since the 17th century. In 1773, Herder coined the term *volkslied* or "folk
song," essentially giving it rational form and conceptual momentum.

The 19th century was tumultuous but dynamic. People searching for
identity and roots, folklorists and field researchers emerging as important
cultural actors, finding purpose and employment working for the state in
efforts to standardize folk culture.

In the early part of the 19th century, Archduke Johann (the subject of
the "Erzherzog Johann-Jodler," a popular yodel standard) stimulated
awareness of Styria's (Steiermark) unique folk heritage, which led to the
publication of censored versions of folksongs. Franz Ziska and Julius
Schottky, two early collectors of Austrian folksongs in 1818, romantically
hoped their collections would "find their way into the world." Academic
rows over the censorship of bawdy songs ensued. Meanwhile, high-culture
composers gave their audiences what they wanted by incorporating
arrangements with Alpine airs (tunes) and faint hints of yodels in their
compositions. The 19th century also saw the rise of the Tyrolian singing
families from Styria who set out to make their fortunes touring in emblem-

On the road with yodel-
ing Tyrolian minstrels.
Anonymous lithograph.

atic folk costumes with a repertoire of clichéd Tyrolian tunes and yodels.
They even toured North America, serenading homesick immigrants with
their standardized yodels and folk songs.

The mid-19th century served as the starting point of commercial folk
(folk pop). Pop evolved precisely out of the activities of these traveling
"families" who played up mediated images of themselves and packaged folk
for commercial consumption. In 1910, Konrad Mautner published
Steyrisches Rasplwerk, an anthology of Austrian folk songs he had meticu-
lously written down and notated to continue this trend, which continues
into the present day in both pop and the more traditional realms of folk
music performed for tourists, where the musicians ingratiatingly play
exactly what tourists expect to hear. This strange détente can be found
everywhere in the world and is characterized by a virtual hybridized cultural diorama that tourists have been primed by commerce to expect. The
daffiest overhyped regional kitsch actually came via operettas, which often
incorporated and then morphed various folk songs. They were particularly
popular between the two world wars, as were the syrupy *"heimat* films"—
sentimental B-movies that spoon-fed the audience melodramatic father-
land fare.

The landlocked isolation of Austrian mountainfolk, teamed with the
generous use of yodeling in Austrian music, has created a body of musical
works quite different from Swiss yodeling. *Juchizn*, the Austrian variant of
the Swiss *jüüz*, is described as a series of distinct short yells, each with its
own (utilitarian) meaning; it's going to rain, or time for dinner. It is charac-

terized by a distinctive male use of falsetto. Austrian yodels are seldom austere, and in an entertainment milieu they're anything but plaintive and mystical.

Yodeling began with a single voice melody, and it remains common for a single voice to start a song. A second voice came along, then a third, and sometimes a bass line. Austrian yodeling generally appears as a refrain to lyrical verses. But as in Switzerland, some yodels are *just* yodels. There is also polyphonic yodeling "with parallel thirds and triads."

Austria's contemporary pop music is characterized as a variation of Anglo-oriented pop. Contemporary music is more global and mongrel. Austrian pop prefers to mimic popular world forms: rock, disco, new wave, trip-hop. The songs are "made" Austrian by the addition of various ornamental exoticisms and ethno-fusion spins—a yodel refrain tossed in for good measure. This *Volkstümlichmusik* is considered by many folkies, musicians, and reigning hipsters to be nothing more than the audio branch of the tourist industry, manufactured sonic kitsch. Austrian commercialized folk music represents a dubious hybrid of folk and professional, of kitsch and earnestness, of irony and tastelessness—Nashville comes to Austria. But it also holds the germ of new possibilities, perhaps in a manner not unlike how John Coltrane reinvented pop standards.

Hipsters can reuse *schläger* pop with distancing amounts of irony and satire. This is the struggle: part homegrown in its need to come to terms with the invasion from within (nostalgia and past) and a second struggle with the invasions from without (Anglo-pop-rock, Eurovision schmaltz, and global languages versed in laptop electronica, street rap patois . . .). Austrian musicians have often turned to self-parody as a strategy to cleanse their souls of everything that binds Austro-musicians to various tiresome traditions. Among others, there was Hans Albers's "Alpen Rap," which narrates the tale of a New York producer who comes to Austria looking for the latest untapped trend in ethnic chic—yodeling music.

1980s New Folk Music—which seemed to counter the falsified old in a similar manner that New Folk in the United States tried—looked for a way back into some kind of authenticity. It's described as "a mixture of Anglo-American 'folk' with German-Austrian alpine *Volksmusik*, combining these with elements of jazz, *Schrammel* (19th-century Viennese restaurant music genre), rock, blues, punk, and hip-hop." This is most evident with the progressive band Attwenger, who sound both folksy-earthy and totally confrontational *alien* with their unique hybrid of punk and Trio-like electronic hip-hop. Tongue-in-cheek irreverence wins them some elbow room, while hearkening back to traditional standards offers an element of roots and continuity. The Zillertaler Schürzenjäger (Zillertal Apron

HUBERT VON GOISERN

I am a 'real' folk yodeler as well, because folk music is what you feel it is.

Hubert von Goisern (b. Hubert Achleitner, 1952) knew at age five that he wanted to be a conductor. But his early trumpet lessons, music teacher, and life in Bad Goisern, Austria, all proved to be too stifling for this wandering spirit. What this wandering, this curiosity, this love of music launched was a new genre that was neither Eno fourth world, Peter Gabriel all world, or Alan Lomax primal world. He has composed a body of work that draws the Alpine ambiences of his Tyrolean spa town youth together with what he has found on his world excursions.

Von Goisern, as self-taught multi-instrumentalist-singer-yodeler, took up the accordion—his trademark today—with the help of his grandfather and has fused the mid-1980s Alpinkatzen sound with the music he heard in Africa, Asia, the Americas, and Europe. The Alpinkatzen tromped around Vienna, gigging in empty bars and apathetic clubs, eventually producing their first record in 1988, *Alpine Lawine*, with a version of "Kokain Blues." Sabine Kapfinger joined the band and brought the essential ingredient: yodeling. The Alpinkatzen's second CD went gold, and in the early 1990s Von Goisern invited press and label reps to the snowy peak of Dachstein to accept his gold record in three meters of snow. Hubert said simply, "I'm at home in the mountains. Here my ideas for songs occur." He toured Austria with a group of Tibetan artists and eventually ended up traveling to Tibet, witnessing Chinese oppression first-hand. A second trip led to a

continued on the next page

Von Goisern in Africa: Yodeling as world music. Photo by Hannes Heide, © Lawine.

Hubert von Goisern, continued

meeting with the Dalai Lama, which eventually led to the 1998 release of his *Inexil* (*Tibet Project*) CD with four Tibetan musicians. In 1998, the Dalai Lama came to visit Austria upon Von Goisern's invitation. In May 2001, Von Goisern was awarded the Amadeus Music Award for Best National Artist Rock/Pop. In his acceptance speech, he criticized the Austrian music industry and radio stations for not supporting Austrian artists. After a successful 2001 tour, Von Goisern went to West Africa and Egypt. In Egypt, he shared the stage with it's most popular star, Mohammed Mounir.

Von Goisern comments:

> Yodeling, of course, is integrated into my music, but it's not especially exposed. The yodeling in my songs is natural and almost always included . . . I draw from all of the traditions I know, among them the folk music of the Salzkammergut, like Mozart, Schubert or Mahler did before me. Through my journeys, came new traditions—jazz, rock, and blues. All assembled themselves in the creative process, and something original arose, and yodeling is a part of it . . . although I also released a few songs without words, only with yodeling, too.

Von Goisern's music has evolved into an organic pastiche of influences. Part of his style is defined by his dynamic globe trotting, creating a respectful yet easy dialectic with foreign musics. Some Peter Gabriel, some bluesy riffs, funky reggae rhythms, and African folk are audible, as well as some techno and ambient flourishes. But don't forget the unsexy flugelhorn, Styrian accordion, and his yodeling. Afro-Alpine ambient blues rock? As he himself observes, "Yodeling can go beyond any border, as it is a form of communication everybody deeply knows and everybody therefore understands. Yodeling can be mixed with any type of music—jazz, blues, reggae, rock, and its origins will still be present without conflicting with the music. . . . The people are reached by the music."

- *Alpine Lawine*, Ariola, 1988 (1993).

- *Omunduntn*, Ariola, 1994. A tribute to his hometown adapted from Hoagy Carmichael's *Georgia*.

- *Wia die Zeit Vergeht*, Ariola, 1995. Includes "Da Juchitzer."

- *Gombe*, Ariola, 1998. Includes "Anreisejodler" and "Abreisejodler."

- *Eswaramoi*, Ariola, 2000. Includes "Iawaramoi (Steirer)," "Anreisejodler," "Da Juchitzer," "Abreisejodler."

- *Trad*, Lawine, 2001. Austrian folk songs and yodel songs.

- *Poika*, Lawine, 2002. Wonderful CD-single that combines modern studio techniques and yodeling.

Chasers) from the Tyrolean Ziller Valley combine elements of Benny Hill with Riders in the Sky, and a tongue-in-cheek Spinal Tap element, to create humorous novelty songs that appropriate and parody established commercial folk styles including yodeling.

But what about "authentic" yodeling? Austria has literally hundreds of local yodeling clubs and choirs. These groups can be found in small rural villages, larger towns, and the most cosmopolitan of cities. Most of them compete annually in a series of regional festivals in solo, duet, and group categories.

The "Kufsteinlied" is a standard song (often with yodeled refrains) that has been covered by hundreds of Austrian and non-Austrian singers and yodelers since the mid-1950s. It covers typical territory: the beauty of the countryside, some swaying waltz sounds, and yodels. The a cappella group 4Xang renovated "Kufsteinlied" in a deconstructionist manner, while still managing a soundbite of respect for the original.

There are some unique contemporary hybrids in Austria, be they popular, experimental, or hip soundmeisters like Zabine and Von Goisern, who mix cool newness and retro-beats with a special ethnocentric nod to folk musics, taking musical elements and devices and incorporating them into modern styles. They sound simultaneously very Austrian and very other—the most delightful element of pop music at its best. The scene and sound is characterized by combining folk music idioms with pop affectations, to create a world music of innovation while echoing traditional folk sound elements.

SELECTED AUSTRIAN YODEL REGIONS

Switzerland's institutionalized *jodelfests* are nonpareil, but Austria also supports many *jodelfests*. Austrian yodeling has more recently been influenced by modern Alpine trends. They were also irretrievably altered by the introduction of modern recording techniques.

Salzburg Province in central-western Austria is home to plenty of yodels or *Ludler*. Pongau is a prime location for the subject matter of many yodel songs. "Bin a Lustiger Wildschütz" by Pongauer Viergesang is a quartet yodel about the common subject of poaching. Pinzgau is also known for its yodeling enthusiasm. Pinzgau *juchzers* were almost alone in their daring use of the deep tritone (an interval spanning 3 tones, considered *diabolus in musica* by the Vatican, sinful and not recommended because of its ungodly difficulty) prior to 1900. The themes often involve adventures in the mountains and carefree lifestyles. Salzkammergut, a mountainous lake region that includes Salzburg, is also noted for its yodeling. The *kuah-melcher* (Salzkammergut dialect for cow milking) is a slow, ponderous,

THE SOUND(S) OF MUSIC

The Sound of Music, producer/director Robert Wise, 20th-Century Fox (1965), is based on the real-life story of Baroness Maria von Trapp. Or, more convolutedly, an adaptation of the Rodgers and Hammerstein Broadway musical, which produced Ernest Lehman's screenplay, which was based on the German film *Die Trapp Familie* (1956) and on the Howard Lindsay/Russel Crouse book, which was based on Baroness Maria von Trapp's 1949 autobiography (*The Von Trapp Family Singers*) about the harrowing tale of the family's escape from the Nazis. A joyous wholesome rendition of the fourth-hand truth, then.

Sound, nominated for ten Academy Awards, surpassed *Gone with the Wind* as the biggest box office hit ever until *The Godfather* (1972). "The Lonely Goatherd" is more than just a joyous yodel song. It also introduces the Plummer-Andrews love entanglement through the puppet theater tale of the goatherd meeting the girl.

- *The Sound of Music* (Broadway version), various performers, Sony Broadway, 1993. Originally titled *The Singing Heart*, Rodgers and Hammerstein's last collaboration opened on Broadway in 1959 and was a Broadway hit, running for 1,443 performances. It starred Mary Martin in the Andrews role, for whom the yodeling numbers had originally been written.

- *The Sound of Music* (film soundtrack) various performers, RCA, 1995. Music by Richard Rodgers, lyrics by Oscar Hammerstein II, makes for that rarest of events, an engaging, nonirritating musical.

- *Singalong Sound of Music* began in New York and is sometimes presented in the magnificent Ziegfeld Theatre. It has also had extended showings in Amsterdam courtesy of the Meezing Bioscoop (sing-a-long cinema). It's a cross between cocooning and going out. Fun happening with some therapeutic healing thrown in?

The Roots of *Music*

- *An Evening Of Folk Songs With The Trapp Family Singers*, Decca, 1956.

- *At home with the Trapp Family Singers*, the Trapp Family Singers, conductor Franz Wasner, Concert Hall, 1950s.

- *The Best of the Trapp Family Singers*, MCA, 1973.

Swiss-style yodel song, which features a harmonic blending of voices that creates an enchanting melody, although the second part is more up-tempo with obvious virtuosic yodeling. The Pongau region's "Da Küahsuacha" is a *kuhreihen* cry that ends with a *juchzer* sung in the highest register possible by the yodeler. "Nachgesang" is a nice Christian Austrian yodel from the Salzburg region. A popular yodel song is "Auf der Alm is koa Bleibn."

The Schneeberg region in Lower Austria is also known for its yodeling. "Uberlaurenziberg" is a melodic yodel with humorous lyrics about losing one's girl friend while tobogganing. In the area between Styria and Hungary, yodels are *jugitzen* or *Almer*.

Styria, in central Austria, is one of the most renowned yodeling regions. Here yodeling is often referred to as *Wullazer/Hullazer*. There are "three- and four-part homophonic yodels, other multipart mountain pasture songs, and the *Almschroa*, a solo dairymaid's yodel." Ennstal is home to the *Spiagjodler*, a well-known Alpine *jodler*. The influential *Schottisch*, a polkalike dance popular in this region and northern Austria, is known for its feverish pace, which seems to send people into foot-stomping ecstasy with women shrieking and men yodeling.

Tyrol, in western Austria (including Italy's Dolomites), is *the* most famous folk music province of Austria and, other than Switzerland, is perhaps the region most commonly associated with yodeling. It is also where "real" yodeling can still be found, although "it is difficult to distinguish between older yodeling styles and several recent waves of commercial yodels." Tyrol is the country's most touristic province because of the Alps. It is home to the *ländler* dance song with its eight-bar time structure and the yodels based on this genre. "Hahnpfalzwalzer" by Tiroler Kirchtagmusig, a local dance band, is a Tyrolean dance song that includes yodeling. The yodeling here is less about work and more about merry-making, promenading, and love-making.

Vienna introduced its own variants of folk music and yodeling (*dudler*) as rarefied by the sophisticated surroundings of 18th- and 19th-century Viennese culture. R. J. Neuwirth's "Uhudler-Dudler" is a humorous yodeling song that plays on the Vienna word for yodeling—*dudler*—and the unwise mixing of various kinds of wine. The *dudler* is a bit like what Tin Pan Alley did for (or to) cowboy and hillbilly yodeling—gave it a professional sheen. *Dudler* are often highly dramatic, histrionic, operatic, over-the-top yodels, the oral equivalent of rococo. Austrian yodeling uses triple meter and arpeggiated melodies in major keys. Many yodel songs here use the Alpine verse-vocable refrain form. Austrian yodels are often accompanied by ensembles consisting of accordions, dulcimers, zithers, string instruments, and/or various horns.

Although yodeling is not often associated with dance music, the joy of a particular dance might lead to spontaneous yodels (the woo-woo of the techno dance floor; the yip-yip of the cowpoke dance floor). The history of most formal dances (such as the waltz) is folk dance becomes formalized as ballroom dance, from common folk to uppercrust but then eventually back again. One way composers gained popularity was by including pop themes/leitmotivs in their work. This often led to the inclusion of yodel themes to evoke a pastoral ambience, to hearken back to some deep-seated folk archetypes.

SELECTED TRADITIONAL FESTIVALS WITH YODELING

Alpine Austrians sometimes live inside the stereotype created for them by tourists and outsiders. Women often still wear the *dirndl* (full pleated skirt, tight bodice) and traditional apron, bonnet, and puff-sleeve white blouse. The men still wear *loden* (collarless jackets), green felt hats, suspenders, and shorts deep into winter. Although tourism is an important industry, the rural concerns remain herds and harvests. The traditional meal is still the basic variation of meat and potatoes plus desserts like strudel. Folk rituals continue to serve a function somewhere between tourist spectacle and ceremony in the many local festivals. They still celebrate ancient traditions such as the arrival of spring, which maintains a decidedly pagan aspect to it and often involves yodeling and cowbell chiming.

Adventsingen

The Salzburger Adventsingen is the main event of the annual Salzburg Christmas Festival. It was instituted in 1946 by folk music pioneer, and collector of Austrian folk songs, Tobi Reiser who decided to create an event to distract World War II survivors from their suffering. The event now attracts more than 40,000 spectators annually and has evolved into a dramatized Christmas oratorio with hundreds of amateur and professional performers and folk musicians. In 1964, Wilhelm Keller wrote new arrangements of folk songs and composed cantatas that combined folk music with modern music. Add to that a large chorus of yodeling shepherd boys, and you have a spectacle of epiglottal proportions. It has helped preserve the pure yodeling of smaller groups in Bavaria and Austria.

Assumption

Rural folk celebrate the Feast of Assumption on August 15. It's marked by herders and milkmaids (*Almerinnen*) and their grazing herds being fêted by townspeople, outsiders, herders, and farmers from the valleys below. This inevitably leads to merry-making, drinking, singing, and yodeling on the hillside pastures or in herders' huts. Austrian herders can be either men or women, as are the yodelers: the men handle the herd on the treacherous upper pastures, while the milkmaids handle the herds on the lower grazing fields.

Fasching

This occurs during Carnival season in January and has mystical connotations related to paganism. There are parades of elaborately and grotesquely masked people in Tyrol and Salzburg—similar to those in Appenzell. It's the classic human drama of good (beautiful masks) versus evil (ugly masks) "and the struggle of fertility and life against the desolation of winter, which is always a symbol for death." There are rituals that try to arouse nature from its deathly sleep with stamping feet and much clamor. In Bad Ausee

ALPINE HONORABLE MENTIONS

Alpenrebellen, a now-defunct band of acid punks, had a 1994 novelty "hit" with "Country Bumpkins," an unsentimental love song, with emotion mitigated by decidedly irreverent oompah-wave sound. Their work includes wild stretches of yodeling by Milker Räp Sepp, rudimentary rock accordion, some rapping cattle, and yodeling in the style of latterday Elvis—uh oh, must be the thin-air?

• *Endlich Samma Wieder Do*, Kiddinx, 2002

• *Das Beste der Volksmusik*—Alpenreblellen, kiosk, 2000.

Bairisch Diatonischer Jodel-Wahnsinn (Bavarian Diatonic Yodeling Madness) was an inspiring German trio who broke up in 2000. Over the period of a decade and a few CDs, Monika, Otto, and Josef managed to create a lovingly controversial and entertainingly subversive body of songs that satirize the self-serious of the folk scene. They are also adept at a great many traditional musical instruments including zither, concertina, trumpet, sax, alphorn, bagpipes, harmonica—the list goes on—all played in an unconventional manner. They managed to inject a spirit of verbal anarchy and snide cabaret satire into the standard folk and yodel songs, giving it the dynamism of scat under fire, or yodeling on the run. Bonzo Dog Band in Bavaria with yodeling?

• *Sägenliebe*, Lawine, 1999.

• *Aus Tiefster Brust*, Lawine, 1995.

BavaRio combines the unimaginable: Bavarian brass, traditional *zwiefacher* rhythms, and yodeling with cool Brazil sounds. Wolfgang Netzer's Bavarian-Brazilian combo commits near-sacrilege and furrows some brows. There are rules but no regulations, there are frameworks but no taboos. The band of four Bavarians plus the Brazilian percussionist Marcio Alves create an Alpa-nova sound that will have you dancing with your head and thinking with your body. It's an audio hybrid that blows hot and cold, ice cream in an oven, but sounds strangely organic. The yodeling intuitively wraps around the swiveling rhythms.

continued on the next page

Alpine Honorable Mentions, continued

Josef Waldmann plays traditional hackbrett and handles the yodeling, which is decidedly melodic and unostentacious on "Berge." Think Weather Report backing Joao Gilberto in a Biergarten.

* *Baraba*, Lawine/Virgin, 2001. World music from an uncharted territory, complete with some swinging yodeling.

Trio Eugster is a popular Swiss Schlägergruppe that makes generous use of yodeling in their repertoire of pop-torch ballads. They are among the most popular in this German tradition. Alex, the trio's chief songwriter, led the family trio of Guido, Alex, and Vic. They had many hits with his compositions, the most famous of which is no doubt "Kafi mit Schnaps" (Coffee with Schnapps). Others include "Moderne Alp," "Hinder em Mond," and "Sitzed Si, hocked Si, nämed Si Platz." A wonderful example of the more serious side of Alex Eugster is his melancholy *jodler* "De Herbscht-Jodel" on the compilation *32 Beste Jodellieder*, SRG-SSR, 2002.

* *Das Komponisten Portrait*, Alex Eugster, Phonoplay, 1998.

* "Kafi mit Schnaps" 7" Single, Trio Eugster.

* *Feierstunden*, with Trio Festivo, Trio Eugster, 1998.

* *66 Original Swiss Hits*, 2–CD, K-Tel, 1999.

The Hardroasters perform Austrian "roots" music where the roots end up under some cynical urban hip-hop pavement. They produced a heady-headless hybrid—a reggae-yodeling version of the Temptations' psychedelic-soul-era "Papa Was a Rolling Stone." They were part of a mini-movement of young bands—street, urban, satirical, and funny—who were out to prove that Austria was not all somber clean-scrubbed Alpine hillbillies and not just Falco and Mozart. Irreverent yet rootsy, often straying far from home, but don't call them late for dinner.

Maria & Margot Hellwig, this very popular trad-clad Bavarian mother-daughter act has been singing/yodeling since 1963. Franzl Lang "discovered" them in Bavaria after hearing their pure yodeling. They've produced some 600 songs and 100 records of their earnest-yet-polished and very popular solo and duet folk-style yodeling and *schläger* discs.

* *Heimatabend*, Baccarola, 1970s.

* *Mein Liebster Jodler*, Maria Hellwig, East-West, 1981. She has the operatic lungs to reach the furthest mountaintop and shake the edelweiss off its stem.

Klostertaler is an Austrian band that does a well-known gospel yodel version of "Oh Happy Day." They also have an acid jazz number "Duke Johann, You Can't Dance Well Wearing Lederhosen and a Hat," a spoof of the yodel standard "Erzherzog Johann-Jodler."

continued on the next page

Alpine Honorable Mentions, continued

- *Das Beste,* Koch, 2003.

Zabine (b. Sabine Kapfinger, 1974) is a yodeler whose voice travels well beyond her native Tyrol. As a member of the Alpinkatzen, she introduced Hubert von Goisern to yodeling as a vocal technique that might cast one both forward and back. The Alpinkatzen convinced her of the power of their enthusiastically post-mod-trad music. It was

Zabine: A yodeling Björk from Austria? Photo by Sabine Grudda, © Lawine / Virgin Records.

their unique menu of traditional mixed with pop, experimental, and musics from faraway worlds that etched the universal aspect of yodeling into her heart. The disparate parts, the conflicting rhythms, somehow harmonized and communicated with one another in a numinous funk. Her debut *Transalpin* is not unlike Von Goisern's: sophisticated, shimmering with ambient and housey wanderlust while remaining rooted in the sounds she grew up with—yodeling, accordion. The title cut contains a dozen tendencies that must all come together by sheer audacity and the belief that it can be so. It's a busy, noisy and dense affair, a United Nations of sound with yodeling mixed into accordion, digeridoo, thumpy beats, with plenty of studio reverb and even some trendy Daft Punk vocorder-altered vocals.

Her world travels have taught her that strangers to yodeling are inevitably astonished by its sonic uniqueness. Although her world vision is macroscopic, her early life is psycho-geographically microscopic. She's from a peaceful Tyrolian village. Her roots are insular and spectacular, local and pastoral. Make no mistake, the Tyrol has shaped her vocal cords, and they are in the shape of a yodel. She grew up with pop and Elvis—and yodeling.

She's a jane-of-many-musical-trades with hints of Bjork–Ofra Haza-like universal cosmopolitanism. Zabine believes that one needs an element of cosmic faith to successfully combine the universal with the local, the cosmic with the microscopic, and that's her mission. "I will integrate the entire world into my music, piece by piece," she vows, "because all these different cultures are enormously suited to me." Indigenous house-yodeling as remixed by Coldcut?

- *Transalpin*, Lawine, 2001. Ethereal yodeling plus drum and bass, folk music rap, all fused together with strands of ambient, drones, mantras, digeridoo, Tibetan flourishes and African percussion.

SELECTED GERMAN-AUSTRIAN YODEL DISCOGRAPHY

- *Adventsingen zu Salzburg,* various performers, Telefunken, 1978.

- *Arabella,* Richard Strauss, conductor: George Solti, Vienna Philharmonic. Polygram video of 1977 performance.

- *Auf der Alm*, Alfons Bauer und seine Musikanten, Europa 1960s. A zither player and popular interpreter of traditional Bavarian folk music.

- *Bavarian Yodeling Songs & Polkas*, various artists, Olympic, 1975.

- *Castles on the Rhine,* Vico Torriani, London, 1960s.

- *The Cuckoo in the Wood / Old Vienna Yodelling Dance*, Mina Reverelli, 10–inch 78, Parlophone, 1949.

- *Greetings from Austria*, various performers, Monitor. Includes many yodel songs.

- *I Remember Bavaria*, various performers, Fiesta, 1960s.

- *Jodelerfolge,* Uschi Bauer, Koch Präsent, 1989. German pop-star does covers of traditional material.

- *Jodler und Schuhplattler,* various performers, Koch Präsent label, 1990. Austrian yodeling.

- *Kermesse en Bavière*, Toni Witt with Michael Berger, RCA-Gala, 1969. Typical beerhall good-time atmosphere album.

- *Lustig und Fidel / Merry & Carefree*, various performers, Peters Int., 1979. Some of Germany's biggest pop-stars including Heino, Bauer, and Maria Hellwig.

- *Lustige Musikanten,* various performers, Polygram/Fontana, 1985. German folk music and Franzl Lang compositions.

- *More German Drinking Songs*, various performers, Legacy International, 2000. Recorded live in Bavaria, Munich, Heidelberg, and Berlin.

- *Music from Austria: vol. 3, Folk Music*, Mica, 1999. Stylish high-design book with CD sampler that offers a perfect introduction to Austrian folk music.

- *The Music of Bavaria,* various performers, Passport, 1995.

- *Music from the Tyrol: Jodler Songs*, le Groupe Tirol, Playasound. *Jodlers* with accordion and contrebass accompaniment.

- *Pepi, Pepi, Du Bist Mei Spezi,* various performers, Basilisk, 1997. Classy collection of "Dudler and Salonjodler" from Vienna (1902–1953).

continued on the next page

Selected German-Austrian Yodel Discography, continued

- ***Südtiroler Akkordeon und Jodler***, Frieda Wilhelm with various performers, Elite Special, 1960s. The sonic resonance of the accordion actually suits the yodel well.

- ***Yodeling in the Tyrols***, Karl Zaruba Ensemble, Inge and Rudi Meixner, and the Fürk Yodler Trio, Vanguard, 1963. High dramatic yodeling plus some lovely duet polyphonic yodeling and some kiss-and-yodel love songs.

- ***Ein Zillertaler Heimatabend***, ORF/Philips, 1960s. Kitschy cover accompanies good, healthy, beer-soaked fun.

- ***Zipfel eine Zipfel Ausse***, Duo Pinguin, Tyrolis 1970s. Wacky duo's light-pop Lederhosen-Lounge with bouncy choochoo train hammond organ accompaniment.

- ***A Zünftige Musi: Bavarian Country Music***, various performers, RCA-Victor. Includes traditional Baviarian standard polkas, dance songs, folk songs, and *jodlers*.

the celebrations turn profane and animated, with men dressed as women banging on drums for the day.

Michaelmas

Michaelmas is another festival related to herding, occurring mid-September when the herders and *Almerinnen* bring their herds off the mountain pastures in preparation for the coming long winters spent in the valleys. Local villagers come up to greet the herders with their cattle all decked out in floral wreaths and headdresses. In the village the *Almtanz*, the homecoming dance, is danced, and there is much revelry, yodeling, and playing of the zither and ocarina (egg-shaped wind instrument).

Perchtenlauf

Perchtenlauf is a folk celebration normally held on January 6, the date of the Christian Epiphany holiday, but is observed later in some areas. Masked townspeople run through the streets shouting and yodeling, beating drums, and generally making noise to symbolically drive winter away. The name of the holiday derives from *Perchten*, the old wooden masks worn during the celebration and handed down from generation to generation. A similar tradition also exists in which people walk through the town cracking whips to drive the cold weather out.

4

Where Yodels Are Jodeled Beyond the Alps

A mountain cry in high falsetto . . . known right across Central Europe, and by way of the uplands of the French Massif Central links with those of the Pyrenees, with those of the Spanish Cantabrian Mountains, which themselves continue westwards to peter out in the Riflido of the Galician coastal heights.

—Louise Witzig

Although Alpine yodeling is Europe's most recognizable yodeling, people elsewhere in Europe yodel as well. European women from Scandinavia to Romania have stretched their epiglottises in songs connected with vernal and autumnal festivals. In Scandinavia, the Czech Republic, and Slovakia, women herders maintained the pastures and sang "songs interspersed with yodels, calls, shouts, and signals . . . songs for communication across mountain ranges." Yodels are sporadically heard in countries like Italy, France (*Iouler*, yodel), and Spain (*papagayo*). Yodeling even made substantial inroads into pop music in both Belgium and the Netherlands after World War II—some of it was just armchair tourism for the exotic Alps or a yearning for all things American, but some of it was on (or for?) the money.

CENTRAL AND EASTERN EUROPE

GEORGIA

An old non-slavic culture that lies pinched between the Black and Caspian Seas (technically part of Asia), Georgia shares a rancorous northern border

EASTERN EUROPEAN HONOR ROLL

Igor Stravinsky once remarked that the style of folk music sung by the Georgian group, **Elesa**, meant more to him than all "of modern music." He probably heard the ancestors of Elesa, a nine-man (sometimes eighteen-man) Georgian choir of rough-hewn, retirement-age men. Their melancholic melodies are embellished with cry-like yodels that echo Georgia's embattled history. Georgians sing in an egalitarian style reminiscent of Pygmy vocalizations: everyone is equal, everyone has a chance to shine. Elesa features several singers who specialize in *krimanchuli* (quixotic, high-pitched yelping yodels). Elesa's disciplined singers rarely move more than their lower jaws when singing their powerful *krimanchuli*. However, a tradition of improvisation means that they never sing the same way twice; they're constantly updating their traditional repertoire to include contemporary realities.

Elesa's members are all blue-collar and agricultural workers from Guria, in southwestern Georgia. For more than three centuries, these people have been orally passing down their polyphonic yodel-embellished songs in part because most of them still cannot read music. The texts often involve the workaday realities of herders and farmers. They drink and sing their polyphonic drinking songs to relax. Their work songs serve a function similar to American "Negro" holler-songs, and the "Negro" chain gang rhythms recorded by Alan Lomax. They create a work rhythm, alleviate the humdrum aspect of everyday life, and fortify the human spirit.

Macha Otmar (b. 1922) is a classical Czech composer who incorporated the moods and styles of Moravian folk songs into his early compositions. This formed the basis for his ventures into modern tradition-bound compositions. He has composed for various operas, television programs, and film soundtracks. His series of "Lachian Yodel Songs" are an example of wind instrument interpretations of the pastoral *naturjodel*.

Ianka Rupkina has been singing for more than 40 years. For 35, she was the primary soloist for the Folklore Ensemble of the Bulgarian National Radio. She also founded the renowned Bulgarka Trio and sings with the "Mystery of the Bulgarian Voices" project.

The **Rustavi Choir** has been devoted to promoting Georgian folk music and dancing since 1968 under the direction of Ansor Erkomaishvili, who discovered much of their 300–song repertoire in various Georgian archives. Each of the 12 male soloists in this popular polyphonic vocal ensemble hails from a different region, each representing his region's unique style and song. It's a veritable national unifying force especially in post-Soviet times of increased polarization among regional cultures. Georgians also think of them as cultural ambassadors; having thus far toured through some 40 countries. Plus they sound amazing— clear, precise, and moving. Their complex harmonies involve subtle shifts as they dig deep into the authentic, all in a spirit of improvisation; in other words, they don't sound like some dusty folk exhibit.

• *Table Songs: Georgian Folksongs II*, director: Ansor Erkomaishvili, Sony Classical, 1995. Polyphonic songs sung as dinner table toasts.

• *Georgian Voices*, Nonesuch, 1991.

with Russia and a southern border with Azerbaijan, Armenia, and Turkey. Georgia was independent until the Russian tsar annexed this inaccessible, mountainous terrain. Georgia was then part of the Soviet Union until 1989. Georgians don't have much in common with Russians or any other culture for that matter, except for some everyday work songs they share with their Armenian neighbors. This is because Georgia lies at the heart of the treacherous Caucasus Mountain Range. Georgia's resistance to outsiders, especially since Joseph Stalin's grandiose displacement of entire peoples, has remained high. They say Georgians sleep with one eye open and one finger on a trigger.

Georgia's most important musical tradition is probably its a cappella polyphonic singing. Voices cleave into three or four layers, each with its own tempo: the higher the voice, the faster the tempo. The bass lays the groundwork: slow, melancholy. The second level is higher and joins the basic rhythm. The most dramatic aspect, however, occurs at the highest register where yodeling voices weave in and out, with a soloist issuing mercurial yips and shrill jaunty departures from the static bass line. This style is *Krimanchuli*, a highly evocative, ornamental, and stirring yodel sometimes characterized as a "distorted falsetto, distorted jaw." It arose from the area where wine making may have originated—southwest Georgia along the Black Sea, bordering Turkey.

Georgia's culture feels Italian; its people spend a lot of time around the dinner table, eating, drinking, storytelling, reciting poetry, singing, and yodeling. There are boasts and toasts. Some of these toasts involve elaborate table songs. They remain a vital part of the culture because of their improvisational nature. Many of the songs are for three parts: the speaker (*mtkmeli*) leads, while the middle singers form the principal section, with the top voice as follower (*modzakhili*). The *modzakhili* can be manifested in a variety of voices, ranging from a rooster sound to its most renowned form, the *krimanchuli*.

The peasant/herder Svans (some 35,000) live in the steep-sloped, dense-forested heart of the Caucasus, in an isolated valley in the shadow of Mount Elbruz (5642m/18,500ft). An isolated people with unique music, they live communally and own land collectively. Each commune maintains its own sacred (pagan) sites where rituals and music are still performed, despite Christianity. The men sing the public, religious and polyphonic songs, and thus define the Svan sound. Despite their isolation, Svaneti songs are a potpourri of styles, including Christian hymns. They practice their own three-part polyphony: the lead voice introduces melodic fragments, determining the song's text, tempo, and pitch; while the head (*mec'em*) and chest (*bani*) voices follow, entering simultaneously. These

SELECTED EASTERN EUROPEAN DISCOGRAPHY

- *Albanie: Polyphonies Vocales et Instrumentales*, Chant du Monde, 1988.

- *The Bistritsa Grannies and their Grand-Daughters*, Gega, 2000. Traditional pastoral singing passed along maternally in the Bulgaria's Shoppe region.

- *Czech, Slovak, and Moravian Folk Songs*, Monitor, 1962. Moravian Teachers Chorus.

- *Folk Songs from Czechoslovakia*, various artists, Folkways, 1956. Includes numerous traditional pastoral songs.

- *The Folk Music of Rumania*, Olympic, 1974.

- *Memory,* Georgian Voices, Boheme, 2003. Representative 3–part polyphony songs.

- *Géorgie: Polyphonies de Svanétie*, various performers, Chant du Monde, 1994. Svaneti perform their unique three-part polyphonies with lead vocalist introducing the song with melodic fragments, which also involves yodel-like ornamentation.

- *Music from Albania,* various artists, Rounder, 1993, Field recordings include some polyphonic yodel-like techniques.

- *Rumania, Vocal Polyphony of the Arumanians*, Chant du Monde, 1990.

- *Table Songs of Georgia*, Tsinandali Choir, Real World, 1993.

- *Vocal Traditions of Albania,* various artists, Saydisc, 2000. Documents a 1995 nationalistic festival in Berat.

parts are sung by more than one singer, often by entire sections of choirs. The opulence reminds some of Bulgarian or Turkish vocals.

ALBANIA

Albania's music remains mysterious because it is—to say the least—underdocumented. Albania's combination of natural beauty, exotic remoteness, and Iron Curtain isolation has contributed to this nation's mysterious, unyielding reputation. Fact gives way to legend because of its rugged terrain and because Albania was a skittish Stalinist state from 1945 to 1989, suspicious of both East and West. Albanians, the oldest Balkan race, probably descend from the earliest pre-ancient-Greek, Aryan immigrants. Their Thraco-Illyrian language is distinct from the rest of the Balkans. The Romans ruled Illyria for some 600 years. Albania was a "backward" country until 1945, wracked by feuds, poverty, illiteracy, and disease. Albania strove to alleviate these ills during forty years of communist rule. And yet, when the borders opened in 1991, the country seemed like a geographical time capsule, a rusty bit of antiquated modernity—a strange diorama of another world—neither capitalist, nor communist, neither west nor east.

Until quite recently, Albania could be divided into north (the Ghegs, Kosovo, and Montenegro), south (the Tosks), the coastal region (the Labs and Ams), and the Aromuns, related to the Romanian Vlachs—plus the Roma (Gypsies). The Tosks live in the shadow of the Dinaric Alps and sing polyphony, usually two singers performing yodel-like vocalizations, accompanied by a bass drone voice. The Labs also sing polyphony, not unlike what one hears throughout Eastern Europe. Groups gather in a semicircle, with three soloists in the middle. The harmony section sings a drone (*iso*: Byzantine Greek for extended single note), forming the atmospheric backbone. Some believe *iso* is a vocal imitation of Greek church bells; others insist it's precisely the reverse. Atop the thick drones, we hear the first soloist, the *ia merr* (beginner), with a second replying to the first. The third sings nonsense syllables, adding vocal-textural complexity. Singers in the Pogoni region perform a style of polyphony that is also practiced by locals in Vlach and Slav communities. It is characterized by a pentatonic structure with three vocalists—one sings the *klostis* (embroiderer's) part, embroidering the melody with yodels.

BULGARIA

Bulgaria lies in the middle of the Balkan Peninsula. Three thousand years ago, Thracian tribes inhabited Bulgaria. Greek and Roman writings described it as the land of muses, singers, and musicians. Memories of mythical Thracian musicians can still be found in traditional Rhodope Mountain folk culture. Bulgaria was founded at the tail-end of 7th century and unified two ethnic groups: proto-Bulgarians and Slavs. Music during this period was pagan with much of it concerning changing seasons, fertility, and so forth. In the 9th century, Bulgarian churches began adopting Byzantine service chants. During Bulgaria's annexation by the Ottoman Empire (1396–1878), indigenous music was outlawed. The surreptitious singing of folk music helped Bulgarians maintain their identities. Little documentation exists, but traditional village folk and church music served as rallying points in their liberation from the Ottomans and influenced new forms of sophisticated musical culture. Emigré and outlawed musicians reintroduced vocal and instrumental folk music, which is opulent, textured, and varied due to Bulgaria's many cultural influences.

Each region maintains its own musical identity. Polyphony is found in the Pirin, Rila, and Vitosha mountain areas. Even today, village people sing work songs—ritual songs that accompany funerals, births, and weddings—

and many still play traditional instruments like the shepherd's pipe. Many of the songs employ asymmetrical rhythms (5/16), which Béla Bartók called "Bulgarian measures." Women sang field songs during harvests and added ornamental solos with their miscellaneous vocalizations, including a periodic yodel. Men stuck to narratives and ballads.

Pirin, in Southwest Bulgaria, has many songs that are sung by two groups of three women. One group commences with a melody, with the second voice floating atop the melody. This process of call-and-response results in a lush intertwined choral sound. Dissonant intervals are introduced between the first and second voices. This produces rapid changes of pitch and yodels with sharp bell-like sounds, an aural allusion to cowbells jangling from the necks of grazing cattle in the Pirin valleys.

The Rhodopie Mountains of southern Bulgaria, home of Orpheus *and* Bulgarian Muslims, is marked by its musical variety. Most songs have simple rhythms but complex pentatonic melodies, which give them a majestic awe-inspiring sound. The slow melancholy songs are generously ornamented and usually concern the herder's lonely life and his dreams of returning to civilization. They are often accompanied by Rhodopy horns and country boys blowing on *pandores*, or shepherd's whistles. Shopluka, the Shoppes Mountain region around Sofia, the capital, has two groups that engage in dynamic call-and-respond singing that includes lyrics and vocables. One group attempts to create those sharp intervals involving yodel-like vocals that remind listeners of cowbells.

Northern Bulgaria, between the Danube to the north and Balkan Mountains to the south, is home to Turks, Romanian Vlachs, and Serbs who sing songs based on one or two tones and characterized by simple rhythms. The songs are mostly of the shepherd-harvesting variety with an incantatory quality, The songs are remnants of a time when people still (rightly) believed that music influenced nature (herds, crops). They include periodic insertions of high-pitched yelps and yodel-like calls performed by one or two soloists.

ROMANIA

In southeastern Europe, along the Black Sea, between Bulgaria and Ukraine, and bordering Hungary, Moldova, and Yugoslavia, Romania is one of the poorest countries in Europe, pillaged for decades by the corrupt Ceauşescu regime. He was overthrown and executed on live television in late 1989. Romania's infrastructure remains antiquated, and, since 1989, its economy has worsened while corruption has increased.

Religious music was gloomily Byzantine until it began to incorporate local folk styles (15th–17th centuries). Russians may have introduced polyphony in the 18th century, something Romanian composers began wholeheartedly incorporating into their compositions. The uniquely Romanian *doina* are melancholy Romanian folk songs, not related to any particular custom or rite. Lyrics usually involve the four "L's": love, longing, loss, and loneliness. But the songs are not depressing; they're spunky and life-affirming and sung whenever a singer feels like it. Bartók described the elements that comprise the *doina,* known under various names as "long" or "prolonged" songs about "slopes," "forest," or "farewells." Both vocal and instrumental *doina* exist in a wide variety of formations and accompaniments. *Doina* often include dramatic flamboyant vocals and chromatic melodies—resembling Georgian table songs. In some regions, the *doina* involves glottal sounds (Marmures) or yodels called *haulit* (Oltenia).

BOHEMIA

Some yodeling is found in Bohemia in the Czech Republic and in Slovakia, near the culturally porous Bavarian border where Ernst Kiehl has noted cross-border yodel sharing. This certainly calls for more research, especially since these countries share borders with both Austria and Germany.

LOWLAND YODELING: THE HIGHS OF THE LOWS

THE NETHERLANDS

Dutch yodeling? Ridiculous? You bet. There are no mountains here, although there are some steep skateboard ramps, formidable dikes, and impressive speedbumps. And yet, there has been a fair amount of yodeling in the Lowlands: weird, anomalous, it shouldn't have happened, but it did and does.

The Dutch have a long boisterous history of barroom singing in brown cafés. These smoky bowers offer a raucous ambience where they sing their *smartlappen* (tearjerkers/torch songs) with beer glasses swaying precariously in sweaty hands. These songs are emotionally positioned somewhere between humorous and tragic, often heavy on schmaltz and bathos; *smartlappen* have high kitsch value. The advent of radios and record players changed the nature of popular music, here as elsewhere. It led to a boom in song culture. Dutch cabaret and revues were big in the 1920s and 1930s and have remained so up into the present. Jazz was popular in that period but became even more so after World War II.

But what was genuinely odd was the emergence of Hawaiian music as a popular Dutch genre in the late 1920s, continuing on into the early 1960s. In fact, when all of Holland was celebrating the end of World War II, the

LOWLAND HONOR ROLL

De Alpenzusjes (Alpine Sisters), Dutch/Belgian duo debuted in 1980 in the province of Limburg with their own brand of Lowland yodel-laced pop throughout the Netherlands, Belgium, and Spain and as far away as Tunisia and Australia. Besides "Tirool, Tirool, Tirool," they scored a near-hit in 1986 with "De Tiroler Babysitter Song" recorded with Trio Kwatsch. In 2000, De Alpenzusjes celebrated their twentieth anniversary with the CD *Feest Met De Alpenzusjes.*

Eddy Christiani, first Dutch pop star and creative electric guitarist, wrote "*Ouwe Taaie*" during World War II with the refrain: "jippie jippie jee." As Toni Smith notes, "Because it was about a cowboy it was considered a secret anti-German song." He also played in Tom's Prairie Pioneers, who did plenty of kitchy cowboy numbers. But the yodeling was minimal. Christiani also wrote a song recorded by the great French accordionist Marcel Azzolla called "Rocky Mountain Yodel."

De Drie Musketiers in 1948, performed a Dutch version of the Andrews Sisters's yodel hit "Toolie Oolie Doolie" ("*Als na Regen de Zon Schijnt*") with Henk Dore handling the yodeling.

Johnny Hoes (b. 1917) of Weert (Limburg) is the mysterious godfather cum Phil Spector of Dutch song. A purist and idealist, he has never compromised his mission of Dutch songs for Dutch people. He's been active since World War II, when he began organizing parties for Allied soldiers after Limburg was liberated in 1944. He wrote his first song, "Cowboy Soldaat" (Cowboy Soldier), that same year. He has had his fingers in every Dutch musical pie since and has aided countless singers on their paths to stardom. He's been a producer/label owner since 1973 (Telstar), publisher, singer, songwriter, radio DJ, and honorary sometime cowboy. He has written hundreds of songs (including yodels) for many performers in every genre of Dutch music, as well as producing their records. A few of the many yodel discs (excluding Jodel Jerry's) he has written songs for and/or produced for Telstar include:

- *Cowboys en Meisjes*, various performers, 1973.

- *Alpenbal*, various performers, 1970s.

- *Jodelfeest bij Gerald Fuchs*, 1970s.

- *Feest in Tirol*, various performers, 1970s.

- *Bergen van Tirol*, Helma en Selma, 1997.

Jodel Jerry (b. Ger van Geylswijk) remains a mystery. There's not much out there on him anywhere, although from the 1950s to the 1970s he was very active, working under a number of hats, cowboy and otherwise. He sings Dutch versions of cowboy standards, yodel songs written or translated by other Lowland cowboys like Johnny Hoes ("Ik voel me Rijk als 'n Koning"—I Feel Rich as a King and

continued on the next page

Lowland Honor Roll, continued

"Little Joe") plus his own compositions. He has a deep, broad repertoire of yodel songs, including "De Jodelende Cowboy," "'n Cowboy uit het Westen," and "Jodel Boogie." His recordings are all in various stages of neglect, obscurity, and *unissuedness*. I had no luck trying to contact him. He sang solo and as part of De Jodel Jerry's and Jodel Jerry & De Prairie Rosjes. Because he's a good yodeler and the songs remain interesting, he certainly bears further investigation. Some other yodels include "de Jodelenede Cowboy," "Ver in Arizona," "Het Jodelende Boertje," and "In de Jailhouse."

- *De Jodelende Cowboy*, Telstar, 1970s.

- *Het Beste van Jodel Jerry*, Telstar, 1970s.

Bobby Klein was a child wonder in a kid's cowboy outfit. Although his singing can be annoying, as most children's singing is, his yodeling is surprisingly accomplished and robust. "De Zwitserse Cowboy," "Ouwe Bles," "Een Drent in Tirol," "Oh, Mooi Tirool," "de Cowboy Song," "Cowboy Johnny," and "Jodelin' Bobby" were some of his yodel hits in the 1950s.

Dutch boy yodel wonder, Bobby Klein. From *Tuney Tunes*, March 1955.

    Paul Ostra (1899–1978) debuted as a cabareteer in an operetta in 1923. He wrote hundreds of songs and ran his own theater company for years. He also starred in the 1961 film *Hunted in Holland* by Derek Williams. However, his most yodel apropos theater piece was the musical *Tyrol, Kunt U jodelen?* (Tyrol, Can You Yodel?) with music and lyrics by Ostra. He performed in it as well, singing the finale, "Kunt U Jodelen," introduced by the following dialogue:

    Yvonne: Where were you?
    Charl (Ostra): I was lying down on the Jungfrau (literally "Young Woman,"
        an Alpine peak). I was a young man. But she remained ice cold. I
        couldn't get any movement out of her.
    Yvonne: What do you think of the mountains here, Charl?
    Charl: Fantastic, I can see quite a bit from these overgrown mountains.
    Co: Yeah, but there's plenty of bald spots as well.
    Yvonne: Can you yodel, Charl?
    Charl: Yodeling, what's that?
    Delsing: You really don't know young man? (yodels)

continued on the next page

Charl: Nice, shall we do some together? Here we go then.
(Yodel song)

Pater Moeskroen was born as a folksy rock band in Amsterdam in 1985. The group combined serious musicianship with some tangibly dynamic Mano Negra-like sounds. Their kinetic stage dynamics plus some deliriously ridiculous lyrics made them popular in the 1980s. They produced eleven albums and six singles.

• *Heimwee*, HKM-records, 2001.

• *Diddelidee!*, self-produced, 2001.

Kitty Prins (1930–2000). The mysterious Belgian cowgal known as "Texas" Kitty Prins is a memorable yodeler who has all but fallen off the map into a purgatory known as society's amnesia. She yodeled and wrote original songs, like her worthy yodeler "Just a Little Lovin'" and some in a Hank Williams style like "Did You Miss Me." Two of her compositions, "A Song Called Hope" and "In the Dust of Dying Day," appear on Ragnar's CD *Honky Tonk Memories*. She died of cancer at age 70.

• *Super Piraten*, various performers, JBS, 1990s. Several Kitty Prins songs on volumes 1 and 5.

Bertus Staigerpaip, contemporary humorous singer with a Brabant accent had a number of Dutch Top 40 (*Tipparade*) hits. In 1990, Staigerpaip got into trouble for writing a satirical song about vacationing Germans in the Netherlands that was deemed to be in bad taste. In 1999, he took part in an evolving house-dance CD series with a piece of manufactured kitsch called "Aprés Ski Jodelie" for the 1999 Carnaval festival.

Ben Steneker, Godfather of Dutch Country and Dutch country music pioneer who began his career in 1959. In 1973, he founded the group de Country Stones. In 1998, he received a lifetime achievement award in Vienna(!) for his life-long dedication to the promotion of American country-western music. His first hit was with Lydia & Her Melody Strings, a cover of "Send Me the Pillow You Dream On."

De Twee Jantjes were Johnny Hoes and yodeler Jan Hendriks. Formed after World War II, they perfomed a number of cowboy-like yodel songs such as "Lasso Joe" and Zwerver Langs de Prairie."

De Twee Pinten (Two Pints of Beer) were a humorous vocal pop duo from Den Bosch (active from 1969 to 2001) as guided by founding father Wim Kersten (1924–2001), who served as one of the two "Pints" (1969–1974) with Joep Peters. Theo Van Veghel replaced Kersten in 1984. They had numerous hits in the 1970s on Philips. They also did lots of cabaret. Their debut album, *Geef Mij De Liefde En De Gein*, reached #7 in the early 1970s. Between 1977 and 1980, they had two Top 40 hits, one of which was "Jodelodelodelodelohitie," (CNR), written by Hennie Vrienten and Tom America.

continued on the next page

Lowland Honor Roll, continued

André van Duin (b. Adrianus Marinus Kyvon, Rotterdam, 1947) discovered his forté early on: making people laugh, using his red hair to advantage, becoming the class clown who could do perfect parodies of popular songs. In 1964, he won a youth talent contest on TV. He later worked at an insurance company by day and rehearsed his skits and songs by night. He evolved into a sort of Dutch version of weird Al Yankovic. Besides his robust television career, he has produced hundreds of recordings, like his 1973 B-side "De Tiroler" (CNR). But it was in 1972 that he produced his memorable yodel satire single "Angelique" (CNR), a Dutch version of the Roger Miller song, "Swiss Maid," that Del Shannon had a hit with. It tells the tragicomical tale of a lonely girl who yodels so loudly she starts an avalanche (author's translation):

Bob Vrieling: Genuine Belgian cowboy yodeler. Album cover detail.

> Because of all that racket
> in the mountains of Switzerland
> the snow started to shake
> . . . yodel ay eee ooo, she sang
> when suddenly an avalanche came tumbling down
> Jodelohohohohehehohohee . . .

Bob Vrieling is Belgium's "other" yodeling cowboy. On the cover of his hit album *Prikkebeen* (1970), Bob is sitting next to "his" white horse on a bale of hay, dressed somewhere between a Hayseed Liberace and Conway Twitty after a Nudie's shopping spree. But Vrieling's yodeling is very accomplished and the cowboy-style singing fairly tolerable. "Prikkebeen," his only hit, reached #250 on the Belgian Top 350 for 1970, ahead of, among others, James Brown and King Crimson. The lyrics, edging toward Merle Travis drinking songs, are about a man with a still and a stash of illegal gin. Some other Vrieling yodelers: "Als Ik Door de Alpen ga," "Het Jodelmanneke," "De Jodelende Cowboy," and "Het Jodel Hoedje."

- *Prikkebeen*, Telstar, 1978. Includes numerous yodel songs written by Bobbejaan Schoepen and Vrieling himself. The yodeling is an odd yet effective hybrid of cowboy and Swiss influences.

music everybody played was Hawaiian. The (Dutch) Kilima Hawaiians were all the rage. Dutch accordionist and writer Toni Smith notes that three exotic proto-world-music styles emerged in the postwar period—Hawaiian, Alpine, and cowboy—all three of which, of course, have their share of yodeling and share other similarities as well. They are all about desirable other places, as mythic-imaginary or unattainable terra exotica, an important detail in the early years after the war. The pseudo-cowboys met the ersatz-Hawaiians . . . well, you can imagine—and this was before hash brownies and "coffeeshops"!

Youth-targeted popular music blossomed in the 1950s, with the emergence of the youth-as-cultural-consumer demographic. Popular torch songs sung rollicking sing-along style with accordion accompaniment by the likes of Johnny Jordaan and Willi Alberti competed with the new American imports. Jazz, blues, swing, country, and rock-n-roll filled the charts and led to the phenom of Neder-knock-offs (my term), Dutch bands taking big Anglo hits and putting Dutch lyrics to them—something the Lowland cowboys had already been doing.

When it comes to folk music(s) and pop culture, one realizes that musicians swim in a very muddy stream: where the mud begins and the water ends is impossible to determine. The Netherlands, because of its history as a centuries-old trade center, has seen its folk traditions become popular song, become pop. Foreign influences are almost impossible to distinguish from the indigenous. One hears French *chanson*, German *schläger*, U.K. pop, and hybrid reggae-world musics, alongside American jazz-blues-country, and so on. Add to that the music from the former Dutch colonies and recent immigrants, and you have a full spice rack of tastes and tendencies. And so the Dutch pop world has seen its share of wacky potential malapropisms that went beyond kitsch to forge a kind of ersatz folk. The Dutch and Belgian yodelers have their own snug, little subgenre of music that *no one* will seemingly *ever* take very seriously, sadly enough.

Yodeling carved out a certain part of flatland culture, rediscovered by a select few later as perfect kitschy romps into aberrant bad taste. Any yodeling in pop songs was considered exotic, mythic even. Today, yodeling is basically considered marginal and corny. And even in the immediate postwar era, you had countless parodies: the Dutch have a special fondness for wacky-parody songs. A good example is André van Duin's parodies of samba, polka, rock, yodeling, and everything in between. Focus had a "worldwide" hit with the first prog-rock (symphonic bravado?) single to include yodeling refrains. It casts a light over pop's shoulder, back to the 1950s when indeed there was a verifiable Dutch yodel presence. I'm not ready to call it a scene, but a sputter of releases generated some hits and some admiration for its main representative: Olga Lowina, the Mary Schneider of her day.

BELGIUM

The earliest surviving evidence of Belgian music is a 10th-century liturgy. Much of what is now known as Belgium was covered with monasteries and churches (and eventually breweries) where Gregorian music could be heard. Folk music was popular throughout the country—folks sang and folks listened. The first collection of folk songs dates from the 14th century. Harmony and part-singing developed in the region around Liège. The oldest surviving polyphonic work is a 13th-century two-part carol from Tongres. Dutch composers dominated the 15th- and 16th-century polyphonic music scene. The harpsichord dominated the 18th century. The advent of sheet music led to the proliferation and standardization of folk music. The 19th century was dominated by the violin and Romantic Movement-influenced compositions. The 20th century saw the radio become an important factor in the dissemination of music, leading to the emergence of a pop culture based on record sales.

Belgium is famous not only for the internationally renowned French-speaking singer-poet-composer Jacques Brel, jazz harmonica player Toots Thielemans, and the Singing Nun Jeanine Deckers ("Dominique"); but also for Franco-rocker Johnny Halliday and the kitschy new-waver, Plastic Bertrand. Belgians were also important in the emergence of electronic and electroacoustic experimental music plus the explosion of techno, industrial,

DE MIGRA'S

Toon de Migra (b. Toon van der Burgt, 1937) is a full-blooded accordionist—or, as they say in the Netherlands, "in heart and kidney." He was twelve when he got his first accordion, albeit a cheap one but something to fool around with at least. Nobody could separate him from his accordion after that; he's been clinging to one for 50 years now. He lived in Mill, Noord-Brabant, until age 38 when he moved to his present home in Uden, halfway between Eindhoven and Nijmegen.

In the 1960s, after hearing Olga Lowina yodel, he took the big step that would turn his passion into his profession: he founded De Migra's Orchestra (never more than four members). He was immediately struck by Lowina's robust yodeling. "I thought 'first class,' I've gotta learn how to yodel myself," remembers Toon. He began listening to Bavarian music and got totally hooked during a

continued on the next page

De Migra's, continued

time when Lowina was a pop star and yodeling had become a mini-rage. The yodel was featured heavily on a number of their LPs and singles but they were never a yodel band. "The yodel was just something to help me earn a living with," Toon says.

De Migra's recording career kicked off an impressive stretch of Dutch Top 10 hits, including their first single, "In de Vreemde" (Abroad), which reached #6 and also floated around the Belgian Top 40. They also had a yodel hit with the Austrian standard "Het Stadje Kufstein." De Migra's remained regular visitors to the Top 40 into the late 1970s. They had two gold LPs and were regulars on TV and radio, as well as doing the usual tours through the Netherlands, Belgium, Germany, Spain, and Canada.

De Migra's as a duo came to a sad end in 1990 when the drummer died. Toon continues on accordion, often backing local dialect troubadour Nico van der Wetering. He also appears regularly with the youthful Band zonder Banaan (Band without a Banana) with

Toon de Migra, yodeler-accordionist from Holland's highest hills. Photo by Astrid Mali. Courtesy of Toon.

whom he has produced a new CD, which includes an unusual version of the yodel standard "Het Stadje Kufstein." Toon has also recorded it with pop-rock band B.Z.B., and it recently appeared on a new *Tiroler* CD, a compilation of Dutch musicians performing in the Tyrolian style. At age 65, Toon hopes to continue squeezing the accordion and squeezing out a few yodels along the way. You can find him every Saturday night at the Feesterij Barouge in Uden.

- *Gouden Alpenhits*, Discount, 1999.

- *14 nieuwe successen*, Bovema, 1980s.

- *Weer in Tirol*, Bovema, 1979.

- *Country en Western*, Rainbow, 1970s.

- *Jodelen in Tirol*, Negram, 1970s.

OLGA HELENA LOWINA VAN PUTTENMUSTERS

I have an iron throat, I don't need a microphone, and I have the stamina to sing for hours.

—Olga Lowina

Olga Lowina (1924–1994)—check out the book's cover—was one sturdy dirndl-clad, Wagnerian-operatic belter, who deep into her sixties was still able to amaze people with her vocalizing prowess, an untutored singing voice of crystal. They called her the "Nightingale with a Throat of Iron," but it wasn't all mastery and volume.

Lowina's self-effacing reminiscences glow with bemused pride, as if she'd been handed a gift that she never quite knew how to explain. She belted out her octave-crunching yodels before large crowds without the aid of a microphone; she didn't *need* one. Although proud, she'd quickly add: "you don't need to have an attitude just because you were born with a special talent." She recognized her talent at a young age growing up in Boekelo (province of Twente) just before the outbreak of World War II when she'd sing along quietly to her brothers' cowboy orchestra, the Krontjong Serenaders. "I was always yodeling along with them, and I suddenly discovered I had what it takes to do this kind of singing." This led to some early local gigs.

Lowina was an artist, although not everyone's idea of an artist. And Lowina was a pop star, an unassuming one who loved giving audiences what they wanted: pathos-drenched tearjerkers. Lowina's singing, gilded with an obligatory healthy lungful of gymnastic yodel refrains, somehow found its way into many Dutch hearts and ears. She came to prominence after World War II during a time when all inspiration and longing was fulfilled by other places—mostly North America. But there was also a flat-land fascination for everything snow-covered—the Alps, Tyrol. It all seemed so peaceful and free there. This Dutch obsession inspired a slightly fever-pitched yodel rage. Lowina was the perfect unofficial Dutch tour guide to take money-strapped postwar Lowlanders where they could ill-afford to travel. She also served as the perfect soundtrack for returning mountain vacationers who wanted to extend their vacation moods by a few days.

Lowina met her manager, Lou Marti (stage name for Marinus Maria van Putten, a performing clown, seventeen years her senior), in 1946 at one of her concerts. He recognized her talent and predicted: "You're gonna be my good luck charm." They got married, and he devoted his life to promoting Lowina and writing her material. Her first record on Decca in 1948 included four yodel numbers that ignited a veritable mini-yodel craze. She sang with the John Holshuisen (later Woodhouse) Edelweiss Band. Woodhouse played that irredeemable execrable schmaltz that was anything but "easy" listening. He also wrote some of her material. If anyone wonders why Lowina was not more famous, I'd look at her choice of collaborator as the culprit. No one doubts that she was an accomplished yodeler, but one can only imagine what she would have sounded like in more able hands of someone like exotica-meister Martin

continued on the next page

Olga Helena Lowina van Puttenmusters, continued

Denny. She had certified yodel hits in 1950 and 1951. In 1957, she was voted most popular female yodeler in Germany, beating out mega-star, Maria Hellwig.

Olga Lowina's "Mijn Moeder komt uit Zwitserland" (My Mother's from Switzerland) from the late 1950s was released at the height of the yodel mini-craze. Despite Lowina and Holshuisen's proper disposition as family-oriented enter-tainers, they also wrote "Hoog in de Bergen daar woont Sinterklaas, trioladiedieo-laadiehie / Die smeerde z'n reet in met Zwitserse kaas, trioladiedieoladiehie." (High in the mountains lives Santa Claus yodelaydeeoo / He spread Swiss cheese on his rear yodelaydeeoo). It's a bawdy number with yodeling that you can easily imagine Benny Hill singing—or Bolle Jan, if you're Dutch. *He's* famous for his satirical détournements of popular songs using obscene imagery and innuendo.

Olga Lowina didn't visit Tyrol until some twenty-five years after her career took off in 1951. When she first visited, the Tyroleans were perplexed by this foreigner, from the flattest and lowest of lands, who had taken up their beloved yodeling. But she was earnest, convincing, and there in the Tyrol she held court; whenever she stepped out on the town, people on the streets would request a yodel. She always obliged, because if anyone ever felt it was her des-tiny to yodel it was Lowina. She was declared an honorary citizen of Steinach, Austria, in 1978.

Following the 1960s British invasion spearheaded by the Beatles and other mop-topped teens, Lowina found the traditional pop world thrown upside down. Invasion, revolution, and a befuddled sense of ostracism. But feisty Lowina didn't take her new-found oblivion lying down. With her release of *16 Successen* (16 Greatest Hits) in 1983, she engineered a comeback series of tours, and she was never again to disappear from the public ear. She pretty much did not leave the stage—until right before her death at age 69. She produced more than twenty 78s, five singles, and seven LPs full of yodeling, on Telstar, Philips, and Decca. Pretty much everyone knows who she was. Somewhere around 1980, Lowina played the same stage that Nina Hagen had tread many times, the famous Paradiso, one of Amsterdam's top music venues. In 1984, she remembered that concert: "young people found it a little strange at first, all that yodeling. But after about three songs, they were crazy for me yelling 'Olga, Olga, Olga!'"

Her husband died in 1993, but Lowina continued yodeling despite being diagnosed with liver and kidney cancer. Her death was big news in the Netherlands but also in Belgium, Germany, Austria, and Luxembourg. At her memorial service in 1994, in Schiebroek, outside Rotterdam, where she lived most of her life, mourners could view Lowina's signature red Tyrolean hat placed on her casket and were serenaded by her "Droomland" (Dreamland) emerging from the crematorium's speakers. She never got rich but she lived, in her own estimation, a charmed life. And as people left the memorial service they heard her yodeling, yodeling all the way to heaven: "Hola hola hola hie—tierie / Hola hola hola hie—tierie."

continued on the next page

Olga Helena Lowina van Puttenmusters, continued

- *De 20 Grootste Successen*, Polydor, 1996.
- *Het Beste Van Olga Lowina*, Telstar, 1994.
- *Ozejodletzo*, Tyrolis Musik Verlag, 1993.
- *Zestien Successen van Olga Lowina*, Polydor, 1983.

and quirky experimental music (Stellla). And, of course, there's Adolphe Sax, inventor of the saxophone.

But when it comes to yodeling, there are basically only three of any notoriety: Bob Vrieling, "Texas" Kitty Prins, and Bobbejaan Schoepen, who's a mighty fine yodeler but pretty famous. Vrieling is less remembered than he ought to be, and it's a shame that there's almost no information out there to be found on Prins.

SCANDINAVIA AND THE NORTH COUNTRY

Scandinavians don't yodel in the strict sense of the meaning: rapid movements from chest to head voice. But they do have related vocal calls. There were once many examples of *viehlockrufe* (cattle calls) to be found in Iceland and Scandinavia. Scandinavian cowherds use signals related to yodeling called *kulning,* which means " . . . to communicate with the herd over distances amounting to . . . even a few kilometers by means of calls: wordless acoustical signals . . . with specific subfeatures primarily concerned with pitch and intensity." However, Megan Lynch, of Web site *Yodel Central*, noted that it is

> significantly different in sound from yodeling. Although it uses the same high vibratoless voice, it doesn't use the same sound patterns nor does it descend much into chest voice. I'd class it as related to yodeling by dint of its origins and original function, but the similarity ends there. . . . Yodeling involves the ascent into the head voice, descent into chest . . . The *kulning* I've heard (on Frifot's *Summersong*) stays in head voice almost the entire time and doesn't really accentuate the difference when it does dip into lower notes.

Kulning (like *joiking* and *kulokkar*), is not "music" per se, but an acoustical signal of the ancient herding culture, serving as calls to domesticated cattle and as signals between shepherds. "The governing principle steering the overall course is pragmatic. Shall the cattle leave for grazing, or are they to be called back? . . . *Kulning* is a matter of near-field commanding . . . and distance-field signaling to the cattle." Nonetheless, it sounds a lot like yodeling.

SELECTED LOWLAND DISCOGRAPHY

- *18 Gouden Piratenhits Deel 1* (18 Golden Pirate Hits: vol. 1), Multidisk, 1990s.

- *De Allermoiste Jodelliedjes*, various artists, CNR.

- *Cowboys en Meisjes*, various artists, Telstar/Parade, 1973. Collection of Dutch cowboy music, some of it eerily "genuine" sounding.

- *Dominique*, Soeur Plus!, Dureco/Dutchy Publishing, 1980s. 12–inch single includes "Yo! Deli (Yodel Mix)."

- *Geplukt & Ongeplukt*, Willie Batenburg, RPC Entertainment, 1993. Idiot-savant, Batenburg was proficient on twelve instruments and mangled classics like "Jambalaya" and "Don't Fence Me In," tossing in some half-hearted twisted yodels, the way you might toss a few crumbs to pigeons in the park.

- *Lichtende Sterren*, various artists, MFP/EMI, 1970s. Includes Stella Bos's "Mexico," a Dutch song done Mexican style with a *piñata* full of Mexican clichés and a pretty *feliz* "Meks HEEEEEE co" yodel refrain.

- *Nederland Piratenland*, Dureco, 1981.

- "The Show" Dizzy Man's Band, Harvest, 1973. Dutch hit single, entertainingly annoying.

- *Slijpers Disco Polonaise + De Jodel Disco*, Telstar Maxisingle, 1981. Disco remix medley plus old yodel songs.

- "The Yodel Sire," Jaap Koning.

In Norway, a principal folk song style is the *saeter*. Loosely translated, it means upland summer grazing pastures (*fäbod* in Sweden). The vocal music associated with pastoral lifestyles (like Alpine) included many work songs like milking songs and calls aimed at particular herds—"goat calls [*geitlokkar*], cow calls [*kulokkar*],"—with similar communication functions as yodeling. There were also shouts (*laling*) and hollers (*huving*), which served as a long-distance communication tool effectively replacing horns. *Kulokkar* is the general term for herding calls that include yodels, shouts, and songs within a melodic framework characterized as somewhere between talking and singing "performed with a type of falsetto technique using an extremely tense larynx." The epiglottal stops and abrupt changes are present, which hint at the existence of migration patterns between the Balkans and *Samiland*. It's certainly possible that Norwegian herders were familiar with Alpine yodeling. A Norwegian "*Gjeitelok*" (goat call) has its roots in the Alpine *kuhreigens*, according to Claudia Luchner-Löscher, in its structure, function, and the fact that it includes affec-

BOBBEJAAN SCHOEPEN

Bobbejaan Schoepen is a "legendary singer and performer from the days when Flanders was still known as the Wild West and the Belgians all wore Stetsons and cowboy boots." He's a flamboyant Belgian yodeling cowboy singer from the muddy plains of Kempen, Flanders. He's maybe the only yodeler in the world—other than Dolly Parton (whom he counts among his friends, coincidentally)—to have an amusement park named after himself. Schoepen's certainly only the second yodeler to ever have a hit with a whistling song (Ronnie Ronalde is the other). If you've ever seen the Eurovision Song contest, it's inconceivable to think that a whistling song would even be entered. But in 1957, Schoepen, the Belgian entry in the Eurovision contest, performed the whistle-song "Straatdeuntje," which he supposedly picked at the last minute, rehearsed once, and then performed on

Bobbejaan Schoepen, cowboy whistler-yodeler and amusement park owner. By permission of Bobbejaanland.

stage. He didn't win, but no whistling song has ever stood a whistle of a chance to win this Miss Universe–like pop contest. As some kind of comeuppance, "De Jodelende Fluiter" (The Yodeling Whistler)—"when he yodels, well, then he doesn't whistle (yodeling)"—became one of his numerous hits; it combines whistling *and* yodeling. His yodel hits include the American-cowboy-influenced "Yodel-ee-yodel-ay," and "De Jodelende Koe" (Yodeling Cow) with Rina Pia.

Popular from the late 1950s into the early 1970s, many of Schoepen's hits were Flemish versions of American-style country hits, especially Elton Britt's which he sang in English and Dutch. He recorded for RCA as Bobby John, and he's often credited with opening the Belgian door to American country music. His biggest hit, "Café Zonder Bier" (a cover of "Pub without Beer" by Slim Dusty, himself an Aussie imitator of American country music yodeling), has become a Belgian standard. In 1960, Schoepen had a #1 hit with "Een Hutje op de Heide" (A Cabin on the Heath). By the end of the 1960s, he was popular from the Netherlands to Indonesia, and had recorded with Josephine Baker, Gilbert Bécaud, Jacques Brel, and Tex Williams. He'd performed on Grand Old Opry and the *Ed Sullivan Show*, and for Queen Elizabeth II.

In the late 1960s, tired of touring, Schoepen settled down to start a "small" business: his own amusement park, Bobbejaanland, on a swamp in Kasterlee, with an American cowboys-and-Indians Western theme. He suppos-edly still performs his whistling, guitar-picking, yodeling, and crooning there.

continued on the next page

Bobbejaan Schoepen, continued

In 2000, Schoepen, with 20 Gold records, was inducted into the Flemish Music Hall of Fame.

• *Het Beste van Bobbejaan Schoepen vol. 1–2*, Telstar, 1995.

• *De Bobbejaan Story*, Bobbejaan Schoepen, Telstar, 1970s.

• *Double Gold*, BMG. 40 tracks, many with yodeling, 1990s.

tionate calling of the cows' names. These *lockruf*-like vocals or calls were recorded in Norway and Finland by Sichardt. The Norwegian *rop* (call), *huingar*, or *lokk* also include the *lockruf*'s characteristic leaps and plunges, and a closing portamento that glides smoothly through its last notes.

Swedish and Norwegian women have always been the herders in their respective cultures. Like their mainly Alpine male counterparts, they led their herds from the farm into the higher mountain pastures each summer. Women also milked the cows and produced the butter and cheese. They developed a series of sophisticated vocal signals (as well as some blown on horns and the *lur*, a wooden trumpet) with which they communicated with their herds or other herders. The calls are intricate and involve subtle differences in signal to communicate various situations, warnings, or emotions. The songs and music "can be heard up to three or four kilometers through the deep forests." The signals—or *kulning*—involving mostly head voice falsetto (tight larynx), creating "a very high and penetrating sound," were also used to warn their herds or scare off predators. The songs and music once performed a mystical function as a spell to protect their cattle from evil spirits.

Nineteenth-century Swedish folklorist Richard Dybeck, like Switzerland's A. L. Gassmann, was "fascinated by the strong affinities between the music and its soundscape," particularly in the sound of the *kuln*. In true back-to-nature Romantic language, Dybeck said "The song in the forest, the forest in the song." Anna Johnson notes that the "*kuln*'s falsetto may consist of quick short snippets or longer ornamented stylings that include improvised words, sharp calls, or real song phrases." It's not, strictly speaking, a yodel, because it lacks the characteristic glottal switch—although there are a great many variations, which leaves room for speculation that some may very well have veered off into what might be considered a yodel by any other name. The sound was very effective and loud but also acquired aesthetic embellishments beyond mere function over time to please the ears of both senders and recipients.

These signals probably date from the Middle Ages, maybe earlier, making them Sweden's oldest vocalizations. Although the technique as utility signal is disappearing, they can still be heard in some outlying regions of Sweden (*joddla*, yodel) and Norway and have until recently still been passed along orally from one generation of female to another. Just to reiterate, *kulning* and yodeling have much in common *but* they *do* differ: "While the kulning articulation is characterized by high larynx position in combination with an exceptional constriction of the pharynx, the yodel technique shows a lowering of the larynx and a very wide pharynx area." In fact, kulning shares much with operatic singing in the way loudness is accomplished.

The Sami, the indigenous arctic people of Finland, Norway, Sweden, and part of Russia in a region called *Samiland,* are the main vocal practitioners of *juoi'gat* (also *juoi'kat, jojking, yoiking*). Sami (Saami) is the more accepted name for these people formerly known as Lapps or Laplanders, which is somewhat akin to "redneck." The Sami have different roots from other Europeans. They originally came from Central Asia in prehistoric times and began speaking a version of the Finno-Ugrian language some 2,000 years ago. Despite some 18th-century studies on the Sami, they remained basically unknown to other Scandinavians.

For some 10,000 years, Sami culture has been intimately integrated with their habitat, the Arctic landscape of snow and ice, short growing seasons, and the midnight sun. By the 18th century, the semi-nomadic Sami were competing with foreign interlopers like fur traders (moose and other game), miners, and homesteaders for this savage land. Carolus Linnaeus described them as being totally dependent on their reindeer herds. And in relation to the herding of the reindeer, they employed their herder's calls, or *yoiking*. He described their lives as "content and happy" with "few illnesses." Linnaeus also noted that they were *too* idle, with too much leisure time, which seemed to leave them, in his eyes, unmotivated to improve their lot.

Reindeer herders are one of the smaller but more distinctive Sami groupings because of their unique vocalizations. Sami *yoiking* is one of the oldest musical styles still practiced within European borders. Finnish composer Ilpo Saastamoinen, who studied the music of the Sami and other Arctic inhabitants for some thirty years, was heavily influenced by *yoiking*. According to Doris Stockmann, *yoiking* is a vocalization "where melody and verse are of equal importance." It allows the Sami to sonically hitch their consciousness to their natural surroundings: an organic audio connective tissue. These calls are improvised while singing and can express feelings of sorrow, hate, or love: "To sing *yoik* means deeply identifying yourself with someone or something." *Yoiking* is characterized by

> improvised non-strophic type of singing, using special vocal techniques on
> short melo-rhythmic motives. . . . It consists mainly of solo performance, and

SELECTED NORTHERN DISCOGRAPHY

- *Grieg: Piano Music Vol. 7*, performed by Einar Steen-Noekleberg, Naxos, 1995. Includes "St. Thoemas Klukke-Loeten Fra Valders (St. Thomas' Yodel from Valdres), Norwegian melody for piano No. 146," ED 108/146 and "Norwegian Mountain Melodies (154) for piano. Edvard Grieg (1843–1907) was inspired by folk music he heard while wandering the mountainous Norwegian countryside.

- *Song from The Cold Seas*, various artists, producer: Hector Zazou, Columbia, 1994. Cold melancholy songs by far-northern singers. Includes Wimme Saari and also Lioudmila Khandi whose "Yakut Song" is a yodeling cum throat-singing tour de force from northeastern Siberia.

- *Summersong*, Frifot, Chill, 1999. Per Gudmundson (fiddle and bagpipe), Ale Möller (mandola, hammered dulcimer, flutes), and Lena Willemark (vocals and fiddle). Modern trio heavily steeped in traditional songs.

- *Wimme*, Wimme Saari, Rockadillo, 1995? Saari, being from a family of Sami yoikers, naturally *yoiks*—contemporary style.

probably has its roots in shamanic recitation, which played an important role in Sami rituals and beliefs before Christianization but has since been totally extirpated.

Because the Sami sang their *yoiks* and drummed to achieve religious ecstasy the "church looked on [the] *jojk* as 'the song of the Devil' and banned it well into the 1900s." Holy-minded sanitation was also the fate of the Swiss *naturjodel*. But *yoiking* and yodeling have other details in common. The *yoik* has a distinctive way of dividing the octave range with a full voice that differs from, and is separated from, either a low-register voice or a high-register falsetto.

The *yoik* was once a common audio tool (along with various horns) used in Sami daily life: herding, hunting, fishing, agriculture. But Stockmann also describes *yoiking* as a textless mnemonic technique for "recalling to the performer's mind certain situations, places, humans . . . connected in one way or another with the singer's life." *Yoikers* employ key words and improvised vocables of "different sound qualities" to trigger memories; it "sounds a little like Amerindian chants and song," notes Sam Fuqua. Some of these one-tone recitations are reminiscent of Siberian shamans who employ "an upper or lower minor second vibrato on vowels of long duration . . . and a rhythmically highly variable . . . motivic structure." Some of the more expressive styles dart breathtakingly between a throaty to a normal singing voice or from a low whisper to a sudden high-volume blurt.

In the 20th century, the *yoik* was reintroduced by intellectuals and supported by local youth cultures. It has reemerged as an articulate way to express contemporary Sami concerns. Contemporary *yoik*-influenced progressive and pop music has had a sizeable impact on pop culture with the amazing vocal group Värrtina, Lena Willemark solo and with Frifot, and Angelin Työt, a modern Finnish female group of *yoikers*. Mari Boine Persen, a prolific Norwegian singer, has become an unofficial spokesperson for Sami culture. She performs a hybrid of local and world music, incorporating sounds and instruments from oppressed peoples in other parts of the world. She uses an African drum with her *yoiking*, and this conjures up images of Sami shamanism. But the problem of the *yoik's* survival has nothing to do with the perception that pop is tarnishing its folk purity. It probably has more to do with the way Christian missionaries tried to stamp out all pagan rites that might compete with Christian iconography. With the arrival of Christianity, *yoiking* fled underground.

Do Brits Yodel?

There's no real history of yodeling in the British Isles although there are hints of yodeling-like sounds among some vocals in Ireland, Scotland, and . . . Devon. I talked to avant-garde vocalist Phil Minton after a performance in Amsterdam. His vocals are closer to an exorcist about to give birth to a trombone than yodeling. But he has been known to yodel on some of his more than fifty releases. He explains: "I grew up in Devon and that's how everybody spoke. People speak with yodels in their voices." He gives an example of yodeled conversation; there is decided head-to-chest movement. He says that his mother used to yodel to him. People also sang to the accompaniment of bagpipes, their voices emerging as yodels as they mimicked the bagpipe sound.

Britain did, however, produce some yodelers who gained some renown far beyond the shores of Britain. Locating any yodeling activity in the United Kingdom means stepping inside the music halls: the British version of general variety entertainment and vaudeville. This is where artists like Bert Terrel, Ned Tucker ["The Yodelling Ploughboy," 78rpm on Radiophone, 1930s], and Harry Lester [1895–1993] and his Hayseeds took to the stage. The Hayseeds were an early country-western-style band, featuring wacky characters like Arabella and Goofus, who was known to slip in a yodel now and again (on songs like "Bell Bottomed Trousers"). Their hillbilly-style was popular among radio broadcasters. Some other Irish and British singers who sometimes yodeled include Rose Tynan, Brian Coll, Houston Wells, Brian Golbey, Ronnie Winters, Sydney Devine, Ron Jones, Terry Edwards, and Tony Goodacre.

MEDITERRANEAN

None of us suspected that that world of music, songs . . . and poetry over the course of millenia—would be swept away in a couple of years . . . by the voodoo of 'progress'.

—Vittorio de Seta

In a country noted for its opera, culture, history, and beautiful countryside, you'd think there'd be more documentation concerning Italy's folk music and *Gorgheggiare* (Italian yodel) with its ancient application of the alphorn-fa. There is some data but very little of it about the yodeling that once existed and may still exist; if it hadn't been for Alan Lomax, there'd be even less. Some say Italian culture is being held hostage by its glorious past, living in a shadow the culture and tourism industries can ill afford to let go of. When you think about culture in Italy, your mind may mull over Fellini and De Sica for a second, but in no time your mind is reeling back a century or two to a Venice at its operatic and gilded apex. And yet, when you talk about folk music, there is apparently no Italian-version of Folkways Records, and there is no audio equivalent of Florence's Uffizi.

Granted, there has been some interesting DJ, experimental, and dance music to emerge from Italy, but who are the folk singers, the Guthries, the pop stars? Despite a famous song history: from dance and lyric songs to ballads and Rossini operas; plus Giuseppi Verdi, Antonio Vivaldi, Giorgio Moroder (disco's "inventor"), Ennio Morricone, Nino Rota . . . and then who? Am I making my point? Actually there's probably some good, deep, or amazing material out there; it's just not getting out far enough.

Several regions of Italy have experienced some indigenous yodeling. The northern border is, after all, shared with Austria. With its grazing herds and Swiss-like scenery, you'd expect to find yodeling there. "If you're in the mountains you need an instrument or a high voice to give signals," Barbara Bachmann-Geiser noted during a conversation in Bern, Switzerland in 2002. "And that's the *naturjodel*, but also the *jauchzer* this burst, this shooting of about one-octave very high and very loud. That's the most normal thing, I'm sure you have that in the Dolomites. Because you need it. It's an instrument, it's a tool." Some "cattle calls survive as do, in the Alpine area, a small number of yodels, to which native scholars have given little attention." Tuscany, Sardinia, and Corsica apparently also have some cattle call yodels.

Pure chance led me to a wonderful CD of—you guessed it!—Italian yodels: *Italie: Chants de Toscane* collects three singing groups, each representing a different area and style. The Grosseto Singers from Castel del Piano, near Grosseto, perform some amazing Italian twists on yodeling.

SOME PROMINENT BRITISH YODELERS

Charlie Drake (b. Sprigall, 1925) is a diminutive London-born actor and comedian who had a hit with the Bobby Darin vehicle "Splish Splash" plus novelty hits like "I'm Too Heavy for the Light Brigade." He eventually came into the capable hands of Beatles producer George Martin. He had some success with the suggestive Benny Hill–esque "I've Lost The End of My Yodel," (Capitol) in 1963: A man on a mountain climb "slipped and ripped my yo diddle ay de lee," where the "yodel" becomes the obvious euphemism for a penis.

G.H. Elliott (1882–1962) began recording in the 1910s, including some yodels and songs that made generous use of falsetto. According to Paul Hazell,

> He would often sing a verse then a chorus, then another verse and finish with a second rendition of the chorus. On the second round, he would sing descants, throw in wavers in his voice, phrase the words differently, strengthen his voice and add voice breaks. It was a very effective way of adding a climax to otherwise mundane songs.

Elliott was an effective vocalist and "coon" singer who produced some good records into the 1950s.

Frank Ifield (b. 1937) was born in Coventry, England, to two Australian parents, during World War II. His formative years were spent in rural Australia, outside Sydney. Here, while milking the cows, he first heard hillbilly yodeling on a radio program. He was immediately mesmerized. Ifield recorded his first disc at age 13, and returned to live in Coventry in 1959 (until 1986). He had his first U.K. hit (#22) with "Lucky Devil" in 1960. The yodeling "I Remember You" was a #1 single on the American charts in 1963, which he followed up with "Lovesick Blues," another #1 hit. He was so popular then that in Liverpool the Beatles were his opening band. This eventually led to an album called *The Beatles & Frank Ifield On Stage*, which was originally titled *Jolly What* and is now considered one of the most prized pop collector's items in existence.

Around that time he sang and yodeled "She Taught Me to Yodel" for Queen Elizabeth II. His yodeling style is gentlemanly, like Frankie Laine or Bing Crosby doing country: smooth and warm, right where country and popular used to meet. A "semi-country thing" as Ifield himself describes it. "I started off in my early career being very influenced by people like Hank Williams, Hank Snow, and that type of performer. Wilf Carter was one of my favorites at that time."

- *Frank Ifield Remembers the Great Favourites*, EMI-Australia, 2000. Marked 50 years of performing.

- *Frank Ifield: The Best of the EMI Years*, with Vic Lanza and Thierry Pennetier, EMI, 1991.

- *Frank Ifield Sings Country & Classics*, EMI Gold, 2002. From his 1950s heyday, including some rare cuts of his versions of country faves.

continued on the next page

Some Prominent British Yodelers, continued

Ronnie Ronalde (b. Ronald Waldron, 1923), is a diminutive English-Scottish whistler-singer who yodels with a booming tenor voice and a lot of heart. He grew up poor in London's Islington and earned extra money for the family by whistling down cabs for local pub jockeys. Ronalde has been yodeling since the late 1920s. His first recordings came as part of singing troupe (Arturo) Stefani's Silver Songsters back in the 1930s. His early solo discs as "Ronalde" were whistling 78s released in the United Kingdom. His career hinged on, of all things, his virtuosic whistling. He had studied birdsongs and learned to mimic calls so accurately that by the time he was twenty he was known as one of the world's best whistlers. He can whistle basically anything from pop songs ("Tip Toe Through The Tulips") to classical pieces (Handel's "Largo").

According to author and Ronalde expert Paul Hazell, he learned to yodel "from his grandparents who used to sing 'I'm a Yodelling Boy' as a duet at parties. The song has English lyrics but is sung to the tune of 'Zillertal du Bist mei Freud.'" Ronalde cites Roy Rogers as a big influence and also fondly remembers as a boy the milkman announcing his delivery with a "Milk-o-oo-dee." Ronalde broke through in the 1950s ("Yodelling Rag" became a hit in 1953) with his unique combo of singing, whistling, and yodeling, entertaining audiences with his classical-, cowboy-, and Swiss-style yodeling. Hazell writes: "Columbia executive Norman Newell was in a pub one evening [during the 1950s] when Ronnie came on the radio singing 'If I were a Blackbird.' Newell noticed the whole pub quieted down to listen to the performance. Within days he had approached Ronnie to become a Columbia recording artist." He eventually moved to New Zealand in the early 1990s where he stumbled upon a fanatical fan base for his deliriously tuneful, ornithological and epiglottal utterances.

- *Around the World on a Whistle* volumes I–II, Australian EMI. Plenty of yodeling.

- *The Ronnie Ronalde Collection*, HMV 1990s. Includes "Yodelling Waltz" with singing, whistling, and yodeling!

- *Ronnie Ronalde: Magic of*, EMI, 2001. Collected from 1950s–60s recordings.

Harry Torrani (b. Harry Hopkinson, 1902–1979) is very unjustly underdocumented, for someone of such stellar repute. He is considered England's best yodeler by those who know or care enough to judge. He could wag his epiglottis with the best of the world during his short recording career. From 1932 to 1942 he recorded some fifty songs, most of which included yodelings.

One story tells how Torrani guided a ship he was on through thick English Channel fog with his piercing yodeling. It is said that his voice was so purely sweet that women cried during performances. Apparently his voice remained forever boyish never cracking into manhood.

Harry grew up poor in a Wingfield mining family. He got his first notice as a singer in a church choir, and as a teen won a talent contest. Torrani joined a touring group that took him around the world. He changed his name from

continued on the next page

Some Prominent British Yodelers, continued

Hopkinson to Layton, but later, with a new manager, he expanded his yodeling repertoire and changed his name to the more exotic-sounding Torrani and began to make his mark on the world's stages. Reports note that wherever he sang and yodeled people were transformed. In 1935, he serenaded yodel fan, Adolf Hitler; while in the United States, he yodeled for Franklin Roosevelt. Shuttle yodel diplomacy anyone?

Torrani sang, yodeled, and accompanied himself on guitar. He wrote most of his own songs and yodelers of the day covered his "Mammy's Yodel!," "Mississippi Yodel," "Yodel All Day," and "Yodeller's Dream Girl." Torrani was often billed as the "Singing Puzzle" because he commenced performances hidden behind a scrim, so that when he let out his amazing soprano yodel many mistook him for a woman. This caused some nagging speculation about his gender during his career. Torrani retired from the yodeling circuit in the late 1940s but continues to influence yodelers like Frank Ifield and Australian yodeler Rex Dallas.

- *Yodelling to You*, Bronco Buster, 1999, compiled by Paul Hazell. Most of the 20 tracks were written by Torrani.

- *Harry Torrani: Regal Zonophone Collection*, 3–CD-set EMI, 2000. Includes all of his own compositions plus just about everything he covered.

George van Dusen (b. George Harrington, 1905–?) was a yodeler about whom not much is known and not much has been preserved or documented. We do know he was a singer-yodeler with some hits in the 1930s. He was in his eighties when in 1988, his 1937 "It's Party Time Again" (Bri-Tone) became a freak novelty Christmas hit after a music publisher had found a dusty version of it in a flea market and engineered its rerelease.

- "Cobbler Waltz" Van Dusen yodeling with accompaniment.

- "Yodelling Mad Lost Mountaineer."

The Grosseto area of the Ombronne Valley has been very successful at maintaining its traditions. Their unique vernacular, performances, and vocalizations feature polyphonic vocals accompanied by the Tuscan equivalent of yodeling, "bei-bei." The town of Castel del Piano perched on the slopes of Mount Amiata is where "bei-bei" survives in its most characteristic form. The yodeling of Gardellini del Fontanino feature vocals that imitate various musical instruments. It's not so unlike the "trallallero" vocalizations of Genoa and some choral singing on Sardinia. The "bei-bei" which seems to have a rhythmic function, sounding almost mesmerizingly like a train. It can be performed by a trio or a larger number of voices divided into three voices: the "primo" solo tenor, "bei-bei" the medium yodeling voice for many singers, and the "holda" or bass voice.

Italian vocal music consists mostly of lyric songs or ballads. There are some nonstrophic songs, wails, dirges, and work songs that are traditionally and romantically set in pastoral surroundings, and Italians' nostalgic subconscious. These songs, like children's books, always end up down on the farm. Several work songs (and calls) include those that control herds *and* kill boredom: "In Italy, Spain, and the Mediterranean islands, mule-drivers moved goods down the road with special non-strophic songs that combined melody with whoops and calls."

However, work songs in urban and nonagricultural settings started to emerge in the Middle Ages as people moved into towns in search of gainful employment. Most trades developed their own song repertoires. This has been noted in studies in Belgium, the Netherlands, and Denmark. Soldiers, miners, railroad workers, lacemakers, and children's nurses all had their own songs. A few trades include the phenomenon of workers singing *while* they worked (rather than merely songs *about* work). This includes Atlantic seamen, who, in a strange twist of fate, were "probably influenced by African [perhaps yodeling] slaves in the West Indies."

There are also obscure, underdocumented spottings and notations of yodels in France. "Do they yodel in the Pyrenees?" Bachmann-Geiser asks rhetorically during the course of our conversation. "Certainly!" As they also do in parts of Spain.

SELECTED MEDITERRANEAN YODEL DISCOGRAPHY

- *Faiddi*, Agricantus, Compagnia Nuove Indye, 1999. Palermo's Agricantus are veterans of Italian songs and are still peripherally beholden to traditional sounds, although they're decidedly modern. Features Swiss-born vocalist, Rosie Wiederkehr.

- *Folk Music from Italy*, various performers, Folkways, 1956.

- *Italian Treasury: Folk Music & Song of Italy*, Rounder, 1999 (1953), compiled by Alan Lomax. Includes: "The Bells of Alpine Cattle" and "Jodoler (Yodeling Song)" from the Piedmont.

- *Italian Musical Odyssey*, various performers, Putumayo, 2000.

- *Italie: Chants de Toscane*, various performers, Arion/Maison des Cultures du Monde, 1984/91. Features mountain polyvocal accompaniment called "beibei"; its tone and vivacity not unlike Tyrolean yodeling.

- *Polyphonies of Sardinia*, Chant du Monde, 1992.

5

From India to Down Under

In Chapters 5 and 6, we'll travel beyond the confines of Europe to visit other indigenous yodelers in Hawaii, Melanesia, Latin America, Papua New Guinea, the Solomon Islands, and Africa. Even in India, in some "Bollywood" flicks, we find a propensity to break into Hindi yodeling, which is characterized by an eruption of wrought-up, deliriously shrill warblings. Yodel clubs exist in Buenos Aires, South Africa, Australia, New Zealand, but, even more incongruously, in Seoul (Korean Yodel Association, founded in 1979) and Japan (Jodler-Alpen-Kameraden), where they *yoderu* (yodel).

ASIA: FROM BOLLYWOOD TO INDONESIA

I don't pretend to know much about Indian music. We're talking about an area of the world that holds one-fifth of the world's population, so attempting to sum up Indian musical traditions in a few pithy phrases is futile. Instead, I'm going to zoom in on what probably qualifies as the most prodigiously vibrant untraditional of musical genres, Indian and otherwise: Bollywood film music. Bollywood produces 800 films annually complete with a requisite soundtrack because Indian film music, *filmi sangeet*, must do more work than its Western equivalent. Bollywood soundtracks serve as placeholders for all that is sensual, erotic, and forbidden; the soundtrack must paint an evocative if abstract soundscape of the carnal. And just as it may seem cheap for Hollywood directors to evoke the 1960s by injecting a few clichéd sampled seconds of sitar, Bollywood filmmakers have made a veritable subgenre out of appropriated western genres. It's great fun to see

KISHORE KUMAR: "THE BING CROSBY OF INDIA"

his voice wrapped its magic around India

—Amit Kumar, his eldest son

The only Bollywood yodel most Westerners might be familiar with is "Zindagi Ek Safar Hai Suhana Yahan." It's featured in the 1971 film *Andaz* (The Gesture) and appears on the compilation *Bollywood Swinging*. The song may be familiar to Western ears because a version of it was featured on the soundtrack of Mira Nair's film *Mississippi Masala*.

According to radio DJ Rob Weisberg, "Kishore Kumar was one of the handful of big star singers in India during the so-called golden age of film music (1950s–70s) and unlike many of his fellow 'playback singers' he also acted in films." Kumar (1929–1987) was a polymath, jack-of-many-trades: funnyman, serious actor, script writer, director, composer, and, as the liner notes on the *Hits of Kishore Kumar* album proclaim, "the only film singer who has yodelled his way into the hearts of the younger set." He's second only to Dilip Kumar (no relation) as far as his fame as a singer goes. Kumar had no professional training as a singer; he just winged it and discovered he had a knack for ululation. In fact, his singing-yodeling has a kind of untutored bold abandon to it. He often just tossed odd babbling jazz-scat remnants into the rhythms and then improvised with inspired patter and yodeling.

On "Zindagi," Kumar's voice emerges out of a miasma of orchestral strings to sound almost like a Rai (Arab pop) star. His yodeling is robust, satirical, and kinetic and is complimented by the naughty call-and-response laughter of his female partner, furthering its suggestive randiness. Kumar also yodels in *Chalti Ka Naam Gaadi*, a film starring his brother, Ashok Kumar, and someone called simply Cuckoo! The yodel song, "Baabuu Samajho Ishaare Hauran Pukaare Pam Pam Pam," is sung by Kumar, Manna Dey, among others. Kumar was a true Peter Sellers–style eccentric. He once placed a sign proclaiming THIS IS A LUNATIC ASYLUM in his front lawn. He apparently also talked to his trees. Kumar didn't smoke or drink but had a soft spot for sweets. He died of a heart attack in 1987. There are many CDs to choose from.

- *20 Best Songs of Kishore Kumar*, Includes "Zindagi."

- *Golden Hits of Kishore Kumar*, HMV, 1991.

- *Hits of Kishore Kumar*, Angel Records, 1970s. Includes "Zindagi" and interesting liner notes.

and hear country, rap, Elvis, psychedelic rock (ironically containing obligatory sitar) or disco through Indian ears. Their cultural grafting efforts are, however, strictly hi-turnover and can be simultaneously amazingly off-kilter *and* tremendously right-on.

"Modern Indian music continues to incorporate elements from contemporary western pop," notes Peter Manuel, to the extent that most film cabaret scenes feature rock bands, and amidst all the synthesizer, bass, and guitars the only "traditional" Indian touch is usually the "characteristically ornamented" vocals. Indian vocals are distinguished from other vocals by their unique ululations: "Indian ornamentation and melodic nuances are quite distinct from the characteristic styles of, for example, Greece, Southeast Asia, or the Arab World."

North and south Indian films have their own trademarks and main-stream gestures. North Indian films are in Hindu-Urdu, the lingua franca of major motion pictures. Most soundtrack lyrics appear in Urdu, and many of these appear in *ghazal*, or poetic rhyming Urdu. The songs are less indige-nous and more Western (featuring closed structures). The songs also appear in *qawwali*, used in Sufi music and usually accompanied by percussion, har-monium, and hand clapping. The singing may include "virtuoso coloratura improvisations, which alternate with a group refrain." Coloratura vocals fea-ture virtuoso-like rapid scales, arpeggios, trills, and even yodeling.

While Kishore Kumar is the acknowledged Jimmie Rodgers of Bollywood, other, less-renowned Bollywood singers veer into heart-stop-ping epiglottal leaps and coloratura falsetto, like Chandra Babu and Rajagopal. The low-budget *Dhoondte Reh* (director Kumar Bhatia, 1998) includes the yodeling song "Na Tum Bolo" by Jatin-Lalit and Majrooh Sultanpuri. There is probably much more to Bollywood yodeling than Kumar. Due to timeframe and budget restraints, I was unable to take my research any further. This area is ripe for further research.

There are yodel-like vocalizations in other parts of Asia as well. For instance, traditional Tibetan folk songs include various mountain and pas-toral songs. As in other mountainous areas, the rural Tibetans often work in isolation, often as herders with little human contact. Peasants and shepherds sing their mountain songs in their free time and their pastoral songs while they're working the pastures or tending the herd. The songs kill boredom and amuse. The solo songs are fairly unstructured and rhythmically free, and they include a wide range of sounds. They employ a good range of tones with sig-nificant dramatic leaps from chest to head with plenty of playful embellish-

SELECTED ASIAN DISCOGRAPHY

- *Living Music of the Steppes: Instrumental Music and Songs of Mongolia*, various performers, Multicultural Media, 1999. Twenty tracks of instrumental and vocal music from Mongolian nomadic shepherds. Including nine Köömiy songs featuring throat-singing. Some of the pieces feature dramatic yodel-like vocals.

ments and stretched notes that remind some of the expansive uninhabited land. The subject matter is often pastoral or about life, love, or Buddha. Typical work songs include those that accompany the milking of cows, the plowing of fields, the preparation of harvests. It seems that, not unlike American cowboy yodel songs or Alpine songs, the killing of loneliness or the serenading of one's herd is of essential concern. And wherever that happens, one can almost assume that there are going to be outbursts of yodeling.

Indonesia plays host to some genuine yodeling. Between East Timor and Bali lies Flores, an island rich in musical traditions and incredible instruments like stringed tube zithers (varying from one to nine strings), and wooden xylophones used with drums during healing ceremonies. Flores' *Mbata* songs are call-and-respond songs that involve a male vocalist whose singing is answered by another singer or chorus. *Mbata* songs often include gong and drum accompaniment. The vocals in the Manggari region of Flores "can incorporate yodeling, and stories abound of singers sitting on opposite hillsides, competing with one another across ravines."

HAWA–EEE–AAA EEE–AN YODELING

Everybody does it in Hawaii / A yodel ay-hee, olay-hee, hee
—Jimmie Rodgers, "Everybody Does It in Hawaii"

The origins of Hawaiian yodeling are intertwined with the origins of Hawaiian slack-key guitar. The many examples of how yodeling influenced the sound of slack key guitar, steel guitar, and ukele—and vice versa—are similar to the chicken-or-egg debates regarding the evolution of the alphorn and yodel. As Elizabeth Tatar notes "falsetto songs . . . were often played on steel guitar." How did this come about?

Polynesians first visited Hawaii around A.D. 400, and lived there peacefully until the year 1000. Then the Tahitians arrived and introduced their customs and strict social order. Powerful chiefs and priests established an authoritarian feudal system. Struggles between nobles and inhabitants ensued. Island inhabitants associated song with *mana* or cosmic creativity. English explorer James Cook, in 1778, was the first Westerner to visit the islands. He named them the Sandwich Islands. Chief Kamehameha I (1758–1819) traded sandalwood for Western military hardware and emerged as Hawaii's indisputable ruler, leading to a century of monarchical rule. Nineteenth-century American whalers used Hawaii as a port of call and established all the affiliated "industries": bars, prostitution, entertainment. The first American missionaries arrived in 1820. Churches and

SELECTED HAWAIIAN YODELING DISCO/VIDEOGRAPHY

- *Aloha Festivals Hawaiian Falsetto*, various singers, Mele, 2000.

- *Capitol of the State I'm In*, director Joe Dawn, Don Ho Video, 1997. Includes Ho's "Yodel Medley."

- *Hawaiian Country,* Island Breeze, Island Breeze Productions, 1995. Some chants and yodels sung in Hawaiian and English.

- *Hawaiian Rainbow,* video, producer Neil Abercrombie. Mug-shot, 1987. Includes history and music of non-Western cultures in Hawaii.

- *Her Second Album*, Karen Keawehawaii, Kaleolani Records, 1981. English and Hawaiian yodeling.

- *Images of Hawaii*, Various Artists, M & H Hawaii, 2001.

- *Kaliuwa'a*, Palolo, Hanaola, 2000? Falsetto plus ukelele versions of early rockers.

- *Ki Ho'alu: Seattle Style Hawaiian Slack Key Guitar,* Ledward Kaapana, Gary Haleamau, and others, Northwest Folklife, 1990s.

- *Legends of Falsetto: Classic Island Sounds*, Hanaola, 2001. Classic 78s from the 1930s–50s. Extensive liner notes.

- *Local Folk,* George Freitas, MGC, 1997. Hawaiian popular music.

- *Pualeilani*, Kahaliïa, Cosmo International, 1993.

- *Randy Parker and Mauka Moves*, Randy Parker, Mauka Productions, 1988. Includes "Pali Yodel."

- *Shores of Anini*, Punaluïu Blend, Punaluïu Blend, 1991. Includes "Teach You to Yodel."

- *Slidin' on the Frets!*, various artists, Yazoo, 2000. Includes "Pame Sti Honoloulou" by Bezo's Hawaiian Orchestra. Rewired ukulele traditionalist Dr. Jazz says their yodeling "does not seem to be Hawaiian but more nonsense syllables in the 'traditional' yodel style."

- *Songs of Hawaii*, Hawaiian Melodies, 2000.

- *Vintage Hawaiian Music: The Great Singers—1928–1934*, Rounder, 1989. Selected by steel guitar master Bob Brozman, with many written for falsetto and yodeling.

schools were built; reading and writing were introduced. Christianity became the predominant faith. Hymns were introduced and Hawaiian traditions were discouraged. Missionaries colluded with the monarchy to cleanse Hawaii of "evil" influences. Hawaii would never be the same again.

In the mid-1800s, relatives of the missionaries created a lucrative sugar industry. Chinese, Japanese, Portuguese, Puerto Rican, Korean, and Filipino temporary laborers were hired to work on the sugar plantations. How yodeling came to Hawaii is still debated. Some believe exuberant 19th-century missionaries brought their Latin American influences including hymns, polyphony, and "the Western scale, but the Hawaiians preserved their high falsetto style of singing, which is similar to yodeling." Chanters effortlessly slid from high tenor into falsetto. Numerous early European seafarers' journals made note of the natives' "pleasant" vocals.

British explorer George Vancouver offered Kamehameha II (1796–1824) a herd of cattle as a gift. The cattle multiplied and roamed far and wide, ultimately becoming a nuisance. Kamehameha recruited professional Mexican and "*paniolo*, or Spanish-Indian *vaqueros* [cowboys], from Southern California." in the 1830s to bring the herds under control. These flamboyant cowboys brought along their Spanish guitars and singing styles. Hawaiians loved the cowboy guitar sound and fell under the spell of the cowboy songs. The *vaqueros* ultimately accomplished their mission and upon their departure left their guitars behind as gifts to the locals. The space of a few 19th-century years saw the introduction of two essential musical imports: the guitar and Western falsetto.

Tatar offers concrete evidence that falsetto and yodel techniques were introduced by two missionary voice teachers, Henry Berger and Theodore Richards, who also conducted a boys' choir that sang native songs with some yodeling embellishments. Richards supposedly even got Chief Kamehameha III (1813–1854) to yodel.

Apparently, by 1890, Hawaiian falsetto and yodeling were already popular, and by 1928 yodeling was all the rage. These Mexican and missionary-introduced falsetto styles may have just further highlighted the native version. Hawaiians easily applied their falsetto to Western song structures. Most of the falsetto comes from the island of Hawaii, where the cattle ranches were located and the Mexican and Portuguese cowboys worked.

Locals also loved the guitar. However, they were not too keen on the dynamic flamenco style, which didn't suit their dispositions. So they slowed it down by retuning the strings to an open tuning of the major chord, which gives the harmony a sunny, laid-back feel that better suited their daily lives. Conventional history notes that Joseph Kekuku (1874–1932) put the guitar on his lap in 1885, and at age 11 began experimenting by running a comb and other objects across the strings to introduce the trademark glissandos of slack key guitar: a hybrid of Polynesian sounds applied to a Latin-European instrument. Maybe it was a combination of the heat and the weight of the guitar; after all, Hawaiians do prefer a much smaller guitar. A century later, Hawaiians had developed a unique slack-key style that depended on a steady bass-line on the lower strings, with melody and trickery plucked on the higher strings, like American bluegrass and folk. Jimmie Rodgers was one of the more influential country musicians to incorporate Hawaiian sounds in his songs to successfully capitalize on an earlier rage. Most popular music styles were influenced by the Hawaiian sound, from hillbilly to Broadway show tunes. By the late-1940s, Hawaiian music was popular worldwide.

Jimmie Rodgers cowrote "Everybody Does It in Hawaii" with his sister-in-law Elsie McWilliams, in 1929, with Joe Kaipo, a genuine Hawaiian guitarist. Rodgers also recorded "Moonlight and Skies" with the faux Hawaiian group, Lani McIntire & His Hawaiians. This was world music (with a touch of exotica's fudged authenticities) at its most rudimentary. The Hawaiian slack-key guitar played on the lap eventually evolved into the (electric) steel guitar, which is responsible for one of the most recognizable (and annoying—that whine!) sounds in country music. Meanwhile, in Hawaii, King Bennie Nawahi returned the favor by producing his own

HAWAIIAN HONOR ROLL

Gary Haleamau [b. 1950s?] was born into a musical family and raised on the slopes of Hualalai on Hawaii Island. Inspired by his slack-key, guitar-playing father, grandfather, and great-grandmother, Haleamau took up a guitar at an early age. As a youth, Haleamau began performing the Hawaiian and *paniolo* music that was a Haleamau family tradition. At the age of 12, he won a recording contract on Pumehana Records. He appeared at the thirteenth Annual Border Folk Festival in Texas and the 1984 National Folk Festival with his Hawaiian Cowboy father and Clyde Sproat. The single "Morning Dew" / "Home Pumehana" was released in 1978. In 1987, Gary released his first album of slack-key and falsetto, *Big Island Style* (Liko). Since then, he has played Hawaii, the American mainland, and Japan, captivating audiences with his guitar playing and his sweet falsetto voice that soars into effortless yodeling. He often performs with his wife, Sheldeen, a dancer and former Miss Aloha Hula. "Hawaiian Yodel" displays his yodeling virtues.

• *Best of Gary Haleamau*, Liko, 1994. Includes "Yodel."

continued on the next page

Hawaiian Honor Roll, continued

Raymond Kane (b. 1925) is the most famous living slack-key guitarist. His gentle Hawaiian style is a not-so-strange blend of Polynesian and Latin-European styles. And when Kane sings about Hawaii's natural beauties, his gentle gravelly baritone voice is a combination of soul and physiology (he suffers from asbestos-aggravated emphysema). His first recordings appeared in 1961, and by the 1970s he had become one of the prime beneficiaries of the traditional-folk revival. His singing retains hints of Mexican *cancion* and is peppered with his unique Hawaiian yodeling as he sings about Hawaii's natural beauty. His yodeling may have been influenced by the Mexican *huapanguera* and the cowboy "YEEE-Haw" presence in Hawaii.

• *Punahele*, Dancing Cat, 1994. In trademark *nahenahe* (relaxed) style, he mixes standards with original songs, singing some duets with his wife Elodia.

Genoa Keawe (b. 1918) Honolulu native recorded over 140 singles, many with her characteristic crystal clear yodeling during which she could hold the high note for a legendary two minutes.

• *By Request*, Mele, 1998.

Prince Leilani of the Kalani Peterson Trio was a renowned yodeler. Two examples of falsetto with extended yodeling are "Maui Girl" and "Ku'u Pua Loke."
  Lena Machado (1903–1974), "Hawaii's Songbird," was discovered at age 16 "perched in a mango tree singing." She was very influential in the 1930s and 1940s as singer, falsettist, composer, and all-around entertaining Renaissance woman. Other females to employ the glottal break include Nani Alapai, Lizzie Alohikea, Rose Tribe, Leinaala Haili, and Genoa Keawe. Machado's highly acclaimed soprano-falsetto was unique; it included dramatic vocals with an emphasis on the break, "executed only on vowel sounds"—a yodel, in other words. She was also famous for her "'ornamental articulation of the consonants." Her voice would break at certain consonants. "Another characteristic . . . [was] yodeling at the cadences." She employed a vast arsenal of effects and embellishments to create a rich, variegated, and fascinating vocal style. Her songs weren't all style, however; they also included interesting, risqué, and humorous (sub)texts. Many singers have covered her songs. Bill Aliiloa Lincoln names her as his falsettist inspiration. She was also a formidable musician, playing all the traditional and nontraditional string instruments. She was very popular and toured throughout North America, Asia, and the Pacific.

• "Holo Wa'apa," South Seas.

• "E Ku'u Baby," "Holo Wa'apa," "Ei Nei," "Ho 'onanea," and "Kauoha Mai" are examples of Hawaiian yodeling with large dramatic leaps and emphasized glottal breaks.

Hawaiian blend of jazz, blues, and hulas.

Singing is central to Hawaiian music. Popular singers perform the *leo kl'eki'e*, an indigenous version of falsetto (coined in 1973) with a similar emphasized break between normal voice and falsetto. Hawaiian-style falsetto, like yodeling, emphasizes and *exaggerates* the very break between registers that conventional singers are taught to file down to imperceptible. The falsettist, like the yodeler, exaggerates the break through repetition. "Though partial yodels are more frequently used, especially at song endings, there are a few songs and some falsetto singers who feature continuous yodeling."

Hawaiian melody sounds unique because songs often begin with a dra-

GEORGE KAINAPAU

> They didn't believe a man was singing; they always thought it was a woman.
> —George Kainapau commenting on his falsetto

George Kainapau (1905–1992) was already performing on stage as a toddler and touring the Hawaiian Islands with famed guitarist Sol Hoopii as a teen by the 1920s. By the late 1950s, he was a regular at hotel ballrooms. Kainapau, *the* most famous Hawaiian falsettist, was the ambassador of Hawaiian yodeling, popularizing the style both in Hawaii and elsewhere. He called his falsetto "a gift from God" because he just did it, having never had any formal training. His tenor was famously clear and high, ascending effortlessly into a falsetto and often emphasizing the glottal break, all of which became his trademark. He often inserted a yodel at the end of a phrase and could hold a breath for, well, breathtakingly long.

His impact on the legacy of falsetto was immense, influencing the likes of Bill Lincoln, Joe Keawe, David Chun, and Kihie Brown, all of whom sang in his shadow. His influence reverberates way beyond Hawaii's beaches. Indonesian falsetto singer Hoegeng Santoso claims to have learned to sing by listening to Kainapau's discs until "the grooves were worn through." Japanese falsetto singers Katsuhiko Haida and Mineo Shimizu also claim to have been greatly influenced by him. Kainapau's "Ku'u Ipo Rose" includes falsetto, yodeling, and steel guitar imitations of his vocal ornamentation. His many accomplishments include helping to establish the Hawaiian Music Foundation to preserve Hawaiian folk culture and music. Kainapau yodeled in a number of films, including *Bird of Paradise* (King Vidor, 1932) in which he warbles his sunny falsetto in the theme song "Mauna Kea." In *Flirtation Walk* (Frank Borzage, 1934), Kainapau performs mellifluous yodels in "He Mana'o Ko'u Ia 'Oe" with Sil Hoopii. While in *Waikiki Wedding* (1937), Kainapau sings Oscar-winning "Sweet Leilani" with Bing Crosby and graces the film with his trademark yodels.

- *Holiday in Hawaii*, Decca, 1960s.

- *The Golden Voice of Hawaii*, Decca, 1965.

matic surge, a yodel-like burst consisting of large one-octave leaps. There is also a Hawaiian quavering that comes from the rapid ascending-descending movements of the voice by successive thirds or fourths. This uniqueness may have to do with vocal training or with the transmission of various traditions. As the physiological details of how a yodel works continue to mystify the experts, so it remains with Hawaiian vocals as well. Falsetto in the world of improvised Hawaiian vocals became yet another detail to play with; some singers even made it their trademark.

Micro-Mela-Polynesian Yodels

Among the hundreds of slivers and island fragments that comprise the South Seas (including Melanesia, Micronesia, and Polynesia), there are some very strange and under-documented applications of falsetto and yodeling. These are the fabled places thousands of vacationers fantasize about running off to, the settings of adventure movies starring people like Errol Flynn and stories by Robert Louis Stevenson and Jack London, but also of nuclear weapons testing.

Falsetto use is common among these far-flung atolls, and of course, with any creative use of falsetto, the yodel is only a glottal stop away. Melodies containing yodels are fairly common in parts of Melanesia and Polynesia. Falsetto and yodeling are not just employed to arrive at new sounds but also to converse with spirits and invoke divine results.

In New Guinea the yodel forms part of the aural terrain—pleasant entertaining background music. The Huli of the Southern Highlands Province, Papua New Guinea, sing two types of yodels: solo (*ú*) and collective (*íwa*). Both involve an alternating head-chest voice song among the men. They also sing work songs involving repeated phrases and yodels with a fixed timbre (tone color):

> Yodeling is an important musical activity of the Huli. . . . Solo yodeling helps people communicate across mountainous terrain. Men yodel whole statements; each ends with a high-called *u*. Purely yodeled signals also occur *á–ú–á–ú* 'Where are you?' and *háko háko* 'I'm here'. The solo yodels often deal with love, laments, storytelling, legal issues, and magic spells.

Like yodelers in other cultures, workers sing their work-yodel songs to kill the drudgery or set a helpful work rhythm. The Huli's "collective yodeling occurs when men work together. It synchronizes individual actions, informing listeners of the activity in progress." This is not unlike descriptions of Alpine yodels, Sami herder calls, and African-American slave work songs. And like Pygmy work-related yodeling, they are integrated into a structure of interlocking calls.

Some specific Huli yodels include:

- "*Nògo u*: a yodel performed by men toting butchered pigs back to a mourning observance. It signals that death has been appeased and now mourning can become celebration.
- *Gèla*: a yodel performed during fertility rites.
- *Iwa*: a warrior or laborer's (fast) yodel after a victory.
- *Màli ìwa*: a yodel by male dancers to announce their performance.
- *Àliwa*: A boy's yodel to announce approaching rain or cold weather. It's also used to teach boys how to yodel.
- "Women have solo and collective calls. In rage and excitement, a woman shouts *hèagola*! Women walking to their gardens may call *heao*." They don't employ falsetto and thus are not considered real yodels by locals.

Ethnomusicologist Jacqueline Pugh-Kitingan notes that the

> Huli say thoughts form in the heart, rise in breath from the lungs to the mouth, and roll off the tongue as words. Language determines musical structure: linguistic tones affect melodic tones (in Hawaii as well) and linguistic articulation determines musical pace and rhythm. Where context or instrumental technique disallows linguistic articulation, music imitates yodeling—the precursor of human speech, according to Huli myths.

Just as in Hawaii, where the steel guitar sometimes imitates the yodel, so it is with the Huli when they play their *Susap*. This ingenious wind instrument is made of bamboo and twine and functions as a kind of jew's harp.

Men from Papua New Guinea's Chimbu Province are judged by their singing voices, not their looks—there is hope for future Roy Orbisons! Within their culture, the yodeler is highly revered. In this province, yodeling still serves as an important form of long-distance communication (the introduction of the mobile phone not withstanding) in the mountain regions. Yodeling still announces deaths, visitors, gatherings, and the like.

Post–World War II global pop influences seeped into indigenous Papua musical styles with string band music—the ukulele was especially popular—in the 1950s. The songs were mostly twangy "guitar songs . . . minstrel, western and hillbilly songs." One Papua song recorded in 1955 even featured an English-language text with a local melody, "'Carry Me Back to Ole Virginny' complete with hillbilly and Hawaiian-style yodeling."

As some yodeling in both North America and the Alpine region is said to mimic various animals, most commonly birds, the *Kauweawèt*

MICRO/MELA/POLY YODELOGRAPHY

- *De 'Aré'aré: Un peuple mélanésien et sa musique*, Recorded/documented by Hugo Zemp and Daniel Coppet, Ocora, 1978.

- *Irian Jaya: Music from the Mountainous Region of Western New Guinea (Irian Jaya): A Documentation in Sound of the Vanishing Musical Cultures of the Eipo and Their Neighbors, Artur Simon Museum Collection, Berlin*. Six-CD-set, 1990s.

- *Iles Salomon: Musique de Guadalcanal*, Recordings/documentation: Hugo Zemp, Ocora, 1994.

- *Iles Salomon: Musiques intimes et rituelles* Recordings/documentation: Hugo Zemp, Chant du Monde/CNR, 1990.

- *Music of Biak, Irian Jaya*, Recordings: Philip Yampolsky, Smithsonian/Folkways, 1996.

- *Music of the Huli, Papua Niugini*, various performers, Musicaphon, vol. 4 in *Music of Oceania* series. Vocal music covers variety of yodel styles (*u, nogo u, iwa, mali iwa, gela, aliwa*, and *healo*).

- *Papua New Guinea Music Collection*, various performers, edited: Don Niles and Michael Webb, Institute of Papua New Guinea Studies, 1987. Documentation plus eleven cassettes.

- *Polyphonies des Iles Salomon*, Recordings/documentation: Hugo Zemp, Chant du Monde/CNR, 1990.

- *Primitive Sounds: An Authentic Sound Picture of New Guinea*, various performers, compilation/recordings: James L. Anderson, Hibiscus, 1971.

- *Voices of the Rainforest*, various performers, producer: Mickey Hart, recordings/documentation: Steven Feld, Ryko, 1991. You will hear some clear examples of Kaluli yodeling as they respond to the birds, waterfalls, and frogs.

(*Takoetamesso*) people of Papua likewise sing melodies that incorporate various birdcalls. According to Jaap Kunst, the "Komasa [of Papua] is an expert in this respect; more or less sweet twitterings alternate with highly realistic turkey-like gobblings and the quacking of ducks." The sounds may have a religious basis. Other Papuans ornament their songs with the voices of animals. Falsetto is usually sung by men. It is also sung by the Irumu, Managalasi, Maring, Sursurunga, and many other peoples; "yodeling . . . occurs famously among many peoples of Irian Jaya" in West Papua.

A 1936 expedition led by Dutchman Anton Colijn and Jean Jacques Dozy, a geologist, encountered the Mountain Papuans, the Kapaukos of

Irian Jaya. This was the Kapaukos' first encounter with Westerners. So, with bows and arrows aimed, they stood facing the strange interlopers in total harrowing silence. Then one among the expedition, someone experienced in these kinds of encounters, broke the tension by breaking out into dance and some hearty yodeling. The local Kapaukos gleefully followed suit.

The inhabitants of one of Vanuatu's five islands (located in the Southwest Pacific, formerly called New Hebrides, pop. 22,423, 90% Tanna) are said to be excellent yodelers. While "walking in the forest or working in the gardens men (and sometimes women) yodel to attract the attention of others, who may be several hills away. Men yodel just for the fun of making themselves heard. Yodels are distinctive . . . by sound alone, people can easily identify the yodeler." The Tanna in this region have many string bands, formed by teenagers who play guitars and ukeles: "Singing with these bands, males often use falsetto, recalling traditional yodeling."

Yodeling can also be heard on the Solomon Islands. Savo is one of the Solomon Islands where a type of singing occurs that involves a movement from chest voice (*neo laua*) to head voice (*taga laua*) that ascends into falsetto. The yodelers are sometimes accompanied by bass drone voices. The northern Solomon Island is host to vocalizations that Von Hornbostel compared to Swiss yodels. The people signal by using a combination of "falsetto, flexible-sliding pitch changes, extraordinary legato techniques, light melodies and voice interchanges."

Guadalcanal is the largest of the Solomon Islands. There are several mountains that peak at 1,800 meters (5,600 feet). Here we find the Solomon capital of Honiara, a port town of 35,000, inhabited mostly by Melanesians and Polynesians from Kiribati. Numerous indigenous yodeling variants survive, despite Christian missionary attempts to eliminate indigenous folk expression. Some vocal styles use drones with two soloists weaving melodic flourishes above it. There is also musical growling and some accompaniment by a local variant of the panpipes. Polyphony also exists and includes melodies over the drones: "The songs of Guadalcanal also feature two solo vocal parts having wide ranges and frequent and rapid change of register, a kind of yodeling."

East Polynesia (Cook Island, Society Islands, and other French Polynesian islands) also has its yodelers. Vocal ornamentation may accompany any of the six recognized vocal styles, including spoken recitation to repeated mesmerizing pattern phrases. A yodel can form a part of most of these styles "with a break in the vocal line to emphasize the shift between vocal registers." (See also the section on Hawaii.)

HEAD VOICE DOWN UNDER: AUSTRALIA AND NEW ZEALAND

Australia was once the world's largest penal colony, "settled" as it was by Irish and English convicts who had a choice: live out their days in a British gaol or ship out to Australia. New Zealand, as legend goes, was discovered in the 10th century A.D. by Maori explorer Kupe (their Ulysses), arriving from Polynesia with his people in enormous ocean-faring canoes. The Polynesians (Maori) settled there shortly thereafter. The first European to set eyes on the region was Dutch explorer Abel Tasman, who journeyed around the islands in 1642, in search of the legendary southern continent. In 1769, Englishman James Cook put down anchor along the coast, claiming it for Britain. He gave names to the places he visited and helped produce the first maps of the region.

Both the indigenous populations of New Zealand (Maori) and Australia (Aborigines) have their own musical traditions; neither includes yodeling, although the Maori sang their war songs "in a lashing microtonic falsetto," which sounds like "excited cackling in a barnyard." Maori music also has a long tradition of song and chant. There are some examples of aboriginal country music, such as Dougie Young, an aboriginal balladeer from the 1950s, and Harry Williams and the Country Outcasts, who highlighted aboriginal concerns in a conventional country-music style. However, most yodeling in Australia and New Zealand entered the country through either Swiss/Alpine immigration and/or European immigrants who adopted American cowboy music.

There are two major Swiss-immigrant yodeling groups. Baerg-Roeseli, Inc., is a nonprofit Swiss Yodel and Folklore Group, and proof that the Alpine community exists in Australia. Located in Brisbane, their main goals include showcasing the "customs and music of Switzerland." They perform instrumental and vocal music featuring yodeling and *yutzes*. They consider themselves fully integrated Australians who still "love reminding ourselves of the customs of Switzerland." They performed at Brisbane's World Expo '88.

Swiss Yodel Choir Matterhorn, Melbourne, was founded in 1969 by homesick Swiss yodelers. They're dedicated to preserving traditional Swiss yodeling and maintaining cultural ties with Switzerland. Five of the all-male members are from Kanton Zurich, three each from Bern and St. Gallen, one from Appenzell, plus one Aussie. They were the honored foreign guest *jodelclub* at the National Yodel Festival in Fribourg, 2002. They practice every Wednesday and they "do the yodel very quiet," notes Paul Voumard, their conductor.

Australians and New Zealanders have had an affinity with American cowboy/country music since the end of World War II. There are many rea-

Tex Banes (right) is one of many Down Under cowboy yodelers. By permission of Dagmar Binge.

sons for the widespread popularity of country music. Farming and herding remain prominent industries and commonly supply job descriptions for a sizeable portion of the populace. The two islands have long lured Europeans to its shores with their fantastic tales of open spaces, abundance, and unlimited opportunities. While many arrived from England and Ireland during the late-18th and early-19th centuries, they also came from Switzerland, Germany, the Netherlands, and Asian destinations.

Geographically, yodeling makes sense because the countries are awe-inspiringly expansive, something hopeful for those living in cramped or oppressive circumstances in their homelands. Australia and New Zealand, like North America, offered promises of a better life. Psychologically, the countries also maintain that rugged individual image that is steeped in more bravado than truth. We should not underestimate the image making by Down Under popular entertainers as they cultivated attitudes that lend themselves well to cowboy music and yodeling. The (American) cowboy image is wedged somewhere between myth, wishful thinking, lie, and verifiable reality. Show me an economic downturn that has inspired a people's yearning for a simpler past (that probably did not exist), and I will show you

SELECTED DOWN UNDER HONOR ROLL

Buddy Bishop, (1923–1995) "The Wandering Cowboy," was a humorous yodeler born in Tinnonee, New South Wales (NSW), Australia. His first disc appeared on John Mystery Records (1950), eventually switching to Rodeo where he recorded his famous "Farmyard Yodel." In 1977, he was inducted into Australia's Roll of Renown.

Owen Blundell (b. 1960) is a contemporary yodeler from NSW with a lilting mellifluous yodel. At age 14 he heard Frank Ifield yodeling and "I thought it was the funniest thing I had ever heard in my life." But he fell under the spell and rehearsed his yodel sometimes "five hours a day." He released his first album in 1985. He has written some 400 songs, many of them already classic yodel songs. But "I lost a lot of friends because of my new found love of yodeling." He plays "clubs, pubs, festivals and . . . rodeos." He has toured with legends like Slim Dusty and Smokey Dawson and won numerous awards. His yodel duets with Rex Dallas on *Duelling Yodellers* are a must.

- *The Rambler Comes Home*, Selection.

- *From the Heart of the Mountains*, Selection, 1992.

Corinna Cordwell (b. 1975) is an Australian yodeler who does cover versions of renowned American yodelers. She lives along the Murray River in the shadow of the "Australian Alps," north of Melbourne. She began singing and playing guitar at age 9. Her debut album, *Without You*, appeared when she was just 16. The album was nominated for the Australian Country Music Awards in 1991. She has been the recipient of countless awards. Cordwell had a hit single in 1992 with "Till a Tear Becomes a Rose." She has toured extensively throughout Australia and New Zealand. Her "Mocking Bird Yodel" is an excellent example of her soaring and romantic yodeling style.

- *Without You*, CCR, 1991. Includes ballads and yodel songs; guest vocalist, fellow yodeler, Wayne Horsburgh.

- *Forever In My Heart*, CCR, 1992. Many original songs and some covers with yodeling.

- *Over Mountains and Seas*, CCR, 1993. Originals and covers.

Rex Dallas (b. 1936) is from a small mining town near Lithgow, NSW, an area he has returned to in song throughout his career. Dallas grew up listening to the early morning "Hillbilly Trial" radio show and started yodeling at age 7. Rex began performing at local dances and got his first shot at radio when he was just 16. When his family moved to Sydney he busked around, playing the streets, local hotels, town halls, and small outdoor concerts. In the late 1950s, the golden age of Australian country music, Dallas was picked up by a local promoter. His first single, "Bicycle Wreck" (Festival), became a hit and won

continued on the next page

Selected Down Under Honor Roll, continued

him name recognition. It was his yodeling talents, however, that won him a place on numerous TV pop and variety shows in the 1960s–70s.

In 1986, Dallas left Hadley Records and founded his own Briar Records. He also fronted the Dallas family band on their "Happy Hoedown" tours and the "Rex Dallas Variety Show," playing aboriginal missions and reserves around Australia. In 1992, Dallas had a replica coal mine built near the Tamworth, Australia's Country Music Capital. It's named after his song "The Western Main" and serves as a unique aboveground "underground" country music venue and honors his coal-mining heritage (his father, grandfather, uncles, and cousins were all miners). He's the only male singer to ever win a Golden Guitar for yodeling. A good yodel starter: "Here's to All the Aussie Yodellers."

- *24 Harry Torrani Yodelling Songs*, Briar. Honoring one of the great under-regarded yodelers.

- *Treasured Tracks (1960's to 1980's)*, Briar.

- *Duelling Yodellers*, with Owen Blundell, Selection, 1994. Two generations of impassioned yodeling and nary a yodel-free song to be found.

June Holm(s) (1924–1966) was a Brisbane-born yodeler whose entire wax ouevre consists of six songs. But they're six very evocative songs that feature a clear, uncompromising yodel. She is considered a pioneer for country singers in general and women country singers specifically. She won a talent contest in 1942 and cut her only records in that same year with EMI. She went on to perform as "The Yodelling Cowgirl" until 1948 when she married.

Wayne Horsburgh (b. 1955) is an Australian yodeler who straddles two continents, spending half his time in Branson, Missouri. He was forever changed when he first saw Slim Whitman perform in 1973. Twenty years later, Horsburgh was the Western Music Association Male Yodeling Champion.

- *Yodeling for You*, Rotation, 1985.

- *Singing Cowboy*, Rotation, 1991.

- *Yodel-Antics*, Rotation, 1995.

Tim McNamara (1922–1983) grew up in a musical family near Orange, NSW. Some yodeling contest victories brought him to radio and an EMI recording contract in 1948. He hosted the "2SM Show," which was influential in breaking new country acts. He also recorded for the Rodeo, Fiesta, and Picture labels. Known as "The Cowboy Troubadour," he had a warm, mellow voice, and was inducted into Australia's Roll of Renown in 1981. A good yodel intro: "Red River Valley" with the McKean Sisters.

- *Campfire of Dreams*, Arika, 1985.

continued on the next page

Chad Morgan is a Hee-Haw Down Under singer-yodeler comedian with a buck-tooth grin and a winning barnyard yodel. He sings his slapstick comical ditties from the point of view of the many personas he assumes: the henpecked husband, nagging wife, or macho man. His big novelty hit was "The Sheik of Scrubby Creek" (Regal-Zonophone). His "Farmyard Yodel" is par for his giggly course, complete with a one-man chorus of barnyard sounds amongst the genuine yodeling.

- *The Singles and Beyond*, Regal-Zonophone, 2002.

Tex Morton (b. Robert Lane, New Zealand, 1916–1983) emigrated to Australia in 1932, where he became a teen busker and did some tent show work, knocking about until 1936. Morton got his recording break after some Sydney radio performances, producing some sides for Regal Zonophone, the only label specializing in Aussie hillbilly music in the 1950s. He emerged as a very popular yodeling cowboy, the first *real* Down Under hillbilly success story. Although Morton's main influences were Jimmie Rodgers and Goebel Reeves, he developed a unique Australian bush-ballad style that has been much imitated by younger yodelers. Morton's repertoire included cowboy yodels, Elton Britt, virtuosic Swiss-style yodeling, plus stories of everyday Australian life. He traded in Texan iconography for homegrown images: "cowboys become boundary riders." The local scenery soon began to seem organic and inseparable from the sound; hillbilly transformed into "bush ballad." His yodel often "contained more than a few plaintive or laconic syllables." His colorful career involved touring Australia with his own giant tent show where he did some sharpshooting, boxing, whip and rope tricks, and his heartfelt yodeling.

Tex Morton, "The Yodeling Boundary Rider." By permission of Richard Weize.

Morton eventually found his way to North America where he worked as a hypnotist and sometime Hollywood actor. Now regarded as "The Father of Australian Country Music," he won just about every Australian singing award before he died in 1983. His tongue-uvular trills created a unique vocal style; just listen to his "Freight Train Yodel."

continued on the next page

Selected Down Under Honor Roll, continued

- *The Regal-Zonophone Collection*, vols. 1–2, 1990s.

- *Tex Morton Story*, Festival. Morton sings standards.

- *The Versatile Tex Morton*, Festival.

- *The Last Ride of Tex Morton*, Producers Graham and Jason Archer, Attitude Productions, 2001. Documentary traces life of Tex Morton and the birth of country music in Australia and New Zealand.

Gordon Parsons (1926–1990), "The Old GP," possessed all the country music credentials: bushland childhood, strong physique, and strong voice and yodel. Following success on *Australia's Amateur Hour*, Parsons recorded "Back to Those Rolling Plains" and "Where the Bellinger River Flows" for EMI in 1946. He toured with a succession of circus and variety shows and in the 1980s recorded for Selection Records. He is best known for writing the Slim Dusty hit "A Pub with No Beer." He was inducted into Australia's Roll of Renown in 1982.

Buddy Williams (b. Harold Williams, 1918–1986), "The Yodelling Jackaroo," was Australia's first native country singer and Australia's "second central figure" behind Tex Morton. Raised as an orphan on a Dorrigo farm, he became an itinerant bush worker, writing simple bush lyrics, and busking in north-coast towns. In 1939, he successfully auditioned for EMI and recorded six original songs. In 1946, he began touring and didn't

Buddy Williams, "The Yodelling Jackaroo." By permission of Richard Weize.

stop until his death in 1986. Williams's deep love for the bush and its people is reflected in his recordings, many of which have become country classics.

He was influenced by Montana Slim and Goebel Reeves, but it was Williams's rough and tumble orphan past that gave him that existential sense of alienation-displacement that lies at the heart of his songs. He was working class and suffered his share. Williams's limited voice created a certain modest plaintive warmth that the true virtuoso might neglect because of technical polish. He played his vocal limitations to soulful effect—à la Hank and Jimmie—effectively evoking vulnerability, tragedy, and heartache. He was inducted into Australia's Roll of Renown in 1977. In 1980, he won the first Golden Guitar. Try his "Where the White Face Cattle Roam."

TWO AUSSIE YODELING LEGENDS

Slim Dusty (b. David Gordon Kirpatrick, 1927) was the first singer in the world to have his voice beamed to earth from space when, in 1983, Columbia space shuttle astronauts played Slim's version of "Waltzing Matilda." He's Australia's most prolific and best-selling recording artist (100 albums, 5+ million sold) in a career that spans half a century. His house is filled with gold records and awards.

Dusty grew up on an NSW dairy farm where he sang along to his father's fiddling when he wasn't even out of diapers yet. At age 10 he wrote his first song, "The Way the Cowboy Died." The following year he became Slim Dusty, and by age 15 he was performing on the radio and had recorded two songs at his own expense. By 1946, he was already a seasoned veteran of radio, music halls, and tent shows. In Sydney, Dusty recorded his first serious 78–rpm singles (Regal Zonophone), starting with "When the Rain Tumbles Down in July" and followed by a half-century steady stream of singles and yodel songs. His recording of "A Pub with No Beer" became his monster hit and is today as recognizable to everyone in Australia as, say, "Oh Susanna" is in the United States. In September 2000, he sang "Waltzing Matilda" at the closing ceremony of the Sydney Olympic Games. One of his most characteristic yodels is "The Dusty Trail Yodeler," recorded with his Bushlanders, Capitol (72041).

- *Not So Dusty*, Various Artists, EMI, 1990s. A tribute album by some of Down Under's biggest stars including Midnight Oil.

- *"Live" Across Australia*, EMI, 1986.

- *Man Who Is Australia*, 5-CDs, EMI, 2000.

Shirley Thoms (1925–1999), born in Queensland, emerged as "Australia's Yodelling Sweetheart," a trailblazer who helped to popularize yodeling and opened the door for other women singers. She became the first woman to be inducted into Australia's Roll of Renown in 1980.

She began her career yodeling the Tex Morton and Harry Torrani songs that had inspired her in her youth. She won a talent contest performing Torrani's "Mockingbird Yodel" as a teen. In no time, she was plucked from her family to pursue a singing career. Manager Bill Cook recognized her talents and encouraged her to write her own songs and take guitar lessons. At 16, Thoms went to Sydney and recorded her famous "Faithful Old Dog" for Regal Zonophone. During World War II, Thoms toured with some variety shows and entertained troops in Australia and New Zealand, all the while writing new songs. She even toured as part of the Sole Brothers Circus. Here she met John Sole, her first husband. In 1970, after Sole's untimely death, Thoms came out of retirement and recorded

continued on the next page

Two Aussie Yodeling Legends, continued

two albums for Hadley Records and began performing again. She lost a long battle with Parkinson's disease on July 1, 1999, a stack of her philosophical poems by her bedside.

- *Australia's Yodelling Sweetheart*, Hadley, 1970.

- *Complete Shirley Thoms Collection: vols. 1–2*, Hadley, 2000.

Shirley Thoms, "Australia's Yodelling Sweetheart." By permission of Richard Weize.

a population that looks to its cowboys, its cartoon or celluloid heroes for solace and escape.

Although Down Under's country music is a recognized musical style with its own audience and iconographic preoccupations, it remains somewhat of a bastard offspring of American country music. Australia's country singers tend to conform to the genre to ensure participation and acceptance. Australia's formal institutions, it's festivals and Roll of Renown (hall of fame), ensures recognition while it is further legitimized by its award ceremonies. Huge annual country music festivals attract big country stars—both domestic and North American. American continues to sell big, although homegrown singer Slim Dusty outsells most American acts. Author Graeme Smith has pointed out the heretofore-undocumented prevalence of yodeling in popular Australian music. Undocumented because most musical studies concentrate on lyrical content at the expense of nonsense vocables. Of seventy-five tracks compiled for a survey of Aussie country music from 1936 to 1960, sixty-eight of them featured yodeling!

Cowboy songs, celluloid cowboys, and dime novels (Zane Grey) all spoke to Australians. Tex Morton, the first credible interpreter of American hillbilly, instantly became more famous in Australia than his American counterparts. Morton and Buddy Williams, the hard-knock hillbilly singer, effectively replaced American cowboy images with indigenous bushland images. The result was a satisfying symmetry between genuine and fabricated. The (yodel) songs often combined the grittiness of their humble blue-collar origins with the phantasmagoric yearnings stimulated by celluloid cowboys.

The songs, imagery, costumes, and stage framework—Smith notes that both Morton and Williams set up touring rodeo shows—supplied the perfect ambience for their music. Just as in Switzerland and North America, rural iconography has maintained a hold on the mostly urbanized populations' imagination and ur-yearnings for a forgotten past. Morton and Williams created a standard mythological watermark for subsequent generations of farm boys and gals who took up guitar and set epiglottis in motion. Live performances by singers like Reg Lindsay and Slim Dusty helped solidify the Aussie version of cowboy song, the "bush ballad" with its own language and imagery (kangaroos replaced coyotes), its own fetishized epiglottal break, mythologized landscapes, and idealized stereotypes. Bush ballads feature ornamental yodel refrains and phrasing similar to the yodel add-ons of Hank Williams. The yodel's ornamentality gives them an arsenal of extra effects with which to express a greater range of emotions, including a deeper more forlorn bluesiness or a sense of satirical self-effacement. It was the Swiss yodel, however, that inspired the Aussie yodel technically, with its "faster alterations of pitches within an athletic and lively vocal presence." The yodel's jolting anomalous

MARY SCHNEIDER

You make . . . tape loops of her and she just doesn't sound like the queen of Australian yodeling anymore, she sounds like some message from outer space.

—Garry Bradbury, Severed Heads

You yodelers are freaks.

—Howard Stern to Mary Schneider

Schneider (b. 1933), the self-proclaimed "Queen of Yodelling," has nerve, moxy, and a voice. She has other saving graces as well. She takes the varnish off classical music while she is busily polishing it. There have always been people who have taken the perfume out of classical music—Spike Jones, Looney Tunes, the Marx Brothers, Victor Borge—but seldom has there been someone with her earnestness—and show-biz savvy.

When she began yodeling classics, she did it because she loved the music and saw it as a challenge. While Spike Jones was a true iconoclast, Schneider is the ultimate bad-fashion ingénue who took it all seriously and then was able to laugh at herself and convert this unintentional humor into *haute* concept and fame. Her *Yodelling the Classics* became a worldwide cult hit, in part no doubt because of her sheer unmitigated unselfconscious audacity of taking two unlikely musical styles and forging them together.

continued on the next page

Mary Schneider, continued

On a live American TV show, she yodeled a Kylie Minogue number; on the *Howard Stern Show*, she yodeled "Stairway to Heaven." When asked by Stern whether she yodeled during sex, she responded with classic élan: "Of course I yodel during sex, I yodel at all times"; Stern laughed. On this epiglottal blitzkrieg stateside tour, she also yodeled on TV shows *Good Morning America*, *The Today Show*, *E Entertainment*, and CNN's *Showbiz Today*. She yodeled at the German Film Festival in Berlin, dueted with Bryan Ferry, and appeared on Jean-Paul Gaultier's TV show *Eurotrash*.

She first got hooked on yodeling listening to yodelers like Tex Morton and Slim Dusty on the radio. Six-year-old Schneider would yodel along under a backyard mango tree. One day that epiglottal leap just happened: "But I don't know how I first did it—I just did. No one taught me how." Schneider's mother encouraged her and sister Rita early on; in 1944, their mum insisted they enter a radio talent contest. They won and were offered a recording contract. By 1956, Mary and Rita had recorded (arguably) Australia's first rocker, "Washboard Rock 'n' Roll," written after hearing early Elvis and Bill Haley tunes. They blossomed on TV and radio and toured with a unique makeshift musical instrument called the Schneiderphone, built by their brother out of a washboard, cowbells, bicycle horns, and cymbals, which created a sound like a one-man band on a rampage. In 1972, the sisters decided to go their separate ways.

But Schneider, with a strong desire to spice up her recording career, wanted to do opera. She was already experimenting with jazz and blues, but soon started concentrating more on her yodeling, which is inspired by Harry Torrani, Minna Reverelli, and Elton Britt. But it was not until the 1990s that the notes began to fall into place—the international zeitgeist was ready! Or was it!?

For a time she lost interest in yodeling. "I began to think it was uncool," said Schneider. "Who wants to yodel? I wanted to do jazz." But then, ten years after going solo, she began recording yodel discs. When they went platinum in Australia, the yodeling aria was written on the wall, or at least on a sheet of sister Rita's notebook. Rita helped put words to some classical pieces like the "Skater's Waltz." Her version of Toranni's "Mocking Bird Yodel" was included on *Yodelling Crazy* on EMI in 1992. And in 1994, *Yodelling the Classics* came out on Dino.

- *Yodeling the Classics*, Koch Crossover Music, 1997. Standard classical soundbite selections of Bizet, Mozart, Offenbach, Brahms, Beethoven, Sousa, and Strauss, with ample outpourings of yodeling, accompanied by Tommy Tycho's lush orchestral arrangements.

- *Sound of Yodelling*, Paganini, 1991.

- *Can't Stop Yodelling*, Colstal, 1986.

- *Magic Of Yodelling*, Bluebell/K-Tel, 1981.

character also gave yodelers a surprise weapon, enabling them to lighten a mood or augment a song with extra significance, depending on the yodel. The Swiss heritage continues to be maintained here by vestigial guardians of genuine folk music, the Swiss yodel club.

Buddy Williams's forlorn yodel style replaced the standard "yodel-ay-ee" syllables with his unique "Cooee" yodel. The sound comes from a European interpretation of an Aboriginal vocalization. It now serves as Australia's equivalent—I suppose—of the Rebel Yell, effectively creating a syncretic icon of sound, space, inhabitant, and listener, which could unite Australia emotionally.

However, contemporary country is less "dusty" and more commercial than it used to be as it upgrades its crossover appeal à la Nashville. This divides camps into keepers of the genuine (conservatives) and the renewer-progressives (modern beats, electronic gadgetry, hairstyle updates). Although, as in Nashville, this progressive-conservative polarity becomes totally skewed when one notices that the authenticators are often actually more progressive-improvisational than the renovators. Smith further notes that performers concerned with sales demographics tend to leave their epiglottis packed away because in the strategy "to promote Australian country music to a broader audience, the yodel tends to be a source of embarrassment." Even Slim Dusty now limits his yodeling—less is more?

Australian country is complex, embodying both distinction and mimicry, slavish imitation and audacious originality. The yodel, according to Smith, has been much more than just some "habitual and optional decoration"; in fact, it has been a "crucial and powerful act of performance." And yet, fewer yodels per disc per capita per set per concert are currently being performed. Yodeling has been victimized by new historical and national imperatives to become less mythological and more realistic, less escapist and more "honest" regarding white Aussie relations with the land and the indigenous populations. The yodel has sometimes been too closely linked to a stereotype of so-called hillbilly trash—unenlightened and naïve—you heard a yodel and you raised your eyebrows. Escapist fare perhaps, but Aussie country musicians insist it's genuine roots music and intimately interwoven into the Australian identity. Not unlike Swiss yodelers who claim to be the voice of "real" Switzerland, Aussie yodelers find themselves marginalized as politically and culturally conservative by ever-more urbanized tastes.

And yet, yodeling persists in part because of the diehards. One can argue that it persists precisely *because* the yodel remains a compellingly curious vocalization that can still enchant and entertain. New Zealand's Topp Twins, for instance, are hugely popular, combining hayseed slapstick, melodic country, and yodeling. Meanwhile, yodel contests remain popular at country music festivals.

TOPP TWINS

Lynda and Jools Topp (b. 1958) are two wild and crazy cross-dressing yodelers. Well, it gets even more complicated: Lynda and Jools are identical lesbian twins who grew up on a real farm, in New Zealand, singing to their cows—and that's the *udder* apocryphal truth! Don't forget that they play spoons, sing tuneful Kiwi country-blues, play harmonica, change costumes at breathtaking speeds, and, oh, they yodel.

Topp Twins, Kiwi lesbian yodelers. By permission of management.

A strange "wholesome" cabaret hybrid, indeed. Sounds more like sleazy sideshow material? Well, not at all. The fact that they please mainstream crowds is a testament to their magical crossover potential; lesbians are people, yes, and funny at that!

And to think it all began when, as little girls, they first heard Shirley Thoms, Jean Holmes, and Patsy Montana yodeling on old 78s at a neighbor's house. Lynda became instantly enchanted and vowed to learn to yodel. The sisters would walk home together from their neighbor's house and try to reconstruct the lyrics, hamming up the yodel parts. And when they first yodeled publicly they were just 10–year-old snot-noses. The Topps are immensely popular—their singing is serious, their cabaret is not, and it's all interactive—fans are plucked out of the audience to join them in a yodel refrain or play fall guy. They do their hog-jowl hayseed best at Hee-Haw humor and succeed. They are hip and odd, camp and kooky, and not without political agendas. In the 1980s, the Topps were on the forefront of major issues: anti-apartheid, nuclear-free New Zealand, Maori land rights, and gay rights. Their harmony-charmed bellowing voices remind me of blues belters like Big Maybelle but with a tender Emmylou Harris underside.

- *Grass Highway*, Topp Twins / EMI, 2001.

- *Two Timing*, Topp Twins, 1994. Includes "Yodelling Accordion."

- *In Search of the Lonesome Yodel*, New Zealand TV documentary devoted to tracing history of New Zealand yodeling from early roots to "techno-yodel" and "square-dance rap" through the eyes of the Topp Twins.

SELECTED DOWN UNDER YODEL DISCOGRAPHY

- *The Australian Country Yodelers*, 1990s. Compilation includes many Australian big-name yodelers.

- *Australian Hillbilly Music*, Tex Banes with his Hayseeds, Cattle, 1990s. 1940s-50s singer-yodeler with accordion, fiddle, and steel guitar backing.

- *Back to the Mountains*, Max McCauley, John ten Velde Records, 1990s.

- *Born to Be a Cowboy*, Roger Tibbs, John ten Velde Records, 1990s. Tibbs is most famous for his "Yodel Boogie."

- *Bushland Yodel*, Smilin' Billy Blinkhorn, Cattle, 2000. This excellent Canadian yodeler moved to Australia where he had a robust if short-lived career in the 1940s.

- *Country Music Comes to Town*, Reg Lindsay, Columbia, 1961.

- *Country Music in Australia*, various artists, Selection, 1977.

- *Country Music in Australia, Sounds About Australia*, includes twenty volumes of various Aussie performers and yodelers.

- *Country Music in Australia 1936–1959: The Regal Rodeo Collection*, EMI, 1993.

- *Country Music Jamboree*, Reg Lindsay, Universal Summit. Mostly standards.

- *Country Requests and Yodelling*, Colleen Honeyman, CH. Includes a mix of traditional ballads and yodel songs. Honeyman grew up in Australia and early on became a regular on the Dick Cranbourne 3DB Country and Western Show. In 1984, she won the Victorian Yodelling Championships and is today considered one of Australia's leading yodelers.

- *Dusty Country Road*, Brendan Dugan, RCA 1985. New Zealand singer.

- *Happy Tears*, Melinda Schneider, 2002. Includes the lines: "I was born in 71 / Policeman dad and a yodeling mum / I am proud of where I'm from / And who I've become."

- *Hot Shot Country*, Reg Lindsay, Festival, 1970s. Lindsay on vocals and guitar with unlisted accompaniment.

- *Kiwi Yodels: 24 Golden Yodels*, Four New Zealand yodelers including Roger Tibbs and Kitten.

- *The Man from Nulla Nulla*, Shorty Ranger, Hadley, 1976. Aussie does some yodeling.

- *Reg Lindsay Favorites*, Reg Lindsay and Heather McLean, Columbia, 1960s.

- *Southbound*, Roger Tibbs, John ten Velde Records. "New Zealand's Yodeling Man."

- *Way Out on the Sunburnt Plains*, various artists, Dee-Why West, 1960s.

- *Why Country Songs Are Sad,* Desrëe-Jlova Crawford, Rich River, 1970s.

- *Yodeling Cowgirl*, Kitten, Dominion/K-Tel, 1995. Kitten is an exuberant Kiwi yodeler who prefers yodeling to singing.

6

African Yodeling Beyond the Rainforest

For those who thought the yodel was solely a European or cowboy thing, think again. Yodels are found pretty much everywhere but Antarctica—and maybe a hardy ethnologist will discover yodeling penguins there someday as well. In a strange instance of what-comes-around-goes-around, when Africans in Nairobi first heard Jimmie Rodgers they declared him a demigod for whom they wrote numerous "chimirocha" songs. But even before Africans ended up in the Americas, it seems African yodeling has had more resonance, presence, and enthusiasm than previously assumed. In this chapter, we'll examine some of these yodeling traditions, beginning with Africa's yodeling superstars, the Pygmies of Central Africa.

THE PYGMY: HUNTER, GATHERER, SURVIVOR, AND YODELER

The yodeling and hocketing of Pygmy singing has served as an icon of social and musical utopia.

—Michelle Kisliuk

A German children's book dating from 1821 portrays a yodeling Bushman and a Swiss boy frowning with fingers in his ears, complaining about how a Bushman's yodel sounds like a pig's squeal. If this portrayal wasn't so absurdly pathetic and common—until quite recently—it would almost be funny. But what saddens me even more is the fact that the Pygmies' habitat lies increasingly splattered—shrinking, and under siege—across some of the world's most war-torn territory. They are not the cause of these conflicts, being, as I understand it, accommodating and peaceful to the point of being systematically victimized, indentured, and sometimes even *eaten* by their taller neighbors. They're indeed often the victims of ethnic strife, realpolitiks, and genocide.

"Pygmy" is Greek for "'people pertaining to the *pygmé* [the distance from the elbow to the knuckles] who repeatedly warred with and were defeated by cranes." Pygmies are commonly believed to be the earliest inhabitants of Central Africa, perhaps as early as around 7000 B.C. Homer, in the 8th century B.C., calls Pygmies "men a cubit high." Around A.D. 1100, Bantu tribes began migrating into the forests of present-day Cameroon. Westerners called Pygmies *Negrillos* into the 1930s. Anthropologically speaking, Pygmies are people who grow no taller than 1.5 meters (less than 5 feet); the slightly taller are called Pygmoid. While the term "Pygmy" usually applies to inhabitants of equatorial Africa, the Kalahari San (Bushmen) are equally as short. According to author Alex Shoumatoff, "about a hundred and forty thousand Pygmies live in Africa. . . . they are considered the largest group of hunter-gatherers left in the world." Other figures range between 100,000 to 500,000, depending on the guesstimater. The Pygmy lifestyle is not exactly conducive to accurate census-taking.

Shoumatoff continues: "Pygmies may have originally lived in the savannas of the Upper Nile and, according to the physical anthropologist Carleton Coon, may have been driven into the forest by a drought that affected both their water supply and their hunting." They're nomadic and live in Central Africa's equatorial marshes and forests, surviving by hunting (men) and gathering (women). Over the centuries, Pygmies retreated into the region's dense rainforests to hide from the Bantu tribes. They (prefer to) remain in the rainforests. Pygmies have managed to maintain their essential independence and migratorial lifestyles despite the incursion of the West (beginning in the 16th century) and despite slavery and the massive geopolitical maneuverings caused by colonialism. They depend on incantation, faith, and the spiritual strength they find in their singing and yodeling. As Pierre Sallée has noted: "Their vocal polyphonies are their communication with the forest, which in sending back an echo puts them in touch with its strange denizens."

Pygmies speak a Sudanic and/or a Bantu language. They're said to be the only people not afraid of the forest, but they remain legendarily shy. The rainforest is their home, their source of food, shelter, and spiritual well-being. They seem "almost supernatural, entertaining a relationship of almost disturbing intimacy with nature." Their taller neighbors exploit the Pygmies by underpaying them, ridiculing them in public, and even enslaving them. Some Pygmy tribes have turned to a sedentary lifestyle in

FRANCIS BEBEY

I was the tallest pygmy in this forest.

—Francis Bebey, "Pygmy Divorce"

Music is the outward and audible manifestation of inward biological functions . . .

—Francis Bebey

Francis Bebey, African renaissance man and "tallest Pygmy." By permission of Toups Bebey.

The late Francis Bebey (1929–2001), the son of a Protestant minister, became a composer and performer, a prize-winning novelist, radio journalist, filmmaker, and something of an undervalued all-around cultural omnivore, not to mention a formidable musicologist who wrote intelligently and passionately about African music. Bebey was born on the outskirts of Douala, a Cameroon seaport. He grew up with books and music, learning to play Pygmy flute, African *sanza* thumb piano, and guitar in his youth. Bebey went to college in Cameroon and studied music at the Sorbonne in Paris and New York University. He was influenced by local musicians but also by jazz—Ellington and Armstrong ("The first time I heard Louis Armstrong, I went crazy," Bebey noted in a 1979 interview. "I bought his records like smokers buy cigarettes.")—and the classical guitarist Andrés Segovia. His own music blends African rhythms with Western, Asian, and Latin influences.

To manage this fusion during the colonial period meant overcoming the prejudice against his native "primitive rhythms." Bebey envisioned using Western technology and resources to disseminate African culture. Along the way he sang traditional African songs and ballads, in French, Douala, and English; performed rumbas, modern classical, pop, and makossas; played a wide range of instruments; and yodeled. Bebey's yodeling is Pygmy in vocal style but is used as a refrain in a Western song structure. Bebey produced some thirty records, wrote many songs, and later turned out to be a composer as well. In 1994, his "Kasilane" was commissioned and premiered by the Kronos Quartet.

Bebey earned his living as the head of the UNESCO music department in Paris. In 1974, he quit this post to pursue his writing and composing. He wrote drama and fiction, and published a dozen novels, short story collections, and books of poetry. On top of all this, Bebey was a reputable musicologist as well, publishing the popular study *African Music—A People's Art* (1975). He died of a heart attack in Paris at age 72.

continued on the next page

Francis Bebey, continued

- *Sourire de Lune*, Sonodisc, 1997.

- *Akwaaba: Sanza Music*, Original Music, 1984.

- *Travail au Noir*, Sonodisc, 1997.

- *Dibye*, Sonodisc, 1997.

- *Pygmy Love Song*, Makossa International, 1982. Portrays everyday Pygmy life in a humorous and enlighteningly charming manner.

- *La Condition Masculine*, Sonodisc, 1991 (1975). Includes the classic domestic drama, "Divorce Pygmée."

- *Mandolo / With Love (Works: 1963–1994)*, Original Music, 1995. Compilation of "greatest hits," out-of-print recordings, and unreleased material.

response to a shrinking habitat because of deforestation, governmental decree, or economic necessity. The Ba-binga are now farmers, often ending up in subservient relationships with local villagers. They remain, however, steadfastly more traditional and nomadic than other indigenous peoples—loyal only to their kind and their forest. They remain a demographic anomaly that disturbs bureaucratic minds. In fact, many host nations have tried to curb their nomadic ways, preferring them to settle down as tax-paying citizens, as army recruits, and ultimately as reliable consumers.

Their lives are hard; mortality rates are high (but not any higher than that of urban Africans). Their lives are fraught with danger but also with adventure—both important in the formation of an intensely and organically spiritual relationship with their habitat. Many of the Pygmies live communal lives—sharing and nonhierarchical egalitarian attitudes prevail. Their nomadic ways mean few cumbersome possessions; housing is informal and easily constructed in a few hours.

All of this has had an impact on their musical traditions, which includes a form of yodeling. Their nonvirtuoso, nonhierarchical exchanges of lead solos and yodel improvisations is aural evidence of their social organization. Once a performance begins, musical leadership shifts, and different voices move in and out of the background. Daou Joiris and Susan Kent, among other ethnomusicologists, see this as a reflection of the Pygmies' egalitarian society: "Egalitarianism permeates . . . not only the social and political organization, economics, and division of labor of these societies but also their ethos or worldview—in other words, every facet of culture and behavior." The "Pygmy musical style and practice," according to Thomas Turino, "grows out of, and reflects, the specific egalitarian nature of Pygmy social and economic life." Francis Bebey noted that "African music . . . is common property." Family units are open and community based. Children are often introduced to the entire community and made to feel comfortable around everyone; neighbor women might even nurse babies not their own.

Bebey further pointed out that African vocals should not be judged by Western standards of technical excellence, because singing among Pygmies serves a different function. First of all, "the objective of African music is not necessarily to produce sounds agreeable to the ear, but to translate everyday experiences into living sound." African singing adjusts itself to the situation and ambience more than, say, the confines of a composition. The nature of singing is also less hierarchical and more egalitarian. Bebey continues, "any individual who has the urge to make his voice heard is given the liberty to do so; singing is not a specialized affair."

YODEL TRIBES

After many years, I'm still trying to get a handle on the different spellings of the many Pygmy tribes. Are the Ba-Aka, B'aka, Bakola, Baka, Bibayak, and the Aka the same people? I've come to understand that "Pygmies are classified into four groups according to their spoken dialects: the Ba-Binga, Ba-Ngombe, Ba-Mbuti (BaMbuti), and Ba-Benzele Pygmies," in the words of Ashenaji Kebede.

Ba-Binga

The Ba-Binga (M'Benga) live north of the Congo River, in the forest west of the Ubangi River. They have adapted to the ways of their neighbors but still maintain many of the traditions including hunting and gathering activities. Bebey notes that "polyphonic shouting, in which women's voices predominate, is one of the original traits of Pygmy vocal technique. Alternation between polyphonic shouting and polyphonic singing is a characteristic feature of Babinga musical composition."

The Babongo, Akoa, Bakola (Aka, Baka, BaAka, or Bibayak), into the 1970s inhabited the border territory between Gabon, southeastern Cameroon, and the Congo. They're related to the Ba-Binga Bangombé who live along the Sangha River. According to Mauro Campagnoli, who lived with the Baka, they are being forced into sedentary lives because of the effects of massive deforestation. Michelle Kisliuk notes: "Since the 1960s . . . these Pygmies have become more involved in farming." BaAka perform music to accompany their dances. The "Makala" is a playful improvisational song that includes "interlocked and yodeled sections." The Aka Pygmy yodelers produce highly complex vocal works that can consist of anywhere from a few to a dozen overtones in the high register while, in the low register the tones have a range of intense and homogenous overtones.

Ba-Benzélé (Ba-Benzele)

This group lives along the Sangha River, a tributary of the Congo River, as hunters of water buffalo, gorilla, warthog, gazelle, and elephants. They leave their habitat only once a year to trade with local villagers, sometimes exchanging their goods to pay rent for the land they live on. The Ba-Benzélé have many ceremonies that include a wide variety of vocal styles, most prominent among them yodeling. Their songs often deal with the dangers of the hunt, and so they sing special songs to protect them during their hunting trips. Through their yodeling, they express gladness and gratitude to the forest and animals.

Ba-Mbuti (BaMbuti/Bambuti)

There are some 40,000 Ba-Mbuti divided among four different Pygmy groups who live in the Ituri equatorial rainforest. The nearly 30,000 Mbuti (Mbouti) are hunter-gatherers and call themselves *Ba miki ba ndula* ("Children of the forest"). They live deep within Zaire's dense sunless rainforest of very tall broadleaf trees, which is fed by the Ituri and Congo rivers. Each Ba-Mbuti group has a unique relationship with a different Bantu tribe; the Mbuti live in close relation to the Bila tribe. Colin Turnbull suggested that they spend a good deal of their existence in a tense patron-client relationship with their sedentary Bantu neighbors.

Nevertheless the Ba-Mbuti have found it useful to adopt the language of their trading partners. The Mbuti, for example, trade their extra meat for cultivated foods, iron tools, and weapons from the Bantu farmers, fishermen, and entrepreneurs. The Mbuti resent the fact that these villagers are partly responsible for the disappearance of their forest. The Bantus often clear entire swaths of forest to make room for new farms and villages.

The forest remains essential to the Mbuti. One cannot separate the forest from their vision, ceremonies, art, music, and dances. Their ceremonies are performed to honor the guardian spirit of the forest, *Nzambi*, which protects them and is considered "naturally good." They "associate divinity with the forest, itself living and divine"; the forest provides them (or used to) with everything they needed, including affection. Colin Turnbull notes, "Song . . . is believed to attract the attention of the forest and to please it."

The Mbuti perform numerous complex polyphonic songs that speak to this god in various contexts. Their repertoire of songs is as vocally complex as anything heard in Africa. Kebede believes that "some of their perform-ance styles remind us of contemporary European avant-garde music at its best." *Elima*, a girl's rite of passage, and *Nkumki*, a boy's right of passage, are celebrated with singing, yodeling, dancing, and a tug-of-war game between the sexes.

Other Groups

While the Baka, Ba-Mbuti, and Ba-Benzélé have been popular and amiable subjects for research and recording, the Asua Mbuti Pygmies (not yodel-ers) and the Sua Efe Pygmies from the Epulu area in Haut-Zaire province appear to be underdocumented. This also goes for the Twa (Batwa), who live in the high mountains and plains around Lake Kivu, in the Congo, Rwanda, and Burundi, in a symbiotic relationship with their neighbors, the pastoral Tutsi and agricultural Hutu. I know very little about the Tswa (Batswa) who live, fish, and trap in the southern wetlands along the Congo River and who have adopted the culture and language of neighboring tribes.

Pygmy music is basically vocals with almost no instrumental accompa-niment, except for a few instruments borrowed from neighboring villages like the Bantus (Gabon), who have a long history of intermarriage with the Pygmies. The Pygmy yodel has two distinct sounds or approaches: the more "brutal" version involves "glottal attacks, grunts, hums, and shouts combined with upward and downward releases." The second is more melodic and is "sung melismatically with trills and tremelos, repeated tones by rapid up-and-down vocal glides." In general, the yodels are belted out, and the various yodelers—especially among the Bibayaka—harmonically adjust to one another within fanfare (short ceremonial tune) formulas, with the yodels serving as embellishments. Various yodeling jousts (not unlike rappers and Jamaican toasters) allow individual yodelers to playfully outdo one another for the solo finalé.

Pygmy yodeling is characterized by a deep, round, full-timbred chest voice that ascends into a pinched falsetto. It sounds a bit like a flute, with yodels sung on "Ah eh" (chest) and "ee" (falsetto). The nonlinguistic sound "erupts in broken vocalizing of pure sounds: the voices, entering succes-sively, adjust to one another in 'canons' and 'imitations,' to which the musi-cal code lends the significance of responses by shaping them to its forms."

Pygmy polyphony often involves finding a harmony between the lead (female) yodeler and those who follow her lead. In three-voice yodels, the yodelers converge to create a melodic line that involves the two timbres of the chest and falsetto pitches. Bebey notes that the "African singer alternates head and chest voice like a game of hide-and-seek in a labyrinth of rhythm."

AFRICAN YODEL HONOR ROLL

Bles Bridges (b. Lawrence Gabriel Bridges, 1946–2000), "Mr. Entertainer" was a popular South African (Afrikaans) singer called by some—with no ill will—the Liberace of Afrikaner culture. Despite a fairly small (white?) audience, he managed to sell millions of records. A legend here but nowhere else, Bridges was something of a good-natured troubadour with a superb voice who managed to combine his Irish background with American-style country in his native South Africa. "I Am the Eagle You're the Wind" was his biggest hit. He performed (politically incorrectly) at Sun City in 1987. Many of his songs were cowritten with his wife, Leonie. If he was southern Africa's best yodeler, it begs the question: how many other southern African yodelers are there? Representative yodel: "Sy Leer My Om te Yodel" ("She Taught Me to Yodel," in Afrikaans).

Thomas Mapfumo (b. 1945), the "Lion of Zimbabwe," is that nation's most popular musician. He grew up in the countryside with his grandparents, waking up before dawn to tend the cattle and do his chores before school. Mapfumo's lyrics reflect his people's concerns: rural hardships, young soldiers fighting Zimbabwe's war for independence, and a rising sense of indignation at the white rulers who had for generations systematically devalued Shona culture. Mapfumo has emerged as a world-renowned musician who combines electric instruments and elements of big-band jazz with traditional rhythms, Shona yodeling, and reggae influences.

Mapfumo performs a version of a native music called *mbira*, the name of the resonant thumb piano native to Zimbabwe. *Mbira* music links Zimbabweans to their past, especially through its use in spirit possession ceremonies. The music incorporates three styles of singing: *kudeketera* (poetic lyrics), *mohonyera* (growling drones involving closed throat set at a certain pitch), and *huro* (yodeling). As a soloist, Mapfumo alternates between lead and backing vocals himself or interlocks vocals with an accompanist. Shona yodeling, or *huro* (throat), is sung with an "open" throat and includes sharp and loud, rapid alternations between two different vocal registers. The best example of *huro* use is Mapfumo's "Pidigori," which is based on a traditional Shona *mbira* piece.

- *Chimurenga Collected*, with the Blacks Unlimited, Nascente Worldwide, 2001.

- *The Singles Collection 1976–1986*, with the Blacks Unlimited, Zimbob, 1996.

Zap Mama, a fourth-world a cappella group, formed in 1990 by Marie Daulne, performs a dynamic lilting style of Afro-global vocalese. Their scat-yodel alloy fuses influences from many corners of the world, effectively linking tradition with invention, meaning with exuberance. Their early work was anchored by Daulne's indebtedness to the Pygmies. Daulne was born in Isiro, Zaire (formerly Belgian Congo), in 1960 to a Belgian father and a Zairian mother. In the early years of Zaire's independence from Belgium, Simba rebels killed her Walloon

continued on the next page

African Yodel Honor Roll, continued

father and imprisoned her Bantu mother. Daulne and siblings were delivered to the Pygmies, who offered the children shelter until their mother was released. Daulne and family eventually made their way to Brussels.

Daulne remembers her mother at home, singing Zairean songs and exposing her to polyphonic singing. However, Daulne's Pygmy interests were aroused, ironically enough, by the ethnological records of Pygmy music that shook loose her memories and led her to her roots. She traveled back to Zaire in the mid-1980s to do field research, something she and the group continue to do to unearth the incredible sounds of forgotten Africa. Hearing the music in its context and reimagining her past, Daulne found inspiration in Pygmy melodies. She returned to Europe thoroughly inspired. She went on to study jazz and vocal polyphony.

Daulne embodies the spirit of "real" global music, as opposed to those self-aggrandizing touristic skimmings of riffs and flourishes. Her music is roots music, although the precise location of those roots remains in doubt because she is at once true to roots and nomadically willing to go where inspiring sounds are found—including deep inside herself. Daulne once said "I feel at ease wherever I am. I'm a nomad." That fairly describes their/her music as well.

Daulne and Zap Mama released their first album in 1991 on Belgium's Crammed label. It presented an up-tempo a cappella mix of enchanting Pygmy music and yodeling, Central African and Arabic pop tunes, Afro-Cuban rhythms, and American soul and gospel, and it became hugely successful. Daulne remains the only original member of Zap Mama. Zap Mama is, after all, her vehicle.

- *Zap Mama: Adventures in Afropea*, Crammed, 1991/1993. Eclectic mix of yodels, bird sounds, sirens, African chants, doo-wop, and madrigal.

- *Sabsylma*, Luaka Bop, 1994. Best-selling world music CD successfully fuses Pygmy influences with a broad array of sonic inputs.

- *Seven,* Luaka Bop, 1997. A move away from acoustic a cappella to incorporate electronics and instrumentation.

- *A Ma Zone*, Luaka Bop, 1999. Daulne moved to the United States and worked with musicians like Cameroonian saxophonist Manu Dibango and Speech from Arrested Development to produce a jaunty, urbane disc.

A five-voice yodel (*mbény*) may involve drumming accompaniment. The Bibayaka also perform some dialogues with spirits like the *Kosé* (envisioned as a foliage mask) who dances and speaks through a palm tree tube from inside a foliage-covered hut while the women address him with various yodels. The *Tsinghi* is a forest spirit the yodelers address with their yodeling calls. *Tsinghi* reigns during the elephant hunt and appears in foliage costume.

Ituri and Bantu-language tribes (Ba-Aka and Ba-Mbuti) perform a hunt preparation ritual called a *yeli*. Female participants gather the ritual

S. E. ROGIE: AFRICAN BLUES MAN

S. E. Rogie (Sooliman Ernest Rogers, 1919/1923?–1994), singer-guitarist from Sierra Leone, left behind a distinctive hybridized sound that is best characterized as reverse inspiration. He morphed a baritone voice, highlife, and traditional West African guitar playing (known as the "palm wine" style) into a sound that included slick country pop; he was a big fan of smooth satiny voices like Pat Boone, Bing Crosby, and Jim Reeves. But more interestingly, he had a yodel that was snatched right from the overwrought throat of Jimmie Rodgers. He actually began his career as "The Jimmie Rodgers of Sierra Leone." Rogie discovered the strange crossroads of (country) Western culture and that of his native land, a nation founded by British slaves in the late 18th century. He came to symbolize that crossroads, that harmony of disharmonious cultures by creating a body of work that represents the Sierra Leone's isolated yet convivially multicultural character.

Different sources give different birth dates for Rogie, as well as conflicting biographical information. From what I can gather, Rogie grew up in Fonikoh, near the Liberian border, far from the interracial hubbub of the capital city of Freetown. Orphaned at seven, Rogie took on countless manual labor jobs to survive. At age 18, he discovered a Jimmie Rodgers record in his brother's collection. Rogie soon fell under the Singing Brakeman's spell and began imitating Rodgers's playing and singing. Not long thereafter, Rogie emerged as an itinerant musician and could be heard busking on Sierra Leone's trains and streets.

In 1955, Rogie made his first recordings and did his first radio shows, while continuing to work as a tailor to support himself. He eventually founded his own label, where he recorded his forlorn love songs on a crude, mono, reel-to-reel machine with makeshift cardboard-box percussion accompaniment. He sang in his native Mende, but also in French, English, and Krio (an English-based Freetown Creole lingua franca). His palm-wine style of guitar playing plus his warm vocals produced several hits in the mid-1960s: "Go Easy With Me," "Koneh Pehlawo," and "My Lovely Elizabeth" (the most popular Sierra Leonese song ever). He was also known for his unique yodel. In 1965, he formed the Morningstars, an electric backing band for his acoustic guitar, lilting vocals, and twangy yodels. Rogie eventually toured the United States, ending up in California where he spent sixteen years teaching African culture. In 1988, he returned to Sierra Leone, where he died in 1994 just after the release of *Dead Men Don't Smoke Marijuana*.

- *Palm Wine Guitar Music*, Cooking Vinyl, 2002.

- *Dead Men Don't Smoke Marijuana*, Realworld, 1995.

materials—herbs, barks, and leaves—and burn them; the direction in which the smoke plumes point helps guide the hunters to their game. Ethnomusicologist Daou Joiris notes, "Rites performed in order to attract game are very elaborate in the *yeli* ceremony. Powerful hunting attributes accompany the 'yodel' polyphonies." And to call game into their midst "the *yeli* spirits . . . stay in the bush and start dancing when they hear women singing *yeli*." The Pygmies drink a honey-based "pot liquid," which "reinforces the 'yodel' songs' capacity to attract game." Their polyphonic yodels involve hockets or repetitions of short patterns of call-and-response yodels that create cyclical patterns, which take melodic shape as different voices enter. The yodels are punctuated by a variety of grunts, hums, trills, and tremeloes and glottal attacks or "rapid opening and closing a section of the throat called the glottis," which creates "an interrupted or quavering sound." This allows them to communicate with spirit worlds.

Other non-Pygmy Africans who yodel, some probably because of past contacts with Pygmies, include:

- Some tribes in Ethiopia, the place where some anthropologists believe the Pygmies came from.
- The Khoisan, the lighter-skinned indigenous peoples of southern Africa—the Khoi (Hottentots) and the hunter-gatherer-farmer San (Bushmen).

SELECTED AFRICAN DISCOGRAPHY

- *Anthology of World Music: Africa: The Ba-Benzélé Pygmies*, Rounder, 1998.

- *Bayaka: The Extraordinary Music of the Ba-Benzélé Pygmies*, CD/Book, Ellipse, 1995. New Jersey–native Louis Sarno lives among the Bayaka and was free to record songs and rituals previously unheard by Western ears.

- *Central African Republic.* UNESCO, 1999 (1983). Folk/traditional music from seven Central African Republic ethnic groups.

- *Echoes of the Forest: Music of the Central African Pygmies*, Ellipsis Arts. Recorded/noted by Colin Turnbull, Jean-Pierre Hallet, and Sarno. Showcases polyphony and yodel styles.

- *Gabon Musique des Pygmies Bibayak*, Ocora. Field recordings (1966–1973) by Pierre Sallée, 1984. Stunning display of vocal styles, including some yodeling examples.

continued on the next page

Selected African Discography, continued

- **Heart of the Forest**, Baka Forest People, Hannibal, 1993.

- **Homeland**, Putumayo, 2000. Miriam Makeba (1932) is not only a world ambassador but a legend who was exiled from her native South Africa for thirty years; she yodels on "Masakhane."

- **Mbuti Pygmies of the Ituri Forest**, Smithsonian-Folkways, 1957/62. Unadulterated, unromanticized field recordings by Turnbull, featuring yodeling and hocketing.

- **The Music of the Ba-Benzélé Pygmies,** Musicaphon/UNESCO, 1978. Recordings/notes: Simkha Arom. Some good examples of Pygmy hocketing, polyphony, and yodeling.

- **Music of the Rainforest Pygmies**, Lyrichord, 1999.

- **Musique Centrafricaine,** Recordings/notes: Charles Duvelle, Ocora, 1962. Includes two Ba-Binga Pygmy songs.

- **Musique des Pygmees du Gabon et des Bochimans du Botswana**, CBS, 1976. Includes lovely music, hocketing, polyphony and ritual-oriented yodels by the Baka Pygmies, ¡Kung, Tannekwe, plus folk music from Gabon.

- **Musique du Burundi.** Recordings/notes: Michel Vuylsteke, Ocora, 1968.

- **Oceans of the Heart: A Celebration of Music from Asia and Africa**, various artists, SOAS, 2001?

- **On the Edge of the Ituri Forest**, ILAM, 1998. Hugh Tracey's 1952 recordings.

- **Polyphony of the Deep Rainforest**, Victor, 1986. Documents music that is essential to the Ituri Pygmies of Zaire.

- **Pygmy Attitudes**, Toups Bebey & Paris Africans, Buda Musique, 2001. Francis Bebey's youngest son produces a decidedly "Paris African" urban sound, with firm nods to his African roots.

- **Remember Me**, Virginia Teal, Teal Records, 1960s. "Tennessee Yodel Polka" and others sung in English and Afrikaans.

- **Shona Mbira Music**, various artists, Nonesuch, 1977. Vocalist Mude Hakurotwi, a big influence on Mapfumo, often sings *huro*, or Shona yodeling.

- **Turnbull's Music of the Rain Forest Pygmies**, Lyrichord. Originally released in 1961, its selections include the Mbuti influence on the music of neighboring peoples.

- The Mangbetu of the Democratic Republic of the Congo imitate some aspects of Pygmy polyphony.
- The ¡Kung, southern Angolan hunters-gatherers, use yodeling for anywhere from one to four voices, which are used to produce two or more melodic lines at the same time. In southeastern Angola, the ¡Kung sing San music using extensive yodeling. Their vocable music imitates animal sounds, especially bird calls.
- The San of southeastern Angola, Namibia, and South Africa employ polyphonic vocals and yodel a cappella with plenty of vocables and bird and other animal sounds. Their multipart singing also includes hocketing, much like the Pygmies, although with different musical principles and purposes. "Both Khoikhoi and San yodeled as they sang." The Khoikhoi are a short dark-skinned people related to the San, numbering 55,000 mainly in Namibia and in southwest Africa.
- The Gogo and Bushmen of Tanzania use "elements such as poly-phonic vocal music, yodeling." Although they're unrelated linquisti-cally, the two groups practice similar vocal styles, probably meaning they received it from earlier inhabitants. Because there is no domi-nant tribe or ethnic group, Swahili is the lingua franca, which allows Arabs, the Portuguese, and Bantus to communicate.
- The Shona of Zimbabwe and Mozambique include some 9 million Bantu-speakers who speak five dialects. John Kaemmer notes, "the Shona practice of yodeling suggests influences from the Pygmies, who probably inhabited the area before the arrival of Bantu-speakers." The Shona play the *mbira*, which they use to accompany singers and yodelers. A humming bass voice with or without *mbira* is often ornamented with yodels.

LATIN AMERICA

Many West Africans in the 17th through 19th centuries became unwilling immigrants, brought to the Caribbean and the Americas to work as slaves in the various European New World colonies. They brought with them their musical traditions—including yodeling—and little else. The Spanish also helped disseminate the yodel in the New World. This became most evident in the songs of the Mexican *vaqueros*, some of whom purportedly taught the early American cowboys how to yodel. In any case, the mix of African and European influences made for a unique and potent hybrid yodel.

Latin American music is mainly influenced by four cultures: Native peoples, African cultures, and the Spanish and Portuguese. In Argentina,

TARZAN'S JUNGLE YODELS

(A) noise like blowing on a comb covered with paper
—Mordaunt Hall's description of Johnny Weissmuller's yodel in
a *New York Times* review of *Tarzan, the Ape Man*

The true power of Tarzan's yodel can best be illustrated by an apocryphal story of something that (may have) happened during a celebrity golf tournament in Havana, Cuba, in 1959. Johnny Weissmuller was driving some friends to the tournament when his car was ambushed by anti-Batista rebels. In a bind, the quick-thinking Weissmuller decided to—you guessed it—belt out his famed Tarzan yodel. The stunned rebels recognized the yell and realized

The yodel heard round the world. By permission of Burroughs Memorial Collection.

they'd ambushed their hero, Tarzan. They quickly apologized and personally escorted Weissmuller and entourage to the tournament.

Edgar Rice Burroughs's lackluster descriptions of the howls in his Tarzan books betray their true power, the resonance of which were only fully realized when Weissmuller began belting them out. Burroughs describes it as an animal's scream: "She heard sounds issue from his throat—sounds identical with those issued by the apes." An eviscerated ape-like scream, then. But Weissmuller, in all his grace and human complexity, managed to convert this brutish ululation into an elegant yodel that sounded more like the enchanting song of a Lorelei than the shriek of a savage beast. How did this most famous of cinematic yells come to be? With athletic élan, an almost superhuman moral poise, and a "vivid train of imaginings that his man-mind wrought."

Peter Jonas Weissmuller, born June 2, 1904, in Freidorf (at that time, in the Austro-Hungarian Empire), grew up in the coal-mining town of Windber, Pennsylvania. Windber is situated in the Alleghany Mountains somewhere in the anonymous nowhere east of Pittsburgh. It's a modest town whose history is buried in coal dust.

The Weissmuller family moved to Chicago, and shortly after World War I his father died of brown lung contracted from working in the Windber mines. Johnny eventually quit school and worked as a bellhop and elevator operator. But it was during his adolescent Windber years that Weissmuller learned something that would change the course of (recorded) sound forever. During the

continued on the next page

Tarzan's Jungle Yodels, continued

shooting of his and MGM's first Tarzan film, *Tarzan, the Ape Man,* in 1931, it quickly became clear that Weissmuller was the ideal choice for the part, despite Burroughs' objections. To the producers, this beach bum who, after his retirement from competitive swimming (five U.S. Olympic gold medals), had worked just hard enough to get by had something beyond acting—he had presence. In fact, BVD, maker of men's underwear, also noticed his allure, signing him to a lucrative contract to don their undies in ads. *Ape Man* costarred Neil Hamilton as Harry Holt and the alluring precode Maureen O'Sullivan as Jane Parker.

The idea that necessity was a spur to invention was never truer than in these early days of sound film. The elephants used in the film were the more easily trainable Indian elephants. However, their ears were too small and their tusks too short, which meant that for accuracy's sake the Indian elephants were fitted with artificial ears and tusk extensions. MGM also found fifty dwarves to play the Pygmies, which, of course, is almost pure synchronous poetry considering that both *real* Pygmies and the *not-so-real* dwarfs (see *Snow White*) yodel! Furthermore, the film's climax required that the elephants, summoned by Tarzan's reverberating yodel, stampede a Pygmy village.

This unique cry was personally "designed" by Weissmuller himself. As he recalled in a TV interview: "When I was a kid I used to read all the Tarzan books, and they had a kind of shrill yell for Tarzan . . . when I finally got [the role of Tarzan], they were trying to do yells like that. And I remembered when I was a kid I used to yodel at the picnics on Sundays, and I said, 'I know a yell!'" The sound producers at MGM took Weissmuller's jungle yodel—Aaahhhh-eeeeeeee-aaaahhhh-eeeeee-aaaahhhh-eeeeeee-aaaahhhh!—and reportedly mixed in an odd potpourri of other unrelated sound bits such as the sound of a "hyena's yowl played backwards, a camel's bleat, the pluck of a violin string, and a soprano's high-C." This strange mix became so distinctive and so associated with Tarzan that it became an obligatory trademark, to the point that almost every post-Weissmuller Tarzan has had to lip-synch it.

At Weissmuller's funeral in 1984, rumor has it that six of the pallbearers were of the chimpanzee persuasion and that PA speakers were blaring his jungle Alpine yell for all the mourners to hear.

for instance, the Spanish influence dominates and has done so for more than 400 years. (But maybe a fifth culture should now also be added. The American or transnational taste-shapers like MTV have an economic imperiousness that certainly ensures a certain amount of influence, cash register conformity, and accommodation. The pop singer Shakira, for instance, is certainly heavily influenced by North American musical styles.)

Less well known is the fact that many non-Spanish/Portuguese Europeans have also emigrated to South and Central America over the centuries, among them Dutch, Italians, and Germans. The Germans emigrated to Argentina, Brazil, Chile, and Paraguay during a period of open immigration during the late 1800s and early 1900s. Many German (yodeling?) Mennonite farmers, some of whom had lived in Russia, emigrated to Paraguay. There are also two other (perversely) interrelated people(s) who fled to South America: Jews escaping Nazi persecutions and, interestingly enough, many Nazis who fled for their lives after the collapse of the Third Reich in 1945. The Germans brought their music, their polka-like *schottisch* (somtimes ornamented with yodels) but their most obvious musical import into Latin America was the accordion, which the tango is inexorably associated with today. The Italians who emigrated from the Dolomites also brought along their accordions. Whether the yodel came over with some of these immigrants is highly likely, although documentation seems to be lacking. There are some German singing organizations in Southern Brazil, although it is not known whether they yodel.

But perhaps the most important influence is the African musical contribution. In Guyana, a diminutive nocturnal gremlin-like spirit known as the *bacoo* wreaks havoc on Georgetown and other communities. They reportedly live on bananas and milk, throw rocks at homes, and are able to move large household objects. They remain trapped in sealed bottles until the bottles are uncorked. Once the *bacoo* escapes havoc is sure to follow, although a satisfied *bacoo* usually obeys his owner's commands. "*Baku*" in some West African languages means "little brother" or "short human," but it may also stem from the word "*bacucu*" or "banana." In West Africa, the shorter peoples—the Pygmies and Bushmen—are often believed to have magical powers. The *bacoo* may have come to Guyana via Suriname and, before that, from Africa. This belief was transmitted to Guyana, probably during the times of the slave trade, and perhaps by native interactions with Pygmy slaves or via slaves who were African rivals/neighbors of the Pygmies. So, Pygmies—or at least their image—sailed across the Atlantic and became part of Latin America's cultural-spiritual narrative. This is somewhat echoed by something that Welles Goodrich, an expert on a cappella music, noticed:

> You may be amazed by similarities in sound that developed on opposite sides of the globe. I once received a tape from an anthropologist, which was a field recording of the women of the Orowari tribe in the Amazon basin. These people had been visited only once or twice prior to this contact, yet the recording of the women singing their *festa* [party] songs sounds exactly as though they had been sung by the Pygmy women of Burundi.

That there are peoples in Central and South America with songs that involve the characteristic movement between chest and head voice is not

SELECTED LATIN AMERICAN HONOR ROLL

Joao Bosco is a Brazilian singer-songwriter-guitarist, who has found many appreciative ears lately, mostly because of his creative blends of jazz samba with swinging forays into bossa nova. He combines a distinctive poetic-scat vocal style, which sounds like bebop à la Ella Fitzgerald with the percussive Brazilian *batucada* sound. Bosco's throat produces a quirky yodel that warbles in falsetto before it plunges into chest tones. Bosco is best known for his "O Bebaido e a Equilibrista" ("The Drunk and the Tightrope Walker"), which was written during Brazil's long period of military dictatorship. The song was chosen as Amnesty International's theme song.

Anna Maria Kieffer works mostly outside Brazil in the rarefied realm of experimental vocalization, but her work is firmly rooted in Brazil's traditional music. As a musicologist, she has done research on Brazilian classical music and how this music incorporates and expresses its mixed-culture background. As a singer, she has worked with people like John Cage. She's currently working on a research project involving five centuries of Brazilian vocals.

Ways of the Voice, with Belgian Leo Kupper (Pogus, 1999), includes music inspired by Brazilian Indians and the musical themes of travelers and anthropologists who have been coming to Brazil since the 16th century. It also features two pieces that involve orchestral arrangements of tropical bird songs, where she responds to the calls of jungle birds with a series of aviary-esque yodel-like calls. Kupper's and Kiefer's collaborative work involves metalanguage or electronically enhanced and parsed esperantos. These investigations extrapolate outward from Dada and sound poetry. Language beyond logic enters a psychic sphere where new forms of vocalization are in order; this language includes Dada, chants, birdcalls, hollers, and yodels. "To communicate the incommunicable," Kupper notes, "it becomes necessary to create a new register, to break, with different sounds and form the cage where words were imprisoned." "Récit 1" uses the calls and cries heard in Brazilian markets, while "Anamak" is inspired by indigenous calls and cries. "Annazone" uses birdcalls and deals with the audio delusions of misperceiving natural calls as human vocalizations in a rainforest.

Shakira (Mebarak) is a Colombian pop singer who has emerged as a major world pop star. Photos have her looking like some shiny Barbarella-meets-Britney doll; or some polished offspring of Charo. The heavy-handed production values on her CDs stink of carpetbagger: add a smash of this, a dash of that, polish and edit until there's not a human quirk left. But Shakira can really sing, that's the shame of it all. She sings in Spanish and English and her material is all her own—although I hear plenty of copped riffs and melodies. Just as she is about to sink in a morass of sweeping, epic orchestration, snappy synthetic house beats, whiney rock-guitar licks, and mega-pop clichés, she glides into some very touching . . . yodeling! Especially on "Pienso En Ti" (*Pies Descalzos*, Columbia, 1996).

LATIN AMERICAN DISCOGRAPHY

- *A Bad Donato,* Joao Donato, Blue Thumb, 1971. Latin jazz ensemble features Donato on piano and organ. Includes "Cade Jodel?"

- *Canciones de mi Padre,* Linda Rondstadt, ?, 1987. Mostly traditional Mexican music, including Mexican yodeling, or *huapanguero,* on "Mi Ranchito." Also on "Tu Solo Tu" from her *Mas Canciones,* 1991.

- *Dominican Republic,* various performers, Allegro, 1999. Popular and folk music, includes "Yodel Merengue."

- *In Person at El Matador Pelé: Sergio Mendes' Favorite Things,* Sergio Mendes, 2–CD-set, Atlantic, 2001. Jazzy sambas plus "Jodel."

- *Los de Azuero (Traditional Music from Panama),* various performers. Music from the relatively isolated Azuero peninsula. Women sing the *Saloma,* a kind of beautiful high-voiced yodel. Men perform a *Grito,* a bizarre barking shout.

- *Merengues Festival,* Juan Campolargo, Sounds of the Caribbean, 1973. Includes "Merengue a la Tirolesa (Yodel Merengue)."

- *Sambou Sambou,* Pacific Jazz, 1965. Joao Donato on piano, includes "Tim Dom Dom" and "Jodel."

- *Sounds of the Caribbean,* various performers, Delat Music, 1998. Includes "Yodel Merengue."

in doubt. These peoples also include a number of *North* American tribes. The problem with uncovering precisely where and who the yodelers are is part cultural hegemony, part economic. Despite the fact that the West has absorbed much of its incredibly rich musical culture, South America is often the forgotten continent when it comes to music research and documentation. There's yodeling, but where?

In a bout of bittersweet irony (involving some guilt-inspired justification) we realize that slavery in all its earth-shattering and heart-rending suffering, displacement, and decimation of entire peoples *did* produce at least one positive byproduct: incomparable music. In North America, of course, there's blues, jazz, rhythm and blues, et al. But it's almost impossible to think back to a time before Calypso (Trinidad), Reggae (Jamaica), Mariachi (Mexico), Salsa, Tango (Argentina), Samba, Bossa Nova (Brazil), Mambo, Chachacha, Bolero, and Rumba (Cuba). All of these styles have African roots. What a somber ball this earth would be without this music.

There are many hot yodel-spotter sites throughout the region. Mexican falsetto is not uncommon at all. Much of Mexico's music is influenced by Caribbean styles, which in turn were influenced by African slaves. Mid-

16th century Mexico was already home to 20,000 African slaves. In some areas of Mexico, people sing *huapanguero*, the yodel Mexican-style. Mexican *vaqueros* may have introduced falsetto into Hawaii, and they may have served as the falsetto teachers of many North American cowboy singers, especially in Texas. *Rancheras* are Mexican country-western songs, usually characterized by soggy tear-jerking lyrics featuring hard-drinking and working-class settings that romanticize rural life. A variation is the *huapango*, the folk music of Mestizos in eastern Mexico but also a pop musical style characterized by the generous use of falsetto. The most famous example is Ritchie Valens's "La Bamba."

Haiti, an island rich in African culture, features its own yodeling tradition, according to pioneering ethnomusicologist Harold Courlander: "African singers often use falsetto—even moaning in falsetto! In Haiti . . . [they] may begin a traditional dance song in falsetto and drop to a natural voice." Well, that's pretty much our basic no-frills definition of a yodel—the rapid movement from head to chest or vice versa.

Cuba is musically hip *and* inspiring; it has been "flavor of the month" since the new millennium. That it deserves it is not in doubt. What *O Brother Where Art Thou?* did for bluegrass, the *Buena Vista Club* did for Cuban music. It's also somewhere one might hear evidence of yodel-like activity. After all, "African and Spanish cultures have been juxtaposed throughout Cuba since the 16th century." Voice is used in a variety of ways, "holding a tone, cutting it off, sliding into a falsetto for accent, shading the tones to fit the song." And once you've come this far, yodeling is the next step.

The *Mestizo* are people of Spanish, African, and indigenous background. Their music often incorporates local themes, indigenous sounds, and European instrumentation and chord progressions, often combining orchestral instruments with traditional indigenous instruments like *Kenas* (flute) and panpipes. This is evident among the Colombian *mestizaje* who incorporate African influences like call-and-response styles and the use of vocables. These influences are still evident throughout much of Central and South America and can be found in many of the mixed-ethnic styles. There is much evidence of hocketing and interlocking of melodic and percussion sections, characterized by dense overlapping textures, which often include vocal embellishments including yodel-like activity. Marimba music is based on *ostinato* (repeated melodic phrase) with an allowance for improvisation. A soloist may sing in an interlocked manner with the percussion or the female chorus—an African remnant—and the women sometimes burst into a flurry of yodel-like embellishments.

Millions of Africans came to Brazil during the period 1538–1850, probably more than any other single region in the Americas. They came from

Nigeria, Dahomey, Gold Coast, Angola, Mozambique, and Sudan. And they played an essential role in the development of what evolved into Brazilian music. The indigenous pre-Columbian *Bororo* people of the Lower Xingu River in north-central Brazil sing hunting songs that are characterized by a "yodel-like larnyx technique" that sound an awful lot like a yodel: "oh-ee oh-ee aye-go."

7

Transmission and Transition

How [the yodel] got to Jimmie Rodgers is the real question.
—**Ranger Doug, Riders in the Sky**

How and when yodeling came to the New World is a subject of some speculation. Most conventional wisdom pins the yodel's transmission from Europe's Alpine region at no earlier than the 1820s. The fact that this is 200 years after the first European settlers arrived begs the question: Could the yodel have stowed away and arrived much earlier, say, among the first waves of Germanic immigrants in the 1670s? Or did the yodel sneak in with the Scandinavians in the 1660s or with the first African slaves in the 1620s? Most experts do not want to negotiate the possibility of an earlier date.

And even *ur-lier*, could the yodel have been something Native Americans passed on to the first European interlopers? There may be some flintlock sparks of evidence that point to American Indian songs and chants as a yodel source. The possibility that they may have yodeled is supported by various descriptions of their vocal styles. Professor of Navajo Studies, Charlotte Frisbie notes that Native American melodies were decorated with a variety of vocal ornamentations including "vocal pulsations, falsettos, nasality." Pioneering ethnomusicologist Curt Sachs observed that, "the Apache act [out] the songs of smaller birds in falsetto, while that of the slowwitted lumbering giant is intoned in a gruff voice." Perhaps most telling is European observations of the "high and piercing" quality of their chants, which is certainly how non-yodel-lovers might complain upon hearing a yodel today. Native Americans also commonly employ(ed) vocables.

So, we've basically distinguished many of the elements necessary for yodeling except evidence that they highlighted the break between high and low; this *may* have occurred but simply went unnoted.

Native Americans were themselves influenced by contact with their new immigrant neighbors. Harold Courlander cited a study by ethnomusicologist George Herzog, who noted that "Africans . . . had numerous contacts with Indians in various parts of the country (there were a number of Indian slave owners) . . . [and] curiously enough . . . at least one group of Cherokee Indians took over elements of African music from the Negro slaves."

Native Americans also had contact with Swedish immigrants and the rowdy unkempt Finns who settled along the banks of the Delaware River. It's conceivable the Nordic pioneers brought their herder calls and *kulning* along. New Sweden, composed of some 110 farms, existed as a Nordic outpost for nearly twenty years before being gobbled up by the Dutch and immediately thereafter by the English in 1665. The total population of New Sweden probably reached 1,200 by 1697, including Swedes, Finns, and Norwegians, but also Germans, Danes, Frisians, and Dutch. However, the only "real" yodeling Scandinavians are the Sami, and they were not represented among these pioneers.

SLAVE SHIP TRANSMISSION

While some immigrants to the New World were escaping religious persecution, others came to make a killing in the fur trade or chose the adventure of a new life over prison. The African slaves (like British convict labor) came because they had no choice. Large-scale agriculture developed so quickly during the early 17th century in the southern colonies that the indentured servant population (whites) couldn't keep up with the boom. Landowners turned to the African slave trade to provide the necessary workers. In 1619, the first Africans set shackled foot on British North America in Jamestown. The slave population exploded, and by the 18th century approximately 15,000 slaves were being delivered annually to the colonies, which was only a small proportion of the *total* slave trade that was mainly concentrated in the Caribbean. The principle source for African slaves was the "Slave Coast" between Sierra Leone to the north and Angola to the south, including numerous regions inhabited by Pygmies and their trading neighbors. This leads me to believe there may have been a few stray yodeling Pygmies among the slaves, although most estimate the numbers were low. Their neighbors, the Bantu, were captured in much greater numbers. The notion of the yodel's entry into the New World via the Africans (perhaps indirectly via tribes influenced by Pygmy song or even by some direct transmission) is substantiated—somewhat—by various sources.

"In Negro tradition the falsetto has an esthetic value placed upon it," observes ethnomusicologist Harold Courlander. "African singers often use falsetto . . . as an informal style for singing solo and in small groups, and men singing at work in the fields or forests may sing to themselves in this register." But Courlander slams on the brakes on my reckless, heedless conclusion that Africans may have been one of the transmitters of falsetto and yodeling into North American popular music genres. He quickly adds that this falsetto more likely comes from "Mexican yodeling cries." Courlander concludes—perhaps too hastily—that "the cowboy song with falsetto effects stems from a different tradition than the Negro falsetto and the two do not seem to be related." Both John Greenway and Bill Malone, however, cautiously suggest that "Negro influence again may have been a contributory factor, particularly through the field hollers and the work shouts." Malone (among others) also suggests that the yodel may have been influenced by Mexican songs, which are characterized by hillbilly-like shouts and wails. "The blue yodel," Malone suggests, "may originally have been carried into the lower South by cowboys returning to their southern homes from brief employment on the ranges of the West."

Despite his backpedaling about African sources for American yodeling, Courlander proves to be a poetically creative ethnomusicologist who stitches together "a cry from a distant hill" in Nigeria with the work cries of a peasant "in a mountain field, emit[ting] a liquid quavering sound which slid up and down . . . and ended abruptly with a 'hoooo-ooooo' that echoed across the ravine. Almost before the sound had died, there was a response." Courlander manages to fuse this with a Cuban call and cries heard in the southern states, to create a long organic chain of "melodic calls, unexpected wordless birds of sound." He believes these utilitarian vocables and emotional cries voiced a soul music of the fields—of melancholy and ennui. The melodies were improvised and were "often ornamented and employ many African vocal devices, such as yodels, echo-like falsetto."

And where did one hear work calls? In rural areas, but also in cities, where food vendors, paperboys, and junk sellers all had their own calls. These are "sometimes sung with elaborate ornamentation." Courlander observes. "In white rural areas of America, cattle calls are common place, as they are in Europe." One begins to notice a kind of ur-vocal, a universal voice, a proto-world music that includes what sounds suspiciously like a yodel as one of its distinguishing features.

AFRICAN–AMERICAN INFLUENCES ON
EUROPEAN–AMERICAN CULTURE

The United States has a unique situation—a politically unempowered (black) minority musically dominating the (white) majority. As Alan Lomax observed: "the tremendous enthusiasm of all Americans, no matter what their prejudices, for Negro folk music and the profound influence of this music on American culture." Which makes this mutually beneficial musical relationship all the more vexingly ironic, because the more noticeable the bleeding and hybridizing, the more vociferously the various black and white cultures and nationalities began "safeguarding" what they perceived as their ethnic identity from erosion and melting-pot disappearance, sometimes with a unique racially demarcated fervor. And yet, as author Gene Bluestein notes, "despite the fact that the United States remains one of the most racially segregated societies it is without a doubt the most integrated musically."

This "tremendous enthusiasm," teamed with an appreciation for the exotic, is perhaps what led landscape visionary Frederick Law Olmstead to note the strange vocals he heard in South Carolina, some years before the Civil War. Upon encountering a railroad slave crew festively gathered around a fire along the railroad tracks, he heard: "Negro jodling" (sic) that sounded like a "bugle call" or the "Carolina yell." This "yell," also called "whooping" or a "howl," Olmstead further described as "a long, loud, musical shout, rising and falling, and breaking into falsetto." "Sounds of this general type," according to history professors Shane White and Graham White, "were ubiquitous throughout the slave South, certainly from the mid-eighteenth century."

Author Lydia Parrish has transcribed this vocalization in the sheet music to "Ole Tar River" as "O—e-e-e." Parrish further notes that during her childhood—the early 1900s—the Georgia coastal islands area was still rife with singers who employed "the trick of dropping from a high note to a low one on a prolonged one syllable word." Olmstead later heard a call emerge from the crew encouraging the others to "come now, echo! Roll away! eeho-eeho-weeioho-i!" as they returned to their work. These "calls of the open spaces" are usually called "hollers" and were often employed to circumvent a master's ban on conversation among slaves or otherwise to break the silent monotony. White and White report:

> Frederick Douglass . . . observed that "apparently incoherent" slave songs actually held "deep meanings." In saying this, Douglass was not alluding primarily to their lyrics. The meanings to which he referred were to be found,

rather, in what he termed the "wild notes" of the singers, the "tones, loud, long and deep," every one of which constituted "a testimony against slavery, and a prayer to God for deliverance from chains."

DJ Sam Fuqua offers another definition: "hollers . . . were used to get your voice across the hollers, hills, and valleys in the southeastern part of the United States." This is a conflation of the colloquial "holler," as in "hollow," meaning shallow valley, with "holla" as in "to shout." So, holler as both noun and verb: a holler hollered across that holler. Fuqua echoes hollerer Leonard Emanuel, who insists hollering is not yodeling. Fuqua, however, does admit that yodels and hollers *are* "very similar—[hollers have] the abruptness emphasized and the pitch changes of yodeling. It's maybe not as musical. Maybe that's why they call it hollerin'." I sense very little difference between a holler and a *naturjodel*. In fact, listening to hollerin' and then to "Negro" field hollers and Pygmy yodels, I begin to sense there's an intimate connection between them that has something to do with transmission and absorption among African slaves and rural Southern whites.

Courlander notes that blues and jazz may have borrowed some elements from field hollers but that "ornamentations and free melodic and rhythmic elements heard in field calls may also be heard in prayers, spirituals, blues, and solo worksongs." The stew keeps on cooking when we realize that these railroad worker or chain gang songs "are deeply rooted in tradition." But whose tradition? Courlander believes the melodies may be European, the beat depends on the work pace, while the harmonies may be either African or European. But the genre of singing-while-you work is thoroughly African. As Kebede notes, slaves employed "many African vocal devices, such as yodels, echo-like falsetto, tonal glides, embellished melismas, and microtonal inflections." This commingling makes analyzing the distinct ingredients of the musical stew Bluestein calls "an unlimited number of possible syncretic configurations" or what Whitman called "the teeming nation of nations" a daunting task.

Although Africans, mostly as slaves, had been present in the American colonies since the mid-17th century, the black-white leapfrogging musical symbioses began to truly heat up in the decades after emancipation. Blacks began adapting European ballads as "secular story songs." Leadbelly adapted "John Henry" as a heroic folktale employing the cadences and rhythms he'd heard working the fields and railroads with workers who killed the workday's monotony with the "trance-like repetition" of their hollers. As the workers and prisoners "hollered to themselves in the empty fields the deepest, most primitive roots of their racial heritage seemed stretched in ageless pain"—a bulls-eye definition of the blues, which pinpoints the time and area where hollers, combined with storytelling ballads, evolved into blues. Even as Africans began finding their "place" in American society, historians White and White note that they continued "to employ calls that contained either no or very few English words; if a few such words were included, they tended to function as syllables in scat singing, as pure sound, rather than as vehicles for the conveying of information."

Black settlers also headed west after the Civil War. Lomax noted, "the Old Chisholm Trail was lined with Negroes headed for Topeka and Emporia, Kansas, to get a free farm and a span of mules." About 5 percent of the total cowboy population was black, while many more were farmers. As Bebop trumpeter Kenny Dorham (1924–1972) remembers growing up near Fairfield, Texas:

> When a cotton-picker was taking his last sack of cotton to the scale for the day, one might hear him yodel, Ye-o-dle la-de, ye-o-dle, la-d-o-dlela-de-o-dle la dee. In later years, I heard Charlie Parker yodel on alto saxophone and after Charlie I heard Julian [Cannonball] Adderley yodel the same melody on his horn. A lone cowboy at the end of a day on the range could be heard yodeling.

Dorham makes an important observation that connects black and white, jazz and country. Like their white horsemates, black cowboys were often taught the ropes by Mexican *vaqueros*. Black cowboys sang specific songs to calm their herds. They also sang Irish ballads, to which they added their own lyrics and "extra musical devices." Lomax recorded many of these songs in places like East Texas, but he also captured the gandy dancer and muleskinner hollers, not to mention songs like Moses Platt's "St. James Hospital," a British ballad reworked with lots of "field-holler-style whoops." The railroads were built by "Negroes," Mexicans, Chinese, and Irish settlers, each with their own repertoires to express their various feelings: thirst, exhaustion, pain, melancholy, regret . . . And it's in this "babeling" stew that Frederick Douglass swore he heard African vocalizations.

By the early 1900s, blacks were considered among the most proficient and enthusiastic practitioners of yodeling in America. Several black singers were highly regarded and became renowned for their yodeling techniques. Black blues singers at the time known to periodically yodel included Tampa Red, Stovepipe Johnson, the Mississippi Sheiks, plus numerous Cajun singers who lent a frightful scream to their yodeling. Although yodeling is found on black jazz and blues discs, it was never considered a "Negro" thing, which may have as much to do with the underdocumentation of black performers as the overdocumentation of whites.

IMMIGRANT SHIP TRANSMISSION

That yodeling may have slipped into the New World via the once idealistic portal known as Pennsylvania offers some compelling and entertaining possibilities that have yet to be fully researched. If we set aside the Swedes and Dutch as essentially not of primary yodeling interest, we are left with early German immigrants. Somewhere along Route 501 a mile or two north of Lancaster, you can take your eyes off the road and catch a glimpse of forgotten panoramas, old landscape paintings of a time when all was pastoral and arboreal. Squint a little, and you can see in the not-so-distant distance the grey-blue undulating foothills that lead into the Appalachians. This may have been the "seedbed" of what came to be known as hillbilly, cowboy, and eventually country music.

Some say that the "first man to explore the county was a representative of the German Mennonites from the Swiss Alps, far from any town or village." If we conveniently forget the original inhabitants, we might shake our heads "yes." The Germans were indeed among the first immigrants to come in substantial numbers, coming from the Pfalz (Palatinate in English) region in southwestern Germany. The Pfalz (present-day Baden, Alsace, Würtenberg, and Hesse) hugs the left bank of the Rhine, along the northeastern border of France, just downstream and in the shadow of the Alps as the Rhine runs through Mannheim. The Protestant Pfälzer (Palatines) were mostly industrious farmers grateful to God for giving them another chance after decades of devastating oppression and strife (1618–1689). They fled, sailing on German ships filled with provisions—peas, oatmeal, and beer—out of Rotterdam to the New World, becoming in effect refugees of both war and religious persecution. In 1738, Lieutenant-Governor George Thomas described Pennsylvania as "the Asylum of the distressed Protestants of the Palatinate and other parts of Germany." Late 18th-century Pennsylvania was predominantly a German-language enclave ripe for the consumption of culture stimulated by *heimweh* for the *heimat* (homeland).

Pennsylvania was the prototype for the subsequent enthusiastic America ("Send me your wretched yodeling slaves, your yodeling persecuted herders"?) welcoming its strangers to a strange new life. The first interested parties were mostly from the fervent fringe of the Christian faith. Collectively, these persecuted sects became known as the Pennsylvania *Deutsch* (later mangled to Dutch). These early immigrant-pioneers were Mennonites, Amish, Dunkers, and Moravians who had fled religious persecutions in southern Germany and Switzerland. Many of the early arrivals spoke a Swiss dialect. They settled in an area roughly between

Turn-of-the-century minstrels, Franz Reilhofer's Alpine yodelers. By permission of James Leary.

present-day Philadelphia and Lancaster. Many descendants of these settlers have maintained their simple earthly ways as well as their own German dialect.

Although these Germans were—and still are—noted for a certain ascetic sobriety, "there was little prejudice against music on the part of most of the religious sects." Germans were neighbors to many Irish and Scottish immigrants, among whom drinking and singing became shared amusements. These "newcomers brought their folk culture into Pennsylvania as the early settlers had theirs. Each colonial immigrant group had been free . . . to follow its own folkways." Although religious, "the Germans of Pennsylvania were in the habit of singing work songs from the old country." And that some of these work songs may have involved frivolous and playful ornamentation such as falsetto and yodeling is not *that* far-fetched.

Leonard Gross, a Mennonite archivist, comments:

> [My] hunch is that the [yodel] came to North America with the first emigration of Swiss proper. And they might have been other than Swiss Brethren, of course. My wife, who is Swiss (her father, a Mennonite minister—Walter Geiser—living in Tavannes, could yodel well), says yodeling goes way back into Swiss Brethren tradition. . . . It would seem obvious that Swiss Brethren, migrating directly from Switzerland to North America throughout much of the 19th century would have brought some yodelers with them.

By 1726, some of these early German settlers—those most disturbed by ungodly behavior—were already migrating south into the Shenandoah Valley

THE YODELING MAKLEY MATRIARCHY
OF JACKSONVILLE, FLORIDA

The Makley Family, Florida's yodeling matriarchy. Photo by Pamela Milam. Courtesy of the Makley family.

The Makleys, three generations of yodeling women, annually yodel and teach tin-eared types (me) how to yodel at the Florida Folk Festival (FFF). It's easy. Yeah, it's easy to win a grand prix if you happen to be a champ driver in a Ferrari. They're the kind of gifted, entertaining, and yet unself-conscious performers we used to call genuine folk; after all, they've "never performed professionally." Their entire recorded output is one track on an FFF compilation. That's a shame—but things could change. Makley yodeling began some sixty years ago in New Hampshire. Representative yodels include some unique five-part family-harmony yodeling on "Sleep, Baby, Sleep," "Swiss Lullaby," "Swiss Moonlight Chalet," and their original "White Springs Yodel."

Elroyce "Mom" Makley was the Makley yodeling matriarch until June 7, 2003, when sadly she passed away during the final stages of editing this book, and only a month after her life partner "Uncle Ray" Sine, a Rebel Yell-style yodeler, had passed away. Will there be yodeling in heaven now? You bet. She played harp and often managed a triple yodel. Lucinda Makley is the oldest of the Makley sisters but the last to learn to yodel. She began when she was well into her forties. She's only recently rejoined the family in Florida, where she and her husband have "retired" to pursue a mellower lifestyle. She recently wrote her first yodeling song. Ruthanne Makley is the second of Elroyce's daughters. She "fronts" the Makleys. Bettina Makley, in her mid-forties, the

continued on the next page

youngest daughter, began yodeling at age 3. Bettina plays guitar and helps write the music. She also performs with her own group, Under the Water Lilies. Emily Anne Mason is Elroyce's granddaughter, Ruthanne's daughter. She turned twenty in 2003 and is majoring in graphic design at college.

Elroyce recalls:

I first heard yodeling as a child, growing up in New Hampshire, over the radio, and at local shows—at fairs, etc. I heard a lady on the radio, a country singer—Georgia Mae was her professional name—when I was about 12, and I thought I could do that. I tried, and was successful, and have been yodeling ever since. I had *no* encouragement, and most of my friends and family didn't even know I could yodel—until years later, when I performed on the "Ted Mack Original Amateur Hour."

I spent 30 years raising 6 children and taking care of an ill husband. So, I didn't even think of singing outside the home and church, until we moved to Florida, hoping my husband's health would improve, and I first saw the FFF, and decided to audition for it . . . and I was accepted then and there. My two daughters, Ruth and Bettina, had a separate audition later, and we did our first performance together about 1972.

Ruthanne continues the story:

When we first performed at the FFF, I sang harmony with them but did not really yodel. The yodeling was the part of the act that interested people the most and we started to be introduced as yodelers, so Mom and Bettina encouraged me to learn. Our final yodeling number—"He Taught Me to Yodel"—had three verses and there were three of us in the act at the time, so they insisted I do the first verse. I did, yodeling badly for years before I finally learned to really break my voice. They gave me plenty of encouragement and basically threw me to the wolves at the same time . . . so I eventually learned to yodel.

Bettina had a different experience of being introduced to the ancient art:

I was three . . . My older brothers were picking blueberries in the mountains. My Mom and Dad and I went to pick them up. Mom went up the mountain to get them, while Dad and I waited at the bottom. After a while I heard my Mom call out with a yodel. I answered her by imitating her. After that, of course, I was encouraged to yodel . . . for anyone who would listen. When I was in first grade, they took me around to all the classes to yodel for everyone. It was a novelty . . . especially for a little kid. Later on, I can remember several times being threatened by bullies. Did they want my lunch money? Nope! They wanted me to yodel!

As the youngest and newest member of the clan, Emily Anne reflects on how she was brought into the tradition:

continued on the next page

The Yodeling Makley Matriarchy of Jacksonville, Florida, continued

I think I first asked my mom to teach me when we were swimming in the Suwannee River one year at the FFF but I was too shy to even try. I didn't sing with them until I was about 8 and I didn't start yodeling with them until . . . I was 14. . . . It's virtually impossible to even create a yodel if you don't have proper breathing techniques. I consider myself lucky to be classically trained because I already know how to use my diaphragm to project my voice without it sounding like it's being pushed. I also know . . . how to minimize tension in my vocal chords.

When I first started yodeling, it was more of a pressure-to-continue-the-legacy thing than anything else but when I started yodeling more and more for lots of different people, it became one of my defining qualities. So now, it's both a legacy thing and an interest.

* *Remembering Old Friends: A Florida Folklife Sampler (1975–1987)*, Florida Folklife Foundation, 1992.

of Virginia, some moving even further south into the Carolina Piedmont. The further they journeyed from their original settlements, the more unconnected they grew from their native culture and religion. Restrictions against alcohol consumption and merriment gave way to more relaxed attitudes toward diversion: "The Germans, push[ed] past the English into the interior" and mixed with "a flood of other nationalities—Scotch, Irish, Welsh, Ukranians. Tradition has preserved some of their folk songs, games, music, and ballads. Characteristically, the music retains the flavor of the folk songs of the country from which it derives, while the lyrics are often in dialect or in broken English." Evidence reveals literally hundreds of *Deutsch* folk songs. Would it be too much to assume that a few of these were yodels?

Germans either continued migrating onward and outward, looking for even more bucolic isolation, or they moved further inward guarding their traditions and language, amazingly enough, until World War I, when it became very *un*popular to be German. Adolf Schroeder notes that the "strong local folk tradition and local pride . . . was maintained in the United States and resulted in numerous . . . musical . . . clubs in urban areas based on provincial origin." The industrial revolution and other European upheavals further exacerbated dissatisfaction and precipitated a second wave of "German" immigrants in the early- to mid-1800s.

The first Swiss to set foot in the New World was a Bernese man tagging along with French Huguenots, mid-16th century. The Swiss settled in South Carolina, Maryland, and Pennsylvania during the 17th century.

NON-COWBOY HONOR ROLL

Louis Alder was a Swiss immigrant who emigrated to Monroe, Wisconsin, from Appenzell, and founded the Monroe Yodel Quartet (1921). Because of his sweet pastoral yodeling, the group became known as Lou Alder and His Swiss Yodelers. Imagine twelve men harmonizing around Alder's soprano leads. Adler's most representative yodel is "Swiss Mountaineers Yodel" (Gennett).

Charles Anderson is a fairly unknown vaudeville yodeler who recorded a number of singles in the early 1920s. In 1913, he was already a performing in vaudeville, described as a black "yodler of note" with a "golden voice" and "perfect yodeling" abilities. He ululated between a broad range of sideshow acts including magicians, acrobats, freaks, and dancing girls. Yodelers like Anderson "were yet another curiosity from mysterious faraway lands." His singing-yodeling is accomplished and, yet, unremarkable, ultimately a bit fettered by his Al Jolson–minstrel style—a sound of its time. His falsetto, the pseudo-bluesy trill and timbre of his voice remind me of Bessie Smith outtakes, although you get the feeling he's not taking you anywhere with his embellishments and affectations. Some examples of his yodeling include "Sing 'em Blues," and "Sleep, Baby Sleep."

Rudy Burkhalter (1911–1993) grew up in Basel, Switzerland, where he learned the accordion, yodeling, and alphorn. He became a renowned composer, promoter, and teacher in Wisconsin. At age 18, Burkhalter joined the renowned Moser Brothers from Bern, replacing an alcoholic accordionist who forgot his songs after a few drinks. He also yodeled and played clarinet, as the Mosers barnstormed across North America, playing Swiss clubs and small joints. He played in a number of other bands and was the music teacher of Betty Vetterli and the Edelweiss Stars, local accordion-yodel acts.

In the mid-1950s, Burkhalter wrote songs for a *Mickey Mouse Club* serial, *Adventure in Dairyland,* starring Annette Funicello. In the series, a Swiss farm boy teaches two American kids to yodel. Burkhalter wrote "Will You Teach Me How to Yodel": "Teach me how to yodel / and fill my heart with joy / (yodeling)." He retired in 1978, but continued to "blow the horn and sing and yodel" until his death.

Fred Burri is a second-generation Swiss-Californian, who grew up surrounded by Swiss music and yodeling in Portland, Oregon. He spent some eighteen years as the "Disneyland Yodeler," serenading audiences with his dramatic ululations at the Matterhorn attraction. In 1995, he participated in a documentary about the Matterhorn, which detailed his connection to the Disney attraction.

Shirley Abbott Clark is a Portland, Oregon, yodeler who began singing with her local Swiss choir at age 12. She performed with her mother for many years along the Pacific coast, Canada, Ohio, and Wisconsin. After her mother died, Clark continued performing and has yodeled on radio and TV.

The Edelweiss Stars is a seven-member yodel-singing group from New Glarus, Wisconsin, composed of local yodelers Dorothea Widmer, Margaret Wild,

continued on the next page

Non-Cowboy Honor Roll, continued

Kathleen and Marion Zentner, plus two men, one a native of Burgdorf, Switzerland. They began performing in 1950 and have released several records. They performed throughout the Midwest as well as in Disney's *Adventures in Dairyland.*

- *Anniversary Album,* Bright. Includes *Dairyland* selections.

- *Edelweiss Stars,* with Rudy Burkhalter, Cuca.

Anna Gempler (b. 1924) is a Swiss-American accordionist, student of Rudy Burkhalter's, and yodeler from Monroe, Wisconsin. She learned accordion at age 4 and learned to yodel from listening to Moser Brother discs. She was not even a teen when she began yodeling and performing at parties in her parents' cheese factory. She went on to perform yodeling duets with Dorothea Widmer of the Edelweiss Stars.

Sandy Gernhart, from Vancouver, Washington, is a second-generation Swiss yodeler who has worked on film soundtracks and collaborated with The Polkatones. She performs both traditional Swiss yodeling and improv vocals, combining innovation and tradition.

"East Side" Dave Kline is from the undulating hills in the heart of German and Swiss immigrant territory near Kutztown, Pennsylvania. Kline was first smitten by yodeling in the 1970s when he heard bluegrass masters and a singer named "Uncle Fudd." He was also influenced by *Snow White*, Roy Rogers, Slim Clark, and Patsy Montana. He traveled the Alps to learn more about the world's uplands, and became fascinated by "mountain music," his name for a fusion of Alpine and Appalachian mountain musics. His combination of enthusiasm for both yodeling and Alpine outdoor sports gives his music a robust passion.

> I'm appreciative of [yodeling] as . . . practical communication. I was leading a ski group around a section of Italy's Dolomite Mountains when thick cloud cover rolled in creating a white out. In order to lead everyone down off the mountain safely, I would ski down a few dozen meters, then yodel up to the group who would follow the yodel, then we'd rest and regroup, then repeat the process until we arrived in the village far below. The yodel provided both an audio beacon . . . and a psychological boost as it sounded "cheerful" and took their minds off the dreadful conditions.

His yodels are earnest, learned, and he's fully convinced he's communicating with mountain spirits. He has yodeled for audiences throughout Europe and the United States.

> A well-known part of . . . mountain culture, especially in the Alps, is the concept of the Mountain Trilogy. This is a state of being in which the practitioner seeks a perfect balance between the Things of God . . . of Nature, and . . . of Man. Yodeling is important in this trilogy because . . . it touches on all three of the prime areas which empower a soul to move forward to perfection in a less-than-perfect world.

continued on the next page

Non-Cowboy Honor Roll, continued

- *Mountain Spirit,* Mountain Laurel, 2002. Standard and original yodels.

- *Mountain Folk*, Mountain Laurel, 1999. Eight yodels.

Betti Kneubuehl Vetterli and Martha Bernet (both born 1927) were members of the Edelweiss Stars, as well as a popular yodeling duo who promoted Wisconsin's dairy products at concerts. Vetterli, from Monroe, is third-generation Swiss and studied accordion under Rudy Burkhalter. She has yodeled all over North America and in Switzerland. Bernet was born in Leissigen, Switzerland, and grew up immersed in Swiss music. She also performs with the Monroe Swiss Singers. She produced "Chalet in the Valley," a Swiss-language music program on Monroe's radio station WEKZ. Their talent is represented on *Swiss Echoes from Wisconsin's Switzerland,* (Bright).

John Lilly (b. 1954) has come a long way since his youth in the Midwest and his impressionable days as a tour guide at the Country Music Hall of Fame and waiter in a Nashville restaurant, spending his free time hawking his songs. These days, Lilly's talent does not go unrewarded nor unheralded.

"I'm essentially a traditional folk or country music artist," explains Lilly, "my music has roots in traditional country, and branches out to include my own songwriting and . . . blues, folk, bluegrass, and old-time."

Lilly caught the wandering spirit early in life, hitchhiking his way through almost every state; he has essentially lived the sound and played the life—singing, yodeling, promoting, and writing about old time music. He's currently the editor of *Goldenseal*, a West Virginia folk magazine, emcee, and cofounder of "Old-Time Music on the Radio," which promotes traditional folk music. In the mid-1980s, he was a member of the New Southern Ramblers and the Green Grass Cloggers dance troupe as a musician, singer, and dancer.

Lilly is living proof that you don't have to be some tragic ego-flailing character drowning in sorrow and white lightning to be an interesting singer. His sinewy voice seems to haul things—ghosts, tragedies—out of the deep earth. Lilly's interpretations of old gospel-tinged material has a way of burrowing into your guts like a rusty bullet with a sly smile carved into the lead.

He has been yodeling for some twenty-five years now. But the more he yodels, the more he's marginalized as novelty. "I've recently been limiting the amount of yodeling I do in performance," Lilly notes, "because I discovered audiences were 'boxing me in' as a yodeler, and I wasn't being taken seriously as a songwriter-vocalist. . . . Frankly, if I could yodel like Ranger Doug, Wylie Gustafson, or Don Walser, I'd do it all night. Given my simpler style, however, I'm more comfortable rationing it out."

Lilly has a full performance repertoire of yodels. His own yodels—"A Little Yodel Goes a Long Way," "Blue Highway," "Glow in the Smokies," "Wrong Wrong Wrong," "Yodel Our Way Back Home"—are supplemented by Hank Williams's "Lovesick Blues" and "Moanin' the Blues," the Delmore Brothers'

continued on the next page

Non-Cowboy Honor Roll, continued

"Gamblers Blues," and Gene Autry's "Cowboy Blues." Lilly's main influence, however, remains Jimmie Rodgers:

> I always include at least one of his songs. . . . Rodgers made me feel like I could yodel, too. Compare that, for example, with the yodeling of the Callahan Brothers or the Dezurik Sisters, whose showcase yodeling could never possibly be duplicated. Rodgers, on the other hand, seems to invite listeners into his music, welcoming them to give it a try. Effortless, spontaneous, soulful, and simple.

"I learned 'Will There Be Any Yodelers in Heaven?' some years ago from a recording of the Girls of the Golden West." Lilly explains.

> One of my most moving experiences as a musician was singing it at a funeral for a woman in Ohio. She had been a big fan of the band I sang in . . . and yodeling would always bring tears to her eyes. She knew that she had terminal cancer, and it was her special request that I yodel at her funeral. Singing that song in front of an open casket . . . was a serious challenge. I made it through somehow, yodels and all, and never sang that song again.

Is the yodel a good pick-up line or ancient mating call? Lilly thinks so. When I was young and single, the effect that yodeling had on the "fairer sex" became apparent to me. I was at a festival in Indiana, and was scheduled to perform . . . in a few hours. I wandered among the trees . . . practicing my yodeling, oblivious to the world. I snapped out of my trance in time to find a very attractive young woman staring at me, leaning dreamily against a big tree, with a look in her eyes I have seldom seen before or since. She asked me about the yodeling and tried to express herself about it—"You sound like a wounded animal," she said. While that wasn't exactly the effect I was going for, I decided not to argue with her. She and I went on to become very good friends, and she always got that funny look about her whenever I yodeled.

- *Broken Moon*, self-produced, 2000.

- *Blue Highway*, self-produced, 1992. Lilly in his element, dredging up forgotten nuggets, accompanied by master fiddler Ralph Blizard.

The Moser Brothers—father Moser and sons Albert and Paul—were a renowned trailblazing Swiss yodeling "family" that toured North America. In 1928, Burkhalter joined; in 1931, the father died and was replaced by a third brother. Their energetic touring sent them hurling from East to West, from Canada to Deep South. They yodeled and played dance music for the Swiss and German immigrant throngs, eventually replacing their solemn traditional numbers with up-beat, funnier tunes, and even performed minstrel "coon" songs.

They wore clichéd Swiss costumes: short yellow pants, white stockings, leather cow-milking beanies, and traditional embroidered black velvet jackets.

continued on the next page

Non-Cowboy Honor Roll, continued

They performed before a set of three interchangeable elaborately painted Alpine backdrop scrims: a mountain scene, a waterfall scene, and a William Tell theme used during their rendition of the "William Tell Overture." Not exactly a U-2 tour but pretty impressive back then. So impressive, they were hired to perform in the Swiss pavilion at the Chicago World's Fair in 1933. By the time they returned to Switzerland, they were hot stuff, performing in top venues in places like Zurich. They recorded some thirty-six 78s for Victor in New York, as well as some for Odeon and their own Mosertone label. Their songs

The famous Moser Brothers could ham up any yodel. By permission of James Leary.

were elaborate productions that included "singing, yodeling, accordion solos, accordion/violin/bass trios; marches, waltzes ländlers, polkas, slow airs; paeans to romance, cows, mountains, flowers, rural life, and homeland"—no wonder they were popular with homesick Swiss immigrants.

- "Sennenleben Jodler Ländler/Die Lustigen Knaben," 78rpm, Victor, 1920s. Yodel duet accompanied by instrumental trio.

- "Rigilied," Victor, 1926. Rigi Mountain towers over Lake Luzern. Combines virtuoso yodeling with pastoral imagery.

- "Yodel Ländler" / "Longing For the Mountains," RCA, 1920s. Side A: instrumental with yodeling; side B: yodeling with accordion.

- "Jodler-Ländler" / Sehnsucht nach den Bergen," Bat-Wing Electric, 1920s, Side A: instrumental with yodeling; side B: yodel duet with accordion.

- "Zweu Schuemeli" / "Bi ues im Baernerland," Victor scroll. Yodel duet and accordion.

"Yodeling Betty" Naftzinger is from just outside Kutztown, in the heart of Swiss-German Pennsylvania. Naftzinger grew up as Betty Wies on a small farm in this very area in the 1940s. And as any good Swiss farmer's daughter, she did farm chores. She remembers plowing fields as a kid and singing at the top of her lungs. She's almost totally unknown, modest and happy to sing and yodel, given the slightest excuse. A true folksinger. I interviewed Naftzinger in April 2002.

continued on the next page

Non-Cowboy Honor Roll, continued

There she stood, perky 70–year-old American country Swiss miss with a blond beehive, guitar slung over her shoulder with "Yodeling Betty" inked into the leather strap. She's been singing all her life and has only recently taken her yodeling on the road, bringing its healing power to old age homes and hospitals. Betty strums her guitar and goes into "Strolling along in the moonlight . . . roll along old Silvery Moon." And a refrain of joyous yodeling. In fact, her yodels outshine her singing, evidence that yodeling is her access to joy and contentment.

> I learned to yodel . . . driving a tractor. . . . We farmed for a living and when we first got the milk tanks, you know, the milk tank to put the milk in, we had one that you had to wash by hand and it echoed. I mean, when you were washin' the thing, here's the lid and you're stickin' yer body in this stainless steel contraption washin' and it used to echo back. I really enjoyed listenin' to my voice. Yuh know, when I'm doin' it [yodeling] and I'd go in there and I'd start out—DO-RE-MI-FA-SO-LA-TI, DO-RE—on up through a couple of precarious octaves. I could almost do two. But it helped, yuh know, when you were throwin' your voice from one octave to another. It really did help. I had a wide-open space. . . . No one there to hear it but the good Lord and he was there and he enjoyed it. So that's where it came from.

Oregon Peter is from Thayngen, Switzerland, and in 1970 he moved to a dairy farm in Corvallis, Oregon. He's been singing in the Portland Jodelklub Edelweiss since 1983. He was a featured solo yodeler at the North American Swiss Singing Alliance Festival in 2000, Edmonton, Alberta, and at the 23rd Pacific Coast Swiss Singing and Yodeling Festival in 1999 in Salt Lake City.

Lisa Ward-Rieder, born in Switzerland and emigrated to Portland, Oregon, in 1958, now lives in Vancouver, British Columbia. Her yodeling technique is said to be unique in that she creates her own yodel echoes. She performs internationally and, for more than thirty years, has been the featured yodel

Yodelin' Betty, Pennsylvania yodeler. Photo by the author.

soloist at the Mount Angel Oktoberfest in Oregon and for more than twenty years at Oktoberfests in Hawaii! Lisa was chosen as a soloist in the Swiss Television Production "*Gruetzi* Canada Welcome Schweiz."

Christoph von Graffenried (1661–1743) led the first Swiss-Palatine settlers to North Carolina, where they established New Bern. The Swiss settled across North America, many heading west between 1840 and 1900. There are German- and Swiss-immigrant communities in Texas and Indiana, but the largest concentration remains in Wisconsin.

There are more than 400,000 Swiss immigrants in North America, 25,000 arriving before 1776. The Swiss Brethren, Swiss Reformed, Amish, and Mennonites came for religious reasons. Others were lured by this mythical topographical cornucopia. Most blended into American society, while the more particular sects created various homogenous Swiss settlements in Berne and Vevey, Indiana; Highland, Illinois; and several counties in Wisconsin, particularly the towns of New Glarus and Monroe. Swiss Mormons ended up in Utah and Idaho, Swiss Catholics in Indiana, Missouri, and Oregon. Nineteenth-century Swiss secular settlements include Grutli, Tennessee; Bernstadt, Kentucky; Tell City, Ohio; and New St. Gallen and Helvetia, West Virginia.

YODEL HOMES OF NORTH AMERICA

Here we focus less on yodeling cowboys, hillbillies, and blackface performers and more on "other" American yodelers and Alpine traditionalists.

HELVETIA, WEST VIRGINIA

The town of Helvetia, a small Swiss-American community of farms between Pickens and Czar, was first settled in 1869 deep in the mountains

Helvetia, West Virginia: A slice of Switzerland in America. By permission of Augusta Heritage Center.

of central West Virginia. The Appalachian hills may be less dramatic, but they offered the early settlers this self-same Alpine feeling: isolation, fresh air, security with a view. Helvetia's settlers were part of the second or third wave of Swiss immigration, arriving on America's shores sometime in the 1860s and first settled in the unlikely place of Brooklyn, New York. An advance party, following up rumors of bucolic countryside, set out for West Virginia by train, but the territory grew progressively more impassable, until they had to abandon their wagons and continue on foot. In 1869, the first families set out for the location that was to become the future town of Helvetia. They named their new town after the Latin name for Switzerland. Others followed, and eventually this petit town of Swiss immigrants developed a unique Switzerland-away-from-home culture. By the 1880s, they had built a school and a church.

To this day, this rural community, including the town center, with a population of 143, maintains a decidedly Swiss folk-cultural character. Most of the Helvetians are still farmers. Some still speak in the Switzer-Deutsch dialects, engage in folk dancing, singing, and the playing of the accordion, fiddle, and zither . . . and yodeling. Their songs refer to both Switzerland and West Virginia. "They have no direct connection to other Swiss communities," Gerry Milnes, the Folk Arts Coordinator of Helvetia explains, "but they maintain a connection with the Swiss/American Folklore Society in Washington, D.C. Despite its small size, the place is very active with dances, a *Fastnacht* celebration, a Fair . . . "

SWISSCONSIN

Monroe and New Glarus are situated some thirty miles west of Madison, Wisconsin's capital. Nestled in among the region's gentle, rolling hills are several architectural masterpieces designed or inspired by Frank Lloyd Wright. This is bucolic Wisconsin, outpost of the small family farm and home of America's largest German population.

The first Swiss immigrants arrived in Wisconsin in the 1820s. Others, fleeing economic uncertainties, arrived from the canton of Glarus, Switzerland, in the 1840s. The Swiss settled near German immigrants. More came in the 1880s, initiating a cheese-making boom in Wisconsin. By 1900, there were some 8,000 Swiss immigrants in Wisconsin. They were mostly agricultural folks—farming, herding, dairy products—who sang their religious and secular songs and drank their beer, to create a heady atmosphere of revelry tempered, or perhaps fueled, by faith. Church choirs spawned secular glee clubs: a bunch of Swiss guys hanging around singing. They eventually organized a Swiss-American Singers Association and, by the late 1890s, they were hosting music festivals that attracted visitors from around the region.

HELVETIA'S YODELING CHEESEMAKER

Yodeler and "amateur folklorist" Bruce Betler has many connections to Helvetia. "I grew up here in Helvetia." Betler explains. "My father's family settled here in 1872 from the Simmental of the Berner Oberland; my mother's family in 1870 from Windisch in Kanton Aargau—I've been here for five generations." Betler plays a prominent role in the Helvetia's music-making *and* cheesemaking. He's currently producing a distinctive St. Gallen–style *Baergkaese* (mountain cheese). He's also actively involved in the historical and cultural preservation of Helvetia. I was introduced to Betler by yodeler John Lilly.

Bruce tells how yodeling has become an integral part of the town's culture and his life:

> All Helvetians grow up learning Swiss folk dancing and songs. Yodeling is part of some of these songs. I first heard yodeling before I can remember. The Helvetia folk dancers perform a dance called the "Weggis" in which yodeling is part of the verses and chorus. And the village children learn a song called "Mein Vater ist ein Appenzeller" with much yodeling.
>
> Eleanor Fahrner Mailloux yodeled the "Weggis" for the Helvetia folk dancers. It looked like she was having fun, so I tried it. She was very encouraging, so I stuck with it. . . . When in the seminary at the Catholic University of America, I was frequently scolded by my peers and superiors for yodeling in the four-story marble stairwell at Marist College. The guards also hushed me in the U.S. Capitol dome for yodeling at the request of our tour guide. Usually I yodeled outside while looking for the milk cow in the evening on our family farm. During puberty, I had to stop yodeling as my voice was changing. I didn't resume until college when [I was] inspired by the stone walls of St. Vincent Arch-Abbey Basilica's stairwells.

- *Vo Mine Bärge: From My Mountains—The Music of Helvetia*, Augusta Heritage Recordings, 1995. New World versions of some traditional Swiss tunes on fiddle and guitar plus yodeling on about one-third of the 21 tracks by Betler and a host of others.

- *1997 Concert Souvenir*, various artists, Augusta Heritage Recordings, CD/cassette.

- *Helvetia: The Swiss of West Virginia*, one-hour video documentary.

Joseph Rohrer, from the canton of Unterwalden, was the area's first cheesemaker. He "learned to play clarinet while herding sheep." Rohrer would sit and try to imitate the horns and whistles of passing ships on the Mississippi River on his clarinet. Others brought their Swiss button accordions, violins, fiddles, zithers—and well-developed epiglotisses. Typical Swiss sounds filled the Wisconsin air: traditional cowbells and yodeling joined to embellish the joyous noise that "rang out in 19th-century

Monroe Yodel Quartet, typical yodeling Swissconsinites. By permission of James Leary.

Wisconsin." These bells are now a "mute symbol" of the past here in Wisconsin except during special events and annual festivals. Swissconsin festivals were frequently marked by performances of *schalleschotte* that accompanied the melodic yodeling of locals like Rudy Burkhalter or Karl Hofman.

Around the late 19th century, the *jodlerverbande* began proliferating. These men's yodel clubs sang "in praise of the cowherd and his Alpine dairying life." According to folklore professor James Leary, they came from "yodeling strongholds like Appenzell and Bern, who had emigrated in the 20th century."

Twentieth-century Wisconsin Swiss emerged as a demographically heterogeneous bunch: urban and rural, farmer and professional, old (from Glarus or Graubunden) and young (from cities like Bern and Zurich). Swissconsin culture became less insular, livelier and less . . . purely Swiss. Traditions like yodeling, however, continued to be passed along from generation to generation. The early-20th-century bands played traditional Swiss music but also, interestingly enough, "a few pseudo-Afro-American 'coon songs'."

The Monroe Yodel Quartet was founded in 1921 in a cheese cellar where one yodeler communicated his ecstasy to another yodeler upon hearing his own echo. The group eventually became known as Louis Adler and His Swiss Yodelers. Other clubs formed and memberships swelled. In

1960, the New Glarus Yodel Club, including international champion yodeler and Zurich native Robbie Schneider, toured Switzerland with the Swiss Jodelklub Glarnisch, stopping off for a concert in the original Glarus, thus bringing the yodel echo geographically full circle. Meanwhile, Wisconsin resident Rudy Burkhalter, "the Upper Midwest's foremost Swiss American traditional musician," had been performing since the 1920s and eventually passed on the tradition to younger generations.

The yodeling continues in its American-interpreted form as part of the hybridization process that occurs when different cultures rub borders and interests. Besides German influences, the area is also influenced by Slovenian polka music, well known particularly because of Frank Yankovic. The Slovenians share a similar Alpine heritage and sound. Slovenian-Alpine yodeling has gained recognition through the yodeling of accordionist Slavko Asvenik. As James Leary notes, this kind of music has been an American staple of "live and recorded musical ambience for ice skating rinks and ski lodges." Musician Roger Bright, who died in 2001, used to mix Slovenian and Swiss influences and made his recording studios available to contemporary yodelers.

The Swissconsinites, in true Swiss fashion, began institutionalizing and standardizing their characteristic folk culture in order to preserve it. Suddenly there were annual "Cheesedays" and "Volksfests," while New Glarus's "William Tell" performance of Friedrich von Schiller's play became an annual event, along with the "Alpine Festival" with typical Swiss yodeling. In 1965, an annual "Heidi Festival" was added to the Swiss-oriented tourist events. 1986 saw the institution of the annual "Winter Festival," which prominently features quality yodeling and alphorn blowing. No wonder New Glarus is called "Little Switzerland."

ADAMS COUNTY, INDIANA

Berne and Geneva, Indiana, in Adams County—twenty miles south of Fort Wayne, three hours southeast of Chicago—is home to the Old Order Amish. They live in the pastoral countryside of rural Southern Indiana where they've preserved certain folk traditions, lifestyles, and musical instruments, and yodeling is part of that package.

The Amish here, like those in Lancaster, Pennsylvania, are interesting because of their isolation from mainstream America. They're farmers and craftsmen—Berne is known as a furniture center—who maintain traditional ways of farming—no electrical appliances, no motorized vehicles—and grow fields of corn and soy beans through which the Wabash River calmly wends its way north.

The Swiss Amish came from Bern and Emmental, Switzerland, in the 1850s via Strasbourg, Paris, Le Havre, and New York. From New York they sailed north on the Hudson, past Albany and across a near-frozen Lake Erie to Cleveland and finally to Adams County. The family names on the Indiana mailboxes are the same you see in Bern, Switzerland: Burkhalter, Moser, Baumgartner, Stucky, and so on. Here they still sing mostly solemn and simple religious songs and solo hymns. But once you step outside the religious realm, where the people are engaged in their daily activities or during leisure time, they might be found mimicking twangy country torch songs they hear in town, at neighbors, or on the radio. The Amish children who attend regular public schools also secretly listen to this music on cassettes in the school library.

During the course of her fieldwork, folk-music professor Barbara Bachmann-Geiser encountered some yodeling as well. For instance, an 82–year-old woman from Geneva, Indiana, sang "Rigi-Lied" to Bachman-Geiser. This well-known yodel song by Joseph Felder from the Luzern area is about Mount Rigi, a boat ride from Luzern across Lake Luzern. It was notated in 1865 by Eduard Hoffman-Krayer: "jo-lo-re-i-di di di jo-li-o-u—di." Some of the American-German lyrics come from A. L. Gassmann's 1900 version from Küssnacht, Canton Schwyz. The American versions are sung in a variety of registers. Bachmann-Geiser notes that the song is also sung among the Pennsylvania Dutch: the Amish and Mennonites of Lancaster County. Bachmann-Geiser also noted that milkmaids often serenade the cows they are milking with a yodel. It's a common yodel in both Austria and Switzerland. It not only fills idle time but it also soothes the cow while stimulating it into giving more milk.

Yodeling "persists because it serves several important functions," Chad L. Thompson believes. "In the community: it is an accepted form of entertainment in a society that shuns commercial entertainment; it serves as a symbol of separation from the English-speaking world, as well as from the non-Swiss Amish communities; and it serves as an integral part of certain types of social interaction." The Indiana Swiss Amish, according to Thompson, still practice their yodeling, which makes them, "unique in the Amish world." The yodels Thompson heard while researching these communities fell into several types: those without lyrics (*naturjodel*); those serving as refrains in songs with lyrics; and yodeling during the singing of lyrics. Thompson notes that the songs "are typically either in Bernese Swiss or English, but some of the Swiss lyrics have Standard or Pennsylvania-German elements." Perhaps this is because some of the Pennsylvania Dutch Amish moved back and forth between Pennsylvania and Indiana.

The musical environment in the Adams County Amish community is a potpourri of sacred songs, unavoidable American country and pop music,

KEY SOURCES OF THE AMERICAN-ALPINE TRADITION

- Leary, James. *Yodeling in Dairyland: A History of Swiss Music in Wisconsin.* Mount Horeb: Wisconsin Folk Museum, 1991. Documents Swiss settlers in Wisconsin and their music; includes profile of Rudy Burkhalter.

- *Ach Ya!: Traditional German-American Music from Wisconsin*, 2–record set, Wisconsin Folklife Center, 1986. Includes yodels by German-Wisconsin yodelers like Albert Kolberg and yodel duo Elfrieda Haese and Heidi Schlei. Includes waltzes, lullabys, drinking songs, ballads, and polkas.

- *Art-of-the-State*, various performers, DWP of Wisconsin, 2000.

- *Behind Bars*, Happy Schnapps Combo, Exclusive Novelty, 1994. "Wisconsin's Favorite Drinking Band" offers much to endear them to your funnybone. They zestfully mix metaphors, drinks, and yodeling, German-American kitsch culture and serious mayhem.

- *Deeper Polka: More Dance Music from the Midwest*, Smithsonian/Folkways, 2002. Polkas with lyrics, waltzes and *landlers,* and some yodeling.

- *Downhome Dairyland: Swiss Family Frauenfelder,* The Frauenfelders, Wisconsin Public Radio, mid-1990s. This family yodeled in Wisconsin *and* California throughout the 1930s and 1940s.

- *Downhome Dairyland: Yodeladies*, various artists, Wisconsin Public Radio, 1993. Wisconsin Swiss and Austrian musicians and yodelers.

- *Matterhorn Echoes*, Betty Vetterli and Roger Bright, cassette, Bright Productions, 1980s? Vetterli yodels and squeezes an accordion while Bright plays bass and piano.

- *MidWest Ramblin': Traditional and Original Old-Time Music*, Goose Island Ramblers, Wisconsin Folk Museum, 1990.

- *Swissconsin: My Homeland*, various artists, Wisconsin Folklife Center: Ethnic Music Series cassette, 1988. Excellent sampler of Swiss-American music. Half the tracks feature yodeling and are composed of late-1980s field recordings plus some old Moser Brothers 78s. Also features the Frauenfelder Family.

plus a fair number of old Swiss folk songs including more than a few yodel numbers, along with the potential influence of Pennsylvania-Dutch Amish, although most of these songs are being sung less and forgotten more. One of the leftovers is the *jodellied* "Jetz wott i eis joodele," which was written down from memory in *Schwartzs' Song-book.* Also included is Christian Widmer's "Emmentaler Lied" and the *jodellied* "Niena Gates."

THE DOPEY VOICE

In an interesting 1992 handwritten letter from Rheiny Fraunfelder to James Leary, Rheiny recalls the "little history of the Fraunfelder family" including their relationship with Walt Disney. When I received this letter, I thought "too good to be true." So, I checked *Videohound's Soundtracks,* and, indeed, there in the credits under *Snow White* was "The Fraunfelder Family (yodeling)."

Reynard "Papa" Fraunfelder Sr. was born in Wildegg (!), Switzerland in 1895. He and his wife, Frieda (née Fehlmann), from Möriken, Switzerland, emigrated to Southern California in 1923, with 3–year-old Rheiny and younger sister, Betty, in tow. They remained for seventeen years, producing four more children. Reynard was a yodeler but also a lecturer, teacher, choir director, and musician. He passed on his talents to his children and eventually formed the "Swiss Family Frauenfelder" with Rheiny singing tenor, doing comedy, and playing clarinet, while his sister, Betty, sang soprano and played accordion; another sister, Ruth, sang alto and played piano.

They went on the road with their four-part yodeling harmony in the 1930s and performed hundreds of concerts. They also worked for film studios including Universal, MGM, and Walt Disney. At Disney, Reynard put his yodel songwriting talents to work, writing the yodel tunes for *Snow White and the Seven Dwarfs* while Rheiny supplied the yodel voice of Dopey in the "Silly Song." As the Brothers Grimm noted: "Happy led the orchestra and kept them all stepping and puffing and blowing. Snow White tapped her foot and clapped her hands in time to their yodel song." This means that most westerners' first exposure to yodeling was probably the voice of Rheiny!

The Fraunfelders received their share of accolades and awards, and they eventually introduced their yodeling curriculum into California's public schools. In 1940, the family toured the United States, appearing at hundreds of schools, universities, service clubs, and concert halls. They also joined the Chautauqua circuit of touring arts and were even joined by First Lady Eleanor Roosevelt (not in a yodeling capacity, I assume).

In 1943, the Fraunfelders moved to Whitewater, Wisconsin and continued performing on the USO circuit during World War II. The Schlitz Brewing company, maker of a modestly drinkable beer, sponsored them, and they became the "Schlitz Family Frauenfelder." Rudy Burkhalter thought the family's real star "was Betty on accordion and yodeling." Most of the family moved back west to Oregon, to run their "Mel-o-Dee" Ranch. They toured until 1959. Reynard died at age 93 in 1988.

- *"Yodel Polka"/"The Milkmaid,"* Rondo.

- *"The Cuckoo"/"Yodel Ländler,"* Rondo.

- *Snow White and the Seven Dwarfs*, Walt Disney Productions, 1938. Based on "Schneewittchen" in *Kinder und Hausmärchen*, collected by Jakob Grimm and Wilhelm Grimm.

continued on the next page

The Dopey Voice, continued

- *Walt Disney's Snow White and the Seven Dwarfs*, various performers, original soundtrack, Walt Disney Records, 1993. Includes "The Silly Song." The Fraunfelder Family supply the yodeling! The dwarfs also included the able yodeling voices of Wesley Tuttle and Zeke Clements.

YODELING GOES RADIO-ACTIVE

Although the Germans may have brought the yodel to North America early on, the more common theory is that the New World yodel came to North America via various professional traveling shows composed of singing-yodeling Swiss families. By the 1820s, Tyrolean folkloric troupes were busy exporting neat little packages of performers who had played European concerts and now traveled from coast to coast, yodeling for curious audiences. Christoph Wagner notes that these yodelers showed up on America's shores to serenade homesick Swiss and German immigrants in their bars and civic centers—a little bit of home away from home—effectively becoming tourists in their own pasts.

This trend evolved into a veritable mini-craze for yodeling acts during the mid-19th century, with spin-offs of the most successful traveling Tyrolean yodeling family, the Rainer Family from Austria's Ziller Valley, touring throughout North America during the mid-1800s. A proliferation of traveling yodel families exploited *heimweh* to create a subgenre of commercialized folk songs: the best and worst of both worlds. The Moser Family actually *emigrated* to the United States, while other so-called Swiss families were neither Swiss nor families. The Hutchinson Family (the "New Hampshire Rainers") were arguably the Osmond Family of their day. Their fame precipitated numerous yodel parodies. They made yodeling so trendy that even opera divas felt compelled to include a "mountain style" song (yodel) in their repertoires.

Yodeling found its way into the crazy quilt of cultural phenomena known as medicine shows, with their assortment of freaks, quacks peddling elixirs, and singers singing everything from traditional English, Scottish, and Irish songs to Hawaiian and yodel songs. Furthermore, these acts were parodied and used for satirical effect in more rarified places like urban music halls and the far dustier environments of tent shows. Tom Christian was an early minstrel-singer, a "blackface 'coon'" who introduced yodeling on a Chicago stage in 1847: "The full version of *Lily of Laguna* has a yodeled chorus." Others yodelers included minstrel songwriter and author of "Dixie," Daniel Decatur Emmett (1815–1904), and John Hill Hewitt, America's most successful songwriter until Stephen Foster, who probably wrote America's first pop song, "The Minstrel's Return'd from the War" (1825). "Later in the decade, singing families from Austria and Switzerland toured the USA, and Hewitt wrote mountain songs; 'The Alpine Horn' (1843) included a yodel."

The emergence of a popular stage that included vaudeville, cabaret, and blackface performance as well as tent shows, and the new technology of recorded sound in the last years of the 19th century, all helped resuscitate the yodeling art. Here in this land of babel, this ragged quilt of pidgin tongues, and communication difficulties, Wagner claims that yodeling may even have served as some makeshift musical Esperanto. Harold

YODEL HOLDOUTS

There are other Swiss and Alpine groups scattered across North America who remain focused on preserving Swiss traditions. **The United Swiss Singing Societies of the Pacific Coast** presents events, concerts, and festivals with a focus on Swiss folk culture and yodeling. In 2001, they presented a 300–singer mixed chorus performing traditional Swiss song and yodel selections at their 24th Swiss Singing & Yodeling Festival Grand Concert. Yodeling, *ländlermusik*, alphorn blowing, cowbells, and a parade of flags are just a few of the performances at this annual festival.

The Walburg Boys of Walburg, Texas, produced the CD *Alpine Style* (Walburg Boys Records) in 1996 that further establishes a link between Old World European-style yodeling and New World cowboy yodeling. It includes yodels like "Der Jodel-Automat," and "Walburg Jodler."

LeRoy Larson and Janet Sorenson, from Lakeland, Minnesota, have spent twenty years researching, resurrecting, and recording Scandinavian and Scandinavian-American music. They've performed throughout the Midwest, Canada, and Norway and have been featured on National Public Radio's "A Prairie Home Companion" and Norwegian national radio and television. Their concerts include interesting historical information, anecdotes, humor, dialect songs, jokes, and a yodel or two.

- *On Tour*, Banjar, 1991. Traditional and contemporary songs from Norway, Sweden, and Minnesota, as well as some country-western yodeling.

- *Spectacular Yodeling*, Arthur Brogli, Brogli Records, 1990. Sung in German in Salt Lake City, Utah.

Alberta, Canada, also has a fairly large Swiss community and is represented by several yodel groups, one of which, the **Jodlerklub Heimattreu**, was invited as honored guests to Fribourg's 2002 *Eidgenössischers Jodelfest*.

Courlander (among many others) credits radio and phonograph records as two of the main sources of genre hybridization in American music, facilitating both the acculturation and commodification of musical genres. Radio and phonographs framed popular music in new ways: recorded sound on wax cylinders (George P. Watson recorded the first American yodels on wax cyclinder in 1897), on fragile, variable-rpm platters, plus live radio broadcasts. The yodel became a conspicuous part of American music, with the first yodel records appearing at the cusp of the 20th century. Swiss Tenor Arnold Inauen, Jacob Jost and the Swiss-American Male Voice Choir of New York, Fred Zimmerman, Swiss-American yodeling luminary, and Matt Keefe ("Roll on Silvery Moon" / "Mother's Lullaby," Pathés Frères, 1919) all recorded popular yodel records between 1900 and 1920. In fact, the "1920 [Victor] catalog listed seventeen 'Yodel Songs' . . ." These sorts of recordings probably initiated that dizzying process of pop cultural hybridization, which spawns the creative dynamics of popular music. Zimmerman recorded "I Miss My Swiss" with the renowned bandleader Paul Whiteman in 1925, some five years before Rodgers's hillbilly stylings were given Louis Armstrong's jazzy touch.

Swiss records and sounds by Swiss artists like the Bärtschi Yodel-Band and Paul Gerber were also finding their way onto the American market. These records had an exotic allure to the 1920s record buyer, although, probably a good portion of those early record buyers were probably homesick Swiss-Americans. By the 1920s, the enthusiasm for yodeling rose to a near-fever pitch. "Everyone" was trying their throat at a yodel or two. Early recordings exposed people to a variety of yodel styles, from minstrel blackface (Emmett Miller), rowdy white trash (Cliff Carlisle), to the blue and Alpine yodels. This allowed the Alpine yodel to resonate with "new meanings when brought into proximity with the hollers, whoops, and howls of vernacular vocal techniques," notes Graeme Smith, "used by both white and black American singers."

So what can we say with any certainty or bold abandon about how yodeling came to North America? It seems highly unlikely that yodelers could have been kept silent for some two hundred years (1620s–1830s). Bruce Betler agrees "that yodeling was here by the 1600s." Western African slaves no doubt brought their vocalizations to North America. These stylings included polyphonic singing, falsetto, and probably yodeling. There's also reason to suggest that the yodel may have arrived several times: with the slaves, the Swiss/Germans, and possibly others prior to the 1830s, although documentation remains scarce. I think it's worth a long deep glance; it certainly merits further research.

8

The Hillbillies Are Alive with Yodeling

You got to have smelt a lot of mule manure to be able to sing like a hillbilly.
—attributed to Hank Williams

Yodeling possibly first headed "west" somewhere in the drag of the dusty "ornery wind" created by the coattails of Davy Crockett (1786–1836) or Daniel Boone (1734–1820), two mythic restless spirits who journeyed west in the early 1800s. Boone was born in Pennsylvania but is more associated with Kentucky, where in 1769 he blazed the "Wilderness Road" through the Cumberland Gap in the Appalachian Mountains into the "howling wilderness" of Kentucky, where he moved with his family. He ultimately headed to frontier Missouri where he lived out his increasingly disillusioned life, dying there in 1820. Meanwhile certain groups and communities journeyed through the Gap to cheaper secluded land in West Virginia and Kentucky. This became home to a rowdy melting pot of Germans, Scots, Irish, runaway slaves, and white indentured servants. They brought their vocalizations, histories, ballads, folk songs, fiddles, guitars, and liquors. English and Irish settlers employed Biblical imagery and Celtic songs to create a clearing for the eventual development of musics like bluegrass and hillbilly.

Musician Al Hopkins was reportedly the first to use the term "hillbilly" when he told record producer Ralph Peer that his band was "nothing but a bunch of hillbillies." His band, thereafter called the Hill Billies, was the first to combine Hawaiian slide guitar with hillbilly music. Hillbilly is intricately pejorative (like "Lapp" or "nigger") meaning "from the hills" where "billies" (white trash "bumpkins") lived and played music. In 1926, the entertainment journal *Variety* described a hillbilly as an "illiterate white whose creed and allegiance are to the Bible, the Chautauqua, and the phonograph . . . with the intelligence of (a) moron." Even though there was some intensely serious musicianship to be found in the backwoods, the slur stuck and helped prevent hillbilly music from being taken seriously.

Early-1920s hillbilly was not given a twang's chance of survival, given its association with white-trash Appalachia and its stubborn attachment to traditional instrumentation. Country musicians were consistently underpaid, and so most worked day jobs. Industry boycotts against their kind meant limited performance opportunities: basically local dances, contests, the streets, or political rallies. However, radio and records changed all that. Radio provided new outlets for musicians through live performances, especially on the various barn dance programs. Many of the yodelers I interviewed confirmed radio's impact; it was often where they first heard yodeling.

Somewhere along the timeline, between the 1930s and '50s, country "music that had been entirely homemade [and ignored,] became largely store-bought." Country musicians became touring and performing pros. "In the process, authenticity had become commodified": the look, the sound, the shorthand iconography became marketable. George Hay, "inventor" of the Grand Ole Opry radio program, encouraged the cultivation of the hillbilly image via clichés and humor. Hillbilly iconography has endured into the present day and for some has even become a source of inverted post-modern pride: the proud redneck.

The yodel came to country music via one brilliant performer: Jimmie Rodgers. Yodelers like Vernon Dalhart, Riley Puckett, and Gid Tanner all made records in 1924, but it was to be Rodgers's "minstrel show yodel, a sort of fake blue yodel (Swiss yodel, black lyrics)" style that caught fire and soon inspired almost *every* country singer to yodel and every record buyer to buy their discs. Yodeling became not only an obligatory stylistic flourish, but a commercial necessity; in fact, "yodeling became almost synonymous with country music." By the 1930s, "yodelers and balladeers could be heard everywhere, even in New York." Rodgers's distinctive and "infamous blue yodel that defies the rational and conjecturing mind" became the ululating watermark of what a yodel "should" sound like: somewhat melancholy, perhaps mimicking a "lonesome train whistle." However, Rodgers apparently viewed his yodeling as nothing more than a throwaway flourish or, as he described them, "curlicues I can make with my throat."

SWINGING OUT WEST

Meanwhile, further west, logical yet delirious bastardizations such as Western Swing, real dance music for the working stiff—dance, sweat,

RILEY PUCKETT

Riley Puckett (1884–1946), born and died in Georgia, was blinded as a child and as a consequence turned to one of the only employment avenues open to him, music. He distinguished himself by becoming the first important country music star. He was known as an experimental guitarist, forceful singer, and American roots yodeler credited (but not enough) with introducing yodeling to hillbilly music in 1924, three years prior to Jimmie Rodgers. He produced some hundred recordings as a solo performer and with Gid Tanner and his Skillet Lickers.

"The Caruso of the Mountains," Riley Puckett. By permission of Richard Weize.

Puckett headed north with fiddler Gid Tanner in 1924 and recorded some dozen sides both solo and with Tanner at New York's Columbia Studios. In 1925, Puckett was involved in a serious car accident that led to his marrying his nurse. In 1926, in Atlanta's Columbia Studios, Puckett and Tanner joined Clayton McMichen and Fate Norris to record and emerge as the intrepid Skillet Lickers, archetype for all string bands who followed. Although they stuck to traditional material, they performed plenty of vital, quirky music (unusual harmonies and rhythms plus Tanner's trademark wild falsetto)—definitely virtuosos stretching the limits of a form. Puckett's intrepid predilections plus the jazz and traditional influences of the rest of the band created a dynamic chemistry, which made the whole much greater than any of the individual parts. The Skillet Lickers became the band of record, outselling everyone at the time, but they earned their real money out on the road. They recorded some eighty songs until they split up in 1931.

Puckett's rich deep voice propelled the band to fame. His first solo record appeared in 1924. "Rock All Our Babies to Sleep" was probably the first bonafide hillbilly yodel record. Puckett recorded his yodeler "Sauerkraut" in 1926 but had his first hit in 1927 with "My Carolina Home." Puckett later joined McMichen's Georgia Wildcats, performed in his own tent show, and at the time of his death was performing with the Stone Mountain Boys on an Atlanta radio program. When you scour the list of Columbia hillbilly releases in that fecund late-1920s period, you notice endless titles by Puckett; he's a force that has not been adequately dealt with.

- *Old Time Greats, Vol. 1–2*, Old Homestead, 1978.

- *The Riley Puckett Story*, Roots, 1971.

JIMMIE RODGERS

His message is all between the lines and he delivers it like nectar that can drill through steel.

—Bob Dylan

(Rodgers) couldn't read a note, keep time, play the "right" chords or write lyrics that fit. All he could do was reach the hearts of millions of people around the world, and lift them up. They listened, and understood.

—Nolan Porterfield

Rodgers (1897–1933) was known for converting his imperfections into expressive evocations of universal and soulful human detail. That he died at such a young age only made every word even more poignant. And that all except 6 of his 110 songs—two recorded just *two days* before he died of tuberculosis—contain yodeling begs the question: why was he so stuck on yodeling?

"The Yodeling Waterboy," Jimmie Rodgers: Man of many hats and several octaves.

Before Rodgers, yodelers were propped up between the other sideshow freaks. Even Rodgers got ribbed about his yodeling, some suggesting he pop into some *lederhosen* to get in character. However, with each succeeding yodel hit, more and more of the taunters became silent mimics. He stuck to his guns, or better yet, his epiglottis and managed to make an uncool music cool. Plus, in an era dominated by instrumental (string) bands, he helped put vocals back into the limelight. Maybe this is why yodelers feel so indebted to him. That his records were so popular that regular stores could supply your groceries and the latest Jimmie Rodgers and that snobby phonograph emporiums kept a handsome supply of his discs is proof of the breadth of his influence; Rodgers's songs were groceries *and* high art. Rodgers's sense of timing lent his work an uncertain off-balance (eccentric or thoroughly vulnerable?) "artless sincerity." He'd scurry his way through four-bar lines with such haste that they'd come out three. Maybe he knew his days were numbered.

Rodgers was born near Meridian, Mississippi. After his mother died when he was five, he was "brought up in a series of foster homes . . . occasionally tagging along with his dad on railroad runs." As a young teen he tagged along

continued on the next page

Jimmie Rodgers, continued

doing "all sorts of odd jobs, unofficially, as a boy in the railyards and on the trains" including as a waterboy—Hey, little water boy / Bring that bucket round"—and later as a brakeman on various railroad lines. Here he learned his licks while listening intently to the Negroes who sang their songs, hollered their hollers, and picked their guitars. In 1924, Rodgers learned he had tuberculosis, probably contracted from his railroad work. He decided to leave the railroad life behind. Ironically, it may have been the TB that pushed him into music and eventually provided the source for his spine-tingling train-whistle calls that skewered his yodels. After nearly dying in the hospital, Rodgers came back, playing the mud and dust circuit of fairs and tent shows, also doing his share of blackface minstrel performances. Here he may have been exposed to some of the other blackface performers like Emmett Miller or some of the yodeling blackface "coons" (blackface blacks).

His health was already pretty iffy in 1927 when he and his band "made [their] way across the Blue Ridge in a borrowed car to audition" and started recording for Ralph Peer. Three months after his first session in Bristol, Tennessee, Rodgers recorded "T For Texas." Until his death six years later, he was recording constantly, tirelessly, obsessively, performing on radio shows and touring the country in a blaze of busyness, knowing it might end at any given moment or note. Two days after his last song was put down on acetate, on May 26, 1933, he died of a lung hemorrhage in a New York hotel.

Rodgers's success was astounding for its time. His "T For Texas" sold more than a million copies and soon he was earning something absurd like $1,000 per month (this was more than most people would earn in a year—especially during the Depression). He often worked solo, but some of his most enduring songs were cowritten with his sister-in-law, Elsie McWilliams, a gifted songwriter and musician in her own right. She cowrote thirty-eight of his songs including "Never No Mo' Blues," "Anniversary Blue Yodel," and "You and My Old Guitar."

If Duke Ellington is America's Beethoven and Charlie Parker its Mozart, then who is Rodgers? Puccini? Rodgers may actually be more the white man's Robert Johnson. Rodgers did with a skinny, whiney voice something what others of better voice can't and did not do: he infused the yodel with soul or, as Douglas B. Green pegged it, a "cry of pain and anguish." This may have been, according to NIcholas Dawidoff,

> because its falsetto delivery was so different from his singing voice, it was a fine way to apply a certain accent to whatever he was singing about. . . . with the possible exception of the mysterious blackface singer Emmett Miller, nobody could yodel like [Rodgers]. Which prompted some lurid speculation. There were people who believed Rodgers's magnificent yodeling was a by-product of the tuberculosis that was beginning to kill him.

continued on the next page

Jimmie Rodgers, continued

Rodgers, a vagabond-sponge, an omnivore, and Johnny Appleseed, absorbed and recirculated a variety of cultural influences. He found it essential to warp standard melodies, gallop at his own tempo, and fumble some guitar work, adding his own anguished yodel, which came across as heartfelt soul. He was never content with one sound and so recorded with an amazing array of bands and styles, even employing the Dorsey Brothers and dueting with Louis Armstrong. He was the first major (Emmett Miller notwithstanding) white hillbilly to record with black musicians.

His subject matter was heavily influenced by early blues singers. His "Blue Yodel" was basically a standard blues where on the third line of every verse his voice would be hurled upward through a glottal stop into a tense falsetto. In fact, "the identifying characteristics of the 'blue yodel'" John Greenway has written, "are (1) the slight situational pattern, that of a 'rounder' boasting of his prowess as a lover, but ever in fear of the 'creeper' . . . and (2) the prosodic pattern, the articulation of Negro maverick stanzas dealing with violence and promiscuity, often with double meanings, and followed by a yodel refrain." To a lesser extent, this may be true of Rodgers as well. His yodels tend to be linear, almost dagger-like, like twangy short-voweled "i" sounds instead of the richer, more full-bodied "O" sound of the more accomplished yodelers in the Swiss style of yodeling. They seem to mirror not only the desolate foreboding landscape, but also the watermark that the landscape leaves on the human soul. The yodel can express ecstatic recognition of natural beauty, but it can also be plaintive like a coyote's yowl, or the howl of a gust through a bullethole in a dingy window.

Rodgers's genius was his ability to jumble and mix the blues, some yodeling, hillbilly, and Tin Pan Alley stuff, with generous hints of jazz performed with what Bill Malone called "effortless informality." He made the personal sound universal, and he made it seem like he had invented something that already existed: British ballad and blues holler. And his "realness" as blue-collar yodeler helped construct the *myth* of Rodgers as the "Yodeling" or "Singing Brakeman."

Rodgers further transmogrified the influences he absorbed while working beside "hollerin'" blacks into a strange brew of hollers, European ballads, spirituals, and yodels. At the recommendation of producer Ralph Peer, Rodgers actually recorded "Blue Yodel #9" in Hollywood in 1930, with Louis Armstrong and his wife, Lil, on piano (Earl Hines on other versions), with Jimmie Rodgers adding "an alpine yodel to the end of each verse." This landmark/voiceprint instant where yodeling, country music, and jazz fused into a dynamic and sparkling weld eventually spawned rockabilly, impatient younger cousin of country music, which sired rock 'n roll (which died an ignominious death as arena rock). This improbable and famous duet (in a segregated society) presaged the rise of black-influenced white music(s) and the modern

continued on the next page

Jimmie Rodgers, continued

multiple-hybrid known as World music—which is merely the conscious A-side of what had been going on unconsciously for a long time—cultural collaboration. As musicologist Christoph Wagner rightly notes: "A hybrid music was emerging, where T stood not only for Texas and Tennessee but for Tyrol too"— alluding to Rodgers's famous line in "Blue Yodel No. 1." Rodgers was arguably one of the first "world" musicians but, inarguably, a unique American voice.

Rodgers has influenced so many yodelers, including direct imitators like Gene Autry, Ernest Tubb and Hank Snow, Lefty Frizzell, and Tommy Duncan. But also Cliff Carlisle, Jimmie Davis, Moon Mullican, Eddy Arnold, Roy Acuff, Bill Monroe, Stanley Brothers, Bing Crosby, Carl Perkins, Robert Johnson, Bessie Smith, Johnny Cash, Jerry Lee Lewis, and countless younger rockabilly and country singers. They can't all be wrong.

As the train carrying Rodgers's body pulled into Meridian, Mississippi, to take his coffin to the cemetery, the engineer blew the whistle—a long melancholy moan—as a tribute to Rodgers's yodeling.

- *The Singing Brakeman*, Bear Family, 1992. Typical excellent liner notes.

- *Travellin' Blues*, RCA Victor, 1955.

- *Jimmy Rodgers, My Rough and Rowdy Ways*, RCA, 1960.

- *Recordings, 1927–1933*, 5-CD Box-set, JSP, 2002

- *Blue Yodel*, Arpeggio Country, 2001.

- *The Essential Jimmie Rodgers*, RCA Nashville, 1997.

- *The Songs of Jimmie Rodgers*, Egyptian Records, 1997. Tribute album produced by Bob Dylan.

The Blue Yodels

- "T For Texas: Blue Yodel #1," November 30, 1927

- "My Lovin' Gal, Lucille: Blue Yodel #2," February 15, 1928

- "Evening Sun Yodel: Blue Yodel #3," same date

- "California Blues: Blue Yodel #4," October 20, 1928, also called "Ain't No Blackheaded Woman Can Make a Fool out of Me"

- "Blue Yodel #5," February 23, 1929

- "Blue Yodel #6," October 22, 1929

- "Anniversary Blue Yodel: Blue Yodel #7," November 26, 1929

- "Mule Skinner Blues: Blue Yodel #8," July 11, 1930

continued on the next page

Jimmie Rodgers, continued

- "Standin' on the Corner: Blue Yodel #9," July 16, 1930
- "Ground Hog Rootin' in My Backyard: Blue Yodel #10," February 6, 1932
- "Blue Yodel #11," November 27, 1929
- "Barefoot Blues: Blue Yodel #12," May 17, 1933
- "Jimmie Rodgers' Last Blue Yodel," May 18, 1933, also called "Women Make a Fool out of Me" and "Why Don't the Women Let Me Be."

imbibe, forget—was being mastered by innovators Bob Wills and Milton Brown, who introduced drums, horns, and electric instruments into country. They also borrowed heavily from big-band jazz and anywhere else that suited their fancies. Wills incorporated numerous yodels (performed by lead singer Tommy Duncan, among others) into his live gigs. Wills's own delirious, falsetto shout of "Ah-hah" as his musicians performed is itself half-a-yodel.

The West is also home to Tex-Mex and Czech-Mex, musical folk-pop hybrids that emerged from the Rio Grande Valley, which spawned many a bizarre musical adventure with its combination of country guitar, Mexican Mariachi trumpet, Czech folk music, some accordions, German polkas, and . . . yodels. There were also some *real* yodelers about to make their mark; both Elton Britt and Wilf Carter would further escalate the aesthetic value of yodeling.

ELTON BRITT

Elton Britt (James Elton Baker, 1917–1972) born half-Irish, (and perhaps) half-Cherokee in Zack, Arkansas, is regarded as one of the purest and highest-voiced yodeling cowboys. Some call him the "World's Highest Yodeler." At the end of "Chime Bells," he holds a note for a pregnant minute, giving the feeling that his yodel is suspended in some pristine valley somewhere. Yodeler Liz Masterson claims he held a note for some sixty-four beats by her own count.

Britt picked up music from his dad, a champion fiddler, and singing from his mom, an Ozark Mountains native. Britt took up a guitar and learned songs from spinning them over and over again on the family's phonograph. He could spend entire days listening to Riley Puckett and Jimmie Rodgers yodeling. Britt was discovered by a couple of talent scouts behind a plow in a field; they signed Britt to a one-year contract with radio

Elton Britt, an inspiration to many youthful yodelers. By permission of Richard Weize.

station KMPC in Beverly Hills. In no time, he was yodeling on the major radio networks. Britt was just 12 when he joined one of California's most successful country groups, the Beverly Hill Billies in 1929. They broke up in 1933, and Britt and their accordionist, Zeke Manners, headed to New York, where they performed under numerous aliases and recorded some songs. Around that time, Britt won a yodeling contest organized by celluloid cowboy Tom Mix, and he was crowned the unofficial world yodel champion. Eventually, Britt went his own prolific solo way, recording some fifty albums and hundreds of singles for various labels.

In 1937, Britt began working for RCA where he wrote his greatest songs with Bob Miller: "Rocky Mountain Lullaby," "Buddy Boy," "Driftwood on the River" and "Chime Bells," which is based on "Happy and Free Yodel," an English vaudeville song, written and recorded years earlier by Harry Torrani. Britt recorded a huge patriotic hit during World War II (1942), "There's a Star-Spangled Banner Waving Somewhere." The song got him an invitation to the White House—the first country star to be so honored—where he sang it for President Franklin Roosevelt. The song also earned him the first gold record ever awarded to a country singer.

In 1946, Britt had six Top 10 country hits, including his smash hit "Someday You'll Want Me To Want You" (#2, eighteen weeks on the charts). Britt's other yodeling hits include "Patent Leather Shoes,"

"Lorelei," and "Maybe I'll Cry over You," which are all marked by his distinctively clear and soaring yodel. There are numerous schools of yodeling loyalties. There are those who prefer Rodgers (fragile yet soulful); or Montana Slim, with his cowboy songs and his Alpine-style front-of-the-throat yodeling; or Britt, who used the *back* of his throat and combined a bluesy soulfulness with a crisp clarion prowess that cut through all babble and clutter. You sit up and take notice when he yodels! Britt also did numerous duets with yodeler Rosalie Allen, including "Quicksilver" and "Beyond the Sunset." They had a minor hit with Britt's yodel version of "The Skater's Waltz."

During the 1950s, Britt drifted in and out of the music business. He appeared in some TV commercials and, in 1960, ran for president in the Democratic primaries. Before settling down to a life as a gentleman farmer, Britt had one last hit in 1968, his first in eighteen years, with "The Jimmie Rodgers Blues." He died of a heart attack in 1972 in McConnellsburg, Pennsylvania.

A tribute to Britt's yodeling glory is etched into his gravestone, but otherwise he remains North America's underappreciated yodeling paradigm. His vibrant emotional yodel manufactured an entire ambience: "He heard the lonely song of the whippoorwill / he heard the lonely echo." Indeed he did, and I can almost hear his Presidential acceptance speech . . . "My fellow Americans: I have worked hard to maintain that dramatic break between the high and low—yo-de-LAY-EE-OOO . . . "

- *Stars and Stripes Forever*, Cattle. Covers 1933–1951. Essential.
- *The RCA Years*, Bear Family, 1990s.
- *The RCA Years*, Collector's Choice, 1998.
- *Yodel Songs*, RCA, 1955, (Stetson, 1960). Exuberant collection of Britt's backbone-tingling yodels with exquisite production values and exotic orchestral arrangements, plus two Allen duets.

WILF CARTER (AKA "MONTANA SLIM")

Wilf Carter (1904–1996), born to a Swiss Baptist minister and an English mother, was working as a farmhand at age 13 when he spotted a poster for "The Yodeling Fool" in his native Guysborough, Nova Scotia. He snuck in to see this most vocal of human freaks, and decided then and there to become a yodeler. Or so goes the story. "I yodeled upstairs and downstairs, in the parlor and in the apple orchard," said Carter. "Dad couldn't stop me, though he wore out a dozen slippers on the seat of my pants."

The yodeling bug lured him to the Cowboy West of real yodelers. Carter hopped a freight train, joining the tramps and hobos, and found work as a lumberjack before ending up in Calgary, where he landed a job as a ranch hand. Carter was now a real Alberta cowboy and, in the 1920s, he sang every chance he got—in the bunkhouse, around a campfire, or at local gigs. But in 1926, when he auditioned for a Calgary radio show, he was told to "stick to milking cows." Eventually, Carter landed a job as a guide in the Canadian Rockies where he distinguished himself as the Trail Riders' official singer-songwriter. Carter sang on CFCN Calgary in 1933 and came to the attention of RCA-Victor in Montreal.

At his first recording session he sang "Swiss Moonlight Lullaby," a yodel song written during his trail rider days. It was distinguished by his unique yodeling Alpine-meets-Western-scat yodel style. It became a hit in 1933, which helped him land his own New York radio show at CBS. Here he met Bert Parks, who began calling him "Montana Slim"; the name stuck. When he toured the States, he *was* "Montana Slim," everywhere else he remained Wilf Carter. He didn't care what they called him as long as they paid him. Carter toured incessantly and was the most popular singer in both Australia and New Zealand in the 1940s—influencing an entire continent of emerging country singers there. Carter wrote more than 500 songs, many of which feature his signature speed yodel with heavy studio echo effects, which he called his "three-in-one."

- *Cowboy Songs*, Bear Family, 1997. Includes some 180 songs and outtakes, mostly penned by Carter himself. Massive.
- *Dawn on the Prairie*, Cowgirlboy. Recorded 1938–50.
- *Dynamite Trail: The Decca Years, 1954–58*, Bear Family, 1990.
- *Reminiscin' with Montana Slim*, Stetson, 1989.

TOMMY DUNCAN

Duncan (1911–1967) was the most talented of the yodeling vocalists in Bob Wills's Texas Playboys. His early "gigs" were spent singing and playing a cheap guitar for loose change outside a soda stand. He soon got his big chance winning an audition to perform with Wills and the legendary Light Crust Doughboys. Duncan filled the void left in Western Swing by the car-accident death of jazz-country innovator Milton Brown (1903–1936), who began his career in the "Three Yodeliers," a group that certainly yodeled on "I Ain't Got Nobody" (also covered by Emmett Miller). Duncan and Wills left the Light Crust Doughboys to start the Texas Playboys in 1932.

Wills's gift as a bandleader wasn't musicianship but an uncanny management ability to gather and enthuse the right folks to create a swingin', dancin' critical mass. Tommy Duncan sang, played piano, and not infrequently yodeled on some 500 recordings. His piano playing was so wild and dynamically destructive that he left a trail of piano wrecks in the wake of his early touring days. His voice was what mattered, however—a soothing, Bing-like, blues-crooning—and it contrasted nicely with the uptempo Playboys material. He was unsentimental and never feigned pathos.

Although Wills sang his twangy blues numbers and added his signature "ah-haaw" interjections, Duncan did most of the singing—and yodeling— showing his prowess as a blues singer on "Honey, What You Gonna Do," "Blue Yodel #1," and "Swing Blues #1." He wrote many songs and cowrote "Cotton-Eyed Joe" with Wills (1946). His music has been an inspiration to many, including Merle Haggard and Willie Nelson.

- *Texas Moon*, Bear Family, 1996.
- *Beneath a Neon Star in a Honky Tonk*, Bear Family, 1996.

YODELING COMES OF AGE

The folk music stream is pretty muddy by now, lots of mongrel yodeling cowboys who mixed black blues with Celtic ballads and German yodels. But through some process of acculturation and revisionism, with no small amount of commercial opportunism attached to it, the ersatz and manufactured became a benchmark for the authentic, so that now, dipping into the deeper water of the 21st century, we have cowboy yodeling as the genuine authentic deal. This process has occurred in other genres like disco; reviled as fake one day, and authentic and validated the next. Time and longevity heals all shortsightedness. Maybe yodeling will some day be the beneficiary of this corrected vision. Giants of country like Patsy Montana and Bill Monroe were commercial successes and are now considered artists. Canadian Hank Snow became a country crossover star in the 1950s. Singers like Jim Reeves, Patsy Cline, and Marty Robbins had hits that crossed into various markets. Slim Whitman and Eddy Arnold did the same with yodeling.

Hank Williams arrived on the 1940s scene like some James Dean supernova. But he ended up throttling his talent white-lightning fast— dead in the backseat of a Cadillac by age 29. Williams was a truly gifted persona, fusing lyrical content to the mythical aspects of his life like no one before him. He also casually morphed the yodel into something impatient and modern. He interjected his offhand yodel mid-line, mid-word, lending lyrics emotional import and a hint of post-modern divergence from narrative text. His half-a-glottal break probably developed into the strange whooping hiccup yodel, developed by Kenny Roberts and passed along to Jerry Lee Lewis and Bill Haley. These whooping-hiccupping yodels (and their related on-stage dynamics and kinetic acrobatics) became trademark yodel hybrids, characteristic of both rockabilly and early rock 'n roll and seemed to mirror the intensified emotional stress that the times seemed to nourish: pump up the volume *and* the beats-per-minute.

JUMPIN' KENNY ROBERTS

As an "original" and incumbent yodeling king, Roberts has had to constantly defend his turf and title. His brags are like Mohammed Ali's "I Am the Greatest"—true and indisputable. But advertising your prowess comes with a yodeler's epiglottal territory. 2003 marked 60 years of performing for this legendary yodeler. Throughout his long yodeling career, neither his voice nor his boasting withered much. During our various email correspondences, Roberts pointed out that "Kerry [Christensen], Ranger Doug, and Randy Erwin are all great yodelers, but I can still out yodel any of them, even at my age."—no bragging, just something resembling the facts. He's important not only for his yodeling achievements but also for the fact that he led the big leap over country music's barbed wire fence into the fidgety future that came to be known as rockabilly—carrying his octaves to the *other* side. Roberts, born October 1926 (or 1927) in Lenoir City, Tennessee, was *still* out there touring the Midwest–New

"Jumpin" Kenny Roberts, "King of the Yodelers." By permission of Richard Weize.

York–Pennsylvania fairs circuit when I heard from him in September 2002.

Why does a yodeler of his stature have to huff and puff? He remains relatively unknown—marginal—something he should *not* have been. "I've been identified as a yodeler and one of the best voices on ballads in country music," Roberts informed me, and yet, that said, he still felt the need to set people straight. After all he'd yodeled, he was still there at the entrance to the Promised Land handing people his résumé. It is precisely *because* Roberts played cowpie fairs instead of top-notch venues that I am writing this book; to bring just light to this unjust neglect.

Despite all his showmanship, there was a lot of gut-wrenching soul pinned in between Roberts's glottal breaks. All the more unlikely given that he claims to be descended from the Mayflower Puritans and a dozen U.S. presidents, two scrums of characters not commonly associated with soulfulness. His mother died when he was a kid, and he moved to Athol, Massachusetts, where he helped out on his father's farm. Roberts's youthful heroes were Elton Britt, Roy Acuff, Montana Slim, Ernest Tubb, Roy Rogers, and Gene Autry. "I listened to them on the radio and bought their records," he recalled. In 1972, Roberts was asked to replace Britt at a New Jersey concert—quite an honor tarnished only by sorrow because it was the night that Britt died.

Roberts won a talent contest when he was 13 years old and first played with the Red River Rangers on WHAI, Greenfield, Massachusetts, in 1942. It was in April 1943, when he was still only 16, that Roberts recalled, "my dad gave me permission to leave home and join them on the radio. Yes, I grew up fast. At sixteen and a half I joined the Down Homers, a western cowboy group, at $12 per week to perform daily on radio shows at WKNE of Keene, New Hampshire." Yodeling came relatively easy. "I practiced a lot and I loved that unique sound and wanted to do it." In 1944, Roberts tagged along with the group to Iowa where he earned $35 a week doing radio and then on to Indiana's WOWO to do the "Hoosier Hop." When Roberts left to join the Navy in 1944, the group replaced him with Bill Haley. Roberts actually taught Haley some rudimentary yodel techniques and some upright bass, the fiddle, and some Sons of the Pioneers–style harmonies.

After the Navy, Roberts hooked a radio gig at WOWO in Fort Wayne, Indiana, officially launching his solo career. In 1947, he recorded some sides for Vita-Coustic but they gathered dust and were never released, so he moved on to Coral Records. The rise of his sonic falsetto toward some renown really began in earnest in 1948, when he began hosting his own radio and TV shows in Cincinnati, becoming a hero to millions of kids in the Midwest. While encouraging kids to drink their milk, he entertained adults with his yodels and country songs. Roberts became known as the "Jumping

Cowboy" because he could leap several feet into the air while yodeling. And jump he did; just about every show would feature his jumping yodel. Roberts yodel was emotionally versatile, stretching from emotive-bluesy to frenetic, from haunting to buoyant, from downright frolicsome to comical. Roberts's yodel repertoire was eclectic and crowdpleasing. The so-called galloping yodel, which won him many yodel contests was called that because it was so breathtakingly fast. Some claim he was the "world's fastest yodeler."

Roberts often appeared on the Opry stage and on most of the day's legendary radio shows, including NBC's "Prince Albert Show" with Red Foley and Minnie Pearl. Roberts's biggest *Billboard* hits include "I Never See Maggie Alone," "Choc'late Ice Cream Cone," "Wedding Bells," "Jealous Heart," and "Bluebird on your Windowsill." "Choc'late" cast him as a novelty singer, vinyl death for most artists, but not for Roberts. In fact, "Maggie" went gold and was one of the first crossover hits, appearing in both the *Billboard* and *Variety* pop (#9) and country (#4) charts. He was also a jukebox and radio-request fave.

Music writer Paul Hazell notes that, "Kenny was renowned for his voice-break style of singing—where the yodel technique is applied at the end of a line or during a word—much as Hank Williams did on 'Lovesick Blues.' It's especially evident on "Blue," which he first recorded with falsetto yodeling in 1967. In 1996, it was revived by teen country queen LeAnn Rimes. Stories (in *Billboard*) appeared, claiming "Blue" had been written especially *for* Rimes, ignoring the song's history. In 1996, Nashville's IMG-KING label reissued Roberts's original version of "Blue."

Throughout the 1960s and '70s, Roberts's Starday 45s and LPs got lots of airplay and were pretty popular. But from then on American radio went from mediocre to menacingly stultifying, until almost all marginal music fell into the vapid blackhole of middle-of-the-road demographics.

Roberts can be heard yodeling "Yodelaine" (composed by wife Betty-Anne) in *Another You*, a 1991 comedy starring Gene Wilder. The story is that Roberts was hired to write original yodel songs and help teach Wilder to yodel. Roberts also appeared on the game show, *To Tell the Truth* (1974), as the mystery guest, performing his "Galloping Yodel"; NBC's *Today Show* (1992); and the *Joe Franklin Show* (2001), where he yodeled and chatted with Franklin.

I asked Roberts if there is something mystical that happens in that shift between chest and head voice. "Nothing happens. I just enjoy hearing those sounds coming out and pleasing the audience." Roberts took the epiglottal sound of greats and pushed it to the brink of rock 'n roll. Today many contemporary yodelers like Wylie Gustafson name Roberts as a prime influence.

- *Jumpin' & Yodelin'*, Bear Family, 1996. Very jaunty and lucid early 1950s yodeling.
- *Early Country Yodel Songs*, Cowgirlboy, 1991. Includes 1950s–60s recordings.
- *Then & Now*, Longhorn, 1981 (1946). Includes two yodeling duets with Elton Britt, the only time they ever appeared on record together.
- *Tribute to Elton Britt*, Palomino, 1972.
- *Indian Love Call*, Starday, 1965, IMG-KING Records, 1997. Almost all yodel songs.
- *United States, Indiana, Fort Wayne, 1979*, Down Homers. Includes Shorty Cook, Paul Tyler, Guy Campbell, and Roberts. Unreleased recordings dating from 1979.

ETHEL DELANEY: THE "SWISS MISS YODELER"

Ethel Delaney (b. 1926) has been the "Swiss Miss Yodeler" for as long as anyone can remember, and she can still muster a yodel of formidable octave breadth if called upon. The rerelease of vintage Delaney material (*Turning Back Time*) offers a good sample of Delaney's yodeling glory days. She yodels so convincingly that the singing just gets in the way of the next yodel refrain. *Time* is a remastered showcase of twenty-six cuts originally recorded between 1963 and the 1980s. It includes the novelty "Hillbilly Leprechauns," complete with some insane yodeling and munchkin voices.

"My husband Russ came up with the idea to record this song at 15 IPS," explains Delaney, "then slowed the tape to 7–1/2 IPS and re-recorded the yodel at 1/2 speed, which, when brought back to 15 IPS, the end result would fit the Leprechaun image." Some of the songs ("Turn Back the Hands of Time" and "Your Heart Taught My Heart to Cry") were recorded with backing vocals by the legendary Jordanaires. Delaney remembers that the session was recorded in August 1973 at Nashville's RCA Studios. She happened to be recording at the same studio as Elvis. "Lloyd Green who played steel guitar on all my Nashville sessions was able to make the arrangements. The legendary session musician, Charlie McCoy," Delaney explains, "played harmonica on several of my sessions and also played the Hammond organ and bass guitar on a few cuts."

Delaney was born in Crescent, a small coal-mining town in southeastern Ohio (fifteen miles west of Wheeling, West Virginia). "Back in those days you didn't have the constant distractions that children have today," Delaney reminisces, "I spent a lot of time with my mother in the kitchen—watching her sew a dress. . . . When I was 3 or 4 . . . I would hear our radio playing country music—my mother would hunt the dials for the music." At age 5, Delaney started her guitar lessons, began singing, and took up yodeling. Her mother also took time to transcribe the lyrics from the radio and then taught her the words and melody. Delaney has fond memories of her youth:

> My family was very supportive—we got together on our front porch each evening after suppertime. My dad played fiddle, my brother harmonica/vocals [he was 6 years older], all our neighbors would gather around to hear us sing and play. My parents were average people—my dad worked in the coal mines—who couldn't afford an expensive guitar. *But* I did get my guitar. I really applied myself into learning to play . . . and to teach myself to yodel.

"My first appearance on the WWVA Jamboree [radio station in Wheeling, West Virginia] was at the age of 6 or 7." She won first place in an amateur yodel contest when she was 9, which earned her a regular spot on the Jamboree, and she appeared regularly on WWVA's "The Kiddie Program." Here she earned the "Swiss Miss Yodeler" moniker because of her yodeling and her tongue-twisting maiden name, Pocsik (Paw-SICK).

Yodeling came easy to Delaney. Living in the isolated Ohio foothills she could yodel to her heart's content because no one was there to complain:

> We lived *way out in the country*; the nearest town fifteen miles away. When I was 17, I graduated high school and went to work at Sears Roebuck in their accounting department. I moved to Wheeling and lived with a girlfriend where we shared a small apartment. . . . I was also performing on WWVA live each morning before going to work.

Delaney gained confidence by performing for church socials and school affairs: "I would go home on weekends as my parents traveled with me to all of my engagements." It wasn't all work and no play; on weekends she could hang out, and: "Saturday afternoon we'd go to the 10–cent movie matinee in town—about a fifteen-mile drive to the nearest town—to see Roy Rogers, Tex Ritter, or Gene Autry. . . . I especially liked the Rogers movies because he always did some yodeling."

But then, just as things seemed to be happening, Delaney abandoned the performing life to get married. She moved to northeast Ohio where she worked as a secretary. But in 1963, Delaney's husband coaxed her into returning to the yodeling life. Her return to the stage, Delaney remembers, "was marked by that ecstasy, that titillation, one feels when you are once again in the spotlight" and she wondered how she could have ever left. In 1964, Delaney joined the Buckeye Strings (which eventually included her son, Russ Thomas, on drums), who formed a solid backing band to highlight her vocal talents. Delaney cut her first single on the Deco label in Cleveland. "Echo Mountain" was the first song she wrote herself. Many yodel songs followed. While she has enjoyed some success with her yodeling, Delaney sees the yodeler's struggle for recognition as an uphill battle. "I've had songs charted, but the major charts [*Billboard, Record World,* etc.] have always been reluctant to give yodeling the attention that I believe it deserves, as at any concert, stage show, or showcase event that I have seen or performed at, when an artist performs a 'quality Yodel,' it brings down the house."

In 1970, Delaney was nominated for Top Country Western Female Artist by the Country Music Association. While she was passed up for that award, that same year she was voted into Sweden's Top Five of Country Western Female Artists. In June 1983, Patsy Montana personally presented Delaney with the Patsy Montana Cowboy Sweetheart Award on behalf of the Texas Proud Association. This was an immense honor because Montana was her idol. Back in her formative years Delaney remembers listening to the "WLS Barn Dance" Saturday nights. "I'd have my ears glued to hear Patsy Montana and the Dezurik Sisters—all terrific yodelers in their own styles. I never met the Sisters but Patsy and I became friends when we first met in the 1960s in Nashville . . . and remained friends o'er the years and did many performances together." Elton Britt and Rosalie Allen are also influences: "They were both great yodelers both as a duo and as individuals."

"I consider myself a singer-yodeler. I apply the yodel to the melody of the song and use the same tempo as the song. . . . I get great responses from my audience wherever I perform and . . . children are mesmerized by the yodeling." Delaney enthuses, "I always encourage young people to continue yodeling—the more they yodel the better they become." All of her discs are on Ohio Records.

- *Turning Back Time*, 2000. CD of greatest tracks.
- *Sounds of Ethel Delaney and Her Buckeye Strings*, 1987.
- *Heeere's Ethel*, 1975.
- *Goin' To The Country With Ethel Delaney*, 1970.

SOME OTHER COUNTRY YODELERS

Rosalie Allen (b. Julie Marlene Bedra, 1924) is probably much less renowned than she ought to be. She's most remembered for her enchanting yodel duets with Elton Britt. In the 1940s and 1950s she was certainly big enough as the "Hillbilly Yodel Star" to have her own radio show, "Prairie Stars."

Her story is a classic tale of Depression-era hardships. Born into a Polish immigrant family of eleven children in Old Forge, in the central

Pennsylvania coal-mining district, she worked and boarded in a restaurant, helping out the family by sending home her paychecks. And it was during this period that she got hooked into the magical world of yodeling via songs she heard on the radio. She won a contest that dubbed her the "Queen of the Yodelers," a title she used throughout her career. She moved to New York in 1943 with Denver Darling's Swing Billies cowboy troupe. She had several hit records: "Guitar Polka," "Yodel Boogie," and "He Taught Me to Yodel." Try her "Wide Rolling Plains."

- *Rosalie Allen: The Hillbilly Yodel Star of the 1940s*, Bronco Buster, 1990s. Recorded 1944–49 with Denver Darling's band. Includes some yodel duets with Elton Britt and Red River Dave.
- *Queen of the Yodelers*, Cattle, 1983.
- *Yodel Your Troubles Away*, with Elton Britt and Denver Darling, Cowgirlboy, 1992.

Eddy Arnold (b. Richard Edward Arnold, 1918), "The Tennessee Plowboy," was a smooth Perry Como–like crooner. He was country's first crossover star, achieving fame and fortune by polishing away all the blemishes, all the rough-hewn edges, to create a seamless, glossy, country pop sound.

Arnold grew up on a Henderson, Tennessee, farm and was indeed a plowboy who rode to his very first singing engagements on the back of a mule. He tramped around, lived and worked in a funeral parlor, until in 1940 he got his break with Pee-Wee King as his lead vocalist, performing at the Opry and singing regularly on radio. In 1948, he had six Top 10 hits. Arnold first recorded "Cattle Call" in 1944, rerecording it in 1955. It became a monster crossover hit and made him a star. Arnold remained successful until the end of his career with an MOR sound that ruffled no feathers.. He invested in real estate and was pretty much set for life. Arnold was inducted into the Country Music Hall of Fame in 1966.

- *Hillbilly Favorites*, Cattle, 1990s. Rare 1950s transcription recordings.
- *The Essential Eddy Arnold*, RCA, 1996.
- *Strictly Hillbilly Style*, Cowgirlboy, 1990s.

The Callahan Brothers: Walter and Homer Callahan (later Joe and Bill) were born in North Carolina in the years prior to World War I. They were a significant guitar and vocal act in the 1930s and learned yodeling from early yodeling records. They had a number of radio shows around the South. They were influenced by the early yodeling twosome Fleming and

Underrated
"Yodeling Hobo,"
Cliff Carlisle (right)
with brother Bill.
By permission of
Richard Weize.

Townsend, recorded Riley Puckett's songs, and benefited from the yodeling boom spawned by Jimmie Rodgers. They combined gospel, ballads, hillbilly, blues and (Walter's) yodeling.

- *The Callahan Brothers* Early Recordings, Old Homestead, 1974.

Cliff Carlisle (1904–1983), born and died in Kentucky, was known as "The Yodeling Hobo." A formidable blue yodeler in his own right as a tent show and radio performer, he performed in the shadow of Jimmie Rodgers. His first record, a Rodgers-style yodel, appeared in 1930. In 1931, he recorded with Rodgers and released his own kinky barnyard "Shanghai Rooster Yodel." He introduced steel guitar to country and recorded 300+ witty, down and dirty songs about love hurts, scum, bums, and outlaws, all delivered with a biting nihilistic cheerfulness. He often outdid Rodgers at his own game—Carlisle was more savagely hyper-realistic. His sexually insinuating yodel song "The Nasty Swing" was recorded in 1936, while his version of "Footprints in the Snow" inspired Bill Monroe to record it, making it a bluegrass classic. Carlisle remains a true underacknowledged genius.

- *Cliff Carlisle: Blues Yodeler & Steel Guitar Wizard,*
  Arhoolie/Folklyric, 1996.

Claude Casey (1912–1999) born in South Carolina, this entertainer made people laugh for decades as one of the Briarhoppers on Charlotte,

North Carolina, radio station WBT (1930s–1950s). He wrote skits and country songs and apparently could "out-yodel anyone from the Swiss Alps," according to fellow Briarhopper Roy Grant. He toured nationally as the prototypical "Carolina Hobo," a kind of country clown forerunner of what you might have seen on that long-running TV corn comedy show, *Hee Haw.*

Zeke Clements (1911–1994) was an early regular at the Opry, first performing there in 1930. His first single was recorded with Texas Ruby. He had his own band, the Western Swing Gang. His solo work, all recorded between 1945 and 1947, are excellent yodel songs. Zeke was also known as "The Dixie Yodeler."

- *Zeke Clements—Early Star of the Grand Ole Opry,* Cattle, 1990s.

The Delmore Brothers began their careers before their voices had even cracked. Alton was 18 and Rabon only 10 when they won their first fiddle contest. In 1932, they appeared at the Opry. They've influenced many despite being less famous than the Carters, Wills, and Rodgers. With their close harmonies of gospel, Appalachian, and black influences and the Jimmie Rodgers's blues style, they created an edgy style. They were early proponents of "rockin' boogie," a precursor of rock 'n roll. They recorded "Lonesome Yodel Blues."

- *The Hammer Fall,* Bear Family, 1984.
- *Lonesome Yodel Blues,* Delmore Brothers, Old Homestead, 1985.
  Obscure Bluebird material recorded between 1933 and 1940.

Merle Haggard (b. 1937) is a complicated guy—transgressive and confrontational. But he can sing—Sammy Davis Jr. once called Haggard the greatest country singer since Hank Williams. He's also one of the most original and enduring country talents; he plays fiddle and guitar, and he is a bandleader and excellent songwriter. He has a knack for intense, well-crafted songs with sinewy melodies that exude emotional and geo-psychological complexity. He has often used Jimmie Rodgers's Blue Yodel as a tool to add intensity to lyrical content. An in-between-the-words flourish that makes the lyrics knock around in new ways. This he may have learned from Lefty Frizzell ("Brakeman Blues") and Hank Williams. He recently did a yodeling novelty number, "Yo-deling," a duet with LeAnne Rimes. It's a Ray Stevens–style story about a guy named "Yo" who thinks every yodel song is about him. A better sample: "Nearly Lose Your Mind."

- *Same Train, A Different Time: Merle Haggard Sings the Great Songs of Jimmie Rodgers*, Koch, 1990s (1969).
- *Merle Haggard Salutes the Greats*, Capitol, 1980. 2–record set: one side each devoted to Williams, Wills, Frizzell, and Rodgers.

Grandpa (Louis Marshall) Jones was a comic singer who yodeled and wore make up to make him appear twenty years older than he was. His specialty was banjo picking and a folksy singing style that was humorous, twangy, and capable of an occasional yodel. He became a regular at the Opry in 1946. He died of a stroke just after an Opry performance in 1998.

- *Grandpa Jones' Yodeling Hits*, with Ray Edenton, Monument, 1950s.

Light Crust Doughboys. Were they the first super-group? Well, certainly the first commercially sponsored one. Bob Wills, Milton Brown, and "Zeke" Campbell during the 1930s and 1940s forged an inspired fusion of old-time fiddle music and hot swingin' jazz—the roots and future of Western Swing. They were open-minded with a broad repertoire and made creative use of electric guitar and bass. Their vocals are superb—not overly sentimental, but stylish with a tidy edge. Jerry Elliott's and Art Greenhaw's singing-yodeling perfectly balance a respect for the past and a curiosity for the future and is evident on uptempo "Toy Yodeler."

- *The Light Crust Doughboys–Lone Star State Swing*, Cattle. Roots recordings 1935–1941.

Ken and Simone MacKenzie (Ken died in 1993; Simone in 1984) were true pioneers of New England country. Ken's career began at 18 in that yodel hub of Manchester, New Hampshire. Here he produced a weekly radio show and toured New England with his tent show until 1938, when he moved to Maine to continue producing radio on WGAN. In 1941, his wife joined him and they became a duet. He was inducted into the Maine Country Music Hall of Fame in 1978; Simone was inducted in 1984. They were too busy to release records while they were alive, but a posthumous CD is now available. To quote Pierre Brau-Arnauty of Radio Montagnes in France: "Any traditional country DJ who doesn't play this CD, should be hung by Wilf Carters necktie."

- *I'm Following The Stars*, own label, 1995. Compiled from radio transcriptions.

Bill Monroe (1911–1997) was a true giant of American music. He basically linked the blue to the grass with his soulful, inspired mandolin playing. Much of his technique was cribbed from black musicians he watched in his youth. He dueted with his brother in the 1930s but established the ground-breaking group, The Blue Grass Boys, in 1938. His yodel was terse and piercing. He yodeled periodically and quite famously on Jimmie Rodgers's "Muleskinner Blues" in 1940.

- *Blue Moon of Kentucky*, Sony, 1993.
- *Columbia Historic Edition*, Columbia, 1984.

Jesse Rogers (Rodgers; 1910–1970)—Jimmie Rodgers's cousin—tried to use the family name to career advantage. But in 1937, after too much comparison with his famous cousin, he dropped the "d" from "Rodgers." He was a Rodgers fan and was influenced enough to record in his style, but he never imitated his voice. Jesse had only one song that hit the Top 40— in 1949. He ultimately paid the price for being a (lesser) Rodgers. His hillbilly singing and yodeling songs (1930s–1950s) are marvelous, however. "Little Girl Dressed in Blues" is a good example.

- *Wedding Bells*, Cattle. Composed of 26 Bluebird, Victor, and Sonora masters with some yodeling and steel guitar.

LeAnn Rimes (b. 1982) is an amazing Jackson, Mississippi, talent who in 1996, at age 13, covered Patsy Cline's "Blue" and took it to #10. She won a Grammy for Country Song of the Year before she was a high school sophomore. She was 14 when she covered "Cattle Call" with Eddy Arnold. Rimes began singing at age 2, was on stage at age 7, was recording an album at age 11, and by 13 had a contract with Curb records.

- *Unchained Melody: The Early Years*, MCG, 1997.
- *Blue*, Curb/MCG Records, 1996. Includes "Cattle Call," with Eddy Arnold, the guy who made this song a hit. She does some winning yodeling here.

Peter Rowan has a reputation that made him a legend before he was even old. Bluegrass today is in part defined by Rowan's yodeling and singing. He expanded its boundaries to make it into a kind of World music. He played guitar and sang with Bill Monroe & His Blue Grass Boys (1964–67). He is best known for his yodeling on "Mule Skinner Blues".

- *Bluegrass Masters*, Vanguard, 1996. Includes Bill Monroe with Rowan, among others. Recorded at the 1965–1966 Newport Folk Festivals.
- *Old & In the Way* (*Live*), Grateful Dead Records, 1996. Rerelease of 1973 landmark disc that bridged traditional and progressive bluegrass.

Donald "Butch" Seeley (1937–2002) was born in coal-mining country, Wilkes Barre, Pennsylvania. When he was 12, he taught himself to play guitar, sing, and yodel. He won some local talent contests and went on to be a three-time winner on the popular *Ted Mack Amateur Hour*. He developed an electric rockabilly sound and performed on the *Ed Sullivan Show*. He formed his own band, The Seeley Rangers, with his sister. Seeley was "a superb natural yodeler, this specialty usually had Donny's audiences cheering for more," according to Jane Gilday, of the The, who jammed with Seeley and got to know him in the late 1970s. After a heart attack, Gilday notes, "he had a vision: a tiny blue angel appeared to him and told him he had been given a great gift, the ability to sing and bring joy to people and he should use this gift. He recovered and indeed returned to performing, playing anywhere he might be let on stage."

Earl Shirkey (1900–1951) recorded some 78–rpm sides in the late 1920s that highlight his yodeling. He's accompanied by the enterprising guitarist Roy Harvey, who was a member of Charlie Poole's groups. Shirkey, a peach-hauler in South Carolina and Georgia, would set up his stand along the dusty roadside and round up some kids to sell peaches, presumably so he could go back to his yodeling. Shirkey was to be Okeh Records' answer to Columbia's Skillet Lickers. Shirkey even goes so far as to mimic Gid Tanner's trademark wild falsetto on numerous recordings.

- *Roy Harvey: Complete Recorded Works*, vols. 2–3, Document, 2000. Includes Shirkey yodeling or singing on ten tracks.

Margo Smith, a Tennessee yodeler, became an almost instant country star in 1975 with her "There I Said It." Her "Save Your Kisses For Me" and "Paper Lovin'" also hit the *Billboard* Top 10. She had #1 hits with "Little Things Mean a Lot" (atrociously covered by Jayne Mansfield) and "It Only Hurts for a Little While." She's a Master Yodeler and was awarded the title of "World Class Yodeler." Her most popular yodel song is a cover of Patsy Montana's "I Want to Be a Cowboy's Sweetheart." Smith also recorded with Swiss yodeler Peter Hinnen. Smith now duets with daughter Holly and can be found on the Christian Country charts.

Canadian Hank "the Yodeling Ranger" Snow. By permission of Richard Weize.

- *The Best of the Tennessee Yodeler*, own label, 1987.

Hank Snow (1914–1999) was one of country yodeling's big dignitaries—despite having been a Canadian. He sold some 70 million copies of more than 100 albums! He wrote most of his own songs—often about traveling, trains, moving along. His biggest hit, "I'm Movin' On," was #1 for most of 1950. He also defined that Nashville spangled Liberace-meets-hayseed look.

Snow grew up in an unhappy broken home and didn't finish the 6th grade. His stepfather, Snow said, "treated me like a dog. I still carry scars across my body from his beatings." He and his sister fled home, tromping nine miles on a snowy night to another sister's house. He never forgot this and often donated time and money to child-abuse organizations. Snow once remarked, "It changes a child's personality. And it never leaves you."

In 1929, his mom surprised him with some Jimmie Rodgers discs. Snow found his early inspiration in Rodgers's restless wandering songs. He worked odd jobs to buy a $6 mail-order guitar, and in 1933, he emerged as "The Cowboy Blue Yodeler," followed by "Hank, the Yodeling Ranger," but after his falsetto went false he became "Hank, the Singing Ranger." He produced his first record, "Lonesome Blue Yodel," in 1936 (Bluebird/RCA). His subsequent discs sold well in Canada but did not make their way across the border. Snow and his performing horse, Shawnee, went to Hollywood, where he failed to become the next singing cowboy but *did* land some radio gigs in Dallas and West Virginia on WWVA's "Wheeling Jamboree." He only crept into the U.S. market because of Ernest Tubb's support; Tubb even got him on the Opry stage, and that is where he stayed—for some 40 years. In the late 1980s, Snow was dropped by RCA (after 45 years). He became an embittered, disillusioned performer who was lampooned in Robert Altman's *Nashville*.

- *The Yodelling Ranger*, 5–CD set, Bear Family, 1994. Enough Snow yodeling for a lifetime.
- *The Singing Ranger* vols. 1–4 (29 CDs!), Bear Family, 1989–1995.
- *The Essential Hank Snow*, RCA-Nashville, 1997.

Kenneth Threadgill is the Texas Blues singer-yodeler who taught Janis Joplin to yodel! *Singin' the Yodeling Blues*, Claude Anthony Mathews's 1984 documentary, profiles Threadgill.

Ernest Tubb (1914–1984), "Texas Troubadour," beer salesman, and bar owner began his career as an earnest Jimmie Rodgers wannabe. He worshipped JR, even befriending Rodgers's widow who let him perform in Rodgers's suits and strum Rodgers's Martin guitar on stage. She invested in Tubb to help him (and *her*) "go places." The labels on Tubb's early singles said it all: "singing and yodeling with accompaniment on Jimmie Rodgers' own guitar." A fateful tonsillectomy and disobeying doctor's orders early in his career pretty much kaboshed his yodeling talents.

- *Yellow Rose of Texas*, 5–CD-set, Bear Family, 1994. Catch his yodel before it disappeared into conversational baritone. His yodel loss ironically became the key to his success, however. Includes "Jimmie Rodgers' Last Blue Yodel."

Wesley Tuttle (b. 1917) is a forgotten giant of West Coast country. In 1944, he became the second country artist signed to Capitol, and his second record, "With Tears in My Eyes," topped the country charts in 1945. Tuttle was a popular radio and TV star, and a top West Coast session musician, plus a western B-movie star.

- *Wesley Tuttle: Detour*, 4–CD/DVD/Book, Bear Family, 2002. You'll never need another Tuttle disc.

Slim Whitman (b. Otis Dewey Whitman Jr., 1924), Florida country singer and gifted yodeler, has made a career-long series of choices to undermine his artistic reputation. Somewhere along the way all the wrinkles and soul got ironed out. But make no mistake, his choices have led to success and wealth, in part because he shucked his own discs on late-night TV, where he bragged about outselling even Elvis. His truly clarion yodel and his smooth, flexible voice made him one of the first country crossover successes to go onto U.K. and international fame. Whitman's 1952 hit "Indian Love Call" (music: Rudolph Friml, words: Otto Harbach, Oscar Hammerstein II), a song from the popular operetta, *Rose Marie*, reached #10 in the United Kingdom, #2 on U.S. country charts and #10 on U.S. pop charts. "Cattle Call" became a Top 10 country hit in 1955. Whitman had a 1961 hit with the standard "I'll Take You Home Again Kathleen" (1876). All of his hundreds of LPs have been repackaged under various titles. A good Whitman yodeler: "Tennessee Yodel Polka."

- *Rose Marie: 1949–1959*: 6-CD set, Bear Family, 1996. All you'll ever need of Whitman's crooning/yodeling.

Roxanne Ward's documentary *Meet Roxanne Ward "World Champion Hog Caller,"* 1990s, tells how to become a champ caller. First you have to know the difference between a pig and a hog and a call and a yodel. Ward tells how. In her Texas home we meet yodeling teachers Rusty Hudelson, Tania Moody, and Steve Garner who perform a "Hog Calling Yodel" song. Ward also performs her porky-scat singing that booms five miles—about the distance the stench of pig manure travels.

Hank Williams is *the* most famous of country-western singers and needs little introduction. His singing, life, and death are by now a well-known nihilistic hagiography of live-fast-die-young. The soul of Williams's singing hinged on his ability to break his voice, like the crack of an awkward and emotional teen; it is a brittle voice that hints at our individual frailty. His yodeling was used to thwack words in half or stretch the moan of a vowel. Nick Tosches called it "Hank's cockeyed quasi-yodeling in 'Lovesick Blues.'" Williams, one of the best stylists in the Ernest Tubb tradition and under the tutelage of Fred Rose, gave country soul. "Hank couldn't yodel," Tubb recalled, long after death had ended their friendship. "He could break his voice pretty good like he did on 'Lovesick Blues' and other things, but that wasn't a real yodel." His voice doesn't break so much as splinter or fracture, like thin ice cracking across a frozen lake. There are countless repackagings of Williams's material.

- *48 Original Recordings*, Prism, 2003.
- *American Legend: Best of the Early Years*, Universal, 1994.

Tex Williams (Sollie Paul Williams, 1917–1985) was a West Coast swing guy (born in Illinois) who discovered his gift for yodeling as a young strapling, precisely when he did his best yodeling. When his voice finally broke, it broke big-time, down to "a deep, rich baritone . . . and his yodeling days ended." Thereafter, he became known as the guy with that smooth, warm baritone and sense of melody as the lead vocalist-guitarist in Spade Cooley's band. He left in 1946 to lead his own band, Tex Williams and the Western Caravan. He also starred in plenty of forgettable B-movie oaters. He had a huge hit with Merle Travis's "Smoke! Smoke! Smoke (That Cigarette)." He died of lung cancer at age 68.

Bob Wills and his Texas Playboys, Western Swing's standard bearers, were on the cutting edge between jazz, country, blues, and yodeling. Blue collar-intellectual dance music to forget the work week. Wills was an inveterate experimenter, never content with things as they were. His influence deserves volumes. He provided the fertile framework for a number of yodel songs and yodelers to perform within this creative and challenging atmosphere. Wills even managed to squeeze a few yodels from his slender vocal cords. A good example is "Yodeling Mountains."

- *The Bob Wills Anthology*, Sony Music, 1995 (1970s).
- *Take Me Back To Tulsa*, 4-CD set, Proper, 2001.

9

A Cowboy's Yip to a Yodel

Answering the question of whether a real cowboy—the guy responsible for rounding up the herd—is the source of manufactured cowboy yodeling withers down to a lack of hard evidence. Because notations of *authentic* yodeling cowboy songs do not exist, cowboy yodelers did not exist. Cowboys, many insist, didn't yodel until the 20th century when Tin Pan Alley pranced west. However, from an aesthetic point of view, none of this matters; who cares whether anyone was a real cowboy or "just" some professional entertainer? I'd rather listen to fake cowgal Patsy Montana than real cowboy Ken Maynard any day. Then again, yodeling *could* have been part of the "trail" cowboy's daily work routine calls aimed at getting the herding and corralling jobs done. Maybe the cowboys yodeled in the herds by day and serenaded their bunkmates at night, or maybe they just weren't adventurous-creative enough to put song and yodel together.

Many 19th-century cowboy standards became distinctive once they had a yodel refrain tacked on to the chorus. There are many examples: "The Old Chisholm Trail" and "Cattle Call," among many others, were sung (but presumably not yodeled) by blood-and-whiskey cowboys who controlled their herds along the Southwest's cattle routes. Then, at some point, it became popular or commercially expedient to add some fandangled yodel refrains. Maybe they were dedicated followers of fashion, or maybe it just welled up out of their existential loneliness. Although no evidence exists that singing cowboys—the bunkhouse-campfire serenaders—yodeled, it does not necessarily rule out the *possibility*. Whatever the case, many of the standards that the *real* cowboys sang—"Get Along Little

Dogies"—became the very songs that later served as hat racks for yodel refrains.

Yodeler Liz Masterson believes real cowboys probably yodeled:

> it makes sense to me that any kind of herdsman would use this high-pitched [yodel] sound to go across the herd. I mean, if the cattle are all lowing in a low sound—"mwaaawwwnnn"—kinda down there [chest] and suddenly they would do a "WOOOOOoooOOO" kinda thing . . . a high-pitched sound like that would go across the herd. . . . I know that cowboys use [these calls] because even today on ranches I visit, I hear people making these not-so-musical sounds. But definitely you can hear a yodel in them where they're goin' "Weee-Yip Geee-Yip Geee-Yip" to move the cattle along and that can work itself a little more musical "Geee-Yip-ee de deee dee deee yooO dee." So, I think the two can go right together.

Douglas B. Green believes "yodeling . . . was never associated with the cowboy before Gene Autry [1930s] brought it to the screen, except in the handful of cowboy songs of Jimmie Rodgers." This is nothing controversial; this is *the* cow-scrivener cant. He does, however, admit:

> It is probable that when there was singing there was the use of the falsetto voice; a melody hummed in falsetto might generously be termed a yodel, but it is extremely unlikely this ever went beyond the "whoo, whoo" sounds in a song like "Cattle Call." It is conceivable that a kind of proto-yodeling was what Dobie was trying to describe when he referred to "the indescribable whistle of the cowboy," but to the traditional cowboy singer the mournful blue yodels of Jimmie Rodgers or the athletic yodels of the Alps were unknown and unanticipated.

Nonetheless, there *is* evidence to suggest that yodeling was not "unknown" to cowboys. In her 1905 novel *The Spirit of the Mountains*, Emma B. Miles described the prototypical cowboy: "[He] conquers his chosen bit of wilderness . . . fighting and praying. His are the adventures of which future ballads will be sung. . . . His first songs are the yodel. Then he learns . . . songs of fighting and drinking." Miles indeed suggests that cowboys were yodeling prior to 1905. After all, cowboys were already singing on the western plains by the 1830s. The songs "Texas Ranger" and "Texas Soldier Boy" presumably date from that period, and like most of the others, were standard British folk tunes with original lyrics expressing the personal experiences of pioneer-cowboys. So, the West had the songs, the herder job descriptions, the Alpine immigrants, the freed "hollerin'" slaves, *and* the falsetto-singing Mexican *vaqueros*—all ingredients that could have stimulated yodeling.

If real cowboys didn't yodel, then the icon of the cowboy was hijacked by non-cowpokes, only to have future generations of yodelers claim their cowboy résumé roots as part of the authenticity requirements for accredited yodeling. This is especially true of contemporary cowpoke yodelers who want to distance themselves from the disingenuousness of counterfeit Nashville and carpetbagging city folk (like Johnny Mercer who wrote "The Yodel Blues" for *Texas Lil Darlin'*, a 1949 Broadway musical). There are countless "real-life-cowboy-yodelers": Suzy Boguss, farmgirl; Randy Hollar, wrangler; Gary McMahan, cowboy—I could go on. This is not to in any way question *their* talent or sincerity. What it implies, though, is that there is a desire to be associated with *their* version of authenticity. Cowboys want their authenticity verified as cowboys *and* as yodelers precisely because the two have become inseparable integers in the equation of who is qualified to yodel cowboy style.

Cowboy Iconography

The cowboy's *spatful* iconography is a cartoonish balance between appearance and ethics. His songs were straight-shooting: lonesome, existential, moral, and work oriented. Dime novels, Buffalo Bill's spectacles, Teddy Roosevelt, Zane Grey's and other pulp novels, German storyteller Karl May's vision of the West, rodeo gigs, early radio, and records all enhanced the marketable attributes of the cowboy, spawning the celluloid cowboys both silent and singing. John Lomax's cowboy songbooks nudged romanticized cowboys into the realm of official cultural history. Ironically, however, as Bill Malone contends, "the cowboy contributed nothing to American music" except "the fabric of usable symbols, which surrounded him."

Hollywood really put the cowboy on the cultural map. Early cowboy stars Tom Mix, Tex Ritter, and the first celluloid talkie, Ken Maynard (an uncharismatic cinematic presence and tinny-voiced singer), were quickly eclipsed by two cowboys of more professional manufacture, Gene Autry and Roy Rogers. Autry's warm singing and terrific yodeling actually complemented his stilted acting. In the mid-1930s, Autry, "Oklahoma's Singing Cowboy," patterned his singing-yodeling style after Jimmie Rodgers. Autry got his early yodel chops from hosting his own radio show called the "Melody Ranch" in Tulsa, Oklahoma.

The celluloid cowboys may not have been authentic cowboys, but their spangly shimmering aberrations—Las Vegas meets Cow Pie, Texas, on a Busby Berkley acid trip—were never meant to project "cowboy" so much as "entertainer." The 1940s Hollywood cowboy dandy, a cartoon in flesh, spangles, spurs, chaps, and makeup, emerged from a dime novel into a virtual West courting a look just short of androgynous kitsch. And the more that *real* cowboys disappeared from the actual American landscape, the more they crooned and danced inside the magic lanterns of our collective nostalgic minds.

Singing cowboys, combining myth, old melodies, British ballads, and tacked-on yodel refrains, offered listeners an escape from their own hum-drum lives via their fabricated lifestyles, a fantasy life based on cowboy clichés that probably never existed except on celluloid. Anne Wortham notes that, "in 1951, Autry published his Cowboy Code of Ethics, which he urged the movie industry to use as guidelines for cowboy characteriza-tions." It all blended into a sentimental paint-by-number portrait: a dab of Broadway, a brush stroke of jazz, some dabs of Mexican, Czech polkas, German *lieden*, southern ballads, fiddle tunes, and yodeling.

GENE AUTRY

Orvon Gene Autry (1907–1999) was born on a Texas farm in the middle of next to nowhere. It's said he was born on the back of a horse with a guitar in his hand, but we know better. His father showed him the cattleman life while his mother sang to him. Autry's family moved to Oklahoma, where he finished school and did farm and railroad work. Here he strummed his gui-tar and sang when work was slow. He also met Jimmie Long. They formed a duo and wrote some songs, among them "That Silver-Haired Daddy of Mine" and others in imitation of their hero, Jimmie Rodgers. Autry also performed in The Fields Brothers Marvelous Medicine Show during his teens, developing his yodeling and guitar-picking confidence until he became a dead-ringer for Rodgers.

In 1928, confident hayseed Autry ventured to New York to seek his singing fortunes, auditioning for Victor Records, which summarily sent him packing back to Oklahoma. In Tulsa, he sang on radio station KVOO and began being called "Oklahoma's Yodeling Cowboy." In 1929, he returned to New York to record "My Dreaming of You" (Johnny Marvin) and "My Alabama Home" (Jimmy Long) just days before the Wall Street crash. In 1931, "That Silver-Haired Daddy of Mine," a duet with Jimmy Long, became Autry's first million-seller. Ironically, it was Autry's first deviation from the Rodgers's imitation sweepstakes.

Rodgers's imitations aside, Autry had fairly eclectic tastes, but in a period of a few years he shucked his rough-hewn side—the "blue" record-ings, his hillbilly mannerisms, and folksy material—opting for smooth, inof-fensive cowboy pop. This probably had more to do with his business acu-men and the decisions of his producer, the legendary Arthur Satherley, who "discovered" Bessie Smith, Bob Wills, and Blind Lemon Jefferson. "The

Gene Autry,
"Oklahoma's
Yodeling Cowboy."

Last Roundup" was first a *Ziegfeld Follies* Broadway hit before heading out West with Autry recording it in Chicago in 1933, complete with yodeling. It became Autry's first cowboy hit.

In 1934, Autry auditioned at Republic Studios and became their celluloid singing cowboy. He made 100 B-movies and, although he was as stiff as roadkill on screen—"I moved like my parts needed oiling, and I didn't like the way I looked or sounded"—the studio managed to appeal to fans of his music by naming movies after his most popular songs. These flicks were so formulaic that they could be shot in a week, giving Autry plenty of time for his radio singing engagements. In 1940, Wrigley's Doublemint Gum sponsored his show, "The Melody Ranch," and it wasn't long before he was so popular that the town of Berwyn, near his birthplace, changed its name to Gene Autry, Oklahoma. A line of Autry guitars appeared in mail-order catalogues. In 1939, 1 million Dubliners lined the streets to watch Autry ride his four-legged partner, Champion, down the street.

Autry performed regularly to Chicago's WLS—like all good yodelers— until the mid-1930s, when he left for California to stay. Here he honed his cowboy image into a marketable shimmer of outlandish spangly cowboy outfits looking like something scaly stripped off the back of a tropical fish crossbred in a Vegas dressing room. Autry's personal vocal style was one of lukewarmed-over relaxed perfection. It made people feel . . . comfortable, like some tumbleweed Bing Crosby. In 1961, he rode out on his last tour, with The Riders of the Purple Sage.

Autry developed into the personal embodiment of hard work and the American dream. He became one of the most famous men in the world, not only as a singer, songwriter, actor, and movie star, but also as a business executive and real estate owner. He owned radio and TV stations, hotels, cattle ranches, real estate, oil wells, stock, and more. He invested shrewdly and eventually became the multimillionaire owner of the California Angels baseball team, for which he became so renowned most people never realized he had once been a cowboy yodeler!

- *42 All-time Classics*, 3-CD set, Bear Family.
- *Sing, Cowboy, Sing! The Gene Autry Collection*, Rhino, 1997.
- *Yodeling Gene Autry: The Life Of Jimmie Rodgers*, Cattle, 1980s. Originally recorded 1930–1935.
- *Gene Autry, Blues Singer 1929–1931*, Columbia Legacy, 1996. Depression-era recordings reveal Autry's ascension from Rodgers' shadow into a fine melodic singer, lyricist, and yodeler of his own yodels.
- *The Early Yodeling Days of Gene Autry*, Cattle, 1980s.

ROY ROGERS

Guess when I go, Dale will stuff me and put me right on Trigger

Roy Rogers (1911–1998) was born Leonard Slye in Cincinnati, and became a megastar who peaked for nearly a quarter century. He ruled the tube into the 1960s as a be-spurred cowboy (ironically, Rogers was part Choctaw Indian) idol of millions of kids for whom he became a sagebrush-Christian role model—and an incredibly wonderful yodeler.

Rogers grew up on an Ohio farm in Duck Run, Ohio, where his father made guitars but worked in a shoe factory to make ends meet. His father bought a cylinder player (prephonograph) and some cylinders, including one of a Swiss yodeler. Rogers began yodeling back and forth to his mother and sisters while they worked in the fields, employing different yodels for different situations: storm warnings, announcing dinner, and so on. This makes him probably one of the only North American yodelers who actually used yodeling for its original long-distance communication purpose. These early field calls were to develop into a unique smooth and lucid yodeling style.

During the Depression, Rogers journeyed into California's farm belt in search of work. Here "he picked peaches for Del Monte," according to Laurence Zwisohn in the *King of the Cowboys* CD liner notes, "and lived in the same labor camps John Steinbeck wrote about . . . in . . . *The Grapes of Wrath*." Rogers took up performing in 1931, yodeling live on California radio in a cowboy shirt his sister had sewn for him. He joined a local band, the Rocky Mountaineers, and sang "The Swiss Yodel" for a lemon pie. He cofounded the Pioneer Trio, which evolved into the legendary Sons of the Pioneers. Here Leonard Slye became Roy Rogers fronting the Pioneers with his smooth delivery and clear, crisp yodeling. Rogers and the Sons of the Pioneers created some of the most enduring and classically classy close-harmony cowboy music.

Rogers left the Pioneers to become a movie star in the late 1930s. He made more than ninety films with his palomino "Trigger." His wife, Dale Evans, a singer in dance bands, joined Rogers in 1944 and became his maternal sidekick in life, song, and film. Rogers was the first cowboy to transform yodeling into a virtuosic embellishment that was both playful and technically beautiful.

Along the trail, Rogers used his media fame to merchandise his image, open a chain of Roy Rogers fast food restaurants, and thump the pulpit, promoting not only obedience through his Cowboy Code but a Christian message as well. Rogers Club members were encouraged to pray along with Roy's Cowboy Prayer: "Lord, when trails are steep and passes high, help me to ride it straight the whole way through . . . Amen." And he did it all with that charming, winning smirk—goodness and integrity on *six* legs. But, for all his lustrous stardom, Rogers had to wait until 1988 when he was already 77 years of age to be inducted into the Country Music Hall of Fame.

There are countless examples of his exemplary yodeling: the buoyantly sexist and pro-equine "Four-legged Friend," "My Little Lady," "My Saddle Pals and I," "Pony Boy," and "Devil's Great Grandson."

- *King of the Cowboys*, 4-CD set, Bear Family, 1983. Rare archival gems from radio broadcast transcriptions and live performances.
- *Happy Trails: 1937–1990*, 3-CD set, Rhino, 1999. Thorough documentation plus all the song classics and intriguing unreleased material.

WYLIE GUSTAFSON

I think that folks are tired of being beat over the head with the corporate answers to modern music.

Wylie Gustafson is a dynamic catalyst in the renaissance of rootsy yodeling in this umpteenth reinvention of country music. He's popular and his yodeling style's beguilingly smooth. He's on top of his game, plays the Opry, and, when he takes a break, he's not really taking a break because he's tending a sprawling 900–acre ranch outside Dusty, Washington [pop. 11±].

But in April 2002, yodeling entered the annals of corporate litigation history when it was reported that Internet behemoth Yahoo! had settled over the note-poaching of a mere three notes of a yodel that Wylie Gustafson had performed for a trademark soundbyte that Yahoo! uses in its advertising. Wylie had originally been under the impression that the ad was for regional use by the then fledgling, little-known Internet company, Yahoo!. But when this start up went big, international, and global, and it began reusing his yodel in countless TV ads including during the lucrative Super Bowl without due compensation Wylie decided to sue for copyright infringement. And as Gustafson noted in a *Los Angeles Times* article, "Anything with a musical melody is copyrightable. It's not like I'm just yelling or screaming. There is a definite musical structure to that yodel." The two parties settled amicably and quickly, and so the distinctive Wylie yodel will continue to echo as the Yahoo! audio signature.

There must be a physical place in the brain that functions as a conduit, as a place where experience is blended with talent and enthusiasm like a faucet that blends hot and cold—that faucet may very well be the throat of Wylie Gustafson. I asked Wylie if he considered himself a yodeler or a singer who sometimes yodels. He replied:

I consider myself a yodeler. I yodel every day. Whether it's to a crowd or to my cattle. It has become a part of my life. My first contact was my father. He'd yodel whenever he was happy. On top of the ski hill. Out riding through the cattle. I started imitating his yodel when I was about 12 years old.

The yodel impressed me when my dad did it. Then I heard it on a radio station. . . . I was mesmerized! I was inspired to try it. My brother had a record by New Riders of the Purple Sage. They had a song called ["Louisiana Lady"]. That was the first yodel song I learned in the 1970s. I wrote "The Yodeling Fool" in 1989. It has become the anchor of our set every time we perform. It also is kind of a true story about my life.

Wylie believes yodeling is "spiritual" music: "It's an art form unto itself. It can be happy, it can be sad—it's a very emotional thing for me. I use it in our shows to lift the crowd . . . then settle them into a peaceful state . . . all with the style that I choose throughout the set. . . . I yodel to my cattle and horses every morning. They identify me with my yodel and it calms and assures them."

continued on the next page

Wylie Gustafson, continued

Wylie Gustafson and the Wild West have become prominent figures in the modern fusion of infectious country dance music, which seems equally at home in the straw and dung venues as under the disco balls of urban nightclubs. They blend western swing, old-time country dancehall, rockabilly, and folk music. The Wild West is Wylie, Ray Doyle, Dave Reynolds, T. Scot Wilburn, and Duane Becker.

- *Paradise*, Rounder, 2001.

- *Ridin' the Hi-Line* on Rounder, 2000.

- *Total Yodel*, Rounder, 1998.

- *Way Out West*, Rounder, 1997.

COWBOY SWEETHEARTS: CLASSIC YO-DE-LADIES

The 1930s cowboy craze also corraled some wild, free-thinking, yodeling cowgirls. Women dressed up and got down to do some of the most charming yodelin' ever warbled. The most famous was Patsy Montana, but there were countless others. Montana's disciple, Janet McBride, has helped keep yodeling alive well beyond its heyday into the present-day.

PATSY MONTANA

Patsy Montana (b. Ruby(e) Blevins, 1914–1996) needs no introduction. She is *the* most famous genuine-fake cowgal of all time and the first female country singer to have a million-seller with 1935's "I Wanna Be a Cowboy's Sweetheart" (featured in John Sayle's 1996 film, *Lone Star*). Montana began her musical career as a fiddler at the height of Jimmie Rodgers's success. Everyone was sussing out the Rodgers's formula: yodeling, blues, cowboys—whatever it took. Blevins changed her name to Montana, donned some flashy cowboy gear, and began singing and songwriting before setting out to find her own place in the hearts and ears of cowboy yodel fans.

Montana wrote "Sweetheart" in an Illinois dressing room while she was on tour with Gene Autry. It was meant as a valentine to her then-fiancé and as a tribute to a song she loved to sing, "Texas Plains." Although "Sweetheart" is pretty much a carbon copy of "Plains," Montana's tune became original by virtue of her exuberant singing and vivacious conviction. You just never doubted her. That it was sung by a woman didn't hurt either. She broke through the barbed-wire fence that separated her from success on an all-boy's ranch. Montana became a trailblazer, an inspiration to aspiring female singers everywhere including the DeZurik Sisters, Good Sisters, Ethel Delaney, Janet McBride . . . "Sweetheart" has been covered by just about every woman country singer that ever graced a stage or attempted a yodel—Rosalie Allen, Janet McBride, Yodelin' Betty, Manuela, Patsy Prescott, Judy Coder, Suzy Bogguss, LeAnn Rimes—there are literally hundreds of versions of "Sweetheart." And that Montana performed it with such breezy cheery yodeling panache made it all the more effective. Indeed, she blazed a happy trail to the promised land with one long enchanted career. Apparently, she was yodeling right up till just before she died.

That many continue to call Montana a "genuine" cowgal is testament to her earnestness and believability. That she was born in Arkansas and grew up in urban California and never worked a day on a ranch didn't matter. Montana certainly has her own corner in every country hall of fame where she is no doubt labeled a real-life, genuine country yodeling star. Montana produced hundreds of singles as a solo artist and with the Prairie Ramblers—many of these include her yodeling, because she was one of those real yodelers, a singer whose repertoire was fearlessly filled with yodel songs.

- *Very Early Patsy Montana & the Prairie Ramblers*, Cattle, 1981. Very early material, some with yodels, from the 1930s–1940s.
- *Early Country Favorites*, Old Homestead, 1983.
- *Golden Age of the Late Patsy Montana*, Cattle, 2000.
- *New Sound of Patsy Montana at the Matador Room*, Patsy Montana with Waylon Jennings, Sims Records, 1964.
- *The Cowboy's Sweetheart*, Flying Fish, 1988.

JANET MCBRIDE

Montana's greatest disciple is McBride, who has done her time as a yodeler—60 years worth, and she's proud of it. In fact, she's one of only a handful of yodelers who performs almost exclusively yodel songs. This commitment shouldn't go unrewarded in an age where performers commonly groom their talents to marketplace demographics. She yodels, take it or leave it!

McBride recalls the first time she "ever let out a yodel":

My mother had the four of us kids playing four corner catch so that we would stay clean while we waited for a traveling photographer to come and take our picture. We were playing toss with an apple because we didn't have a ball. When it came my turn to catch the apple I missed it and it rolled into the taller grass. I couldn't find it and . . . so as I searched for the apple I started singing a little song and added a yodel to it. When I turned around, I realized that I had just done something totally new. They were all shocked at the "noise I was making." I was hooked from that moment on. It was spring 1942.

She has distinguished herself ever since, on record and stage, has won numerous yodeling contests and sang (but didn't yodel) a duet with Skeets McDonald as part of the soundtrack to the 1963 Paul Newman film *Hud*.

Even now in her later years, McBride continues to tour and yodel. Until 1996, she co-owned and hosted the "Saturday Night Show" (aka the Mesquite Opry) with husband, John Ingram. Patsy Montana thought the club was "like the Grand Ole Opry in Nashville . . . used to sound." In any case, that's where she held court for fifteen years as "boss lady," as Montana described her. McBride remains a yodel missionary of the most effective kind—an excellent yodeler, wonderful entertainer with a vibrant yodel. "I work with lots of young people," she explains, "where I do my best to 'pass on' all the patterns and yodel runs that I have stored up in my brain. I love what is happening with yodeling. . . . I am the person who taught LeAnn Rimes how to yodel when she was just a 7–year-old child." (Rimes personally thanks McBride in the liner notes to *Blue*.)

McBride was born in Inglewood, California, during the Depression, the third of four children. She started early, singing gospel at churches with her siblings as the Lister Quartet. Despite a decade that saw them traveling cross-country back and forth in a beat-up station wagon between California and Chelsea, Maine, throughout much of the 1940s she still managed to listen to some yodeling on the radio. She heard her first cowboy yodeling in 1942, on the radio. Janet remembers being amazed whenever yodeling was featured. "I was very young when I first heard yodeling," McBride remembers "and . . . it was probably the radio station's 'early morning' live cowboy music shows."

She soon had her siblings yodeling as well. With Janet as lead yodeler of the Lister Quartet, they appeared regularly on shows like "Meet the Mike" on WRDO in Augusta, Maine. They also played the occasional local grange or school show, but that was about it. By the time McBride was 14 she was known as "The Little Girl with the Big Voice." She never stopped practicing guitar or yodeling. "I practiced all of the time," remembers McBride, "and it didn't matter to me who was around. I just let it out. My brothers and sister often made me walk by myself on the way to and from school and I would often make all of the neighbors mad. Many trailer courts we lived in, we were moved to an area where we had no close neighbors to disturb."

The Yodeling Queen and the Harbor Playboys. By permission of Janet McBride.

In 1954, brother Don and sister Joan left the Quartet, leaving only McBride and brother Dan. That same year, McBride was introduced to a young sailor, Claude McBride, whom she married in 1955. Claude was impressed and thought Janet was just as good as Kitty Wells. In 1959, Claude took over managing McBride's career, getting her gigs at local nightclubs. (It's beginning to sound a little like *Coal Miner's Daughter*.) But he had greater ambitions. They drove straight down to Nashville to give Webb Pierce and Chet Atkins her demo tape. They liked it, but not enough to offer her a contract.

Claude didn't give up; he approached a local DJ and owner of Toppa Records. McBride's eventually released five singles on Toppa and got some regional airplay. McBride's popularity spread during the early 1960s, releasing records on Galahad, Brookhurst, Sims, and Longhorn. In 1963 and 1964, she carried home the award for "Female Artist of the Year" at the Southern California Country Music Awards (predecessor of the Academy of Country Music).

In the ensuing years, they moved to Texas, Nashville, where she worked as a beautician to support the family, her husband died, she got remarried—to John Ingram, who encouraged her to start singing and yodeling again. McBride began performing on the Grapevine Opry Country Music Show in 1979. In 1981, they bought the place and created the Mesquite Opry Saturday Night Country Music Show. They ran it for nearly fifteen years. McBride only began recording again, however, after being contacted by Dagmar Binge of the German labels Binge and Cattle. This meant that for the first time in her life she had worldwide distribution. It certainly rejuvenated her career! McBride is still writing and recording. But even more interestingly, she has become the mother of yodeling. She mentors young yodelers among whom we can count not only Rimes, as mentioned earlier, but also Lee Ann Womack, Richie McDonald of Lone Star, Tim Rushlow of Little Texas, and David Bradley and Ken Lattimore both of The Sons of the Pioneers. Her CDs are issued on her own label unless otherwise indicated.

- *50 Years of Yodeling with Janet McBride*, 2-CD set, 2002. Fifty-five yodeling songs, 1951–2002.
- *Wyoming Rose*, 2001. Mostly yodeling.
- *Yodelin' Jan*, Binge. 14 songs recorded 1965–1968, including duets with Vern Stovall.
- *Yodeling at the Grand Ole Opry*, Cattle, 1985. Accompanied by Dexter Johnson and the Tennessee Mountain Boys.
- *The Texas Yodel Lady*, Cattle, 1980s. Many original yodelers with the Tennessee Valley Boys.
- *Classic Yodel Songs Collection*, 1998.
- *Yodeling Texas Cowgirl*, 1999. Recorded in Garland, Texas, and dedicated to Patsy Montana. McBride notes: "This project is as close to a tribute as I will ever do." Nine of the songs were written, recorded, or used by Montana in live performances.

SOME OTHER NOTABLE CLASSIC COWBOYGIRL YODELERS

Here's an honor roll of the (sur)real cowboys and cowgirls who've yodeled their ways into our hearts.

Rex Allen (1920–1999), "The Ambassador to the American West," was that rare film star—a real cowboy during the Depression rendered larger-than-life by celluloid. He rode a horse before he could walk and played a Sears mail-order guitar, singing wherever he was tolerated. He had a deep resonant voice that stretched three octaves by the time he was 12. In 1949, he became the last of the celluloid cowboys and by his second movie he had found "Koko the Wonder Horse," his reliable four-legged companion for some 30, assembly-line B-movie westerns! Some were shot in eight days, which allowed him to continue singing and yodeling on the radio and producing records, including the million sellers "Streets of Laredo" and "Crying in the Chapel." After the denouement of the celluloid cowboy, Allen's soothing voice became familiar to millions as a narrator on Walt Disney productions like *Old Yeller* and supplying the voice for Disney characters like Country Coyote. His warm relaxed voice and yodel are very evident on his "With Nothin' to Do."

- *Yodelin' Crazy*, Cowgirlboy, 1980s. Sixteen tracks of his rougher non-pop material from mid-1940s radio transcriptions.
- *The Hawaiian Cowboy*, Bear Family, 1986. Includes mostly yodeling.

YODELIN' SLIM CLARK

A cowboy is anyone who lives that type of life, no matter where he is.

Raymond Le Roy Clark (1917–2000) made more than 100 recordings as a cowboy yodeler and was the spiritual stepchild of Jimmie Rodgers and Wilf Carter. At age 8, he was already playing guitar and singing along to records. He worked as a woodsman before touring central Massachusetts and doing local radio. Around 1938, he got his first regular program on New Hampshire's WKNE. Here he crossed paths with another great yodeler, Kenny Roberts; as fate would have it, both had been members of the Red River Rangers. He later fronted his own band, the Trailriders.

Clark began recording in the mid-1940s in New York mostly for small labels like Continental and Palomino. Clark also hosted his own TV and radio show from 1952 to 1967 at WABI in Bangor, Maine. By 1947 he was being called the "World's Champion Yodeler." In 1965, Clark recorded a few excellent albums for Palomino records. In the 1960s, he starred on "RFD Dinnerbell," a Bangor radio show. He was mostly a solo artist for some sixty years with only his guitar as accompaniment, playing anywhere: town halls, schools, fairs, and rodeos.

Clark sang traditional cowboy, country, and folk tunes, some Montana Slim covers, and original yodel songs often cowritten with Pete Roy. Some of his most enduring songs include "The Strawberry Roan," "Rocky Mountain Yodeler," and "When You're Blue, Just Yodel." He sometimes referred to himself as the "last real singing cowboy." I suppose that was *after* Autry and Rogers died. In any case, he's the *real* thing. He was inducted into the Country Music Hall of Fame in 1996 and, a few months after his death, into the Cowboy Music Hall of Fame in Tucson, Arizona.

- *Yodelin' Slim Clark: In Memory, 1917–2000*, Old Homestead, 2001. Includes selections by family members.
- *Yodelin' Slim Clark*, Old Homestead, 2001.
- *Yodeling Slim Clark Sings & Yodels Favorite Songs* Palomino, 1966.
- *Yodeling Slim Clark Sings Jimmy Rogers* Palomino, 1966.
- *Cowboy and Yodel Songs*, Continental, 1962.

Betty Cody (b. Rita Cote, 1921) was born in Quebec, Canada, but moved to Auburn, Maine, with her large family when she was 9 months old.

Canadian, Betty Cody, not just a yodeling footnote. By permission of Richard Weize.

Her mother sang around the house in a high soprano, and her father, a carpenter, played fiddle and built violins. By the time she was 16, she was playing and singing country tunes on radio station WCOU, Lewiston, Maine. When she was 17, she met the love of her life, Harold Breau (aka Hal Lone Pine). They got married and had kids, among them Leonard Breau, a renowned musician who started out on guitar in the family band. In fact, Betty Cody's life has been unjustly relegated to that of a footnote in the life of son Leonard; she was a gifted singer-yodeler in her own right.

In 1952, Cody began recording on RCA with Hal. Her first record, "Tom Tom Yodel," became a minor hit. A year later, she moved with her family to Wheeling, West Virginia, where she and Hal were featured on the "World's Original Jamboree." "Lone Pine and Betty Cody" also toured the country circuit along the East Coast into Canada until her retirement in 1970. She moved to Maine, where she became a regular on yodeler Ken McKenzie's radio show. In 1979, she produced an album called *Singing Again* and was inducted into the Maine Country Music Hall of Fame.

- *Hal Lone Pine and His Mountaineers*, Castle.
- *Betty Cody's Country Souvenir Album*, Castle.
- *Boy Wonder*, Lenny Breau, Guitarchives, 1998. Includes an interview with Cody.

Carolina Cotton (b. Helen Hagstrom, c. 1930), was born in Cash, Arkansas, to Swedish-American parents. Her family wandered around the

Carolina Cotton, "the only
Daughter of the Sons of the
Pioneers." By permission of
Richard Weize.

West in a beat-up jalopy during her childhood. During her high school
years, Cotton was doing seventeen radio broadcasts and five dance gigs per
week. During World War II, she was given the responsibility of playing
more and more instruments every time another band member was drafted:
"I played the bass fiddle, guitar and so on. Everything but the drums." She
got her name Carolina Cotton while performing at California's shipyards.

In the 1940s, Johnny Murvin introduced Cotton to Spade Cooley, who
needed a female singer for the music in a Hollywood film "and right away
I got the part," Cotton noted, "an eight-bar-yodel in a Bing Crosby picture." On the West Coast she had plenty of opportunities to yodel in clubs
and films and even wrote a lot of her own yodel songs over the years. She
ended up in Tex Williams's band as the lead female singer and also toured
with Bob Nolan and the Sons of the Pioneers, with Cotton claiming "I was
the only Daughter of the Sons of the Pioneers." Her song "I Love to Yodel"
was featured in at least four films: *Apache Country*, in which she starred
with Autry, who yodels her tune; *Smoky River Serenade*, with Cotton starring and yodeling; *Texas Panhandle*; and *I'm from Arkansas*.

- *I Love To Yodel*, various artists, Cattle, 1993. Recorded 1946–1951.
  Includes some of her yodel compositions.

The DeZurik Sisters were a yodeling duo popular between the 1930s and 1950s. Carolyn (b. 1919) and sister Mary Jane (1917–1981) were proto-feminist pioneers. They invaded the male hayseed preserve with an infectiously successful style of singing and yodeling, which included yodeling extremely high notes. They performed some mean scat singing and could re-create the sounds of chime bells and trumpets. But most interestingly was their propensity to sound like yodeling chickens with a full repertoire of trills, whistles, and cackles. Their cackling was later encouraged by their sponsor, Purina, maker of animal feed and pet food to the point where, during World War II, they became known as the Cackle Sisters. They made an early impression on WLS's radio program, *National Barn Dance*, during the 1930s and 1940s and appeared on the Grand Ole Opry in the later '40s. Mary Jane retired in 1948 to become a full-time mother; she was replaced by a third sister, Lorraine. The new duo appeared on the Midwestern Hayride in 1949–50 but broke up shortly thereafter. Carolyn joined her husband, Rusty Gill, and his Prairie Ramblers. They went on to perform regularly on Chicago TV. They didn't record much, although songs from some of their radio shows have appeared on record. One of these was "The Arizona Yodeler," which certainly highlights their entertaining yodeling virtuosity.

The Cackle Sisters were not chicken to yodel. By permission of Richard Weize.

- *The Dezurik Sisters (Cackle Sisters) Original Songs (1930s up) Vol 1*, American Gramophone & Wireless.
- *A Yodeling Extravaganza*, Veteran Series. Precious near-perfect yodel harmonies. Includes radio excerpts.

Shirley Field (b. 1930s) grew up on a ranch in a musical family in Spallumcheen, British Columbia, where people are scarce and the cattle provide an appreciative (if captive) audience. She began yodeling at age 9, after hearing some Jimmie Rodgers discs on a neighbor's phonograph. She lived the young cowgirl life—on horseback— participating in cattle drives and composing yodel songs as a young teen. She learned the yodeling basics from her father who used to yodel on the ranch. She bought a Sears mail-order catalog guitar and she was in business.

In 1950, Field was honored as Canada's Female Yodeling Champion and starred on her own CFJC radio show "The Cowboy's Sweetheart" in British Columbia and, in 1962, played-yodeled on the Grand Ole Opry. She has toured throughout North America and continues to perform at rodeos, cowboy festivals, cattle drives, and Western shows. Her major influence is Wilf Carter, whom she befriended when she was still young. She has also been inspired by Kenny Roberts (her mentor), Roy Rogers, Patsy Montana, and Elton Britt. You can certainly hear it in her impassioned Swiss-cowboy yodeling style. She makes even the most difficult yodels sound and look easy.

Field is now more of a teacher-apostle—her mission is to pass along yodeling to as many young people as she can. She has won many awards including the Will Rodgers Bronze Yodeling Award in 1999 and the Academy of Western Artists Yodeler of the Year (1999). She was inducted into the Cowboy Hall of Fame [2000]—to certify her talent, but one listen will tell you, "I can teach you how to yodel"—maybe not like her but at least you won't stumble over the next glottal stop. She codeveloped the book/CD *How To Yodel the Cowboy Way with Rudy Robbins*. Her records appear on Wagonwheel.

- *Just A Yodel For Me*
- *Seasons Of Our Lives: Country Gospel with Yodeling*
- *Yodeling Memories*
- *He Taught Me to Yodel*
- *Together Again*. Title song written by Buck Owens, with yodeling by Field.

Dolly and Milly Good went through a marketing makeover early in their careers. Two farm gals from Illinois who had developed their western-style close-harmony duets on Chicago's "WLS Barn Dance" were transformed into "The Girls of the Golden West, born in Muleshoe, Texas." They effectively climbed into the saddle of a *virtual* West, willing to go undercover in a fictional biography set in an ersatz West imbued with a kind of synthetic sense of nostalgia. But none of this matters because they were high-spirited fun-lovin' yodelin' gals, and two of very few gals who broke through to any level of fame. So what if they claimed their yodels were influenced by the coyotes they heard howling on the dusty plains?

They sang both "Will There Be any Yodelers in Heaven" and "Will There Be Yodeling in Heaven." They recorded plenty of cowgal songs on Bluebird and Regal Zonophone, including "Whoopee-Ti-Yi-Yo Git Along Little Doggies," "Cowboy Jack," and "I Want to Be a Real Cowboy Girl." "My Love Is a Rider" (1934) is a cute, if somewhat stiffly delivered, yodel song told from a gal's point of view: the sexual connotations of lines like "he wished me to look at his buckin' bronco" are delivered somewhere between rye humor and unwitting naïveté.

- *Songs of The West*, Old Homestead, 1984. Includes rarities and classics.

The Hammer Sisters, Lillian and Ruth, were born in the 1920s and raised in Granby, Missouri. They began performing in the 1930s, using a fiddle and guitar that their father had given them as presents. They learned their songs in a unique way off the radio. One would copy the song's first line and the other would write down the next, alternating throughout the song. The only problem was, it might be weeks before they heard the song again to make sure they had it right.

In the 1940s, they had their own programs on two radio stations in Joplin, Missouri. They also performed with brother Dave in "Dave and the Prairie Sweethearts." In the 1950s, they stopped playing music to raise families and only began playing again with Dave in 1983 as the "Hammer Family" when they were in their late fifties. Dave died in 1993 and they've called themselves the "Hammer Sisters" ever since. Their Ozark heritage music features tight vocal harmonies with guitar and fiddle accompaniment and plenty of yodeling. All recordings are on Hammer Cassettes.

- *Pickin' and Singin' in the Parlor*
- *Echoes from the Hills*
- *Makin' Memories*

Randy Hollar is as likely to be branding a cow's hind end as yodeling. Another of the many real cowboys who yodels, he's been a wrangler since he left his Alberta, Canada, home at age 14. From the rodeo, he drifted into music. Hollar sings country-gospel and adds a fair bit of Wilf Carter-style yodeling (other than God, Wilf's been his main inspiration). He's been yodeling songs since his youth and has dedicated much of his output to covering Carter's songs. All of his discs are on Montana DelVega and include plenty of yodeling.

- *Bunkhouse Ballads*
- *Randy Hollar Salutes Wilf Carter*
- *The Cowboy Collection*

Laura Lee Owens McBride (1920–1989) was the yodeling-cowgirl singer-daughter of Tex Owens. A gifted Western Swing vocalist, by age 10 she was already singing with her sister on dad's own radio show in the late 1930s. She also sang with an offshoot of the Sons of the Pioneers, the Sons of the Range with whom she appeared in some dozen westerns starring Gene Autry. She was a spirited singer who fell in with Bob Wills, for whom she became the first female Western Swing singer in 1944. She recorded on Columbia with the Texas Playboys in 1945. She married bandleader Dick McBride in 1945 and toured with him as well as with Tex Ritter, George Jones, and Ernest Tubb. She also worked with Hank Williams. Her most famous song is "I Betcha My Heart I Love You." McBride was inducted into the Western Swing Hall of Fame in 1987. She died of cancer in 1989.

Laura Lee Owens, Western Swing's first female singer. By permission of Richard Weize.

- *The Queen of Western Swing*, Delta, 1970s. Featuring some of the original Texas Playboys.

The McKinney Sisters (Evelyn, b. 1928; Dean, b. 1930) replaced Laura Lee Owens in the Texas Playboys in the late 1940s. They began their careers as pre-teens in 1940s Alabama by first backing more-famous singers but soon becoming so popular they received their own radio show. They worked with harmonies inspired more by the Andrews Sisters than by any cowgal. They moved to Atlanta to do radio and did some shows with Eddy Arnold, eventually drifting to better stations in St. Louis and Chicago when they were still in their teens. In Chicago, they auditioned for Bob Wills, who hired them in 1946. The tenderfoot sisters moved to Fresno, California, and their smooth close-harmony singing became the perfect vocal complement to the intricate Wills sound. They did one film short with Wills called *Frontier Frolics* in 1946. By the early 1950s they had settled down and restricted themselves to West Coast performances.

- *For Collectors Only*, Kaleidoscope, 1990. Criminally out-of-print disc. Radio transcriptions from 1946 with Bob Wills's band.

The Miccolis Sisters (Mary Fulmer, b. 1922; Ruth Williams, b. 1924) are two sisters from Chicago who warrant more documentation. I looked far and wide for anything and discovered one short bit on them on *CJ Online's T-Town News*. Apparently they worked with Roy Rogers and seemed to have been in awe of that fact. After all, Rogers was a yodeling TV star with a film-star wife and horse. In 1946, they happened to be at a local radio station when Rogers came around seeking local harmony singers for a two-week St. Louis theater engagement.

The sisters came from a large family of eleven kids. They began harmonizing at age 6. They won a watch and some recognition by winning "The Rubins Hour," a local talent contest. They were offered a radio show contract on KMOX, St. Louis, in their mid-teens because they impressed people with their close-harmony singing-yodeling. Mary even won the title of "National Champion Girl Yodeler" around the same time. They toured regional Missouri rodeos, fairs, and war-bond benefits as a cowgirl duo wearing spangly Western outfits and oversized white 10-gallon hats. They eventually got to sing with the likes of Gene Autry and Eddie Arnold. In 1947, they were offered a lucrative deal with WIBW, where they spent seven years as part of the Ozark Ramblers doing radio and local live gigs. Marriage in 1949 apparently throttled their promising careers.

- *Boogie Woogie Yodel*, 78rpm, DeLuxe, 1948.

Tex (Doie Hensley) Owens (1892–1962), a country singer-songwriter, born in Killeen, Texas, was most famous for the cowboy yodel number "Cattle Call," which has been covered by just about everybody wearing a cowboy hat. He was born into a large musical family; one of his ten sisters was the famous Texas Ruby.

Owens was working as a car mechanic in 1931 when he finally tossed his toolbox aside and vowed to become a singer (and yodeler). He sang on and cohosted a radio show, the "Brush Creek Follies," in Kansas City for ten years with his Original Texas Rangers, which included two of his daughters. Here he became known as "The Original Texas Ranger." Owens wrote "Cattle Call" in 1934, while watching the snow fall from an 11th-floor window at a Kansas City radio station as he was about to go on the air. Suddenly his "sympathy went out to cattle everywhere. . . . I picked up my guitar, and in thirty minutes I had wrote the music and four verses to the song."

"Cattle Call" captures the plaintive wail that howls across the flat lands, evoking prairie solitude. It emanated from the calls cowboys employed to announce their location so as not to startle the herds—an ornamental "yip-

Tex Owens had the cattle calling. By permission of Richard Weize.

yip" signal—certainly a chief function of the yodel. Owens's return to music after World War II as a singing celluloid cowboy was tragically truncated when a horse fell on him during the filming of *Red River* in 1950. He broke his back and never fully recovered.

- *Cattle Call*, Bear Family, 1994.

Red River Dave (David McEnery, 1915–2002) is best known as a tireless folk ballad troubadour. For some sixty years, he lyrically chronicled contemporary events. His most famous song, "Shame is the Middle Name of Exxon," was his lyrical letter of consumer complaint about an Exxon service station that had done unnecessary repairs on his van. He wrote about Watergate, the Falklands War, President Reagan, Patty Hearst, and performed his "Amelia Earhart's Last Flight" (1937) at the 1939 New York World's Fair. He formed the fairly renowned Swift Cowboys and made numerous records for Decca, Savoy, and other labels. Dave's most notorious song is "The California Hippie Murders," which retells the harrowing tale of the Charles Manson murders punctuated with some expressive yodeling. Dave offers even better (canine-inspired) yodeling on "Tennessee Houn' Dog Yodel."

- "Tea Bag Romeo" b/w "Tennessee Houn' Dog Yodel," with the Tomahawks, a 45rpm, MGM, 1955.
- *Yodelin' Cowboy Memories*, Cowgirlboy, 1980s. 12 tracks from the late 1940s and early 1950s.

Goebel Reeves (1899–1959), a real cowboy known as the "Texas Drifter," performed in vaudeville and according to author Rick Koster is the singer who welded country to western. He recorded "The Yodelin' Teacher" in 1934 with a wonderful "instructional" spoken intro, in which he describes the yodel as "a musical thing that was discovered over in the Alps somewhere."

- *Hobo's Lullaby*, Bear Family, 1994.

Tex Ritter (Woodward Maurice Ritter, 1903–1974) was a wonderful Texan singer who was lured out of the University of Texas folklore department of John Lomax to pursue a life inside the cowboy myth. He went on to become an early celluloid cowboy, making more than seventy films. He had a warm amiable touch on folk songs like "Rye Whiskey," which came alive with his drunken whoops that mutate into inebriated dog howls and

the hiccup that cozies up to a glottal stop or two. He did his share of yodeling but wasn't closely identified with it.

- *Blood on the Saddle*, 4-CD Box, Bear Family, 1999.

Rusty Rogers was one of the Down Homers, the backing group for
both Kenny Roberts and early Bill Haley. He's yet another New England
cowboy inducted into all of New England's country hall of fames. But he
wasn't just a Down Homer, he was also quite a yodeler in his own right. In
fact, at one time he was New England's Yodeling Champion. For many
years, he had his own radio show in New England and recorded on labels
like King, Cool, Lamb, and Travelers.

- *Yesterday and Today*, Rusty, 1990s.
- *Tribute to the American Cowboy*, Rusty, 1990s.

The Sons of the Pioneers were one of the more interesting cowboy
groups because they overcame the limitations of their genre by sheer creative use of the vocal (and songwriting) gifts of founding members Roy
Rogers, Bob Nolan, and Tim Spencer. Their close harmonies, songwriting,
and ability to maintain a good reputation despite the corny cowboy chic
they were glamorizing all make them admirable. They came into being in
1933 as a trio of harmonizing yodelers, known as the Pioneer Trio, until one
day an emcee introduced them as The Sons of the Pioneers. They performed some incredible songs written by Nolan including his "Way Out
There," which featured their distinctive trio yodel. "The Last Round-Up"
became a big hit in the early 1930s, and Nolan's "Tumbling Tumbleweeds"
is a Western classic that seems to have been written on the wind. Despite
Rogers' yodeling talents, the Pioneers really took off after Rogers left the
group. Their yodel number "The Devil's Great Grandson" was recorded in
1937, while their yodeling and harmony singing in "Way Out There" set the
standard for this kind of smooth-yet-heartfelt style of cowboy vocals. Their
harmonies plus Nolan and Spencer's songs have emerged as the basic foundation of Western music.

- *Sons of the Pioneers: Ultimate Collection*, Hip-O Records, 2002.
  Recorded between 1934 and 1954.
- *Songs Of Sons Of The Pioneers*: Bear Family, 5-CD/Book, 1998.

Sourdough Slim (b. Rick Crowder) was named "Yodeler of the Year" by
the Academy of Western Artists in 2001. He plays accordion and yodels,

sings, and plays a mean guitar, harmonica, and kazoo—and also does some rope tricks, all while decked out in classic 1920s cowboy sidekick garb. Sourdough specializes in traditional western yodeling or those popularized by Gene Autry and Roy Rogers, plus his own compositions. He taught himself to yodel in his Oregon attic. "I was terrible at first, but I figured nobody could hear me up there. You have to be somewhere where you're not intimidated because you think somebody might be listening." His "Yodeling Cowboy" is a nice example of his sweet yodel.

- *The Best of Sourdough Slim*, own label, 2003.

Don Walser (b. 1934) has a reputation as a true underheralded outlaw and best-kept secret that precedes him. Walser has done the time and is now reaping the benefits of being a cause celebre-cum-undiscovered treasure. Walser, the self-declared savior of the "dying art" of yodeling and the singer *Newsweek* cavalierly nicknamed the "Pavarotti of the Plains," was born in Texas in 1934. Walser's fame has come via a slow wide arc of some forty years yodeling and fronting obscure bands—in the 1960s he was "Little Donnie Walser" fronting the Texas Plainsmen—and playing low-recognition gigs. In 1984, Walser moved to Austin, Texas, where his career took off when his Pure Texas Band gained a "punk" following. His renown and robust yodeling now reach far beyond Austin's city limits.

- *The Archive Series: Vol. 2*, with Pure Texas Band, Watermelon, 1995.
- *Dare To Dream: The Best Compilation*, Texas Music Group, 2001.
  Collection of twenty Walser songs.
- *The Official Souvenir of Pure Texas Music*, Sight & Sound
  SouthWest, 1990s.
- *Rolling Stone from Texas*, Watermelon, 1994.

Ray Whitley (1901–1979) was a singing celluloid cowboy with a thin reedy voice and a lazy high yodel influenced by Jimmie Rodgers. He sang, yodeled, acted, but, most important, he wrote some of the greatest cowboy songs: "Back in the Saddle Again," "Lonely River," and many more. Whitley delivered the classic yodel tune, "Blue Yodel Blues," in a style that was more smooth crooner than rough-hewn whiskey-drinkin' cowpoke.

Yodeling Alberta Slim (b. Eric C. Edwards, 1910) aka "the Yodeling Cowboy," grew up on the Canadian prairies where he learned to ride and rope horses before he was 10. He grew up listening to another great

Canadian yodeler, Wilf Carter, on the radio. Once he learned some of Carter's songs, he'd sing them out on the prairie. In Saskatoon, Slim landed a paying gig at radio station CFQC, where he could be heard from coast to coast. Slim usually opened his show with Carter's "There's a Love Knot in My Lariat." He has lived in British Columbia, Canada, since the 1950s. In his heyday, he recorded twelve albums on RCA, many with the CBC Happy Gang Orchestra. He and his wife even had their own traveling circus, complete with elephants, chimps, bears, dogs, and his famous horses, one of whom was named Kitten. Kitten was famous for her fortune-telling abilities!

- *Golden Memories of Alberta Slim*, RCA.
- *Alberta Slim & His Bar X Boys & His Horse Kitten*, RCA.
- *The Best of Alberta Slim*, RCA.
- *Alberta Slim & His Bar X Boys—Canada's King of the Yodelers*, RCA.

RIDERS IN THE SKY:
POST-MODERN COWBOYS

Riders in the Sky, reverent triple-yodelin' buffoonery. By permission of Riders in the Sky.

The Nashville-based Riders in the Sky have been producing their own brand of western yodeling music since 1977. Their music is full of Sons-of-the-Pioneers-inspired harmony, laced with yodeling and littered with infectiously pesky humor. The Wild West has never looked nor sounded so . . . surreal. And yet they have no problem rolling into accurate renditions of classic cowboy songs.

Riders in the Sky (Ranger Doug, Woody Paul, Joey the Cowpolka King, and Too Slim) are renowned for keeping the singing cowboy tradition alive, albeit with a certain irreverent zaniness. Their humor, which verges on a haystack full of Three Stooges and Bonzo Dog Band skits, massages the crowds for the yodeling, which ululates somewhere between slapstick and pure harmonic reverence. Their chemistry is most evident on their intricate three-part Pioneeresque yodel harmonies, fine-tuned over a twenty-year career.

Ranger Doug and the rest of the Sky live in Nashville. Doug is sometimes known as Douglas B. Green, author of many evocative cowboy music articles and the book *Singing in the Saddle*, published in 2002 by Vanderbilt University Press, which summarizes a lifetime's work documenting the great cowboy singers.

continued on the next page

Riders in the Sky, continued

Doug comments on how he got started yodeling:

My mother and her brothers used to sing, and my uncle Arvid yodeled, so I may have been exposed from my very smallest childhood. We moved to California in the 1950s and there I was exposed to yodeling and singing cowboys on TV and at the movies. . . . As a kid I found I could sing falsetto, and when encountering yodeling as a teenager I found I could do it fairly easily, although hitting the intervals and such took a lot of prac-tice; still, it was something I was able to do rather naturally. Yodeling was just something I had heard and was familiar with from my earliest memo-ries. . . . I didn't have a passion for it, but it was always there and fun to do when I started experimenting, vocally.

If I had a yodeling epiphany it was after I moved to Nashville in 1968, when a bluegrass gentleman named Lance LeRoy invited me over to his house to hear some of his old records. He knew I yodeled and thought I might be interested in hearing a guy named Elton Britt, who I was familiar with in a general way but had no idea what he could do. Needless to say, I was totally blown away, agape, agog, and astonished at what Elton did on the album "Yodel Songs." I had to go out and buy that record and learn how to do that! I did . . . [but] learning yodeling is something you want to do in pri-vate, at the risk of alienating family, friends, neighbors, and pets. I used to drive around in my old truck practicing what Elton was doing, though in a lower key. In that way, I progressed from a simple yodeler to a proficient one.

In his work, Doug tries to balance showmanship and what he calls "soul-fulness":

I think many, even *most*, musical styles, from bluegrass to rock to jazz, have an inherent tension between virtuosity and soulfulness. . . . It's an art and it's a craft and there has to be a balance. . . . I personally have never been much in favor of contests, championships, and the like. I realize they're good "hooks" to grab an audience's attention, but I find competitions, especially yodeling competitions, distasteful and have refused to enter or judge them. Music, for me, is about learning and sharing and appreciating, not winning and losing, not about best versus not-best. Plus the old problem of technique over feel comes up in the contest setting; I'd rather just sit back and listen to some music that means something than to be obsessed with technique.

The Riders' complete discography, mostly on Rounder, is immense and easily accessible via the Internet:

- *A Pair of Kings*, 2002.

- *Yodel the Cowboy Way*, 1998.

- *Cowboy Songs*, 1996.

- *Public Cowboy #1: The Music of Gene Autry*, 1996.

10

Modern Epiglottal Frontiers

SCAT-OLOGICAL YODELING

We should never let this sound—the sounds of the hills and mountains—
slip away, no more than I think we should allow the genuine old-fashioned-
type Muddy Waters blues slip away. Why? We Americans don't have nothing
else, musically speaking.

—Ray Charles

The world of blues and jazz includes yodeling. But despite what we know about yodeling in Africa—particularly among the Pygmies—I'm surprised that there hasn't been more direct evidence of Pygmy-influenced vocals in jazz and blues. James Brown's "freeform screams: the Ooooohhoooohh! Aaaaaaaaooooooow," notes Cynthia Rose, "have perplexed Caucasian listeners since . . . 1956." In much the same way that slave hollers spooked whites. Jazz vocals sometimes suggest Pygmy yodeling's influence on "western"-style singers. Afro-American culture historian Robert Farris Thompson has managed to weld the live wires of Old and New World at James Brown's epiglottis. Thompson echoes Frederick Douglass's observations (see Chapter 7) when he notes that "Whites don't realize what that scream is . . . it's a code . . . another language. . . . Brown is more African than the Africans! In his funk and his vocal quality—those growls, those slurs—you hear real Central African stuff: textless displays of verbal energy, as in yodel sounds and screeches." Leon Thomas extended the anthropological "verbal energy" whenever his Pygmy-yodel-scat erupted from the opening at the top of his larynx. This physiological aspect of technique draws us back to Pygmy yodeling not only via ethnomusicological investigation but via ur-soul, or a back-to-Africa spiritual pilgrimage. This is most evident on Thomas's work with saxophonist Pharoah Sanders, especially on "Creator Has a Master Plan."

BLACK, WHITE, AND BLUE

Ray Charles's career trajectory is the obverse of Jimmie Rodgers's. Rodgers was a white man drawn to black music. Charles is a black singer influenced by white music; a consummate soul man with deep roots in hillbilly music. He has produced a number of country records including *Modern Sounds of Country & Western Music* (1962). In his autobiography, Charles recalls that at age 15 in Tampa, Florida, he "worked with a hillbilly band called The Florida Playboys. I learned how to yodel when I was with them."

Charles embodies that porous border between black and white, between hillbilly and jazz. Jazz, meanwhile, serves as an audio alloy of African and European influences, urban and rural concerns. Slaves on the plantations took European music—hymns, Scottish fiddle music, Irish ballads—and transformed it with their African roots (work songs) and chops. This amalgam forged the sonic DNA that became Negro minstrel music. Introduce Africa's improvisationally mischievous rhythms to the standard rhythms of ragtime à la Scott Joplin—which evolved out of both the "Negro" and blackface minstrel show—and one has the makings of the dynamic music called jazz.

Jazz toyed with standard European song structures and the entire conventionalized arrangement of sound through syncopation (introduction of irregular rhythms to the normal rhythm), creating a variegated off-kilter beat, to which odd vocal ornaments were added. In New Orleans, humid incubator of jazz and blues, W.C. Handy became an early purveyor of ragtime, embodying the hybridization of here and there, Europe, America, and Africa. As Giles Oakley points out, Handy often tossed in a Broadway tune or a classical snippet like the popular "William Tell Overture" into his performances. At some point, "jazz emerged out of the amalgam." Its unique sound was an intertwining of its two roots: "the light airy music of ragtime and the heavier, more emotional strains of the blues." This sound acquired some extra bawdy licks via the honky-tonk ambience. Add to that their reworkings of white ballads, their African-influenced work songs, mesmerizing repetitions, haunting hollers, and peculiar vocal embellishments that eluded standard musical notation and were brought in from the (corn, cotton, or tobacco) fields, and one has a many-faceted tapestry of sounds that ranged from naughty to discomfiting, melancholy to joyous. And it's from this environment of sweltering fields, hard work, and escape via music and spirituality that the blues, the music of emancipated slaves, found its palette of emotions, sounds, and purpose.

Evidence that blacks found interesting material in the white repertoire is fairly substantial. That whites in turn found plenty of inspiration to latch onto in the black repertoire has no lack of examples—everything from Jimmie Rodgers to Hank Williams, bluegrass, Western Swing, boogie, rockabilly, right through rock is based on blues chords. Yodelers like Emmett Miller, Cliff Carlisle, and Jimmie Rodgers all copped licks and resonance from their exposure to black idioms. Some even considered Rodgers an honorary "Negro." Carlisle noted "Jimmie . . . reminded me more of a colored person . . . than anybody I ever saw, in a way." And so, the audio chain of inspiration, created black musicians inspired by whites who had in turn learned from the previous generation of blacks. This happened *despite* official U.S. segregation policies and the efforts of white hillbilly musicians to portray themselves as clean of any "nigger" influences in "the deep though often confused nature of our ethnic interactions." Many clandestine, underground collaborations took place between black and white musicians where borrowing, jamming, and ultimately intercultural transmogrification occurred, creating a kind of proto-world music.

YODELING BLUES

Was the blue yodel a Jimmie Rodgers signature or did it indeed come from the blues? This is a question that can never be answered, but there are some tantalizing clues in the legacy of blues recordings of interchange occurring in both directions. Bessie Smith, interestingly enough, often performed a song with minimal-lackadaisical yodeling called "Yodeling Blues," which furthered the strange—but ultimately not so illogical—hybridization of jazz and yodeling. Other examples abound: the Mississippi Sheiks (Chatman family) whose "Yodeling Fiddling Blues" was "a near marriage of blues fiddling and blue yodelling, and thus capitalised on country music's most exciting new sound."

The Sheiks proved how important the simple "Blue Yodel" structure was and how it led to a much-imitated formula for other hoped-for successes. Rodgers borrowed black material, but then someone like Furry Lewis would return the favor. Lewis borrowed lines from Rodgers; instead of "T for Texas," Lewis wrote "M for Memphis, B for Birmingham." He was one of a handful of black singers who covered Rodgers's songs, proof that blacks were interested in what Rodgers had to say *and* how he became successful doing it. Lewis covered "Waiting for a Train" (as "The Dying Hobo"), even attempting some yodeling although he cautions listeners:

EMMETT MILLER

one of the strangest and most stunning of stylists ever to record . . . Miller's debut represented an avant-garde of its own, an altogether otherworldly voice . . . the last mutant mongrel emanation of old and dead and dying styles, the first mutant mongrel emanation of a style far more reckless and free than the cool of scat.

—Nick Tosches

Emmett Miller (1900–1962) was born (and died) in Macon, Georgia. He's America's fount of ur-yodeling, its epiglottal Holy Grail, preceding Jimmie Rodgers, inspiring Hank Williams, Milton Brown, and Bob Wills. But even his closest colleagues eventually forgot him. In author-ethnomusicological detective Nick Tosches's words, Miller was "a white man in blackface, a hillbilly singer, and a jazz singer and a pretty good representation of the schizophrenic heat of what this country [United States], with a straight face, calls its culture."

A vivid expressionist painting of Miller, but what about the facts? Well, there aren't that many: just some forgotten birdseed and half-chewed misbegotten memories strewn upon the superhighway of culture. That's what Tosches had to go with in writing his hagiography. Tosches tries to dig Miller from culture's boneyard, but the lettering on the headstones is weatherworn illegible. Lack of concrete data, however, gives Tosches the opportunity to use Miller as surly bullywhip for his favorite targets: academics, hippies, PC-revisionists, pretentious ofays, and sell-out Beatniks. By the end, Tosches *does* manage to artificially resuscitate Miller—somewhat—bringing him back from a mysterious obscurity to a world Miller never seemed to really inhabit.

It's a mystery why Miller merits such a skinny dossier in American musical history. Maybe Miller just chose the wrong entertainment field at the wrong time. Minstrelsy (blackface or straight-face) does have a seamy, un-PC aspect to it, with its off-color comedy skits and side-show ambience. In any case, from 1919 to somewhere in the 1950s, Miller performed in minstrel shows and made some amazingly interesting records. His unique and sinister world-weary yodeling style—yodeler Randy Erwin calls it "loopy jazz singer stuff"—very likely crawled inside the voices of other, more renowned yodeling voices.

On stage by age 16, Miller became a star with his bluesy vocals, snarling sarcastic cackles, yodels, and flailing falsetto. His knife-twisting vocals included falsetto breaks in the middle of words, something that would later become Hank Williams's trademark. Miller's voice—raspy, and tangled up in deep dark secrets—was unique. But then, where did he get his "wry, bizarre phrasing, his eccentric timing, his startling falsetto flights . . . his uncanny swoons of timbre and pitch" from? Life, genetics, Swiss traveling yodelers, blues singers?

Miller began recording in 1924, three years before Rodgers, with "Pickaninny's Paradise." He pioneered many things that Rodgers would later get credit for, including a bluesy hillbilly style and yodeling with jazz musicians. Although Rodgers performed with some pick-up jazz groups and Louis

continued on the next page

Emmett Miller, continued

Armstrong, Miller sang with Tommy Dorsey, Jack Teagarden, and Gene Krupa—jazz meets country. He covered "Lovesick Blues" (1925) in such an overpowering manner that many, including Rex Griffin and Hank Williams borrowed heavily from his version.

The central event—that may or may not have happened—was the meeting of Jimmie Rodgers and Miller *prior to* Rodgers's first recording session in 1927. Tosches believes—no proof—that Rodgers may have seen Miller perform in Asheville, North Carolina, in 1927 and somehow in the miasma of musical and creative effluvia they may have cross-pollinated one another. But even though this factional/fictional meeting has all the possibilities of a truth, it remains "unknown and unknowable," especially in the grey world of entertainment minstrelsy, which featured whites in blackface, blacks in black- or whiteface, and/or whites singing as blacks singing as whites. Miller may have actually inaugurated the "yodel blues" by fusing yodeling—"that wild rushing flight of swarming inflections"—to blues so that the form bears Miller's voiceprint—not Rodgers's. This is heretical iconoclasm for Rodgers-worshippers—and healthy and delicious speculation, which ultimately, however, leads to many dead ends.

As blackface fell from grace, replaced by other media, Miller, clinging career-snuffingly to it, fell with it not only into obscurity, but also into alcoholism and depression, playing ever-more obscure venues until his death in 1962. While there are a mind-boggling number of repackaged collections of Wills, Monroe, and Rodgers, there is only one collection of Miller's work currently available.

- *The Minstrel Man from Georgia*, Columbia/Legacy, 1996.

"I'm gonna try somethin' now—I may make a failure." At age 70, he doesn't manage much of a yodel but *does* recognize the importance of trying.

Rodgers "proved to be . . . influential on black styles." Mississippi bluesman Tommy Johnson had a notable falsetto leap, and other "Jackson-based singers like Ishman Bracey and Rubin Lacey saw Rodgers often in the twenties," notes David Evans. "Chester Burnett, whose powerful whooping owed a little to Johnson, claims he met Rodgers in the twenties and was given by him the nickname of 'Howlin' Wolf.'" Rodgers's blue yodel may have provided "the basis for Howlin' Wolf's patented howl" notes author Peter Guralnick. Although some observe how similar his "blues howl" is to the "blue yodel" of Robert Johnson. Nick Tosches even suggests—and why not—that Rodgers may have been influenced by Bessie Smith who sometimes yodeled in concert. Mississippi John Hurt, a cowherd from Mississippi, also found inspiration in Rodgers and recorded some Rodgers material.

Tony Russell makes it clear, however, that most blacks *didn't* do that much yodeling: "They had a similar device, however, in the falsetto. The voice was raised an octave, generally in the last syllable of a word, often at the end of a line; the effect was rather of a whoop or a howl than of the see-sawing about the voice's breaking point which makes a yodel." Skip James's "Yola My Blues Away" "was sung—like all his material—entirely in falsetto; apparently blacks use 'yodeling' or 'yolaing' to denote both the techniques." Evans also recorded him singing Rodgers's "Waiting for a Train."

Blind Willie McTell thought that the "the bluest of the white blues are their 'yodelin' songs'." He was probably talking about Tom Darby and Jimmie Tarlton, who had both done prison time—which helped legitimize their blues—and had a big hit with "Columbia Stockade Blues" and "Birmingham Jail." Their "Traveling Yodel Blues" and "Touring Yodel Blues" were testimony to Rodgers's influence.

The colorful white blues singer and twice-governor of Louisiana, Jimmie Davis, "had worked his way through school, partly by teaching yodelling," and when he was on tour he protected his vocal cords with goat's milk. It's amazing that Davis was elected governor at all, because although no liberal integrationist, he wrote and sang some of the raunchiest most incendiary interracial relationship songs—a white guy bragging about making love to a black woman just wasn't done especially by someone in public office! Plus he sometimes recorded with all-black bands (to the dismay of his political supporters). Davis recorded "My Good Gal's Gone Blues" with a Rodgers-influenced blue yodel. Some of his most explicitly sexy material was later covered by that paragon of sagebrush virtue, Gene Autry.

Novelty blues songs arose in the 1930s. They had witty, racy lyrics with occasional yodel embellishments. The best of this genre were by Bill and Cliff Carlisle. They sang about sexual conquests with sinister jocularity and emotional complexity, further enhanced by their snide and cynical yodel refrains. Cliff Carlilsle's "That Nasty Swing" attaches a sleazy yodel to lines like "Place the needle in that hole and do the nasty swing."

Other blues singers occasionally turned to something like yodeling. Robert Johnson is not a yodeler per se, but he does exhale some mighty weary moans and sighs that swirled around inside his chest and collect like howling gusts off a lonely plain—melancholy field hollers or woebegone yodels, then? "Love in Vain" features one chilling example, as the singer moans, "Ou ou ou ou ou ou hee vee oh woe," testifying to the deep emotions that a voice possessed of soul and urgency can express.

Tampa Red (1904–1981) was born in Georgia as Hudson Whittaker (or Woodbridge?). His red hair and growing up in Tampa made his nickname ineluctable. He was one of the early blues arrivals in Chicago and trans-formed rural blues to urban blues, emerging as an influential 1930s urban blues slide-guitarist. His "Worried Devil Blues" is a casual yodel number—not virtuosic, but soulful. He was inducted into the Blues Foundation Hall of Fame in 1981, the same year he died.

SCAT'S A PLENTY

Scat singing is the use of vocables—nonsense syllables—to imitate an improvised, instrumental line. Louis Armstrong is the pioneer of scat; his "Heebie Jeebies" in 1926 is often cited as the first true example of scat on record. Later jazz vocalists extrapolated Armstrong's innovation and made scat rhyme with art.

Yodeling is easily utilized as scat ammo, because scat is partly the human voice's "imitation of musical instruments." "Talking" with a musical instrument—often the trumpet—"Armstrong's jazz . . . consists of mutual imitation between the singing-speaking 'scat' voice and the instruments." Or, as Nathaniel Mackey put it: "impeded speech finds its voice, somewhat the way [Thelonious] Monk makes hesitation eloquent or the way a scat-singer makes inarticulacy speak."

Beginning with bebop, we can trace the experimenters who developed scat-yodeling as an artform—albeit one that existed on the fringes of jazz singing. These innovators range from trombonist/humorist Frank Rosolino, to Swedish-born jazz singer Alice Babs, and culminate in the far-out vocal-izing of the underappreciated Leon Thomas.

FRANK ROSOLINO

One of the finest trombone players . . . he had a superb tone, astonishing facil-ity, a deep Italianate lyricism, and . . . with a wit that literally would not quit.
—Don Menza, fellow musician

Rosolino (1926–1978) was a great bebop-influenced trombonist known for accuracy, clarity, and inspired improvisational mischief. But less well known is the fact that he was an infectious comedian *and* a fascinating vocalist who employed some surprising yodeling.

Music probably saved him from a life of petty crime in his native Detroit. He played in some great bands: Gene Krupa's and Stan Kenton's, for instance. In 1948, while playing with Krupa, he broke out into inspired scat vocalizing on "Lemon Drop." It must have sounded like he was com-municating in tongues to some alien muse. Rosolino also worked as a ses-sion man for Benny Carter, Dexter Gordon, "Toots" Thielmans, Mel

Torme, Zoot Sims, Kai Winding, and many more. He contributed his agile trombone to some seventeen film soundtracks including *The Man with the Golden Arm.*

However, in November 1978, Frank Rosolino took a pistol, went into the bedroom of his two sons, and shot them, before turning the gun on himself. His girlfriend at the time was sitting in a car in his driveway when she saw the gunshot flashes. His precise motivation remains a mystery. Maybe the fact that he had left his wife for a younger woman and that his wife had gone into the Rosolino garage to asphyxiate herself has something to do with it—not to mention that Rosolino was going through financial hard times.

- *The Frank Rosolino Sextet*, Affinity 1990s. Great intro to Rosolino's 1950s solo work, particularly his vocals. "Pennies from Heaven" is kinetic Spike Jones-esque scat-yodeling, with his head voice moving right into a trombone solo.
- *Turn Me Loose*, Collectables 1990s (1961). Includes "Sometimes I'm Happy," "Pennies From Heaven," and "That Old Black Magic," all of which contain a mad admixture of scat, laughter, and yodeling.

ALICE BABS

Was Babs (Alice Nilsson 1924–1999) the half-sister of Yma Sumac? She was only 15 when she broke through with her first hit, "Joddlarflickan (Yodeling Girl)" in her native Sweden. But soon thereafter she fell under the jazz spell. She became very popular after World War II, with her swinging jazz vocals on a succession of hits. She was even denounced by prim Swedish society types as "vulgar" because her untamed jazz stylings "promoted" promiscuity.

By the 1950s she'd become one of Sweden's most renowned movie stars, while continuing to sing her jazz and pop standards. She had a warm and versatile voice, and her yodeling was exuberantly earnest. This is most evident on her wacky "Hilly-Billy-Willy."

In the late 1950s, she toured the world with fiddler Svend Asmussen and guitarist Ulrik Neuman as the group Swe-Danes. In the 1960s, Babs turned to singing Bach and Mozart in churches. She released albums of hymns and spirituals. In the 1970s, she performed in Duke Ellington's sacred concerts.

- *Mittsommernacht*, Bear Family, 1994. Incredible improvisational yodeling and adventurous vocals.

Alice Babs, jazzy Swedish yodeler.
By permission of Richard Weize.

- *Alice Babs: The Collection*, Disky, 2001. Two yodels, including the scattish medley "Varat Gang."
- *Lollipop*, Alice Babs, Bear Family, 1994.

JAZZ-SCAT-YODELING FUSIONS

By the mid-1950s, jazz musicians were experimenting with fusions of jazz with other types of music, from gospel and soul to rock and avant-garde music (through the '60s), electronic (the '70s), and world music (the '80s and beyond). Soul jazz, a subgenre of funky jazz that developed during the mid-1950s through '60s led to fusion experiments by people like Miles Davis and Weather Report (1960s–1970s). A few exceptional vocalists—Bob Dorough, Mose Allison, and Oscar Brown, Jr.—emerged during this time. They had individualistic styles based on phrasing and interpretation but did not really delve into scat—and then Leon Thomas arrives. Sometimes referred to as the "John Coltrane of jazz vocalists," Thomas managed to fuse scat and the African vocalese traditions, and then added his own inspired yodeling style—performing ritualistic vocals infused by spiritual quests, soul music, and Pygmy yodeling techniques.

AMOS LEON(E) THOMAS

It surprises me, it does everything of its own volition. I call it Soularfone. The pygmies call it Umbo Weti. . . . This voice is not me, my voice is ancient. This person you see before you is controlled by ego but my voice is egoless.

—Leon Thomas

The voice projection . . . leads to a wordless yodel sounding not unlike an American Indian call—the moaning of spirits known and unknown.

—Pharoah Sanders

Amos Leon(e) Thomas (1937–1999) is one of the greatest jazz vocalists, but is barely known. Look in most authoritative jazz tomes and you will most likely find Leon Thomas as a mere footnote in someone else's profile; some don't mention him at all. In 1999, he died in a run-down public hospital in the Bronx, New York. "His demeanor was jovial," notes Thomas aficionado Ian Horst, "despite the hissing of various contraptions in the ICU where he spent far too much of his last months." Ignominious is hardly the way an artist of his caliber should have gone out for his last solo.

Thomas grew up in East St. Louis, studied music at Tennessee State University, and moved to New York in 1958. Thomas's early career can be characterized as straight blues-jazz vocals, working with Mary Lou Williams and touring with Art Blakey. In January 1961, Thomas joined Count Basie and sang at the inaugural balls of both President Kennedy and President Johnson. However, he soon turned to more avant-garde stylings. His most famous work is with Pharoah Sanders on *Karma* (1969) and *Jewels of Thought* (1970). In 1969, on "Creator Has a Master Plan," he sang a scat-yodel with wild fluctuations between glottal and melliflu-ous vocables that instantly affected me. This was a man in search of soul. He gave the human voice a power beyond its mere narrative and image-evoking functions. He seemed to be patching into the incredible yodel-ing patterns of the Central African Pygmies, whose vocal traditions he had studied. Thomas believed they'd given him the gift of particularly elastic throat articulation, or "soularphone" as he called it, which enabled him to sing, blending jazz scat, blues styles, and his interpretation of ancestral yodeling.

In the mid-1960s, Thomas became interested in Africa and mysticism not unlike fellow jazz stars Randy Weston and Pharoah Sanders, among others. He collaborated with Weston, Rahsaan Roland Kirk, and Oliver Nelson, all devoted pioneers of sound, and later with a Thomas devotee, Carlos Santana. Thomas seemed increasingly interested in speaking in the language of an elusive people on a troubled continent. But the story of how Thomas's yodeling evolved or, let's say, emerged is fairly prosaic. Sanders heard Thomas perform and asked him to write lyrics for "Pisces Moon." Thomas did and called it "Creator Has a Master Plan."

The first yodeling was actually courtesy of a freak incident involving Thomas attempting to reel in an old debt with a phone call. The deadbeat was definitely incommunicado, and so Thomas decided to try some mental telepathy to conjure him up. From a yoga headstand, he began walking on his hands to the phone to dial this guy's number. "As I crossed the threshold of the bedroom, I transcended," Thomas remembers. "I was one place and my body was another. I dropped to the floor right on my face and my teeth went into my bottom lip. . . . So I couldn't do my own show with Pharoah." Leon performed at the anti-police brutality benefit in New York anyway. "I could hardly open my mouth. . . . I got up on the stage and when it came time for me to scat, this sound just came out. It shocked me. I didn't know where it was coming from. I realized it was me and I realized that the ancestors had arrived." And that ancestral voice was yodeling.

Thomas's solo career was further nourished by Bob Thiele, Coltrane's producer at Impulse. Thiele's Flying Dutchman label was perfect for artists like Thomas, offering total artistic freedom. Here he did some great solo work including *Spirits Known and Unknown* (1969). Thomas's albums were a blend of aesthetic abstraction, vocal improv, African identity, spirituality, and anti–Vietnam War activism and strains of soul-jazz fusion. He was in high demand and even cut a version of "Master" with Louis Armstrong on Armstrong's last album. A stormy personal period led to a spotty musical stretch throughout the 1980s.

Precious Energy (1993) with saxophonist Gary Bartz, although full of hope, marked a downward spiral into melancholy and dissipation, as a fascination with drugs and his struggles to deal with personal devils took their toll. He took up recording again, which culminated in 1998's *Zaius* with Jeri Brown and John Hicks.

Leon Thomas vocals can best be described as exploratory or extrapolatory—extending our knowledge of the unexplainable. He wasn't afraid to engage the overpowering bellow of Pharoah Sanders's or David Newman's saxophones. Direct verbal combat—engaged, struggling, searching—imbued his vocals with substance and prickly charm. The throaty, stuttering leap into inspired equatorial yodel must have been something to witness live: primal elegance and joyous freefall.

- *Spirits Known and Unknown*, Flying Dutchman, 1969 (Europe, 2002). Lyrically mesmerizing version of "Creator" recaptures 1960s zeitgeist. "Echoes" includes some showcase yodeling within a slow jazz-waltz framework.

- *The Leon Thomas Album*, Flying Dutchman, 1970. Soul-jazz plus Pan-African vocals and an engagé Gil Scott-Heron–like proto-rap.
- *In Berlin with Oliver Nelson*, Flying Dutchman, 1971; rereleased RCA-Victor Gold, 2002. Includes an exceptional ode to Pygmy yodeling on "Umbo Weti."
- *Gold Sunrise on Magic Mountain*, Flying Dutchman, 1971. Entire side of incredible roots-improv vocals combining yodeling and Afro-Brazilian percussion.
- *Facets: The Legend of Leon Thomas*, Flying Dutchman, 1973. Best-of album includes some pyrotechnical avant-yodeling.
- *Precious Energy*, with Gary Bartz, Mapleshade, 1993. Thomas imitates various songbirds, wind instruments, Theramin, extended Pygmy yodels, some hocketing, and other techniques. Marred by poor sound and documentation.
- *Anthology*, Soul Brother Records, 1998. 1969–1985 recordings.
- *Zaius*, Jeri Brown featuring Leon Thomas, Justin Time, 1998. Thomas guest ululates on Canadian Brown's sixth album.
- *Summum, Bukmun, Umyun,* Pharoah Sanders, Woody Shaw, Lonnie Liston Smith, among others, Impulse!, 1998 (1970). Two extended compositions with Sanders playing a dozen instruments and Shaw and vocalist-percussionist Nathaniel Bettis both adding some yodeling!

SOME OTHER JAZZ YODELERS

A few jazz vocalists have tried to extend Thomas's yodel-scat inspiration. Eddie Harris (1936–1996), an intrepid Chicago-born experimenter on saxophone and vocals, is one. He ironically got pigeonholed as a commercial sell-out when he landed a hit with music for the *Exodus* soundtrack in 1961. In 1966, Harris turned to the electric tenor saxophone; a sax connected to a Varitone signal processor. He recorded with Les McCann's soul-jazz group, where he became "Mr. Soul jazz on saxobone" (saxophone-trombone hybrid). In later years, Harris incorporated vocables into his act, and these vocals had yodel-like tendencies, which were sometimes compared to Leon Thomas.

Mark Murphy is an improv jazz vocalist from Syracuse, New York. He has a kinetic stage presence and an unpredictable intuitive desire to transform jazz-pop standards like "How Long Has This Been Going On" into something "other" by mangling it with drawn-out forlorn yodels or some

JAZZ AND BLUES YODEL DISCOGRAPHY

- *Birmingham Quartette Anthology*, Lanka Lanka, 1980s. Golden Leaf Quartette do some close harmony gospel yodeling on the standard "Sleep, Baby, Sleep." Also covered elsewhere by black gospel groups, the Birmingham Jubilee singers and the famous Blue Jay Singers.

- *Black Venus*, Josephine Baker, DCC, 1991, and *Josephine Baker*, Sandstone, 1992. Both include "I Want to Yodel."

- *Blue Yodelers 1928–1936*, Challenge 2000. Mostly Jimmie Rodgers, Roy Evans, and Emmett Miller.

- *The Calling: Celebrating Sarah Vaughan*, Dianne Reeves, Blue Note, 1990s. Detroit-native Reeves is a big-voiced jazz diva with range, pitch, timing. Pays tribute to Vaughn with yodel-like vocables on "I Remember Sarah," while on "A Chamada" she employs yodel-like embellishments.

- *Come on a My House*, Rosemary Clooney, Bear Family, 1997. Includes "Rose of the Mountain," (1951), an American version of Hans Lang's "Du Bist die Rose vom Wörthersee." It's a typical lightweight yearning-girl-in-the-Alps yodel song. She died in 2002.

- *The Complete Early Recordings of Skip James*, Yazoo, 1994. Early recordings of this essential, if unsettling, bluesman. Includes "Yola My Blues Away," a howlin' falsetto yodel number—complex sweet sorrow. He yodels likes wind through a broken window.

- *The Complete Recordings Volume 1*, Bessie Smith, Columbia. Includes "Yodeling Blues."

- *The Earliest Negro Vocal Groups, Volume 3: 1921–1924*, Document, 1980s? Includes "Sweet Mama," an agitated proto-soul Al Jolson-esque yodel number by the Southern Negro Quartette.

- *Eddie Heywood & the Blues Singers*, Document, 1995. Includes four yodel songs by tenor yodeler Charles Anderson: "Yodle Song–Coo Coo," "Sleep, Baby, Sleep," and "Comic Yodle Song."

- *From Lake Mary,* Scott Dunbar, Ahura Mazda, 1970.

- *Head Hunters,* Herbie Hancock, Sony (remastered), 1991. "Watermelon Man" uses sounds made by pipes (Hancock) and beer bottles (Bill Summers) to create audiophonic allusions to pygmy yodeling.

- *Kansas City Blues 1924–1929*, various performers, Document, 1994. Includes "Lost Lover Blues" (1928) by Lottie Beaman-Kimbrough and Winston Holmes on vocals, birdcalls, and yodeling. Holmes was a tap dancer, Kansas City promoter, and owner of Merritt Records (one of the only black-owned labels of that period).

continued on the next page

Jazz and Blues Yodel Discography, continued

- *Male Blues of the Twenties*, various artists, Document, 1996. Includes Charles Anderson's "Laughing Yodel" (1924).

- *Memphis Slim and Willie Dixon at the Village Gate,* Memphis Slim, Willie Dixon, and Pete Seeger, Smithsonian/Folkways, 1962 (1990s). This "supergroup" performs "T for Texas (Blue Yodel #1)."

- *Mental Strain at Dawn: A Portrait of Louis Armstrong*, David Murray with Doc Cheatham, and others, Stash 1992. Includes "Yodel Blues."

- *Mississippi Sheiks: Vol. 1 1930*, Mississippi Sheiks, Document. Includes "Yodeling Fiddling Blues" (1930).

- *Mississippi Blues*, various performers, Catfish, 1999. Includes yodeler Tommy Johnson's "Canned Heat Blues." Shrill whistling yodel chills to the bone.

- *Piano Blues, vol. 4 (1923–1929)*, various artists, Document, 1995. "Green Grass," Stovepipe Johnson's medicine show-influenced blues number, includes nasal-punctuated falsetto that yearns toward a yodel. His "Devilish Blues" (1928) also has some yodeling. Also includes Yodeling Kid Brown's "Policy Blues."

- *Roots 'n' Blues: The Retrospective 1925–1950*, various artists, Columbia/Legacy, 1992. Includes The Rhythm Wreckers' "Blue Yodel #2 (My Lovin' Gal Lucille)."

- *Sara Martin in Chronological Order: Volume 1*, Sara Martin, Document, 1995. Recorded in 1922–23, includes "Yodeling Blues" with W.C. Handy.

- *Sugar: The Best of the Complete RCA Victor Recordings,* Louis Armstrong (1901–1971), Bluebird/BMG, 2001. Includes Armstrong-Rodgers duet classic "Blue Yodel #9 (Standing on the Corner)." Available on various other Armstrong and Rodgers compilations.

- *"Yippee-olly-ay-ho"* / "It Might as well be Spring," Paul Fenoulhet and the Skyrockets Orchestra. British big band jazz backed Sinatra and Carmen Miranda, among others during the 1940s.

- *"Yodeling Blues,"* Buck Mountain Band, Okeh/Clarion, 1929. Virginia rural whites do a yodel version of W. C. Handy's "Hesitating Blues," based on a traditional tune.

BING VS. THE ANDREWS SISTERS

The popular style in the new millennium happens to be vocal groups with an execrable propensity for synchronized hyper-kinetic gymnastics and sugar-pop vocals. Back in a *cooler* acoustic era, say mid-1930s to mid-1950s, vocal music was all about relaxing and sipping, harmonizing exterior with interior, highs and lows. The most compelling of the popular vocal-harmony groups was certainly the robustly versatile Andrews Sisters. They synthesized many styles and sounds into popular vocals.

Three gals from Minneapolis, LaVerne (1911–1967), Maxene (1916–1995), and Patty (b. 1918), sang close harmony on 1800+ songs. Their first hit came in 1938 and was the first million-selling record by an all-female group. Their songs weren't just cheery optimism; they had a spunky underbelly of cynical comeuppance as well. They recorded with Guy Lombardo, Jimmy Dorsey, and Sammy Kay, and they performed with Carmen Miranda, Ernest Tubb, Les Paul, and Danny Kaye, among others. But when they were matched with the tuneful crooning of the even more famous Bing Crosby (on forty-six songs) they arguably became the first super (vocal) group. Crosby was huge in every medium—radio, film, and theater—from the late-1920s through the 1950s, a superstar before that term even existed. He transformed the micro-phone into both musical instrument and dance partner.

The Andrews Sisters first recording with Crosby was "Ciribiribin" b/w "Yodeling Jive" (by Raye Prince; Decca, 1939) with the rascally Joe Venuti Orchestra. It reached #4 on the Hit Parade. Along the hits trail, the Sisters scored another yodel hit in 1948. "Toolie Oolie Doolie" sat in the Top 10 for much of the year. It featured the immortal yodel couplet: "The echo gets higher and higher / and soon their hearts are both on fire." The Sisters also recorded many Tin Pan Alley–style cowboy songs. "Rancho Pillow" (1956), near the end of their careers is one such confected aberration: "there are cowboys that keep hopin' / That he'll soon be ropin' / A dream that will one day come true / caaay-yee-peee (Yeeee!) caaay-yee-peee (Yaaaa!) . . . "

In 1950, Crosby had a Top 40 hit with Johnny Mercer's "Yodel Blues." In 1951, the Andrews Sisters again teamed with Crosby, this time to record the incredible "The Yodeling Ghost" with Vic Schoen's lush orchestration. Although this song was not hugely successful, it contains pure pop poetry coming from "that most harmonious ghost": "There's a yodel in the air yet their ain't nobody there / It must be a yodelin' ghost / . . . la doodle ah-yay-da doodle ah-ay . . . "

- *Apple Blossom Time*, Andrews Sisters, ASV, 1999.

- *Bing Crosby & the Andrews Sisters: Their Complete Recordings Together*, MCA, 1996.

cacaphonous cackles and piercing whoops. You can hear this on his album *Songs for the Geese.*

Two European jazz-men have also experimented with this genre. Gebhard Ullmann is a Berlin-based composer-performer who's not afraid to stretch the limits of jazz and new classical to create pastiched and over-dubbed strands of tango, pygmy yodel chants, African township jive, and *gagaku.* Meanwhile, Joe Zawinul, the Austrian jazz-fusionist composer/keyboardist with Weather Report, has more recently begun experimenting with a new type of fusion. His new "Orvieto Project" furthers the sonic melding of World musics. Orvieto's sound is decidedly jazz, fusion, traditional folklore, yodeling, and electric instruments.

Besides these musicians, other contemporary names have also been bandied about: Miles Griffith, Eddie Jefferson, Joe Lee Wilson, Terry Callier. They may have had their "Leon Thomas-like moments," as Ian Horst described them, but, at best, they remain a sporadic sidebar. There has been no systematic employment of yodeling or institutional imperative to yodel as a vocal embellishing scat-additive. In the worlds of blues and jazz, yodeling has remained a technique applied periodically as curiosity.

FROM ROCK TO RAP

> From beginning to the Huckleberry Fin
> If I was to yodel, would you let me in?
>
> —De La Soul, "Let, Let Me In"

The exuberant aspect of post–Workd War II popular music that led to rock 'n' roll is its characteristic irreverence coupled with an almost devout sense of long-term memory loss. Popular music got streamlined to pop music some time after the war. Part of the ballast it had managed to shove overboard was historicity and authenticity. Perspective was basically pinned down to ecstatic Me-here-and-now, the dispensable joy of the oblivious now, coupled to the nihilism (Sartre and H-bomb) of no future.

In our epiglottal context, when you run across a yodel in contemporary pop music you're immediately aware of its lack of history, tradition, and context. It's like everything else in pop—take the insertion of classical flourishes please!—grist for its mill, a patch for a quilt to be dumped tomorrow. Pop music's use of the yodel is basically an anomalous one-off, a freak-show embellishment, applied whimsically willy-nilly; the sonic equivalent of extreme chrome that garnished 1950s American automobiles. Yodeling in pop, however successful, never leads to anything remotely trendy. Focus's mega-yodel-hit "Hocus Pocus," for instance, did not inspire other prog-rockers to emulate its "formula." Pop yodeling remains reassuringly and frustratingly random, circumstantial, and peripheral to historical context.

ROCK AROUND THE CLOCK

A lot of fans may not know that Haley was well on his way to becoming a national champion yodeler when Rock and Roll came calling.
—Alan Lewis, *New England Music Scrapbook News*

Bill Haley, an unlikely pop star with a greasy-hair ringworm pasted to his forehead, made history as arguably *the* first real rock 'n' roller. His name is synonymous with r 'n' r, and yet his cheek-and-jowl looks and ill-fitting tartan suits left him with little glamour and charisma to parlay. He took rockabilly, added some jittery bop, and came up with his take on Joe Turner's "Shake, Rattle and Roll." It made musical history but, despite some early mega-hits, his star faded fast in the United States.

Was Haley a yodeler? You bet! The story starts in, of all places, staid and tidy New Hampshire. During the early 1940s, Kenny Roberts, a teen yodeler from Massachusetts, was fronting the Red River Rangers. The Down Homers, a New England band, were also on the bill. They were so impressed by Roberts that they hired him on the spot. Roberts and the Down Homers remained in Keene, New Hampshire, for a while, performing regularly on WKNE. They eventually moved on to bigger markets in Indiana and Iowa.

In 1946, Roberts enlisted in the Navy. The Down Homers needed a new lead singer. They placed an ad, and a singer from Chester, Pennsylvania, one Bill Haley, responded. Before leaving, Roberts "taught him how to yodel," is how Roberts puts it. Haley even went on to do some solo gigs, billing himself as the "Ramblin' Yodeler." When Roberts got discharged, Haley found himself suddenly unemployed, so he started his own band, the Range Drifters in 1947, while working as a DJ at WKNE.

Haley's earliest recordings have been rescued and released on *Hillbilly Haley* (Bear Family, 2003). They include some illuminating recordings of the Down Homers with Haley on rhythm guitar and yodeling on "She Taught Me to Yodel," recorded circa 1946. In 1949, Bill Haley & the Four Aces of Western Swing rerecorded "Yodel Your Blues Away" in a Chester studio with Haley yodeling at such breakneck speeds that his guitarist, Tony Rice, could hardly keep pace. Other yodel tunes recorded between 1947 and 1950 include "A Yodeller's Lullaby" and possibly "Red River Valley."

MASON WILLIAMS AND THEM YODEL YELLERS

Yodeling is an audio equivalent of the visual of lederhosen.

The 1960s saw pop music break along the great fissure of the generation gap. This demographic is best exemplified by two opposing topical yodels: on the one end, Red River Dave, the topical troubadour, basically blamed "The California Hippie Murders" of Charles Manson on drugs and a permissive society, while the Fugs's "Yodelin' Yippie" sent the weather vane pointing off in an entirely different direction.

The 1960s fostered many unusual and unexpected pop stars, including perhaps one of the most unexpected, Mason Williams. Let's get right to the nut: Williams is famous for one song, "Classical Gas," one of the great anomalous 1960s singles. Williams as an eccentric musician has been to all of the edges and back. ("'You gotta rock the boat,' Thelonius Monk said, which I've always taken to mean you've got to

Mason Williams's yodels are more than just "classical gas." By permission of Mason Williams.

challenge things, especially yourself," notes Williams.) Williams has been many things but seldom a failure or a bore. He's a published poet, lyricist, songwriter, recording artist, TV writer, and visual artist. Williams's special brand of off-kilter humor led him to extended writing bouts for the ground-breaking "Smothers Brothers Comedy Hour."

Williams was born in tornado country, Abilene, Texas, in 1938, and grew up with suitcase in hand, traveling between his father in Oklahoma and his mother in Oregon. Williams grew up during World War II listening to Elton Britt yodeling. In 1956, he and friend and contemporary art giant, Ed Ruscha, drove from Oklahoma City to Los Angeles, where Williams attended college with hopes of becoming an insurance actuary! This mundane trajectory took a lucky detour, when he was infected with jazz fever. He took up piano, flute, and double bass, and he paid for college by working evenings in a record store, where he vowed to "listen to every record in the store" to further his musical education.

In 1959, Williams formed the coffeehouse folk trio, the Wayfarers. In the Navy he formed The Hootenaires. After the Navy, and back in Los Angeles, he began writing songs for the Kingston Trio, among others. They made "Them Poems" so popular that Williams decided to record them himself. Williams

continued on the next page

Mason Williams and Them Yodel Yellers, continued

approached The Smothers Brothers, who recorded some of his comedy songs from his book "Bicyclists Dismount" and ended up writing comedy skits for them. He was nominated for an Emmy but, more important, engineered one of the most memorable conceptual (satirical) art performances ever to grace the airwaves: the "Pat Paulsen for President" campaign during the height of the Vietnam War. After "Classical Gas" won three Grammys (1968), Williams turned to combining bluegrass with symphonic sounds—his "Symphonic Bluegrass."

Williams's first yodel song was "Cinderella Rockfella," a very strange Euro-pop hit for Esther and Abi Ofarim. Middle East-born singers Esther Zaied and Abraham Reichstadt met in 1959 in a Hebrew club. In 1963, they finished second in the Eurovision contest. But their biggest hit was no doubt "Rockefella" with Esther singing-yodeling lead. Williams has produced other unusual yodelers: 1968's "Cowboy Buckaroos" is Riders in the Sky–style broadside humor, "because yodeling was a part of country-western music." This was before he himself could yodel. Back then it was "just an element in a song." He has performed "Buckaroos" "a lot" over the years.

In 1997, Williams wrote "Yodeling in the Valley," which played on the popularity of early 1990s Valley Girl demographics. Angela Pupello, a genuine VG, did the yodeling. It was a demo-only thing, which is a shame because it certainly could have been a novelty hit along the lines of Moon Unit Zappa's "Valley Girl." "I wrote 'Yodeling in the Valley' because I was always a big fan of valley girl lingo." Williams noted in a 2002 interview:

> I thought it was very creative and very funny. I used Pupello because of her expert *valleygirlisms*. She knew nothing about yodeling. She is such a facile singer, though, that she could fake it. . . . I was trying to create an offbeat character along the lines of the great characters that Ray Stevens came up with—"Guitarzan," "Ahab the Arab" . . . I have a good false tenor voice and moving between the two voices is easy for me. I tell people who want to yodel to work on their falsetto singing voice. I also tell them that the pattern of words . . . when yodeling, is important because the syllables greatly facilitate the leaps and returns from one register to another. A relaxed vocal is key. Yodeling is a stereotyping element. Usually used in conjunction with Swiss and other Alpine cultures and Finland, Norway, etc. It's become a signature sound "lick," much as the accordion has for Germans (beer garden), and the Koto has for the Japanese.

- *Them Poems*, Vee-Jay 1964. Includes "Them Yodel Yellers." Record *still* out of print; book republished by Parallel Press of Madison, Wisconsin. Very funny limerick-meets-haiku format poem.

- *Cinderella Rockefella*, Esther and Abi Ofarim, Philips 1966.

- "Cowboy Buckaroos," single, 1968.

- *Music* on Warner Brothers, 1969.

Haley eventually left Keene, joining the Saddlemen to play boogie and eastern swing. They eventually morphed into the Comets and produced the most successful rock 'n' roll record *ever* with "Rock Around the Clock." However, Haley's denouement was a steep, unkind decline. He attempted to rekindle his career off and on over the next twenty years but finally succumbed to alcoholism in 1981.

Bill Haley's capricious stabs at yodeling prior to his rock 'n' roll ascent didn't have much relationship with other yodel songs that broke into the pop charts, such as 1965's monster hit, "Five O'Clock World" by the Vogues. After Haley came Eddy Arnold's 1955 mega-crossover hit "Cattle Call," also a 1955 hit for Slim Whitman; 1960's great "Muleskinner Blues" version by the Fendermen; and in 1961, a pop version of "Wimoweh," "The Lion Sleeps Tonight," became a chart-topper. The Tokens, a Brooklyn doo-wop group, employed operatic flourishes, a Neapolitan choir, and some soaring yodeling. In 1962, Roger Miller's "The Swiss Maid" was escorted to #2 on the U.K. charts by Del Shannon.

THERE'S A YODEL GOIN' ON: SLY STONE

Yodeling has also been discovered burrowed in the world of soul-funk-rock. We have a four-pak yodel mini-trend with Parliament, Sly and the Family Stone, De La Soul, and the Fugees, four yodels spanning thirty-three years. All four invoke the myth, iconography, and sound of the cowboy yodel.

Sly and the Family Stone's *There's a Riot Goin' On* (Epic, 1971) is an incredible album of psychedelic-Vietnam-generation-gap-Manson-Woodstock zeitgeist. It includes "Spaced Cowboy," the inaugural funk/rock/soul/rap yodel. The song remains truly infectious and combustible, and is a genuine yodel: funk and vision like they've never been fused before.

In the summer of 1971, Epic Records was anxiously awaiting the overdue life-affirming record Sly (a former notorious *yodeling* radio DJ!) was promising. But rumors were circulating that the record was heading into anti-pop self-critique à la John Lennon's iconoclastic *Plastic Ono Band*. And so, Epic called on Sly fan Miles Davis to set Sly straight. Davis, a no-nonsense tough guy, visited Sly's Bel-Air house. Here he encountered headstrong Sly surrounded by bodyguards in a swirl of insanity, racial and political tension, cocaine, rumors of Black Panthers, hippie ideals, Sly's schizoid behavior, pimps, and prostitutes. Ultimately, nothing could persuade Sly from his artistic course, not even Davis.

This artistic course produced a great record that includes some highly anomalous vocals on the slow-train funk driven "Spaced Cowboy" with harmonica bridge that is capped with Sly's casual yodeling, which bubbles up

HOCUS POCUS FOCUS

I like "Hocus Pocus," by Focus. . . . It's great. It's a bit crap, really, but it's hilarious.

—Tim Gane, Stereolab

Rapper Ice T, *after* an interview on Dutch TV, called Focus's guitarist, Jan Akkerman, "un-be-lie-vable." But when asked why he didn't mention this on TV, he responded simply, "Hey man, I'm Ice T." In other words, he has a reputation to uphold. When I say to people, "Yodeling—like 'Hocus Pocus' by Focus," it never fails to garner a bemused grin. Focus and yodeling as guilty pleasures? Definitely!

Focus (1969–1978) represents the apotheosis of yodeling in rock music—and like other rock yodelers, they developed their style in a relative vacuum. Focus was well-known for their technical prowess (and serious pretensions). Despite generous applications of flute, jams, and solos, Thijs van Leer (keyboards, flute, and vocals) and Akkerman (guitar) managed to successfully fuse low-brow to high-art, blending jazz strains and rock licks with classical flutey flourishes while still managing some hooky tunes.

Van Leer met Brainbox guitar virtuoso Jan Akkerman in the late 1960s and there was an immediate chemistry. Their first serious gig was for the Dutch production of *Hair*. They took the name Focus and signed with Sire Records. Their first two albums went mega; in 1972, *Melody Maker* voted Focus as "Brightest hope for the year" and "Best foreign group." However, by 1978, after weathering numerous personnel changes, the band ran its course. But the nostalgia market has demanded "comebacks" and cockamamie re-formations. Akkerman and Van Leer *have* teamed up again periodically; in 1993, they played the North Sea Jazz Festival (The Hague), reprising some Focus material including "Hocus Pocus." This signature frentic prog-scat yodeling reportedly covered up their poor grasp of English. And if you can't sing in English, you might as well grunt, groan, and yodel near-orgasmically. "Hocus Pocus" was massive and remains one of the world's most recognizable yodels—an earmark.

- *Focus: The Best of Focus Hocus Pocus*, Red Bullet, 1993/2001. Remastered compilation includes album and U.S.-single versions of "Hocus Pocus."

- *Focus Live at the Rainbow*, Sire, 1974. Recorded live; yodeling clings to the ceiling.

over the top of the mumbling lyrics—an inspired moment in pop yodeling history. Post-"Cowboy," Sly's dream, however, dissipated into drugs, eccentricity, a legendary no-show at gigs that all led to . . . well, no one's quite sure what happened. Sly has made comebacks but he remains a conundrum inside a recluse—both as beneficiary and victim of his own genius.

Parliament is the Sun Ra of funk; they cast mangled-DNA funk into the path of a flaming asteroid. *Osmium*, 1970, includes "Little Old Country Boy" (reissued on *First Thangs*, 1997) with vocals by Fuzzy Haskins. It's a funky-twangy country ditty with pedal steel, Jew's harp, and yodeling. But in true Parliament (Funkadelic) style, it's also a manic frantic woe-is-me tale of a man done in by a woman, complete with crazed ghetto-cowboy yodeling embellishments.

The yodeling torch was passed from Parliament to De La Soul. I may very well have been the first stateside radio DJ to play "Plug Tunin'." I spun this debut 1987 single over and over and still consider their 1989 debut album, *3 Feet Hi and Rising* (Tommy Boy, 1989 [2001]) to be one of the most important albums in rap—nay, *pop*—history. It's barmy, and is drenched in off-kilter rhythms and a multi-culti myriad of dense samples, flubs, and glitches that creates an incredibly rich, human rap record in non-macho, laidback style. It dug rap underground, but it also appealed to a broader audience without selling out. They've gone on to produce three other fascinating discs. "Potholes in My Lawn"—a great rap song about soul, memory, things, and authorship all disappearing like potholes in your lawn—neatly welded two generations of soul together by sampling Parliament's demented yodeling.

The rap/hip-hop group the Fugees rode a lightning-quick ascent to super-stardom in the mid-1990s. Their contribution to the funk-yodel genre is "Cowboy," (*The Score*, Columbia, 1996) It is atmospheric Western theme music that effectively transposes the mythic Wild West onto the contemporary rap world reality with its own history of senseless violence. The yodeling on "Cowboy" is joyously sardonic.

Barrington Levy, born in West Kingston, Jamaica, 1962, spent much of his youth roaming the hilly Clarendon countryside. Here he'd mess with different voices and vocalizations, ricocheting them off the mountainsides and refining his signature "Blue Mountain yodel" embellishment, effectively using the mountains as recording studio prototype.

He recorded his debut single "My Black Girl" in 1977 with a cousin. He then joined the renowned Byron Lee & The Dragonnaires as a back-up singer. By 1979, he had enlisted Scientist to produce his solo material at the legendary King Tubbys studios. Levy emerged as a ground-breaking

MODERN EPIGLOTTAL FRONTIERS

RANDY ERWIN: CZECH-TEX YODELER

It was just dirty hillbilly ramblings on scratchy records

In the hard dry heart of Texas you'll find some of the sweetest voices. Think juice from a cactus during a drought, and you come up with Randy Erwin. His voice is clear as a proverbial bell in a very tall steeple on a very clear day. Erwin's a modest man with an immodest résumé: four critically acclaimed discs, music for film scores including a yodel cameo in David Byrne's *True Stories*. He's performed on the BBC, CBC, NPR, at Carnegie Hall, and at London's Wembley Arena.

Erwin grew up a farm boy on a rice farm in a Czech/Irish–Native American family along the Texas Gulf Coast. When not working the fields, he succored himself by listening to an old Eddie Arnold single of 'Cattle Call' "and I listened to it obsessively around four or five years of age. There was also an album of Beethoven's 5th and I obsessed on that too. So, it was 'Cattle Call' and Beethoven."

He took piano and trumpet lessons until teen adrenaline drove him from a polka band led by, in Erwin's words, "a deaf, big-band trumpet player," to obscure garage rock ensembles and a bad country-western cover band.

> After college . . . during my first job writing advertising copy . . . I started to hear 'Cattle Call' in my mind over and over again. I got out the electric piano that I had carried around since high school and started to sing the verse. Got to the yodel and it came out perfectly formed, in pitch, in nuance, just floating like Eddie, straddling the baritone I had become and the boy soprano who had long since departed.

In Dallas, he became an integral part of an "odd western-swing yodeling clique." In the 1980s, he earned a living as a trick ropin' yodeler (tricks learned from his grandmother in Ganado, Texas). Erwin offers much insight into yodeling's bio-techno-aesthetic aspects:

> For a man's voice to reach the very highest registers possible for that voice, (to) keep it in tune, control the vibrato, shape the phrase correctly, and lend the power to those high tones that a man's large physical frame can produce can be overwhelming for an audience. . . . Control is everything in the yodel, and when you reach a state of maximum control you can be completely free with the technique. . . . Sometimes when I sing I think I feel something spiritual come rushing through me, but that's probably just adrenaline and endorphines flooding my nervous system.

- *'Til the Cows Come Home*, ROM, 1989. Touching yodels. Backed by Brave Combo.

- *Cowboy Rhythm*, ROM, 1992.

reggae singer known for his "Mellow Canary" vocals—pure and expressive. He played his substantial part in the rise of reggae's tawdry side, called dancehall. By the mid-1980s, Levy was working with producer Jah Screw, and together they created some memorable recordings including the classic *Broader than Broadway*. In 1983, Levy had a U.K. #1 hit with "Under Mi Sensi," a pro-marijuana song that included his signature yodeling.

On the album *Turning Point* (Greensleeves, 1992), he produced some good covers, but he broke high into the reggae charts with "Something in My Heart," a duet with Reggie Stepper. "Heart" combines his formidable mellifluous yodeling style with cultural irony, creating that most unusual of cocktails: Caribbean sensuality plus Alpine soul. It comes across organically, convincing you that yodeling is a truly versatile esperanto that makes music(s) universal, global, and comprehensible to everyone.

Po-Mo-De-Lay-Ee-Oo: Post-Modern Yodelers

If we stretch our pop yodels out and take magnifying glasses to our specimens, we observe more bumper-car reaction than historic continuity or organic development in pop music. In country, we see precedent, logical progression, versions, homage. But trying to understand pop yodeling as a phenomenon in relation to its surroundings is counterproductive.

1980s Texas was the site of some wacky and satirical tangents (satire as a necessary antidote to a whole warbly load of commercialized schmaltz), producing mescal-addled cow punks and Rubber Rodeo types. The non-yodeling Cowboy Junkies filtered their western standards and blues through heroin-ennui-restrained Velvet Underground cool. Riders in the Sky do their Firesign takes on western lore. In the post-Byrds *Sweethearts of the Rodeo*, post-psychotic punk era, yodels have managed to emerge from some very warped throats indeed. The yodel, in fact, seems perfectly outfitted to bring out the silly-absurd-irreverent in one and all. There's even a subgenre of goofy songs with tacked on yodels to emphasize the fact that a particular tune is indeed . . . silly (see the Appendices). Take for instance "The Yodeling Veterinarian of the Alps" (*Larry's Silly Songs*):

> Some just stand in silence while some just scratch their scalps
> At the curious ways of the yodeling veterinarian of the Alps . . .
> Yodel-ay-yodel-ay-ay-hoo!

But there are also those who dug deeper beyond mere diversion to hone out modern tributes: Suzy Bogguss, for instance, lovingly reconstructed "I Want to Be a Cowboy's Sweetheart" in 1988 (*20 Greatest Hits,*

2002; see also her "Night Rider's Lament"). And then there's Steve Earle, Willie Nelson, and Sourdough Slim, even Dolly Parton's lucidly effervescent yodeling. Author Hans Ibold even goes so far as to suggest that the rock crooning of U2's Bono counts as yodeling. Many infidels, myself included, think that, despite Bono's good intentions, he's pretty much a nonyodeler and more of a rock wailer than someone "embracing" his purported hero, Jimmie Rodgers.

Into the new millennium, we discover a yodeling renaissance in country (Wylie, Sheldon Williams III, LeAnn Rimes) and in the Alps (post-pop yodelers Lauterburg, Von Goisern, and Edelschwarz). Yodeling remains pop's bastard wild-child, its blazing blipless no-name nova. I won't attempt to connect any dots, dots that do not, in any case, really exist. There is no ululation map, then, to help navigate us through the star charts of pop and rock. To some this will be annoying, vexing, unsatisfying. If by connecting dots, say chronologically, we are suddenly seeing sense and constellations in a random sky full of stars, well, then, I'll be as surprised as you.

Some Other Hick-Rock-Funk-Pop Yodelers

Johnny Dilks combines gritty post-punk attitude and a bent for realism with his love of Western Swing. Dilks is leaning on a bar somewhere between genuine article, drunken brawler, and cynical SOB. He's already swerved through rockabilly western swing and punk, which he calls "rock's real music. It's real emotion. . . . In a lot of ways, old country music was kind of like the punk rock of the 1950s."

He claims he learned yodeling from a "homemade Kenny Roberts record. . . . It had a yodeling lesson on one side and a duck call lesson on the other side. I'm not sure whether Kenny Roberts was doing the duck calls or not." I asked Roberts about this, and he responded by saying he had no recollection of any record of this description. Dilks records with the Visitacion Valley Boys.

- *Acres of Heartache*, HMG/Hightone, 1999. Neo-traditionalist western swing with detours into Cajun and elsewhere. Includes excellent "Yodel 'till I turn Blue."

Bob Dylan has had some brushes with yodeling; check his homage to Jimmie Rodgers. But Dylan actually *yodeling* above a croak *with* Johnny Cash is a frightening thought. The bootleg *Bob Dylan & Johnny Cash*, Yellow Dog Records (1994), is unreleased *Nashville Skyline* sessions material that includes Rodgers' "Blue Yodel" and "Blue Yodel #5." Cash, by the way, also manages a croaky-yodel on his "Been to Georgia on a Fast Train."

Jewel Kilcher (b. 1974) is a poetry-scribbling, indie-pop-rock sensation who yodels on "Chime Bells" and on 1994's "Daddy, She's a Goddess," on *Innerchange Days*, among some others.

Jerry Lee Lewis is the white-trash problem child of genius. His career remains hagiographical despite time spent imbibing with the devil. His transgressive lifestyle is surpassed only by his stage antics and propulsive performances, which are sporadically embellished with hiccuppy yodels. He has a broad repertoire of Hank Williams, Jimmie Davis, and Jimmie Rodgers songs, including "Miss The Mississippi & You," "Blue Yodel #6," and "Carolina Sunshine Girl," with and without yodeling.

- *Live at Gilley's*, Atlantic. Lewis yodels on "Memphis Tennessee."

Laura Love is a Nebraska-born singer-musician who dodges conventional labels. She once declared: "My mission in life is to put the 'yo!' back in yodel." For a while she referred to her sound as "funkabilly," and with the release of *Octoroon* came the label "Afro-Celtic." Her global influences come as much from her self-professed drifting attention span as her intrepid spirit and genetic heritage, an amalgam of African, European, and Indian blood.

Love's first gig was at the age of 16 at Nebraska State Penitentiary. Beginning with pop standards, moving into grunge-blues with the Seattle band Boom Boom G.I., and on to solo recordings, festivals, and headlining shows, Love eventually released three albums on her own label. Putumayo World Music released the *Laura Love Collection*, with Love's riveting live performances impressing critics. She performs a mosaic of funky groove-oriented rootsy "Afro-Celtic hip-alachian" plus bits of soul, rock, Middle Eastern melodies, and highlife grooves.

- *Octoroon*, Mercury, 1997. Precious keening yodels plus pulsating bass and responsive scat plus accordion, fiddle and flute.
- *Helvetica Bold*, Octoroon Biography, 1994. Heady menu of African and Bulgarian yodeling plus percussive bass thrumming.

Elvis Presley had some iffy bouts with yodeling. The documentary *Elvis: That's The Way It Is* (dir. Denis Sanders, 1970 [2001]), includes rehearsals of Elvis bumblingly slurring the "Cattle Call" yodels. He also yodels on "Cattle Call," *One Night in Vegas*, RCA/BMG. In the film

Flaming Star (dir. Don Siegel, 1960), Elvis plays a confused half-breed. Although Presley covered plenty of Eddie Arnold, Jimmie Rodgers, Bob Wills, and Hank Snow, Elvis never mastered yodeling. His casual throwaway yodels on "Britches," were cut from the film version. Elvis's glottal break is brittle, impatient, and tenuous.

Bob Ritchie, aka Kid Rock, grew up on a Romeo, Michigan, horse farm, north of Detroit. His rapabilly-hick-hop is sometimes described as Run DMC meets Lynyrd Skynyrd. Or Eminem meets Merle Haggard? *History of Rock*, Lava/Atlantic/AG includes his insouciant cunnilingual hit "Yodelin' in the Valley."

The Screaming Headless Torsos performed tight free-base hyperkinetic conceptual-noise funk-improv with a periodic yodel slice thrown into the molotov cocktail. Dean Bowman rapped like a champ tongue-twister and yodeled like Leon Thomas with a few other incantatory human vocal emissions thrown in.

- *Fuzelicious Morsels*, FUZE.

Stackridge was an almost-big Brit band of off-beat prog-folky rock that bled into chamber music pretensions. They were arguably the first rock group to incorporate violin *and* flute. Described as clever-silly and perhaps subsurreal, they edged toward parody and were compared to 10cc, Jethro Tull, and Curved Air. They threw audiences audio knuckleballs, including (unthinkable to prog-rock audiences) covering the yodel standard, "She Taught Me How to Yodel."

The Velvet Underground's influential fourth album was released one month after Lou Reed quit the band. The VU (and maybe Iggy Pop) seem to be the ur-root of all post-alt-rock bands. *Loaded* (Atlantic, 1970), includes "Lonesome Cowboy Bill" with its smarmy half-croaked yodel at the end of the refrain's last line—"You got to see him yodel ay hee ho." Theo Dorian, resident New York prog-glam-rock aficionado on the epiglottal play-by-play: "then [he] does a little falsetto octave leap note, like western singers do after a yodeled line." It might be described as so proto-punk nonchalant as to be almost undetectable, a kind of offhand wink-wink sonic allusion to yodeling. It has further been loosely interpreted-deconstructed by Pere Ubu and Frenchly by the girl group, the Calamités. Dorian notes that "Lonesome" served as connective tissue between Reed's lit-glam, psychedelia, and country. "Lou is just using the idiom in a postmodern, ironic way. Unlike your Hank Williams . . . he doesn't actually yodel the 'yodel ay hee hoo'—which is always like an emotional cry that underlines the chorus—he sings it as dryly as the rest of the song, which is funnier." Reed is fully unmasking the myth of the yodel's reality, Roland Barthes–style, undressing it so that it can breathe anew in all its octave richness. Dorian believes its essential elasticity is truly tested in its "one *sung* yodelayheehoo and one note or two of yodel."

11
Be On Your Avant Garde, Yodelers!

CYBERETTO YODELARIO

The advent of digital sampling, the simple reuse of sound via an "electronic digital recording system, which takes samples or 'vertical slices' of sound and converts them into on/off information" was already presaged with the visual sampling strategies of the Cubists, Constructivists, Futurists, and Dadaists. Today's audio alchemists (Eno, Adrian Sherwood, Mad Professor, Norscq, Zazou, Marclay, DJ Spooky, DJ fill-in-the-blank) are ethnomusico-logical bricolage artists, capable of cutting across styles, genres, continents, cultures with great alacrity and an artistic sense of reinvention through reuse. Much of this material was forecast by Can's *Cannibalism*, Holger Czukay's solo work, and David Byrne and Brian Eno's *My Life in the Bush of Ghosts* (1981).

Among the many groups that draw on traditional yodeling in their sampling, Deep Forest tread precariously close to waffling between righteous reuse and colonial plundering. In their context, all depth is surface and all surface is depth; all culture is consumption. Deep Forest's strategy of sampled Pygmy yodel loops dropped into a new-agey ambient porridge of quasi electro-Euro beats and emotion-twinging synthetic strings and panflutes created some controversy in the early 1990s. Hi-tech dance requirements were crossed with some cultural relevance via the West African Pygmies. Shake your booty while convincing you that your soul was being inscribed with the mysticism of an ancient traditional rite: touristic mysticism, then.

The project developed as Eric Mouquet and Michel Sanchez were listening to old tapes of *Forest Hymn: Ethnic Sound Series Vol. 4 Polyphony of Deep Rain Forest* (JVC). The Pygmy chants-yodels inspired them to immedi-

CYBER-YODEL HONOR ROLL

Audio Murphy Inc. produced an Aussie techno-yodel club hit with "Tighten up Your Pants" in 1994, cowritten by diva-yodeler Mary Schneider's daughter, Melinda, who belts out the yodels. "I really think yodeling is hereditary." Melinda observed, "You're just born with it. . . . They just slapped me on the bum and I was yodeling!"

DJ Scram is a Swedish electronic hard-groovy dance-beat musician in the general DJ Shadow/Fatboy Slim, vicinity. "Yodel Groove" is a late-1990s techno-yodel.

The Moody Boys were Jimmy Cauty (Orb/KLF) and Tony Thorpe (KLF) an early 1990s dub project.

• *Recycled EP*, Guerilla Records, 1994. Ethno-dub-dance. Includes African rhythm samples and substantial reuse of Pygmy yodeling.

Roberto Musci and Giovanni Venosta are intriguing sculptural-appropriators who scavenge and scour found-sounds to make unique new sense of them—call it audio Cubism. Listen closely, this is composition of the highest order—the result is beautiful, and their sampling methods are polemical. Sort of the obscurantist thinking-person's *Bush of Ghosts*. Chris Cutler notes that "in both cases, recordings of ethnic music are used as important voices, the rest of the material being constructed around them."

• *Messages and Portraits*, ReR, 1988. Successfully synthesizes world musics (with some yodel samples).

The Orb has been a highly successful late-20th-century ambient dub enterprise. Characterized by a hefty dub bass sound that's coupled to deep exotic ambiences, plus an adept ear for choosing humorous almost haiku-like text snippets. They make generous use of mellifluous, anonymous Pygmy singing-yodeling on "Bedouin."

• *Orblivion*, Island, 1997.

The Severed Heads were smart post-punk—cynicism, distortion, loops, and effects, the perfect antidote to the Reagan years. "Our" version of a bottle of scotch and a game of Scrabble during a drab night that lasted eight years. Garry Bradbury and Tom Ellard were never above slipping in loops of "Sanskrit yodeling records" and were always about usurping/upsetting the dance floor by inserting totally unexpected sounds into the mix—like Mary Schneider's yodeling. "She's a good old standby," says Gary in an online interview with Amey Mazurek (1994), "Mary Schneider. . . . she's strange actually. You make sample loops . . . of her and she just doesn't sound like the queen of Australian yodeling anymore, she sounds like some message from outer space."

Tweezerhead Rebellion is no household name. They're an improvisational California band (1990) with lots of post-Suicide (late-1970s New York

continued on the next page

Cyber-Yodel Honor Roll, continued

art-drone-punk duo)—buzz-saw plus the whooosh of passing cars . . . and yodeling! Michael Meloan is Tweezerhead's vocalist-author-computer program-mer. Guitarist Dana Massi is interested in extended vocal techniques and loves Pygmy singing. Meloan usually stands

> behind the microphone with a stack of [Massi's] written works. Then we let it fly. The yodel track sprang from the notion that the juxtaposition of elec-tronica and yodel might be strange and interesting. I was inspired by busi-ness trips I was making at the time, where we'd roar across the German autobahn at 140 MPH [220 KPH] with the sight of the Alps in the . . . distance.

• *Democracy*, Tweezerhead Rebellion, Placebo, 1993. Includes "Yodel," a studio-enhanced yodel with lots of reverb and echo that sounds like early Wall of Voodoo in Muotathal.

ately begin laying down synth-dance beats underneath. They eventually took the completed recordings to Cameroon's ethnomusicologist, Francis Bebey, who gave them his blessing. To forestall any hints of inappropriate un-PC behavior, they sought to secure the rights to the vocals. UNESCO agreed, as did Hugo Zemp, the audio archivist of the original Pygmy material. Songs were composed with loops of Pygmy yodels as rhythmic backbone, with syn-thetic dance elements woven around the vocal loops. Part of the profits of *Deep Forest*, (Sony/Epic/Celine, 1992) went to the Pygmy Fund.

The soulful dubsters Up, Bustle & Out, on the other hand, effectively retool Pygmy yodeling and water-drumming, allowing the yodel to hover somewhere in a remix between appreciation and appropriation, part indigenous documentary, part cultural dialogue, part fetishistic exoticism. The yodels are lifted, revitalized with effects and reverb, recontextualized in ambient settings to further fuse tradition with technology.

Looking on the bright side, these kinds of World music reuses para-doxically encourage, as Deborah Pacini Hernandez claims, a "deeper exploration of national musics." As people observe other traditions, they are reminded of their own often-overlooked traditions and peculiarities. But all this beauty of reused appropriation does not deafen us to the copy-right arguments of indigenous people. As author Timothy Taylor observes, "The hype surrounding the new global economy covers up, to a certain extent, the fact that capitalism is as exploitative as it ever was . . . and is con-stantly seeking new people around the world to use as cheap labor." The ease with which anyone can master a sampler makes the debate even more treacherous, as all authenticity becomes easy fair game for reuse via public-domain escape clauses. These circumstances are not terribly unique, although perhaps a bit more intensely obvious, say, than the many ethnomusicological gatherers who, in the name of research and knowledge, left the indigenous populations anonymous. The Pygmies on these recordings remain mostly anonymous, while the focus is often more on the adventures of the ethnomusicological-adventurer-gatherer.

To my ears, the most beautiful recycled yodeling samples (heartrending ornamentality?) occur on Dub Syndicate's "No Dog Barks." It interweaves Pygmy yodeling with the sampled voiced of Prince Far I throughout the song as a melody, lending them a sonic aura as plaintive as any lonesome whistle yodel. It also offers Jamaican/Western/London musicians a broader palette with which to paint their sonic portraits. "Bedwood of Perplex" by Doug Wimbish—Adrian Sherwood collaborator, bassist with Tackhead, and other On-U-related projects including Dub Syndicate—contains some effectively enchanting reuse of Pygmy yodels as well. This particular reuse creates a thoroughly psychotropic trip-hop-dub ambience where the Pygmy voices seem to float free of all bodily ballast, a state, no doubt, recognized by many indigenous populations as the thirst for transcending the mundane everyday.

In 1978, Wilfrid Mellers effervescently predicted "that the future evolution of electronic music will steer this product of highly sophisticated technology towards a manifestation of precisely those 'mystical' and numinous ranges of experience which science was to have obliterated." An irony not lost in the shuffle as the works of Le Mystere des Voix Bulgare and Hildegaard von Bingen have in their timelessness been reconstructed by technology to be the very essence of numinous. It's at this glottal stop, located at this particular crossroad of technology and transcendence, that certain yodelers are able to render a way of life as immediate and palpable. Our earlier notion of a yodel's echo caught in the middle of the valley as an example of prerecorded sound lends itself well to these hyper post-modern tactics of appropriation, dissembling, self-reference, and *détourned* function. As it departs *from* it arrives *at*; as it renounces it reclaims. By departing from ethnomusical empiricism and genre-puritanism, the reconstituted yodel may hermeneutically reclaim deep feelings of awareness by destabilizing socially determined contexts of what music *should* do and where it *must* go.

This has already been loosely termed "Fourth World" music by Jon Hassell and Brian Eno. It includes musicians involved in extended electronica, the inventive reuse of dub, and speculative samples that do not necessarily neglect intelligence, to remain tangentially related to the sociopolitical idealism surrounding the notion of no borders, and, by extension, no nationalism, no wars. It's certainly the idealistic effluvia one encounters with musicians like Von Goisern or Ry Cooder: studio as virtual mountain valley where that synaptical instant, that segue between a yodel's high and low where outer integrates with inner and past fuses to future occurs.

Dub (versioning or doubling) is the strategy of reconfiguring Jamaican reggae songs by stripping them of their vocals and then customizing them with delay, echo, and interspliced samples that transform the song into something like an aural psychotropic entry into altered consciousness. Lee "Scratch" Perry is arguably the maddest genius of present-day post-Jamaican dub. Since his earliest Bob Marley and the Wailers days, he has consistently altered the course of sculpted sound by using a welter of mega-sampling splices, extemporaneous scat-*poesie* and mindblowing reverberated howls. His bawdy vocals sometimes veer into demented voodoo yodeling. He's no doubt a tempest in a "tea" pot; somewhere between idiot-savant and jester-genius, he is able to scat effortlessly from subject to subject and pitch to pitch.

Dub expands the space to hoe "the uneasy silence" between sounds. Robin Maconie seems to hint at this when he notes that "most sounds are intermittent and ephemeral, and because of the aural concept of reality, is framed to account for the continuing existence of things that may not always be signaling their presence." To add further speculation to the mix, Joscelyn Godwin claims that "expansion into bigger and bigger spaces slows down temporal events, to the degree that a single vibration, or rotation, of our planet takes a whole day, and that of a galaxy, millions of years." An echo of the original, which in time became the echo of an echo until the echoes of the echoes began to mingle, harmonize, and morph into something completely new and expansive, "dematerializing and eroding the integrity of singers and song." And it is here, at this juncture of technology and deep abiding notions of connection, of inner and outer, that yodeling may function its connective or *mantral* function.

EXTENDING THE "YO": POSTMODERN YODELISTS

> the glossalalian disruption of the irreducible phonic substance is where universality lies . . . in this break, this cut, this rupture. Song cutting speech. Scream cutting song. Frenzy cutting scream with silence. . . . Scat black magic, but to scat or scatter is not to admit formlessness.
> —Fred Moten, describing Billy Strayhorn's work

Perhaps the most hauntingly resonant yodel I've *ever* heard is, strangely enough, a long, conceptual, stream-of-consciousness piece by Brooklyn-based avant-crooner Shelley Hirsch. Her "Haiku Lingo" gloriously evokes the *feel* of the Alps while simultaneously conjuring up New York's palpable

CYBER YODEL DISCOGRAPHY

- *ADDicTiON*, Is-m, BMS, 2001. Techno-yodel piece combines old world with new, in a jolly, up-tempo style.

- *The Ambient Collection*, Art of Noise, China/Polydor, 1990. "Art of Love (7" edition)" remixed by Youth, includes a very wacked amphetamine-cranked-up Swiss yodel.

- *Après Skihut Volume 5*, CNR, 2000. Crazed Dutch dance-mix series includes sing-along schmalz, drinking songs, and snatched-echoes of forgotten hits ("Jodel Strudel") mixed into a non-stop house-beat.

- *Black Ark Experiments*, Lee "Scratch" Perry with the Mad Professor, Ras/Ariwa, 1995. Includes "Thank You."

- *Edelweiss*, Edelweiss, GiG Records, 1988. Cover warns: "A Sound Attack Straight from the Alps." Maria Mathis is the yodeling vocalist.

- *Incursions in Illbient*, various artists, Asphodel, 1996. Illbient is New York's answer to ambient with jazz-soulful elements thrown into a noisier dub mix. "Transient Scratch" contains a recognizable sample of Pygmies chanting-yodeling.

- *Let Us Play!*, Coldcut & Hexstatic, Ninja Tune, 1996. Includes "Timber," a sonic-visual impressionistic look at consumption and deforestation. Complete with a sampled loop of menacing chainsaws serving as backbeats and plaintive Pygmy yodel chorus as the forlorn looped voices of a disappearing habitat.

- *Light 'Em Up, Blow 'Em Out,* Up, Bustle & Out, Ninja Tune, 1997. Excellent Mekons-like trip-hop band combines electronica effortlessly fused to their sonic globetrotting. Includes "Y Ahora Tu," which samples Pygmy yodeling.

- *Manasseh Presents Spectre: The Missing Two Weeks*, Echo Beach, 1999. Includes reconfigured Pygmy yodels on "Covert Dub (Youth Remix)."

- *Never Trust a Hippy*, Adrian Sherwood, Real World, 2003. Provocative jazz-dub-World fusion samples African yodeler-guitarist S. E. Rogie. Noticeable yodel samples: "No Dog Jazz" (remix of "No Dog Barks") and "Majstic."

- *Stoned Immaculate*, Dub Syndicate, On-U Sound/Restless, 1990. Great record by dub's premier post-mod band. Includes enchanting yodel reuse on "No Dog Barks."

- *360 Degrees*, Dreadzone, Creation/Sony, 1993. The debut of this dub-reggae-electronica group includes "Far Encounter," which makes generous use of Pygmy yodeling as a rhythmic element.

- *Trippy Notes for Bass*, Doug Wimbish, On-U Sound 2000. Includes "Bedwood of Perplex."

continued on the next page

Cyber Yodel Discography, continued

- **Under Mi Sensi,** Barrington Levy, Greensleeves 12–inch, 1985. Producer Jah Screw and DJ Ranking Joe recruited Levy to yodel for their first production.

- **The Yodel Anthem**, DJ Da Rick, Jumper Records, 1999. Techno-hardhouse yodeling with a twist: Rick has sonically conflated two entirely different phonemes here: one of the word "yodel" and the other "*Joden*" ("Jews" in Dutch). This was chanted by PSV-Eindhoven soccer fans in a game against Ajax (Amsterdam) in 1998. Sampling plunderphonics here deconstructs anti-semitic football chants to a ridiculous techno (faux) yodel; fans are now heard chanting "Yodel, Yodel, Yodel" for three minutes. Controversial.

- **Yodel Man**, Yodel Man, from the bizarre "yodel techno" sub-genre, which fuses the ecstatic high notes with an ecstatically frenetic dance beat.

- **"Yodel Reggae / Yodel Dub,"** Leroy Gibbs, Trojan single, 1987. Producer: Desmond Rowe.

neurotic ambience. Avant-garde vocalists are expected to take whatever has been already far-flung and fling it further. Extended vocalization is the voice stretched beyond any recognizable fauna, culture, nation, style, or presumption. The most viscerally satisfying experience in an avant-garde context usually occurs when a strange vocalization begins to suddenly sound *very familiar*, passing through all the cultural filters to tickle us in a new internal organ in a new way. Extended vocal techniques have traditionally meant humans stepping out of their humanity to become the birds, wolves, monkeys of their native environments, or vocals that are not traditionally considered music like growling *mbisa* vocals, the glottal mayhem of Indian singers, the yodels that imitate the cuckoo . . .

Extended art vocals began arguably with the Dadaists and Futurists who both experimented with sound, noise, and vocables and served as the predecessors of the sound poets, although the egocentric and impish reaction to hearing one's echo certainly precedes all conscious art. In the 1950s, composers Luciano Berio and his wife, singer Cathy Berberian, began including coughing, laughing, crying, yodeling, and whispering in their repertoire. But this may have been preceded by Spike Jones's use of almost any and every sound imaginable, including gargling arias.

While World Music, Ambient, or New Age musicians must remain somewhat obeisant to history and tradition, the avant-garde and the heretics must by definition position themselves outside of this orthodoxy. That these performers do not fit in is exactly where they want to fit, *must* fit. Their essential measure is the individual as sovereign body, a nation of one, and their national anthems are composed in vocable, an esperanto beyond the cages of logic, what Curt Sachs referred to as an "emancipation from meaningful words." This does not necessarily mean disrespect, arrogance, thievery, or un-PC thuggery; it just means that they believe in a higher calling and that calling is joyous curiosity.

What these vocalists share with yodelers, then, is in essence proof of Heinrich Leuthold's theory of the origin of the yodel: It was born in the human joy and fascination with manipulating the vocal cords and mouth, and listening to the results. It's the human-at-play and play as a remedy or respite from the prevailing doom and gloom of most people's reality. It can be as simple as the "art of making an experience more vividly real by adding an unexpected ingredient on the spur of the moment."

There are numerous strange amalgamations that involve combining the yodel-inflected falsetto with kitsch (Mary Schneider), operatic excess (Klaus Nomi, most famous as a transsexual whose robotic operatics were applied to the *Wizard of Oz*'s "Ding-Dong the Witch Is Dead"), or psyche-cleansing primal scream therapy (Diamanda Galas). Once you transgress the ethno-purist notion that a yodel must be only one thing, and you realize that it can be "any cry resembling this musical mode," new horizons appear. And those who have yodeled, whether they have meant to or not, begin to reveal their true vocal cords: Tiny Tim (tiptoeing, ambiguous-gendered hippie singer), Yoko Ono (primal screams for peace), or Greetje Bijma or Jaap Blonk (conceptual Dutch scat singers).

In this extrapolation of the yodel, improv is applied to new stresses and societal strains offering a certain indulgent release from the constraints of

SOME KINDA BALINESE JAZZ

The higher they are the higher their voices. The pitch is affected by the actual altitude.

I interviewed Shelley Hirsch (b. 1952) at the Cute White Furniture Café below Canal Street on Broadway, near Hirsch's apartment, one month after 9/11/01. Hirsch composer, improviser, and performer—was born in East New York, Brooklyn, an old Jewish neighborhood that is now a crumbling ghetto, frightening emblem of urban decay. Hirsch now lives in the proverbial shadow of the ghost of the World Trade Center. She is best known for her kinetic multiple-personality panoply of voices that seem pinioned somewhere between shamanistic tongues and urban psychosis. It's improvisation of the highest order but also incredibly entertaining bio-melodrama as she stealthily slides from style to

continued on the next page

Some Kinda Balinese Jazz, continued

genre to questionable mental states. Her tools are cabaret, Borscht Belt routines, opera, 1940s swingin' pop, jazz, rock, Broadway musicals, and some post-Dada forays into the abstract frontier of language as pure sound experiments.

Hirsch's first exposure to yodeling came from a number of influences. When asked what was the first yodeling that she heard, she laughed and said:

> I wonder if when I first loved *Heidi* . . . I don't know why it started but I know it started as a teenager. I started listening to that Bulgarian music very early, like 25 years ago at least. . . . In '82, I went to Italy and I was with a friend of mine . . . but we wound up in some tiny little Austrian town where everybody was yodeling and . . . I got a lot of yodeling things. . . . But I also heard lots of yodeling before that. . . . I remember one of the most inspiring records was either on the Folkways series or this French NATO series of herders actually in the mountains calling and yodeling.
>
> Oh, I know when it first started: It's when I first noticed the crack in my voice going from a chest voice to a head voice. And so I couldn't do that Grace Slick song with that crack in my voice. And then I started to savor that crack. So then I said, "What can I do between those two places?" And so, that's . . . how it probably started.

Hirsch believes yodeling is influenced by the "high altitudes" of the Swiss mountains:

> It's the reflection in the mountains, because that's what a yodel is and why all people living in high places have a similar kind of vocal technique. Whether it's people up in the Himalayas . . . Tibet, I mean, all those people are doing that certain kind of throat-singing with that glottal stop, and needing to reflect off, and then hearing it. . . . I want to study how music from different altitudes sounds different. Because frogs sing differently when they're at different altitudes, you know, their pitch rises . . . the higher they are the higher their voices. The pitch is affected by the altitude. . . . But when you think of people in very mountainous areas, also the jobs they had and they needed to communicate and they heard these reflections and then they incorporated these reflections . . . I mean that's basically how it developed. Taking this reflection and bringing it to a more contained environment.

- *Haiku Lingo*, Shelly Hirsch and David Weinstein, ReR, 1989. Lovely, challenging, and somehow oxymoronically *authentic*. "Lingo" combines "extended vocal techniques and quirky synthesizer machinations to produce a distinctly post-Cagean cabaret."

- *States*, Tellus, 1997.

- *Far in Far Out Worlds of Shelley Hirsch*, Tzadik, 2002.

tradition. Yodeling becomes old clay in new hands precisely because it has proven to be a very versatile vocalization: It can evoke both mirth and spirit, both melancholy and exultation, proving its expressive breadth and depth-of-field. How does yodeling sharpen human experience in the various vocalists' strategies to astonish? Cast the yodel into new canyons to receive a satisfactory echo in return. Based on my presumptuous intuition, I include the iconoclastic antics of the Fugs, the inspired heresy of David Wojnarowicz, the yodeling Blake of Ginsberg and Orlovsky, odd vocal techniques from other cultures like Tuvan throat singers, or Cajuns using split-pitch yelps. I include Stimmhorn here instead of in the Alpine discography.

ED SANDERS: YODELIN' YIPPIE?

Well I ride the left-wing airlines / stirring up trouble at night / . . . I'm just a yodelin' yip-yippie / Cay-Yippie yo-de laaay-ee oo de lay dee

There are few American cultural figures I admire more than Ed Sanders. He has managed to combine what is most difficult in American politics and entertainment: levity with gravity, sobriety with intoxication, logic with spiritual investigation. As an heir to the position once held by Allen Ginsberg, Sanders comes across as more truly revolutionary: He does not have that unresolved tension of Buddhist selflessness versus unbridled egocentrism that Ginsberg seemed to embody. Sanders, who's been arrested more than a dozen times for various protest actions since the 1960s, remains a source of political analysis, polemics, critique, but also of enlightening levity. *Tales of Beatnik Glory* remains one of the best novels about 1950s–'60s New York. His *America: A History in Verse* (Black Sparrow, 2000) is an excellent antidote to standard American history books, investing the worker and ordinary people with their own Whitmanesque voice.

Sanders is also a member of the legendary Groucho-Marxist anarcho-syndicalist post-Guthrie/Seeger band, the Fugs, who've been delivering their pithy and timely song parodies—I think immediately of their rewriting of "Rum & Coca Cola," where the refrain "rum and Coca Cola" mutates into "guns and Lee Iacocca"—since the 1960s. They effectively tighten the drawstrings of style and rhetoric between the 1960s and the 21st century.

I interviewed Sanders in October 2001, in Woodstock, New York. Sanders reminisces:

I got my yodeling . . . well, there were country-western shows at auditoriums in Kansas City that I went to see and I was exposed to it there. . . . I didn't really discover that kind of music until after 1953–54. . . . And I really wasn't aware of Jimmie Rodgers until a bit later. Rodgers's yodel was a little thinner than Williams's but I think he could hit a higher yodel note than Williams. . . . Different styles. I like the way that Williams could go

continued on the next page

Ed Sanders: Yodelin' Yippie?, continued

right from the words into a yodel: "I got a feelin' called the . . . ," and then he goes right in "blOoo-odeLAY eee oooz" . . . right out of the vocal right into the yodel—whew!

I used to practice it when I became aware and got all of Jimmie Rodgers's records and Hank Williams's. I got just one or two of them and I used to listen to'm and practice with my autoharp and . . . I sorta had an Irish tenor, in a way. Of course I hit all the notes so, on one record [*Belle of Avenue A*] in 1969 I did this tune called "Yodeling Yippie" [about] a guy riding the airlines to take part in anti-war protests like a cowboy riding a horse only he rides the airlines. [Actor Donal Logue performs a version of "Yippie" in the bio-documentary about Abbie Hoffman, *Steal This Movie* (2000).] So that's about it. When we do Fugs reunions . . . we added a yodel fill there. I do a little yodeling on "I Feel Like Homemade Shit."

Sanders has expanded his yodeling activities over the years:

Jack Collom, who's a fine American poet and environmentalist-teacher, is a yodel aficionado and collects the most obscure compilations of yodel tunes. Anyway, when I go teach at Naropa [Institute in Bolder, Colorado] . . . we have this thing called the "Hummingbird Yodel." We do environmentalist yodeling celebrating the Colorado bio-region. He's pretty good; when you get two people yodeling it's compounded.

Sanders describes his yodeling technique and philosophy:

As an art form, it's a burst-from-the-soul type of art form. It just appears. It's sudden, there's no intro to it. It bursts out and as a burst-out art form it's a little like an Action Painting—the ones that are good knock you off your feet. . . . It's a mimesis but the thing about it is, once you're removed from the primal source then you mutate the source with your own set of vocal chords . . .

And I always tell people that the thing about yodeling is that you figure out what you can do, don't try to do anything else. In other words, study the notes you can hit and the range . . . don't try to go too high . . . there's a perfect midrange yodel that you don't have to go stratospheric with. . . . And then it's just a matter of the old jazz adage: you practice the way you play. And so you practice a lot and get something down. That's what I did with "Yodeling Yippie." I sat down with my tape recorder and recorded it a lot of times and listened to it and it mutated until I was satisfied with it. . . . I pulled my yodel aura to help keep it going. It's sorta like Japanese flower arranging—it's a good thing and you want to keep it going.

- *Beer Cans on the Moon*, Reprise, 1972. Features "Yodeling Robot," a fanciful sci-fi rewriting of *Frankenstein*, in which Frankenstein's monster falls in love with Dolly Parton.

- *The Fugs Final CD (Part 1)*, Artemis, 2003. with two yodels, including "Government Surveillance Yodel."

I include profiles of both avant-garde and weird (novelty) yodelers. And I'm willing to keep the doors open for someone like Gary Smart, who in 1973 produced "Del Diario de un Papagayo," a tape of his multilingual pet parrot singing arias from selected operas!

SOME AVANT-GARDE YODELERS

Lynn Book (b. 1956, in Texas) is a voice artist with a palette of sounds that would warm the ready-made hearts of the noisiest Dadaists. She works with language beyond the confines of logic, the frustrations and isolation of reason-based language. Her work pulsates and writhes somewhere between well-burnished and inchoate. Book doesn't stop at voice, also incorporating other media into her work like text, sound, and film. But Book is very

> deeply engaged with yodeling, as a vocal practice . . . most definitely a glottal-stop aficionado I am. Also as a teacher it is a most instructive vocal production to highlight, especially for Westerners who are too easily seduced and ultimately defeated by the seamless "beauty" of both classical and pop singers of renown. . . . I also host a yodel contest twice yearly here in the context of an evening of new performance works for voice that Voicelab produces in New York.

- *Strange Familiar*, own label, 1995. With bassist Tatsu Aoki. Abstract-expressive vocals with poetics and some yodeling thrown in; somewhere between cavewoman and cyborgienne.
- *Demi Demo*, Voicelab, 2000. "Song of O" contains substantial evidence of yodeling. She makes the voice sound like something that has yet to be fully (re)discovered.

Tim Buckley (1947–1975), a singer-songwriter who came in through a crack in a wall, entering this world—"a blue melody"—yearning for an unattainable world. He ate from the same loaf as Captain Beefheart and Rahsaan Roland Kirk, although, in record stores he's found in the sensitive singer-songwriter section. Buckley's early influences, growing up in Amsterdam, New York, were quite conventionally Hank Williams and singing cowboys. He realized early on that he had a special voice with a range of four octaves. As a young teen, he joined yodeler Princess Ramona & The Cherokee Riders (nowadays an evangelical preacher). But his John Coltrane leanings and flights of fantasy did not suit this standard country combo.

Buckley signed to Elektra, home of the Doors, producing his first album in 1967 at age 19. He moved rapidly from sensation to incomprehensible genius, producing less and less marketable discs that were more and more improvisational and cast adrift from all conventions of commercial song appeal, culminating in *Lorca* and *Starsailor*, which included vocal excursions into nether regions that only alienated earlier listeners. On tour, his extended abstract vocals (barking, groaning, snoring, and yodeling) left his folkie audiences shrugging on some distant shore. *Starsailor's* failure sent him listing off into deep depression, becoming as alienated as his misunderstood jazz heroes. A rock magazine headline at the time said it all: "BUCKLEY YODELING BAFFLES AUDIENCE."

The stakes started coming loose in 1971. He was claiming to be Sly Stone's personal chauffeur and using drugs as creative exploration tools. During this time he bitterly observed, "The most shocking thing I've ever seen people come up against, beside a performer taking off his clothes, is dealing with someone who doesn't sing words. If I had my way, words wouldn't mean a thing." In 1975, he overdosed on heroin. An amazingly luminous singer of primal careening chants—call it confessions of an improvisational hallucinogen eater — was dead at age 28: a man out of time who ran out of time.

- *Lorca*, Elektra, 1970.
- *Starsailor*, Elektra, 1970. Two of Zappa's Mothers turned Buckley on to Cathy Berberian's opera singing, inspiring this amazingly inaccessible record, 16 overdubbed tracks of alien vocal soundings in a language that only Meredith Monk comprehends. His voice careened freely, expressively from chest voice, rising rapidly through three octaves and then plunging down just as rapidly.

DODO HUG CONTINI

> I think a yodel is almost always a welcome and exotic surprise for the audience. At the same time amazing, rare and funny.

Hug (b.1951) is a singer, songwriter, musician, comedienne, actress, and a yodeler. If you gave Nina Hagen a lot of things to do besides warble, you'd have Dodo Hug; she's a multilingual, one-woman Spike Jones. Her songwriting is witty and in the realm of Judy Tenuta. She has an amazingly versatile voice that you know could go one-on-one with Diamanda Galas. Hug is most closely associated with Zurich, having grown up in and around northeastern Switzerland. She started out in the early-1970s doing dinner theater and performing in the streets and pubs. She joined the musical comedy group Tarot (1974–78) and worked in TV, radio, and children's theatre until 1979. In the 1980s, she did theater, music and conceptual work, and she began her own comedy theater, Mad Dodo. In 1994, she began focusing on her music.

Dodo Hug, yodeling beyond the Cabaret Voltaire. Photo by Christian Lanz. Courtesy of Dodo Hug.

Hug started yodeling in 1956 at age 5: "My grandmother often yodeled for me in her kitchen, because I liked it so much. I imitated her immediately. It amazed me that someone could sing so fast and make such a funny giggling sound with her mouth." Today she's often asked to do radio and TV-jingles,

> when they need someone with a sense of humor, who can yodel in a tongue-twisting way, because traditional Swiss yodelers don't see the point of being funny. I'm a singer who sometimes yodels and I try to do my own kind of yodeling. As kids and teenagers, we didn't pay much attention to Swiss folk music. We only rediscovered it, towards the end of the 1970s.

Hug doesn't relate to yodel traditionalists. "Unfortunately," she observes,

> among traditional Swiss yodelers and folk music people, there are too many political conservatives and therefore it is not so funny participating at Swiss yodel and folk music festivals. For example, some years ago, when Cyril [Schläpfer] did this production with Christina Lauterburg, a lot of people didn't like the way they treated folk music. I think it's a pity, because folk music only stays alive, when it is constantly changing and developing and especially is not written down, like in the past, otherwise it'll just die in the archives. Thank god, some of the younger musicians are trying to clear away the dust again . . . and just play.

She has produced some 8 CDs/LPs.

- *Kaleidofon*, ZYT, 2001. Cowritten/coproduced with Efisio Contini. Ambitious potpourri of styles including poetic-surralististic, Fellini-esque, sensitive songwriting, and truly inspired delivery. "Ds Müeti" is full-blown yodeling; "Gwärchegi Kläng" has some lilting yodel flourishes.

- *De la Musique Folie*, Zyt, 1990s. Everything from Patti Smith to European folk and art songs, with periodic applications of yodel flourishes.

Dawn McCarthy

Yodeling's . . . like magic, even the guffawing drunks stop short.

McCarthy (b. 1969) was born in rural Lima Center, Wisconsin, grew up in Spokane, Washington, and belongs to that rich tradition of vocalists who stretch the human voice to something beyond reason, expectation, and commercial feasibility. She has performed throughout North America, in Germany, Italy Poland, Czech Republic, and the United Kingdom. McCarthy's theatrical shows provide her with alter-egos, odd props, and audience participation. She yodels at least once every set "unless someone requests more yodeling. Often it's near the end because it creates such a plateau" that she finds hard to top. "Or I start the set with it to grab the crowd—usually a cappella." It's her ace up the sleeve, "especially when I need to cut through a noisy room. There has been a lot of yodeling on command in the last ten years of my life in a variety of public or private spaces—'we hear you yodel. So, give us a yodel!'—and like a performing dog I jump into it, happy to be a part of such alterings."

- *Faun Fables*, Faun Fables, 1999. Includes yodels on the melancholy "Ode to Rejection," and the magical waltzy "This Bliss."

Dawn McCarthy's yodels stop guffawing drunks. Photo by Katherine Copenhaver. Courtesy of D. McCarthy.

Phil Minton (b. 1940) is an inveterate sound experimenter who has put down his trumpet and pushed aside his piano to mangle a voice that's no longer the sweet soprano of his youth. His throat gets a big work out with jazzy-spasmatic vocals that leave any bel canto fluttering in the flatulent breezes. He grew up with strong socialist leanings in an English mining town. His early works include a recitation of anarchist John Henry MacKay's "I am an anarchist . . . " He has produced fifty records of uncompromising sound. Engagé art plus abstract vocalization with some prole-punk leanings.

- *Trace*, with Roof, Red Note, 1997.
- *Mouthful of Ecstasy*, Victo, 1996.

Shawn Phillips (b. 1943) is an eccentric vocalist (male Kate Bush?) who gets tossed in the navel-gazing singer-songwriters record section. His voice range and promise often outstrip his ability to harness it creatively. He has shown amazing vocal dynamics (unnerving sounds produced by a three-octave baritone to countertenor range), and his recordings often showcase his voice straying into seldom-charted territory. His vocals awe to the point of discomfort. He grew up unassumingly enough in Fort Worth, Texas, and divided his musical interest between folk-blues and classical. He remains an anomaly who's difficult to market. He has produced some fifteen albums. A&M produced a best-of in 1992.

Erika Stucky (b. 1964) grew up in hippie-era San Francisco and moved to Mörel, Canton Wallis, Switzerland, a mountain village where yodeling still thrives. Switzerland supplied her sonic illumination, America her brazen jauntiness, and, oh, time done in Paris enhanced her jazz leanings. Stucky entertains passionately, easily, lovingly, mixing the mountains' magic with their own worst nightmares. She straddles two cultures and numerous musical styles with a cool, clever delivery: cabaret comical like Ann Magnuson but with an awesome jazzy voice. Add the ability to tell a grimy tall-tale and a gift for irreverent phrasing of questionable pop/rock classics like Aerosmith's "Walk This Way." And in all this sophisticated, scowlin', swingin' scat, one finds little sugar cubes of genuine earnestness in a bowl at the end of the formica bar in a town that speaks in yodel.

- *Bubbles & Bones*, Traumton, 2001. Stucky on vocals, accordion, melodica. Includes some yodels—especially on "Zäuerli."

Toby Twining (b. 1958) is a Texan born under a different hat. He's an avant-garde vocalist/composer, and so the world is his audio oyster. He blurs or explodes the distinctions between folk, vernacular, and art. His

Erika Stucky's yodels straddle two worlds. Photo by felix streuli. Courtesy of Traumton Recs.

Modus Operandi is eclectic and panoramic. He became fascinated with the human voice in the mid-1980s and began studying Renaissance madrigals, scat, African yodeling, and Mongolian throat-singing. He moved to New York in 1987 and established his a cappella quartet, Toby Twining Music, in 1990. He has since gone on to great success, winning numerous awards and commissions. Yodeling evident on "Hee Oo Oom Ha."

- *Shaman*, Toby Twining Music, RCA/Catalyst, 1994. Several works incorporate Pygmy yodeling echoes including "Hell's Kitchen Hootenanny."
- *Chrysalid Requiem*, Cantaloupe Music, 2002. With yodeling in "Kyrie."

MARGINAL FUN: HERETICAL–WEIRD HONOR ROLL

I yodel in the nude

—Weird Al Yankovic, "Talk Soup"

Kerry Christensen (b. 1954), self-proclaimed acrobatically epiglotted Victor Borge of Yodeling and self-promoting master boaster, claims on *Hooked on Yodeling* that he is "unquestionably the greatest creative yodeling artist the world has ever known." That's what it says. He's the master of bluster, hubris, marketing, and moxy. Like the best gangsta rapper, he points out "I am a professional yodeler much different from all the other yodelers of the world." But as Flava Flav (Public Enemy) once warned, "don't believe the hype."

Christensen preserves traditions while he's bastardizing them: hitching kitsch to every thread of *kulture*. He does it all; plays Alphorn, cowbell, zither, and accordion; sings Western, Swiss, German, "jazz," "Cajun"; and

AVANT-FRINGE YODEL DISCOGRAPHY

- *Auch Wenn Es Seltsam Klingen Mag*, Auch Wenn Es Seltsam Klingen Mag, Austro Mechana, 1988. Inspired insanity somewhere between Penguin Café Orchestra and the Lettermen. Early vehicle for Austrian sampler-composer Curd Duca. "The Austrians" is a sardonic send-up of the marketing of Austria as a "friendly race" with yodeling as one of its cute attractions.

- *Blue Yodel, Blue Heron*, Jack Collom, Baksun Books, 2002. Well-regarded Colorado poet-teacher from Boulder, Colorado. Highly recommended tall-tale of a blue heron with yodeling, political commentary, a Burl-y Ives voice that glides into yodeling like a blue heron alighting on a pristine lake.

- *The Gab—Gift or Curse?*, Plain People of England, self-produced, 2000. One of Rob Murphy's many sound projects. Murphy creates aberrant "pop" music that mutates and meanders through styles, genres, and strange parts of the world. "Group Sex" contains subtle sampled yodeling that insinuates itself in the background ambience the way a superior perfume operates.

- *The Green Door*, V/Vm, Test Records, 2000. V/Vm hijack popular tunes from house to pop, grind them up, and spit it back out in a way that makes the Residents sound like the Osmonds and John Oswald like Mantovani. The party "tune" "Schwarz-Gelb ist Borussia" is a thoroughly effects-dessicated version of innocent Alpine yodeling.

- *Holy Soul Jelly Roll: Songs and Poems (1949–1993)*, Allen Ginsberg and others, Rhino/WordBeat, 1994. Four-CD set illuminates many sides of both private and public Ginsberg, including a series of "cover" versions of his favorite poet, William Blake. "Nurse's Song (Innocence)" matches Ginsberg's singing with mad-beat poet/life partner Peter Orlovsky's wonderful tipsy yodeling. Ginsberg chants the line—"and all the hills echo-ED"—over and over until it becomes a kind of voiceprint approximation of rolling hills. Atop this drone, Orlovsky ulu-lates his evocatively rambunctious yodeling. It's their poetic sense that trans-forms the hills echoing with laughter to the hills echoing with joyous yodeling.

- *Imaginary Landscapes: New Electronic Landscapes*, various artists, Elektra/Nonesuch, 1989. Compilation features many big-name experimenters: Marclay, Tyranny, Lucier, Trayle. But also Neil Rodnick, whose "Balkanization" feeds Bulgarian/Yugoslavian village music and yodels through a computer music mangling system. The yodels stutter, cascade, waft in and out. "On the Swing" is an earlier version of Shelley Hirsch's "Haiku Lingo."

- *ITSOFOMO*, David Wojanorowicz, Ben Neill "mutantrumpetist," and Don Yallech, NewTone Records, 1992. 2-CD set includes Wojanorowicz's own "Howl," a long complex mindscape of personal remembrances, feelings, and political rage fueled by American AIDS policy. Wojanorowicz died of AIDS at age 37 in 1992. He was a jack-of-all-arts, but he was most evocative with spoken word. Refusing to ignore his impending death, his texts-voice take on

continued on the next page

the air of a long plaintive blues moan, inflected with strange exhaling yodels, yodels that conjure up torture, and fetch our collective angst, guilt, and collusion in events surrounding AIDS. Not for the faint-hearted.

- **PlatterBack**, Westbrook & Company, Jazzprint, 1998. Mike Westbrook: tuba and vocals; story and lyrics: Kate Westbrook; and other accompaniment. This theatrical song cycle recounts the story of a commuter train trip and the interaction between passengers, each with their own reason for traveling. A serious work complete with a well-timed comical song called "The Stiltsville Yodel," with yodeling that devolves into a cacaphony of farm animal sounds.

- **Tongues**, Amy Denio, Fot/Ponk, 1993. Seattle experimenter-contemporary-composer is prone to doing almost anything with voice and sound. Her extra-terrestrial melodies are supplemented by deep-rooted vocals that venture into inventive abstraction, scat, and on the track "Da (Gdye Damskaya Parikmakirskaya?)," she yodels very effectively.

- **Wir Arbeiten Durch**, Rocket/Freudental, own label. Iggy Pop meets Kraftwerk in a head-on collision with the seminal art-drone band Suicide, yodeling in the ambulance en route to intensive care. Rocket/Freudental has been producing DIY post-folk noise and distorto-rock tapes since 1998. Band-member Steng on yodeling:

  > Both of us are big fans of the mountains, especially the Alps, where we go hiking and climbing. We want to point out the differences to the "urban" student scenes in Hamburg and Berlin, so we started to use samples of traditional South German music and the Alps, looking for the real cool things that the country produces! Bring some elements of historical folk music to rock again, to show both the overproduced city's slackers and the dumb and square "folklore-style" [types seen on] television. And not to forget, to entertain people with unusual sounds. I mean, yodeling is unusual sound.

  Their *Meta-Alpinismus* CD includes title cut and "Landser Höllenfahrt," both insanely enjoyable butcherings of yodeling.

- **Yodelling Bear**, Analysis, self-produced, 1990s. Eleven minutes of indulgent ad hoc electronic noodling and freeform sampling. "This is the sound of a Yodeling Bear" goes the incessant refrain in this raw electronic composition that incorporates a repeated and progressively mangled-by-cheap-effects yodel riff.

slips kitschy yodels into the "Stars and Stripes Forever" and "William Tell Overture"! He gives yodel lessons on cruise ships and via his CDs and yet . . . for all his incredible yodeling, his actual compositions and discs verge on the passable: neither dust collectors nor art. Needless to say, Christensen specializes in bravura-style yodeling: fast, acrobatic, sparkling with dazzling vocal pyrotechnics.

Christensen, acrobatically epiglotted Disney
Yodeler. By permission of K. Christensen.

Kerry grew up on a potato farm in Grace, Idaho, and has been hamming it up since age 3. In 1974, he went to Austria on a two-year church
mission. He came back with an armful of yodeling discs: He had *heard* the
light. He began his yodeling exercises in the wide-open solitude while
operating a tractor on his family's farm. In 1984, he won an audition to
become the official Disney World Yodeler (1984–1990) at the German
Pavilion, Epcot Center. His showstopper "Chicken Yodel," with its yodels
clucking off into the bawk-bawk of enraged poultry, makes you believe he's
Mary Schneider's male doppelgänger.

- *Volksmarsch mit Kerry & Emilie*, own label, 1995.
- *Yodeling over the Edge*, own label, 1990s.
- *Yodeling from the Old West to the Alps*, own label, 1990s.
- *Hooked on Yodeling*, own label, 1998.

Derivative Duo: If Weird Al was gay and did parodies of the already
far-gone self-parodic Marie Schneider, and the already-beyond-parody
Tiny Tim, it would probably sound a little like this. Camp falsetto on "Yodel
Lady Tune (Rossini/The Barber of Seville/Una Voce poco fa)" on *Opera for
the Masses*, Derivative Duo, 1993.

Howard Finster (1916–2001) was a colorful character-artist-huckster-
obsessive-preacher-vocalist who managed to become famous via his unself-conscious dynamic nonstop talk and artwork, churning out some
40,000 junk-folk artworks in his lifetime. His 1980s recordings make an
important correlation between hog calling, animal sounds, and yodeling,
especially noticeable on his "Chicken Sounds." (*Old Songs*, Old Gold,

1980s) Numerous Finster tidbits highlight perceptible shifts from chest to head, making us recognize that the holler is essentially related to the *natur-jodel* as work-related vocalizations with falsetto.

F.S.K., an interesting indie German band, worked on the margins between appropriation, invention, joyous noise, challenging music, and an early interest in yodeling. Taking their name from the West German self-censorship institution *Freiwillige Selbstkontrolle* in 1980, the four members of the Munich underground magazine *Mode & Verzweiflung* (Fashion & Despair) produced interesting skewed noisy Camper van Mekons radical pop-folk aberrations. They mangled German beer-tent post-*kuh*-punk yodeling with Brit sarcasm and American bluegrass twang. As one source noted, they brought the Texan Blue Yodel back to its Bavarian roots.

- "Budweiser Polka" / "Cannonball Yodel" Sub-Up, 1990.
- *Original Gasman Band*, 1989. Includes "Trans-Atlantic Polka and Yodel feed-back from the New World."
- *Bob's Car*, various artists, Cracker Soul, 1990s. Of four F.S.K. tracks, one is a "yodel" remix of "Euro-Trash Girl."

The Godz were gonzo author Lester Bangs's (*Psychotic Reactions!*) kind of primal-naïve gods. Their album "has at least two all-time Godz classics": "Riffin'" that "begins with a Tarzan yell, a wallowing harmonica, 'Melons! Get your watermelons!,' a hog call, an LBJ imitation." This kind of insanely brewed sonic stew led Bangs to drool: "after them, the planet will never whistle, hum, yodel, or even sing in the shower quite the same again."

- *Godz*, ESP, 1960s. Spleen-cerebellum-epiglottis rants.

Nina Hagen (b. 1955) remains the singer-mediator between two life-forms: humans and whatever else is out there. She was born into an artistic East German family and combined punk ethos, drugs, and an incredibly pliant voice to create one of the most eccentric personas in rock-pop-punk history. Her early musical training is composed of fronting cover bands' flailing versions of Tina Turner and Janis Joplin. She moved to Berlin, then London, Amsterdam, and finally outer space. Her albums represent a strange mishmash of punk and operatic flourishes à la Queen. Despite some oddly poignant songs, her mid-1980s albums *Nunsexmonkrock* and *Fearless* reflect a period of self-doubt. Her voice soared, gained luster, confidence, and volume, began twisting and turning phrases just short of Yma Sumac in a stunt plane. Her voice changes pitch and tone, dips down numerous octaves only to soar right back through the sound barrier. Sadly she was sent astray by the wrong drugs and wrong producers. And so this amazing voice has mostly been wasted. Should she do an album with Mij?

- *Nunsexmonkrock*, Columbia, 1983.
- *Fearless*, Columbia, 1985, includes some near-yodeling especially on club hit "New York, New York."

Kabouter Plop, Belgian children's television ensemble composed of five endearing aubergine-shaped gnomes who live in a tree trunk and get into Dutch trouble. They've actually managed to produce several dance remix hits. Their most endearing feature? When excited or surprised, the "tentacles" on their jester-style caps with bells go suddenly erect. And they yodel.

- *Sjoebi doebi dabide.* Studio 100, 2002. Includes "Kabouter Jodel."

Mij (b. Jim Holmberg, 1940s) was a street character-cum-musician with a propensity for ravings that sounded vaguely like a Yoko Ono–Albert Ayler spat. Holmberg, an American of Scandinavian-Swiss descent, was rumored to have once been a Muotathal herder! The fascination with Mij involves humans' interest in the duskiest edge of human expression where wacky blurs with serious psychiatric diagnosis. As the ESP liner notes describe it: "The silence in the somnolent park is suddenly shattered by an unearthly scream, mixed with a yodel. Tracing the sound to its source, a shaggy young street musician . . . plucking his guitar . . . playing to an imaginary audience. Invited to record for ESP, he shrugged and the next day, a record was born." It sounds as if some psychotropic lever, some over-consumption of mind-bending chemicals has lent his random concepts, astral musings, and extra-terrestrial observations an almost otherworldly relevance. ET-as-yodeler? ESP's Bernard Stollman noted: "He once told me that he had a terrible accident, with skull fractures, following which he lost much of his hearing, and could see auras. Beyond that, his yodeling is a mystery to me."

- *Yodeling Astrologer*, ESP, 1969.

Yma Sumac (Ima Sumack), one of the most legendary singers of the 20th century, rose to fame with her 1950s landmark *Voice of Ixtbay* album. It's considered the prime example of exotica, an armchair protoworld music that came to the fore (or background) in the 1950s. Sumac is probably a Peruvian singer born in Ichocàn, Peru, in 1920–something. But regardless of whether she's from Peru or Park Slope, there's no denying her legendary vocal range of four to five octaves. Sumac's earliest works include interpretations of

WEIRD-IS-NOT-ALWAYS-FUNNY DISCOGRAPHY

(novelty / religious / children's / odd / unclassifiable)

- *A Cathy & Marcy Collection for Kids*, Cathy Fink & Marcy Marxer, Rounder, 1994. Fink and Marxer do kids songs with real zing. Helpful yodeling hints for kids and glottal idiots like me.

- *A Friend You Haven't Met*, Kevin McMullin, Hungry Hill, 1995. Children's collection includes animal songs and "Yodel Alphabet."

- *And Now It's Time for Silly Songs with Larry,* various performers, Big Idea Productions, 2001. Children's gospel wackiness. Includes Veggie Tales' "Yodeling Veterinarian of the Alps."

- *And Now Shiro Sings!*, Shiro Matsuo, Mistah Saimin Records, 1991. Sung in English and Japanese with ukulele accompaniment.

- *Baby's First Songs for Little Cowboys*, various performers, St. Clair Entertainment, 2001. Children's songs, cowboy standards, and "Yodeling Song."

- *Behind Bars*, Happy Schnapps Combo, Exclusive Novelty, 1994. They call themselves "Wisconsin's Favorite Drinking Band," and there is much to endear them to your funnybone. Imagine an old 1950s German-American lounge ransacked by these beer-barrel boys as they rambunctiously mix metaphors, drinks, yodeling, kitsch, and mayhem.

- *Benefit Concert*, Don Bakos and band, 1997. Covers Steve Allen's "Bahia Yodel."

- *Continental Records Presents Musette on Parade*, various Musette Orchestras, Continental, 1940s. "Let's Drink" by Donald's Musette Orchestra contains some uncredited yodeling.

- *Cookin' Up a Rainbow*, Roger Tincknell, Hairy Bear, 1993. Includes "Yodeling Old Lady."

- *Das Ave Maria der Berge: Alpine Yodel Songs,* Peters International, 1979.

- *Davy Crockett at the Alamo: Songs of the West*, Cowboy Slim and Scotty MacGregor, Palace, 1960s. Includes "The Last Yodel" and "The Swiss Yodelers."

- *Doodoo Wah Live!*, Doodoo Wah, Ballum Rancum, 1997. Includes "Dental Yodel."

- *East 21st Street Song*, Gary Hall, Fishtraks, 1985. Humorous songs includes Riders in the Sky's "That's How the Yodel Was Born."

- *Favorite Wedding Polkas & Waltzes*, Kenny Bass & Orchestra, Roulette, 1964. Includes yodel polka, "Ei ya ei ya oh Yodel."

- "Finn's Mom Yodeling in the Bathtub," Spazz, own label, 1996. California self-declared "power violence" hardcore band. Despite that fact, this piece is funny and, at 13 seconds, perfect for drifting attention spans.

continued on the next page

- *Flat Out*, Buddy Wasisname and the Others Fellers, own label, 1990. This Newfoundland, Canada band reminds me of the Smothers Brothers on speed stuck in the Monty Python skit about the Canadian Mounties; add crazy lyrics and manic yodeling mixed with throat clearing, grunts, toots, and snorts, and you're halfway there. Their "Yodelling Song" is hilarious.

- *Frescoes and Bowling Balls: 47 More Songs,* Lou & Peter Berryman, self-produced, 1996. Includes their renowned "Double Yodel," with post-marital rudimentary hocketing. Apparently they were once married but cannot yodel separately. "When they say that yokel's vocal cords are subtle, / they'd be surprised to find the yokel is a couple."

- *God is Love: The Gospel Sessions*, Ann-Margret and James Blackwood, Art Greenshaw Records, 2001. With the legendary Jordanaires and the Light Crust Doughboys. Includes "The Hallelujah Yodel Lady" performed by former-sex-goddess Ann-Margret: yes, *that one.*

- *God Put a Yodel in My Heart*, Buzz Goertzen, own label, 1979.

- *Grandma Slid Down the Mountain*, Cathy Fink, Canada Kid's Records, 1985. Includes "Yodeling Lesson," "I'd Like to be a Cowgirl," and "The Yodel Polka."

- *Greatest Hits*, Half Japanese, Safe House 1995. Darlings of the self-conscious primal-id UFO-squawk school of no-chord alternative rock. Sixty-nine-track compilation includes a stutteringly hesitant version of "T for Texas." See also "It Got Me," Jad Fair solo-yodeling on a rare 1980s cassette compilation *Sub Pop Lost Music.*

- *Harsh Toke of Reality*, Squirrels, Popllama, 1993. Includes "Edge of Yodeling."

- *Hi-Line Honky-Tonk,* Eric "Fingers" Ray, Montana, 1990. Includes "Yodeling Fool."

- *I Like Cowboy Songs*, Johnny Bond and the Willis Brothers, 1994.

- *Just One Step,* Vincent, Lighthouse Records, 2001. Children's songs includes "Yo-Yo Yodel."

- *Tom Kubis Big Band Plays Steve Allen's "Fast Cars & Fascinating Women,"* Tom Kubis Big Band, Sea Breeze, 1996. Includes Allen's "Bahia Yodel."

- *Let's Have a Party: Diamond Jubilee*, Frank Yankovic and his Orchestra, K-Tel, 1990. Ranger Doug yodels on "Alpine Climber's Ball."

- *The Looney West*, with Bugs Bunny, Daffy Duck, and others, with Michael Martin Murphey, Don Edwards, Rex Allen Jr., Warner Brothers, 1996. Novelty duet singing-yodeling.

continued on the next page

WEIRD-Is-Not-Always-Funny Discography, continued

- ***The Magic Land of Allakazam***, Peter Pan Orchestra and Chorus, Mark Wilson, Peter Pan, 1962. Includes: "I Wish I Could Yodel."

- ***Bill Maraschiello's Magnetic Elixir***, Bill Maraschiello, Starwind Enterprise, 1984. Includes "The Jedi Knight Blue Yodel."

- ***Multi-Cultural Children's Songs***, Ella Jenkins, Smithsonian/Folkways, 1995. Includes "A Yodeling Song."

- ***Nashville Beer Garden***, Angelo Badalamenti, Ranwood, 1983. Composer of David Lynch's *Straight Story* soundtrack. Includes "Yodel, Dodel, Doe."

- ***The Neanderthal Yodeler***, Michael Welch, Illegal Radio, 1984. Included on *TV Willie 1984–1989*, a compilation of Welch's works. The piece is described aptly by Welch: "one of my peculiar favorites. This musical scheme was conceptualized while I was employed in a German band at Walt Disney World . . . in Orlando. While impersonating a musician in the German pavilion, my breaks were consumed drinking repeated cups of coffee and plotting my breakout from Walt Disney World. After hundreds of undistinguishable sets of *Germutlekeit* polkas, that day in 1987 arrived."

- ***Old Time Waltzes and Schottisches***, Gaby Haas, Mayfair, 1950s. Includes "Yodelling Accordion Waltz."

- ***Once an Austrian Went Yodeling,*** various performers, Wright Group, 1994. Children's project includes introductory text and yodeling.

- ***On the Run***, Dr. Hook & the Medicine Show, Pilot/Burning Airlines, 2001. Dr. Hook did hilarious send-ups of pop culture. Includes many of their hits like "Cover of the Rolling Stone" and "The Yodel Song."

- ***Out in the Desert***, Organ Donors, Organ Donors, 1993. Jim Wilson plays and howls some "coyote yodels."

- ***Outdoor Elvis***, Swirling Eddies, own label 1989. Includes "Arthur Fhardy's Yodeling Party."

- ***Polka Festival***, Beny Rehmann Show Orchestra with Walter Ostanek, Quality Special Products, 1991. Includes "Yodel Polka."

- ***Polka Festival***, Bruno "Junior" Zielinski, Liberty, 1959. Includes "Swiss Yodeler's Polka."

- ***Polka Your Troubles Away***, Richie and Tony Vadnal with Bill Srnick, Peppermint, 1970s. Includes "Teach Me How To Yodel."

- ***Reverend Baybie Hoover & Virginia Brown,*** Baybie Hoover and Virginia Brown, Philo Records, 1976. Sacred song collection includes "Lullaby Yodel."

continued on the next page

- ***Sesame Street in Harmony***, Warner Brothers, 1980. Includes James Taylor's "Jellyman Kelly," a yodel so languid, sluggish, half-hearted, and slurred as to almost slide into some kind of hibernational realm—yawn yodeling?

- ***Sex Is for Making Babies***, God Is My Co-Pilot, DSA, 1995. Includes "Blue Yodel #21" by this anarcho-noise ensemble, or is it jazz punk?

- ***"She Changed Her Hi-De-Hi-De (For His Yodel-O-De-Ay),"*** Ted Weems & His Orchestra, Victor, 1933.

- ***The Singing Cure***, Paul Newham, Sounds True, 1998, six-cassette + booklet excursion into the "healing power of song." I don't doubt the healing power of song but . . . Includes lecture-instruction (?) entitled "To Laugh, Cry, and Yodel."

- ***Sing the Gospel***, Thren Family, Faith Music Missions, 1990s. Includes "The Yodel Song."

- ***Sir Oliver's Song,*** Candle from the Agape Force Prep. School, Birdwing, 1979. "Inspirational" version of "Yodel Song."

- ***Ski-Time Music at Chalet Cochand***, Marili and Fritz Tschannen, CKGM, 1950. "Yodel Fantasies no. 1 and no. 2," "Can You Yodel," "Mabili Yodel," and "Swiss Hut Yodel."

- ***Spoonful of Sugar,*** Rocking Horse Orchestra and Chorus, Rocking Horse Records, 1960s. Includes "I Wish I Could Yodel."

- ***Sojourning***, Chalice, Star Song, 1979. Religious-theme collection includes "Yodel Song."

- ***Songs about Animals***, Jerry Bock and Jim Timmens, Golden Record, 1960s. Includes "Swiss Cheese Yodel."

- ***Songs That Move Me***, Ken Withington, JCL Records, 1975. Quasi-religious material. Includes "A Yodel in My Heart."

- ***Studio Tan***, Frank Zappa, 1978. Eddie Jobson (ex-Roxy Music, violin and keyboards) yodels on "Lemme Take You to the Beach."

- ***Times of Wonder***, Stefan des Lauriers, Music Kingdom, 1999. Children's songs includes "Yodeling Frog."

- ***21 Succès Western,*** various artists, London, 1973. French versions of country standards.

- ***Wavy Gravy Vol. 1 — For Adult Enthusiasts***, various artists, Beware, 1986. Weird, rude, crude, and rockin' trailer trashabilly. Includes a great burpy rockabilly yodel by Selwyn Cox, "His Name Is Jesus."

continued on the next page

WEIRD-Is-Not-Always-Funny Discography, continued

- *Whip It Out*, Reach Around Rodeo Clowns, Llist, 1997. "Come Yodel in My Canyon" is naughty Cramps-onian psychobilly—metal meets mental?

- *Yippe-Olé: Westerns Songs the Latin Way*, Melino & His Orchestra, Jubilee, 1958. Cowboy standards arranged for a dance orchestra. Wacky inspired exotica dovetails with cheesecake erotica. Includes "Yodeling Cowboy Cha-Cha."

- *Yodel for a Fish*, Wayne Potash, Orchard, 1999.

- *"Yodel Love Call,"* Bob Regan & Lucille Starr, the Canadian Sweethearts, A&M, 1964.

- *Yodeling Song: Piano Solo*, Ronald Bennett, Myklas Music, 1998.

Indian folk music recorded in Argentina (1943). These songs served as the basis of her numerous Capitol records that were remixed by Denny and Baxter. In 1990, she played the role of Heidi(!) in Stephen Sondheim's *Follies*. Most of her material has been repackaged on CD.

Texas Terri & the Stiff Ones, L.A.'s slut-version of Alice Cooper, have remastered thirteen tracks from their debut plus the bonus track, "Yodel-ay-hee-ho" on their romantically titled *Eat Shit + 1*. It's punk schlock cabaret that would be perfect for *This Is Spinal Tap II*.

Weird Al Yankovic (b. 1959) has for more than thirty years run a cottage industry based on his *Mad Magazine*–like parodies of pop hits and other earsores. He has a good sixth sense for what needs parodying, although he has become so famous that even a devastating parody has become a kind of inside-out honor. "Polka Your Eyes Out" uses that 1950s medley style while draining the stale beer out of pop hits by Billy Idol, B-52s, REM, and Bel Biv Devoe's "Do Me!" Meanwhile, "Polkas on 45" is a discumbobulated hi-speed medley of Devo, Deep Purple, Beatles, Doors, Lawrence Welk, Police, Clash, Who, and many others. It spotlights a yodel satire of Jimi Hendrix's "Hey Joe," and reached #17 on the *Billboard* charts. 1996's "The Alternative Polka" features Yankovic sending up Alanis Morisette's "You Oughta Move" with an inappropriately appropriate yodel refrain.

- *"Weird Al" Yankovic In 3–D*, Scotti Bros./WEA, 1984/1996.
- *Off The Deep End*, Scotti Bros./WEA, 1992.
- *Bad Hair Day*, WEA, 1996.

YODEL SONGS WITH NO YODELING

That's right: there's an entire anti-category of yodeling songs that contain *no* discernible yodeling: ruses, dead ends, head scratchers, conceptual compositions . . .

- *A Prescription for the Blues,* Horace Silver with accompaniment, Impulse!, 1997. Includes hard-bop, yodel-free Silver composition "Yodel Lady Blues."

- *Broadcasting from Home*, Penguin Café Orchestra, Editions EG, 1981. "Yodel" doesn't have much to do with yodeling: there *are* no vocals on PCO albums.

- *Danish Yodel,* Deep Purple, recorded live in Denmark in April 1970. Includes yodel-less "Yodel."

- *Flamin' Guitars*, Speedy West, Bear Family, 1997. Steel-guitar wizard plus Jimmy Bryant formed the Flaming Guitars, who become hugely popular session guitarists. They perform guitar "yodeling" on "Yodeling Guitar."

- *Hi-Fi Fun*, George Liberace, Columbia, 1956. Includes "Yodel on the String."

- *Kleine Jodeljongen*, Manke Nelis. Sizeable Dutch hit from the 1990s; guaranteed yodel-free.

- *Love That Sound from Polka-go-Round*, Louis Prohut, ABC-Paramount, 1959. Includes "Yodel Polka."

- *Music from Penguin Cafe Orchestra*, Editions EG, 1976, and *Still Life*, Penguin Café Orchestra, Decca, 1990. *When in Rome*, Editions EG, 1988. Yodelless yodel numbers guaranteed.

- *Polka-Party II*, James Last, Peters International, 1973. Easy-listening schlock-grinder "Trumpet Yodel."

- *Technicolor Yodel*, Anal Babes. Three minutes of angst–driven sturm und metal drang but no yodeling.

- *In the Studio 72, Live in Switzerland 73, Live in London 95*, String Driven Thing, Ozit Records. Includes Scottish prog-rockers' nonyodeling yodel song "Very Last Real Yodel."

- *Softboys 1976–1981*, Softboys, Ryko, 1993. "The Yodeling Hoover" contains no yodeling but some memorable lines.

- *Yakety Sax Sound*, Munich Beer Garden Band, Fiesta, 1986. Includes "Appenzeller, Polka (Swiss Yodel Polka)."

- *Yodel Cha Cha*, Trio Schmeed, ABC, 1955.

- *Yodelin' Satan*, Rudy Schwartz Project, 1993. Wanton blasphemous spewings plus bad B-movie music and questionable noises, all in the wonderful tradition of tweaking good taste and taking the piss out of bland commercial culture. No yodeling unless it's from some extra sub-terrestrial.

Appendix A

Yodds and Ends
Yodeling Beyond Music

YODELING AS CUNNING LINGUAL

In comedian George Carlin's dictionary of dirty words, the entry for "Cunnilingus" includes "Canyon Yodeling," and "Yodeling in the Gully." Most slang dictionaries include "Yodeling in the Valley." The American FCC handed out its largest fine ever ($23,750) to an American college radio station for broadcasting obscenity to WSUC in New York, when a DJ played Kid Rock's "Yodeling in the Valley." As A. D. Peterkin observes in *The Bald Headed Hermit and the Artichoke: An Erotic Thesaurus*, "It seems yodeling techniques, which involve the vibration of the mouth, throat and tongue, had other uses apart from calling out across mountain valleys."

SPEED YODELING CONTROVERSY

Munich's Thomas Scholl yodeled twenty-two tones—fifteen in falsetto—in one second, on February 9, 1992. Peter Hinnen also claims this record, and on the same day! A 1990 Swiss popular magazine reported that Hinnen had set his sights on Scholl's record at the time of 19 tones. According to some, Hinnen did indeed establish a new world record on the TV program *Supertreffer* in September 1991. On February 9, 1992, he broke his own record by yodeling twenty-two tones on the TV program, *Wenn-schon-denn-schon*.

STICKY YODELING

In 1994, German yodeler Anna Kormesser yodeled long distance to judges via telephone to become one of ten finalists (6,000+ entries) in the Care-Free chewing gum's "Total Yodel Contest." Kormesser said she taught herself to yodel fifty years ago when she was a young girl. As a finalist, she won two packs of chewing gum; the winner won a trip to Switzerland.

THREE YODELING STOOGES

In *Dizzy Doctors* (1937), Larry, Moe, and Curly impersonate doctors and perform outrageous medical procedures, and ultimately join a hiccuping nurse in an improv session of hiccup yodeling. In *Nutty But Nice* (1940), they rescue a girl's abducted dad when he uses yodeling as a distress signal.

ANTI-SOCIAL YODELING

Two "news" flashes in a column called "Weird But True" (July 2002) reported that police in Offenbach, Germany, were called upon to investigate the source of piercing screams neighbors said were coming from a neighbor's apartment. Upon investigation, they discovered a 76–year-old woman rehearsing for her yodeling diploma. Seems she might need some more practice. In Aachen, Germany, residents summoned police to a man screaming in a forest. The screamer's defense: he was therapeutically yodeling away his anxieties, of course.

PROTO-HIPPIE YODELING

Peter Camenzind, by Herman Hesse (1904), is an early coming-of-age novel. This lyrical work deals with the awakening moral and philosophical musings of a boy inspired by pastoral scenery. *Siddhartha* with yodeling, then: "We could go for a walk somewhere, toward evening. Just walk about, talk a little, climb some mountain, and then you can yodel to your heart's delight."

BEATNIK BUMS YODEL, TOO

The Dharma Bums, by Jack Kerouac, is a better-later-than-never spiritual-awakening tale involving Kerouac and Zen-nature poet Gary Snyder, who go on long hikes in the mountains of Washington state to find an equilibrium between Western jazz decadence and idealized Eastern transcendence. Kerouac's rush of enthusiasm conflates nature, wandering, hermeticism and . . . yodeling: "he got to the foot of a mountain, usually with a yodel, before starting to tromp up a few thousand feet." And "when Japhy went to fetch more wood and we couldn't see him for a while and Morley yelled 'Yodelayhee' Japhy answered back with a simple 'Hoo' which he said was the Indian way to call in the mountains and much nicer."

SUPERMODEL EPIGLOTTAL

Heidi Klum—not *the* Heidi—but the glum supermodel apparently let out a yodel on the *David Letterman Show* in 2001 to prove she's just an ordinary fun-loving gal.

TECHNO GOATHERD

Actress Cate Blanchett is rumored to periodically belt out some hefty yodels. At one techno club, Blanchett went into pure improv by launching into her version of "The Lonely Goatherd" hitting every "yo," "aay", "eee," and "OUCH."

YODELING WITH SCHNAPPS

Stephen Earnhart's *Mule-Skinner Blues*, 2002, is a fascinating documentary about a Mayport, Florida, trailer park's delusional denizens. A retired shrimper has always dreamed of making a low-budget horror flick. This serves as the film's subtext; the making of this flick, which includes a motley scrum of ne'er-do-wells: a rock guitar duo, a pulp fiction writer, and a 70–year-old yodeling beauty parlor denizen songwriter, Miss Jeannie, who insists: "I can't yodel without schnapps." She yodels "Muleskinner" in lonesome blues style.

YODELING WITH OTHER SPIRITS

Yodeling Theresa claims that she cleaned up her act after 20 years of abusing drugs, alcohol, and body by becoming a yodeling Christian! She yodeled to the Lord and he gave her prophetic visions which led to her "hit" "I Wanna Yodel for the LORD." Also check out "I'm Gonna Yodel My Way to Heaven."

Sit-com Yodels

There are no doubt hundreds of yodeling specimens in sit-coms. Here's a small sampling: *Seinfeld*, episode 76, Kramer lets out a "Yodel-lay-hee-hoo!" *The Drew Carey Show* used the Vogues "5 O'Clock World" as its theme song. *Sex in the City* included some Mary Schneider yodels in one episode. The *Beverly Hillbillies* (1962) episode "Elly's Animals" included curvaceous Elly May (Donna Douglas) teaching her furry friends how to yodel.

Olympian Yodels

During the 1972 Tokyo Olympics, Swiss yodelers serenaded Japanese Emperor Hirohito, his wife, and other yodeling fans with Olympian epiglottal feats.

Yodeling Secret Agents

Agent 327, a comic book series by Martijn Lodewijk, includes the buxomy and sturdy adversary of Agent 327, Olga Lawina, a play on the Dutch words for "noise" and "avalanche" and Dutch yodeler Olga Lowina. She's rumored to have a deadly yodeling voice that shatters glass.

Two-Dimensional Viking Yodelers

Asterix, the diminutive excitable Viking comic-book hero, endures some exuberant yodeling in both *Asterix in Switzerland* and *Asterix and la Traviata*.

Softcore Yodeling

"Tirolischers" were an entire sub-genre of "bad" softcore porn movies that emerged out of Germany's wacky 1960s–'70s. The main characters were typically Tyrolean or Alpine bumpkins in lederhosen and/or substantially well-endowed blonde pig-tailed Germanic bimbos. The stories usually involved the comic erotic consequences of when simple country folk met city folk. All heck breaks loose au naturel! The titles lend them a certain found-poetry loveliness: *Happy Orgies in Tyrol, Baby, Alpine Glow in Dirndl Skirts, How Sweet Is Her Valley, Make Them Yodel.* Sex as fun and nudity as inevitable, with orgasms commonly punctuated by yodeling.

Speed Yodeling (Ridiculous Heights)

"Canadian Yodeling Cowboy" Donn Reynolds in 1990 entered the *Guinness Book of World Records* when he yodeled a total of five tones—three octaves in less than one second—from the top of the CN Tower in Toronto.

Yodeling May Be Hazardous to Your Health

When the Grateful Dead's Jerry Garcia went into a recording studio in July 1995, he had no idea it would be his last recording session. The session for the Dylan-produced Rodgers tribute album included a version of Jimmie Rodgers's "Blue Yodel #9" with David Grisman and John Kahn.

JUNK FOOD YODEL

A song called "Yodel (Jello Yogurt)" by Douglas Katsaros and Cheryl Smith sounds suspiciously like a jingle for a product that never quite took off. Probably got stuck around the epiglottis.

Junk Food Mystery Yodel

I tried to contact the makers of the fine near-food, the Drake's Yodel, a hot-dog-roll–shaped piece of spongy chocolate cake-oid filled with some cream-type substitute. I wanted to know how they got the name Yodel. I'm still wondering.

Carol "Tarzan" Burnett

The Carol Burnett Show, a 1970s American comedy variety show, usually commenced with Carol Burnett fielding audience questions. Invariably, she'd be asked to yodel her "Tarzan" yell, which she would dutifully reproduce. It often arose like some wounded pterodactyl during skits as well.

Tarzan, King of the Bungle

Denny Miller (not the comedian) starred as Tarzan in MGM's bomb, *Tarzan, The Ape Man* (1959). For his money, the best person he ever heard do the "Tarzan yodel" was Edgar Rice Burroughs's grandson, Danton: "Even better than Carol Burnett [laughs]! . . . I think they 'sweetened' [Weissmuller's yodel] with several instruments and raised the recording a couple of octaves by speeding it up and rerecording it." They tried to get Miller do his *own* version of the yell during shooting. Before he auditioned his yell, he used to practice it on the beach near his Malibu home by screaming at the ocean. It didn't work, and they dubbed in Weissmuller's instead.

Teeny Bopper Yodeling

Jodel-Madeli: Verhaal uit het Buitenland, Aleid Ages-van Veel, The Hague: G.B. van Goor Zonen, 1930s. *Jodel-Madeli: Story from a Foreign Land* is a wonderful story for "older girls," too old for Heidi, about the coming-of-age adventures of the yodeling girl, Madeli Matters, from Appenzell. An indication of the story's theme and ambience, the book's first words are "'Jodelihoo-I! . . . Joecheee-I! . . .'" There are only two problems: the book's in Dutch and out-of-print.

Yodeling as Family Therapy

Emma Jo's Song, Faye Gibbons, Boyds Mills, 2001. Story opens on day of the Puckett family reunion. Emma Jo's family is seen singing, yodeling, and humming on their farm while they complete their daily chores. She's dejected because she doesn't think she'll ever sing-yodel like them. Well, she's wrong. Every happy ending involves a yodel.

Cool Jazz vs. Hot Yodeling

Chet Baker, tortured white-boy savior of hipster jazz, had some humbling early encounters with yodelers. James Gavin notes in his *Deep in a Dream*: "His voice had yet to change, and it sounded as high and neutered as a choirboy's. . . . In 1942 [his mother] started to 'drag' him to . . . kiddie talent shows. Competing against fledgling accordionists, tap dancers, and yodelers . . . Vera romanticized those contests by claiming that Chettie had always won first place. Baker insisted he never did."

DIYY Hitmaking

A musician named Petals used the online "Do It Yourself C&W Song Kit" to produce the inspired ditty, "I Lost When He Won on the Gong Show": " My Pooh Bear said I'd stay with him forever; . . . But who'd have thought he'd yodel on The Gong Show; / But that's the way Pygmies say goodbye."

THERE'S NO STOPPING THEM

More inspired DIY country lyrics by the Streamliners who used "Kirk Lockhart's country song generator" to write "Nixon Didn't Lie." The lyrics read like early Eno-meets-Arlo Guthrie: "I knew deep down I'd stay with her forever / She said to me that Nixon didn't lie / But who'd have thought she'd yodel in my Edsel / She sealed me in the vault and smirked goodbye."

COOPERATIVE YODELING

Yodel-Ay-Hee is a North Carolina Musicians cooperative, dedicated to releasing and promoting Old Time music.

YODEL INC.

Yodel.inc.com promotes home remedies, herbal medicine, and alternative holistic health regimens online.

YODELING IN CHINA

In 1997, Switzerland and China celebrated fifty years of Sino-Swiss relations. At the ceremony, Swiss yodelers performed a few yodels.

STYLISH AND ELEGANT YODELS

Yodel Gown is a Korean company that specializes in the manufacture of gowns and uniforms.

KOREA KRAVES YODELS

The Chalet Swiss Restaurant in Seoul, South Korea, is a success because it serves up live Swiss-style yodeling every Friday and Saturday night.

EURO YODEL, THEY'RE A YODEL

The youthful Romanian entry in the 2000 "Eurosong" contest performed a yodel number. The injudicious choice of song style relegated the contestant to a 17th-place finish.

SILLY PSEUDO-SOUL YODELING

R. Kelly, born-again pseudo-soul-pop singer, was asked in an interview about his yodeling on one song. He admitted that he was just being silly and that he loves "to go into a territory that no man has ever gone musically." The ignorant and egocentric know no bounds!

YODELING INVADES SERIOUS DRAMA

Youth is a recently rediscovered Thornton Wilder one-act play. Sea captain Lemuel Gulliver is shipwrecked on a tropical island. Gulliver drags himself along a beach, exhausted and hungry. He comes upon a spring where he slakes his thirst and then onto a grass hut where in the distance, he hears the lilting voice of a woman yodeling.

HEIDI, INC.

no other Swiss person alive or dead . . . is as well known as Heidi. She's a worldwide brand. We would be stupid if we didn't try to benefit from this and promote ourselves in international markets.

—Gieri Spescha of the Graubuenden Tourist Office

Heidi is more than just a book: it's an institution, trademark, mega-market-
ing convulsion of memorabilia and cultural disneyfication, with entire towns
willing to alter their historical character to get a piece of the action.

The Book: Classic tale written nearly 130 years ago remains charming
and, although it contains no yodeling per se, it offers countless ambient situations where you're swaddled in the *atmosphere* of the herder's life. You almost
feel the crisp breezes on your cheeks, hear the cowbells or the herder's distant
yodel. Flowers blossoming, streams gurgling, the green pastures, the golden
sunlight, the snow-capped peaks . . . The main characters are Heidi, a small
orphan girl, who loves the Swiss Alps, her grumpy yet kindly grandfather, and
Peter, the goatherd. Aunt Dete sends Heidi into the Swiss Alps near Maienfeld
to live with her grandfather. Here she meets Peter, whom she often accompanies on his herding rounds through Alpine pastures. Dete changes her mind
and *sells* Heidi to the Sesemans as the playmate for their crippled daughter,
Clara. Heidi becomes homesick and returns to her grandfather. She invites
Clara to visit. Clara discovers the miracle cure for her disability: fresh mountain air, which slowly begins to reveal its miraculous powers, pale, feeble Clara
transforms into a rosy-cheeked, positive *walking* girl. By story's end you feel as
if you've been listening to an impassioned yodel song: "everything seemed
even more beautiful than she remembered. The peaks of the mountains were
snow-covered, the pastureland and the valley below were all red and gold, and
there were pink clouds floating in the sky. It was all so lovely that Heidi stood
with tears pouring down her cheeks as she breathed in the fragrant air."

The Author: Johanna Spyri (1827–1901), born in Hirzel, was an
unknown Swiss homemaker from a small town overlooking Lake Zurich
when she took up pen and wrote the first "Heidi," *Heidi's Formative Years*.
Written anonymously, it became an immediate success. With *Heidi Might
Need What She Has Learned* (1881), Spyri began using her name. Spyri's
other books include *The Little Alpine Musician* and *Veronica*.

The Success: One of the most-successful books of all time, *Heidi* has
sold umpteen gazillion copies. It's been translated into fifty languages
(Korean and Japanese—they're crazy for Heidi) in some 150 editions,
including a special tie-in edition for the Shirley Temple film version.

The Movies: Heidi has been the subject of some fifteen films, Hollywood
and European, plus a mega-successful Japanese cartoon series with a

continued on the next page

Heidi, Inc., continued

dark-haired, Pokemon-looking Heidi. The 1937 version, starring Shirley Temple and Jean Hersholt, is perhaps the best-known cinematic *Heidi*. In it, Heidi gets to do the one thing everyone always expects her to do: yodel. Temple is a winning, perky Heidi. A charming movie of a charming book deserves nothing less than a charming soundtrack, and Lee Holdridge delivered a light neoclassical score, evocatively capturing Heidi's growing up.

The 1952 Swiss version, directed by Luigi Comencini (1952), gets good grades especially for its fidelity to the book and fact that it was shot at actual locations, while the 1965 Austro-German version excels in its evocation of Heidi's adventures. In 2001, Swiss director Markus Imboden gave us a new version, set in the modern world of skyscrapers and stressed-out single-parent families. Heidi is hip and contemporary—a principled gal with the right coif?

Theatrical Spectacles: There have been countless theatrical adaptations of *Heidi* in Switzerland, Germany, North America, and even Japan. The first adaptation was Swiss in 1908. A second in 1936 was performed some 5,000 times. In 2001, a French version was performed in Lausanne. The American theater has a long-standing affection for *Heidi*: it's recognizable and it sells itself. The first dramatic adaptations appeared in the 1920s; many versions followed. In 1959, Neil Simon coproduced a musical adaptation with music inspired by Robert Schumann themes. 1961 saw a German-American opera called "Heidi in Frankfurt." A 1979 musical included the byline "The musical for the whole family" with a "healthy dose of comedy" and additional historical/traditional folk elements to give it resonance.

The Tourist Attraction: Several Alpine municipalities have bickered over the right to become the *official* Heidi town. It's better for business to milk a book than a cow, it seems. The 100th anniversary of Johanna Spyri's death in 2001 culminated in a herd of events and marketing schemes to hone in on the lucrative children's nostalgia market. You could book special tourist packages on a special train; there are permanent attractions, both historical and dubious. 2001 Heidi-lights included:

- "Heidi Express" train between Landquart and Tirano.

- Six-day "Route My Heidi" tour package, starting in Zurich, winding through Graubünden to Lugano.

- Daily "Peter the Goatherd" parade in Vilters: a boy in traditional costume leads a herd of eighty goats from the village to the mountains and back.

- Internet trails to various Heidi movie locations.

- Touring exhibition at the University of Zurich offers a look at Heidi's career and how she is marketed as a tourist attraction.

You Want Yours Dry?

The Yodel is a mixed drink composed of
3 oz. Fernet Branca, a liqueur
4 oz. orange juice
Sparkling water
    Pour the Fernet Branca and orange juice into a highball glass filled with ice, add sparkling water to taste and stir.

Yodel Hygiene

The Circle of Friends® brand of eccentrically named personal hygiene products includes Niklas & Heidi Yodel-ay-he Shampoo and Heidi & Niklas Yodel-ay-he Body Lotion.

Yodeling of Olympian Proportions

Sami singer Nils-Aslak Valkiapää performed a *joiking* song at the opening ceremonies of the 1994 Winter Olympics in Lillehammer, Norway.

Yodeling Second Fiddle

The United Kingdom's runner-up song for the Eurovision Song contest in 1997 was "Yodel in the Canyon Of Love" (Polygram, 1997) performed by Do-Re-Mi with Kerry. It finished second to some MOR-pop shingle by Katrina and the Waves. The song was Proclaimers' manager, Kenny MacDonald's, first songwriting attempt. Burach's Kerry MacDonald is the featured yodeler. "Yodel" gained some notoriety because a song about oral sex won second place in a straight contest! This made it a modest hit in U.K. gay clubs in 1997.

Picture This Yodel

Jimmie Rodgers's original 78-rpm "Cowhand's Last Ride / Blue Yodel No. 12" is considered to be the first country music picture disc. Rodgers never saw it, however, dying a month before its release in 1933. It features the image of Rodgers wearing a polka-dot bow tie and straw hat. Only a few hundred copies were pressed, and only a few of these survive.

The Yodel Hex of Rex & Tex

Rex Allen, Rex Dallas, Goebel "The Texas Drifter" Reeves, Tex Williams, Tex Owens, Tex Bloye, Rex Turner, Tex Morton, Tex Roy, Rex Griffin, Tex Ritter, Tex Banes, Tex McMahan, Tex Grande, T. Texas Tyler, Texas Kitty Prins, Texas Ruby, Tex & the Horseheads, the Texas Playboys.

Celluloid Cowboys Yodel in Spats and Spangles

Apache Country (1952) includes Gene Autry performing Carolina Cotton "I Love to Yodel"; *Cowboy from Lonesome River* (1944) with Autry performing "Rocky Canyon"; *Cowboy in the Clouds* (1943) with singing cowboys Foy Willingham, Al Sloey, and Shelby D. Atchison, who yodels; *I'm from Arkansas* (1944) with Jimmy Wakely yodeling and featuring Cotton standard "I Love to Yodel"; *In Caliente* (1935); *Yodelin' Kid from Pine Ridge* (1937); *Laramie* (1949) with Elton Britt yodeling "Chime Bells"; *Way Out West* (1937); Laurel & Hardy, with the Avalon Boys Quartet (including Chill Wills) performing yodels; *High C's* (1930) Charley Chase stationed in France; The Ranch Boys kidnap a German soldier to yodel behind the lines; *Song of Nevada* (1944) in which Roy Rogers yodels "A Cowboy Has to Yodel in the

Morning," among others; *South of Santa Fe* (1942) in which Rogers sings "Yodel Your Troubles Away" with Sons of the Pioneers; *Smoky River Serenade* (1947) includes Cotton and The Hoosier Hot-Shots yodeling; *Texas Panhandle* (1945) includes Cotton's "I Love to Yodel," as well as Spade Cooley and Tommy Duncan. This is a miniscule selection of cowboy films with yodels. As Douglas B. Green noted: "There are tons of yodels in the singing cowboy pictures . . . too many to mention, dozens and dozens."

COW-ROACH YODELING?

Joe's Apartment, director John Payson, MTV/Geffen, 1996. Humorous/gruesome live action/animated film follows a naïve Midwesterner would-be actor in New York. He rents a shabby apartment where he is befriended and bedeviled by gremlin-like mean-ass cockroaches. They taunt him mercilessly, and in a moment when it seems they have won the battle for the apartment they have a rowdy cowboy party with taunting, teasing, and *yodeling*.

KUNG-FU YODELING

David Carradine starred as protest singer, Woody Guthrie in the 1976 Hal Ashby film, *Bound for Glory*. He sang Guthrie's songs convincingly and even yodels on two numbers.

DOESN'T THE TONGUE GET IN THE WAY?

The Basenji is a dog that doesn't know a bark from a yodel. In fact, it creates a howl that is remarkably similar to a blue yodel.

BUNCH OF YODELERS STANDING AROUND IN A SQUARE SETTING A WORLD RECORD

On October 8, 2002, 937 yodelers with XXL lungs set a new world record for the "largest simultaneous yodel" by holding their melody for a minute at the Ravensburger Amusement Park near the German town of Meckenbeuren. Most of the German participants were yodeling students. Some Swiss yodelers also joined in to help out. To be acknowledged in the *Guinness Book of Records*, the yodelers had to hold their tune for a full minute. They beat the old world record set earlier in 2002 in Dublin. The yodelers yodeled southward in homage to Switzerland's yodeling tradition.

SELECTED HOW-TO NOSTRUMS AND YODEL CURE-ALLS

I cannot vouch for the efficacy, veracity, or safety of the following audio elixirs and epiglottal nostrums. I'd be wary of anyone who claims the unbelievable. I don't yodel, but in the privacy of my work space I have tried to follow some of these lessons. One unnamed site suggested that if I had "trouble maintaining pitch, try yodeling with a bucket over your head." A yodeler wannabe is probably better off looking for a teacher of the fleshly variety. We can shop online, but yodeling online is another matter.

- **Amish Yodeling Workshop,** 1983, by Fanny Schwarz, who's from the oldest order of Indiana Swiss-Amish.
- *Anyone Can Yodel*, Magnus E. Bucher's twenty-page tract from Big Mountain Press, 1956.
- **Austrian Yodeling,** Family Education Network, Inc. Students explore Alpine culture through maps, folk music, and yodeling.
- **Dieter Himmler,** an "Authentic" Austrian Yodeler (Austria/California), and **Sven Anders Krong**, a "Creative" Yodeler (Massachusetts/California) offer step-by-step lessons with text and online sound files.

- **How to Yodel the Cowboy Way: Teach Yourself to Yodel Like Sourdough Slim**. Slim was awarded the 2001 Will Rogers "yodeler of the year" Award, so you know the man can swing his technique. When you listen to some of the sound clips on his site, you'll soon be out of breath trying to keep up.
- **How to Yodel the Cowboy Way**, forty-eight-page book with sheet music and CD by Rudy Robbins, of the Spirit of Texas band, and Canada's champion yodeler Shirley Field. Field's no slouch; check out her "The Man on the Moon is a Yodeler"! Features basic no-nonsense instructions, simple songs, recorded demonstrations, nice photos, and profiles of famous yodelers including Field, Wilf Carter, and Kenny Roberts. They also offer support via mail or email. Perhaps the best method out there; highly recommended.
- **How to Yodel: A Crash Course**. Does anybody really *need* a crash course in yodeling? No matter, because this is a lively lighthearted course taught by Florian Keller, a pro.
- **Internet Yodel Course.** Website attempts to "get you to smile." Hmm. The instructor claims fifteen years experience and supposedly awards an "official Certificate of Yodelology."
- **Janet McBride**, in her mid-70s now, continues to offer yodel lessons on the second Sunday of each month with The Cowtown Opry Group, near the Stock Yard Area in Fort Worth, Texas.
- **Jodlerschule für Jedermann (Yodeling for Everybody)**: If learning to yodel is more than just a lark or an issue of winning a bet, then get ready for a lifestyle change. It can take years to become a master yodeler using the Swiss method. Think: sacrifice, time, endurance, practice. Immediate gratification here means like, *many* years. The basic course requires an entire reorientation surrounding vocalization because the yodel is unlike any other. Start with motivation, sense of purpose, and then and only then does one begin the *mechanics* of opening the mouth, learning the physics of using vowels and consonants as levers, breathing . . . And, oh, by the way, add in a one-way ticket to Switzerland . . .
- **Learn to Yodel,** Cathy Fink with Tod Whittemore, 2–CDs, Homespun. Wonderful non-cloying cowboy-style yodeling how-to geared toward kids. Bette Midler used this method when she was learning to yodel for her part in the film *Big Business.*
- **U2 Can Yodel**, Kerry Christensen: "I always wished there was some instruction that would make the whole learning process easier," In this CD, he shows you how, and listen to that Kerry yodel! Features his famous "Chicken Yodel." Easy and practical examples for everyone interested in learning Alpine or cowboy yodeling. He's also prominently positioned on the Internet.
- ***The Yodeling Instructional Video***, Rusty Hudelson and Tania Moody "share their yodeling secrets in this fun and entertaining yodeling instructional video." These "World Champion Yodelers" will teach you the basics with step-by-step instruction for both men and women (is it *that* different!?). They offer sing-along exercises, where yodeler-wannabes will learn to find their natural break, plus duet-style yodeling instruction, and don't forget "Father-Daughter yodeling harmonies."
- ***The Yodel Audio Auxiliary Cassette,*** Rusty Hudelson and Tania Moody. "Enhance your Yodeling ability" and "Impress Audiences!!" claims smell like late-night-TV sales pitch. Approach with caution.
- **YODEL!** is the "world's first interactive, animated singing page" and is one of many sites that treats yodeling as a comical crutch. If you can't be funny *without* yodeling, then you're probably not very funny. Best feature is quick listen to a variety of yodels from Goofy to Tarzan, from loon to Basenji.

Appendix B

Selected Yodel-ossary

- **almer:** Austrian yodel song about mountain life and nature. "Alm" means "mountain pasture."
- **alpsegen:** Alpine blessing or *betruf*, litany performed by Alpine Catholics, 1565 to present. The Schwyz versions are thought to ward off evil.
- **alphorn:** *looooong* (5–12 feet) simple Swiss horn of two halves of a carved and hollowed-out tree trunk (usually delicate pine) held together by decorative lengths of vine, twine, or gut string. It no longer serves its original function of signaling herds and other herders. In 1826, the alphorn became an official instrument when Ferdinand Huber tuned three alphorns of different length to different keys to be used in a musical ensemble. Alphorn tunes often involve a *ranz des vaches*, with its enchanting repeated short phrases. Found in Switzerland, Lithuania, the Carpathians (*trombita*), Norway, the Urals, Moldova, and Romania (*bucium*).
  - *Rosa Loui*, Hans Kennel's Alpine Experience, TCB Music. Modern traditional. Kennel on *büchel*, alphorn, and vocals plus accompaniment.
  - *Echoes of a Disappearing Planet*, Dunain, 2002. Michael Cumberland is a master Canadian alphornist and sounder of natural spaces and urban settings. Alphorn interacts with the Grand Canyon, Grand Tetons, and Switzerland. Some conceptual compositions.
- **alphorn-fa:** or the "Alpine blue note," is the sound of the alphorn's "natural F" that does not appear on the temperate scale. In technical terms: the "fourth step of the scale . . . raised by approximately a quarter of a tone [between F and F-sharp in C major], as the 11th harmonic of the natural tone scale, played on the alphorn." Became a standard in Swiss singing and is still commonly yodeled in the Muotathal and Appenzell regions.
- **betruf:** psalm-like structureless prayer call that remains important in Alpine regions where the dangers associated with treacherous terrain cultivated religious or superstitious feelings among inhabitants. Associated with pagan rites and magical cults of shepherds that were later appropriated by Christianity. Often sung through a megaphone of wood [*folle*].
- **chindli:** Swiss-German term for yodel songs that employ the alphorn-fa during the singing of lullabies.
- **coloratura:** flamboyant virtuosic application of trills, runs, falsetto, and other florid embellishments. Also refers to the singer, usually a soprano, who specializes in this

type of singing and to professional vocalists who employ yodeling in their commercial repertoires.

- **cowbells:** elaborate handmade clapper bells of various sizes and tones hung from the necks of cows, and sometimes sheep and goats, to keep track of herds. The sound is inextricably associated with yodeling, Alpine ambience and remains essential to Swiss ceremonies/celebrations. Bells are often carefully chosen to create a complete chromatic scale or distinct pitches and then shaken by decorative straps.
- **dudler:** light, airy, festive Viennese yodel songs about birds, nature, love. Style is characterized by high-culture ornamentation, nonnarrative lyrics, and urban theatrical/operatic influences.
- **falsetto:** affected or unnatural high-pitched voice especially used by men, particularly tenors, to extend the singer's range to a progression of notes beyond his "ordinary" vocal range. Produced by shortening the active portion of the vocal cords, like pressing on a violin string with a finger. Falsetto (literally "false soprano") uses the breath in the frontal sinuses to produce a thin tone. Falsetto often has negative connotations and is sometimes used to create an atmosphere of annoying shrillness or campiness.
- **folklore:** traditional beliefs, customs, legends, and so forth of a people. Involves the oral and/or informal transfer of cultural material that, when passed back and forth, becomes part of the local tradition.
- **folk song (volklied):** generic term for all songs traditionally passed on orally from one singer or generation to the next.
- **gayo:** Spanish vocalization that resembles the yodel. The word derives from the Spanish *papagayo*, meaning parrot.
- **gradhäba:** Appenzell style of unrehearsed part-singing that is neither written down nor of conscious construct. An improvised solo or group yodel song characterized by vocal harmonies, said to have evolved out of psalm singing and often accompanied by *schellensütteln*.
- **gsangl (Schnadahüpfl or Gstanzl):** Swiss dance song consisting of four-line stanzas that are sung to 3–4 time *Ländler* dance tunes.
- **hackbrett:** predecessor of the dulcimer, introduced to Switzerland by Gypsies centuries ago. Composed of a long wooden board with wire strings of different lengths stretched between nails hammered into a board. To play it, one strikes the strings with small wooden hammers with their heads wrapped in wool to soften the sound.
- **hocket:** from Middle French *hocquet*, "to hiccup," a vocal style most commonly associated with Pygmy polyphonic singing. The simple hocket involves two interlocking melodies or two voices singing alternately at different pitches, creating dense overlapping contrapuntal textures of simultaneous melodic lines. Commonly used by the (Pygmy) yodeler to perform variations over.
- **jodelen:** German for yodeling (U.S.) or yodelling (U.K.).
- **jodeller or jodler:** German for a yodeler.
- **jodellied:** Stylized Swiss three-verse song with verses sung to the same music (strophic) broken up by the regular injection of a yodel refrain. Also called a *gsätzli*, the *jodellied* arose in the mid-19th century during the rise of the yodel clubs and civic choral groups in Switzerland and the development of a distinct yodeling style. Words/texts with pastoral themes replace vocables.
- **jodler (jodle or ludler):** Austrian yodel song derived from the herders' and farmers' cries (*jodellied* in Switzerland). Has a symmetrical musical structure composed of two or three yodel verses with agile alternations between chest and head voice. "The . . . vocalization is assisted by such syllables as 'hoh-ee-dyay-ee-ree, ree-dee-ree-ah'."
- **juchzer (juchschrei):** Swiss for yodel as shout of joy. Short penetrating call that uses a sudden burst of falsetto. Textless singing just short of a real yodel. Max Baumann's *Kuhreihen, Jodel unde Jodellied Nach den Gedrukten Quellen* lists these related terms

and spellings: *Aelplerufe, Hirtenrufe, fischerrufe, fruttruf, jodelrufe, locken, beim mähen, schlittenrufe, urruf, volksruf, wanderers ruf, juchzer, jauchzen.*
- **jüüzli:** Muotathal two- or three-voiced yodel.
- **krimanchuli:** Georgian yodeling, strikingly similar to some forms of Swiss yodeling. Requires a unique head voice that undulates quickly between the falsetto and chest voice.
- **kuhreihen:** literally "line of cows," is the call associated with herding the cows together. Said to have originated in ceremonies involving the naming of a farmer's cows, the naming itself being a magical rite that helped create an intimacy between cattle closer and farmer/herder. The *kuhreihen (kuhreigen)* is a *juchzer* of two or three melodies that begin slow and high, moving into a faster tempo and involving calling the names of the herd in terse spurts. Max Baumann lists these related terms: *kuhreihen, kuhreyen, kühe-reyen, cantilena helvetica, ranz des vaches, air suisse, kühreigen, rond des vaches, puchelspiel, alphornweise, chuereihe, kühreihen des sennen und des handbuben.*
- **ländler:** Austrian frisky, lively folk-based waltz found throughout the Alps. *Sound of Music* fans may remember this courting dance as the first physical contact between Maria (Andrews) and Von Trapp (Plummer). The man does most of the work—stamping feet while clasping his thighs and snapping his fingers while the woman spins around by herself. He chases and grabs her by the waist and swings her around. Herma van den Elsen argues that it is precisely folk elements like yodeling and ländlers that help reduce class barriers between employer and servant. Elsen argues, that folk music allows the upper class to rediscover its roots with the people, binding one and all in their common nationality, basic needs, and desires beyond class distinctions.
- **legato:** smooth and flowing song passage performed in one breath with no perceptible pause between notes. Opposite of staccato and thus fairly antithetical to the yodel as well.
- **löckler:** unstructured Swiss melismatic calls (expressive chants/calls sung on one syllable) once performed *en scène* among herds returning home with their jangling bells as happenstance accompaniment. Today *löckler* are sung by groups who gather in a circle—arms around one another's shoulders, heads close together—one singer yodels a melody (*loba, lobela, or liabua*—depending on what part of the country they're from) while the rest accompany with a steady drone. Some believe this is a remnant of an ancient ritual related to a cattle deity.
- **lockruf:** Swiss structureless call tune.
- **mayenge:** yodeled version of a BaAka Pygmy song.
- **naturjodel:** yodel characteristic of the northern side of the Swiss Alps (Emmental Gruyere, Appenzell, Toggenburg, Berner Oberland, and Central Switzerland areas). With its origins in the *ranz* melody, the *naturjodel* is a structureless utilitarian call that helped regulate everyday rhythms and communicated various affairs such as dinner time, wood cutting, returning home, and end of herding season. Its tempos, rhythms, and dialects or use of alphorn-fa define its various characters.
- **ornamentation:** not as frivolous as it sounds, a technique for bringing freshness, uniqueness, and spontaneity to a familiar song. Jimmie Rodgers's blue yodel is ornamentation because it made standard songs sound new and unique.
- **pentatonic scale:** consists of five different tones and can be found in the early music cultures of China, Africa, Polynesia, the Amerindians, Celts, and Scots.
- **ranz des vaches:** French for "cow's procession" (see *kuhreihen*). Refers to a type of Swiss Alpine melody that is either vocalized or played on alphorn. First referred to in 1531, it's used by herders to call their herds. There are some fifty varieties of this Alpine melody. The *ranz* eventually acquired lyrics but doesn't employ falsetto; it is

more sentimental than most yodels in that it openly expresses affection for one's herd.

- **responsorial singing:** call-and-response singing or singing in which a leader alternates with a chorus.
- **ritornello:** Italian, literally meaning "little return," or short instrumental introductions, interludes, now used to mean shorter repeated refrains. For our purposes, the yodel often serves this purpose in songs.
- **ruf:** Austrian musical call used by street vendors hawking their wares. Basic form of communication, also called the *Almruf* (Alpine call) and *Almschrei* (Alpine cry).
- **ruggusserli:** many-voiced yodel, found in the Appenzell region, based on a sincere melody that can be expressed vocally or via musical instruments.
- **schelleschötte (schellenschütten, schellensütteln):** unique style of *zäuerli* accompanied by the rhythmic playing of three distinctly tuned cow bells attached to cow collars that are draped over the performer's arms, producing a very pleasant harmonious sound during the accompaniment of a *naturjodel*.
- **schnelzer:** Austrian yodels that accelerate in tempo.
- **talerschwinge:** Swiss instrumental accompaniment involving three people swirling and rolling coins on end (usually Swiss five-franc piece or silver coins) around in wide resonant earthenware bowls in a steady circular motion using the forearm and hand. The coins create a unique drone that is said to imitate the sound of an entire herd of cows wearing cowbells.
- **turnaround:** short piece of music like a yodel refrain "that occurs between two verses of a song," John Lilly in a 2003 email explains, "or follows the end of one chorus and comes before the beginning of the following verse. It serves to return the song back to the beginning." Commonly applied to Jimmie Rodgers.
- **tyrolienne:** French term for a Tyrolian or generic yodel. Identified by the use of dialect in both title and text. Found in the Tyrol region of Northern Switzerland and Southern Austria and Italy. Simple in form, text, and yodel chorus harmonies.
- **viehläckler:** Swiss cattle call.
- **vocable:** vocals that are not words. Abstract sounds and nonsense syllables produced by the human voice. Includes yodels, scat, babel, neologisms, throat singing . . . Vocables plus melody equals a simple song.
- **voice-break singing:** involves yodeling mid-word or at the end of word, instead of during an abstract yodel syllable. Used to add emotional resonance to a song. Most commonly associated with Hank Williams.
- **zäuerli:** an evocative and plaintive polyphonic yodel sung a cappella, characteristic of the Appenzell region as part of spiritual/pagan celebrations involving masks and rituals. Doesn't officially qualify as a yodel because its often sung entirely in chest voice, lacking the dramatic shift to falsetto. "But for the people of Appenzell it seems to make little difference," Hugo Zemp notes. It still shares many yodel characteristics: "relatively deep voice range, relaxed voice, mostly in a slow tempo, free rhythmic character with extreme drawing out of notes, 'dragging' from one tone to the next, and rising intonation." Other zäuerli include clear falsettos that beautifully distinguish themselves from the harmonious tenor and bass.
- **zwoarer:** a yodel with voices unique to the Scheibbs region of Austria. When the group adds a third, bass voice, you have a *dreier,* or a yodel for three voices.

Appendix C

Other Carriers of the Yodeling Bug

Al & Jean Shade & the Potter County Boys
Al Eagle
Bea(trice) Lillie
Big Chief Redbird
Bill Bruner
Bill Cox
Bill Schustik
Bill Staines
Bob Everhart
Bob Nolan
Bobby McFerrin
Brian Setzer
Bruce Springsteen
Bud Reed
Cactus Pryor
Cathy Berberian
Chris Isaak
Chris Whitley
Colleen Honeyman
Colorado Hillbillies
Cowboy Slim
D. Harvey
Dan Hicks
Daniel Decatur Emmett
Dave Matthews
David Ball
David Bradley
David Houston
David Hykes
David Rea
The Decibelles
Dennis and Don Winters
Dick Flood

Doc Watson
Dolly Parton
Dolores O'Riordan (The Cranberries)
Don Edwards
Dwight Yoakam
Earl Shirkey
Ed Burleson
Eddie Giguere
Floyd Cramer and Anita Kerr
Flying W Wranglers
Frankie Marvin
Gary McMahan
George P. Watson
Glen Campbell
Guidry Brothers
Hal Ketchum
Hank Thompson
Hazel Dickens
Hobo Jim Varsos
Igor Glenn
Ira Louvin
Iris Dement
Jack Guthrie
James O'Gwynn
Jeannie Pierson
J. E. Mainer's Mountaineers
Jerry Lee Lewis
Jerry Smith
Jim Eanes and the Shenandoah Valley Boys
Jim Lauderdale
Jimmy Davis
Jimmy Wakely
J. K. Emmett

Joan LaBarbara
John Crowder
John Herald
Johnson Mountain Boys
Judy Coder
Kathryn Pitt
K. D. Lang
Ken Overcast
Ken Threadgill
KG & The Ranger
Klaus Nomi
Leake County Revelers
Lefty Frizzell
Legendary Stardust Cowboy
Leon Huff
Leon Redbone
Light Crust Doughboys
Linda Lou & the Lucky 4
Little Richard Penniman
Liz Masterson & Sean Blackburn
Lucille Starr & Bob Regan
Lulu Belle Wiseman
Manuela
Maria Muldaur
Mark Brine
Martin Sexton
Marty Robbins
Marvin Rainwater
Meredith Monk
Merle Travis
Michael Nesmith
Moon Mullins
Muzzie Braun & the Boys
New Riders of the Purple Sage
Nilsson
Outlaws
Ozark Mountain Daredevils
Patsy Prescott
Paul Belanger
Paul Evans
Pete Seeger
Piners
Ramblin' Jack Elliot
Ray Campi

Ray Whitley
Red Foley
Reno Brothers
Rex Griffin
Roberta Shore
Robyn Mundy
Roger Miller
Roy Acuff
Rye's Red River Blue Yodellers
Sainkho Namtchylak
Sam Cooke
Sara Carter
Scott Alan Hoff
Sheila Chandra
Sheldon Williams III
Sid Selvidge
Skip Gorman
Soggy Bottom Boys
Sonny Burgess
Sons of the Purple Sage
Steve Forbert
Stew Clayton
Suzy Bogguss
Tasty Licks
Texian Boys
Three Tobacco Tags
Tim McNamara
Tiny Tim
Tom Christian
Tom Swatzell
Tompall Glaser
Ursula Dudziak
Van Williams
Vernon Dalhart
W. Perkins
Wanda Jackson
Wayne Hancock
Webb Pierce
Werner Zotter
Woody Guthrie
Zeke Clements

[I could go on and on and . . .]

Notes

Introduction

"in a truck, with the windows rolled up. . .": Vaughn, 1996, n.p.

"[Jimmie] Rodgers's yodel . . .": Porterfield, 1979, 126.

Chapter 1

" . . . during the remainder. . . ": Twain, 1982, 196.

what Christoph Wagner calls: Wagner, 1998, liner notes.

Sir Walter Scott in 1830 opined: Quoted in Tosches, *Twisted Roots*, 1996, 109.

sung by both men and women: Witzig, 1949, 15–16.

"Yodelling is understood": Zemp, liner notes.

" . . . without texts or words": Baumann, *New Grove*, Internet.

from bass or low chest voice to high head voice or falsetto: Guiet, May 2002 email.

" . . . and expanded resonance space.": Baumann, *New Grove*, Internet.

"the release of one set . . . ": Brown, 1996, 25.

"a stretch is placed . . . ": Ibid.

" . . . full of meanings . . . ": Paraphrasing a theory by Michel Leiris. In "Glossolalias? La
   Glotte Y Sonne Un Hallali!": in Labelle and Migone, 2001, 143.

"loneliness and desire": Montague in Talbot, 1955, 241.

"lul-lul-*La*hee-oo!": Twain, 1982, 195.

" . . . ko kyini kyini . . . ": call: Kebede, 1995, 93.

" . . . 'blues' on his whistle.": Haymes. "The Birds and the Blues," Internet.

Figure 1: Excerpt analyzed is from Jimmie Rodgers, "Blue Yodel #4," The Singing
   Brakeman, Bear Family. Figure 2: Is an excerpt of a Muotathal juuzli as sung by Emmie
   Suter-Gwerder and recorded by Hugo Zemp in 1979 on the Le Chant du Monde label.
   The top line graph boxes indicate decibel ratios at various moments in the songs. Middle
   graph is an expressive visualization of yodel as peaks and valleys. In the notation, the
   falsetto notes are marked in diamonds. This is part of the fascinating research of Franz
   Födermayr and Werner Deutsch at the Acoustic Research Institute, Austrian Academy
   of Sciences in Vienna <www.kfs.oeaw.ac.at>, which has appeared in numerous technical
   journals, mostly in German.

" . . . a difficult rhythmic passage.": Guiet, December 2002 email.

" . . . AY EE AY EE . . . ": Fink, *Grandma,* Rounder, 1984.

The Appenzell yodel: Hoffmann and Delorenzi-Schenkel, 1998, 691.

"As man's manipulative dexterity . . . ": Berman, Internet.
" . . . Muzak into his milking barn": Lomax, liner notes.
The *naturjodel* is often cited . . . : Leuthold, *Volksmusik*, 1985, 85–86.
Here are eleven basic theories: See Baumann, Musikfolklore 1976; and Leuthold, *Der Naturjodel*, 1981, 12.
But as yodel composer Leuthold points out: Leuthold 1981, 12–13. "Silhouette of Horizons" theory: Gassmann, A.L., "Zur Tonpsychologie des Schweizer Volksliedes" (Regarding the Psychology of Sound among Swiss Folksongs).
they had so much more to talk about." Leuthold 1981, 14.
"While pagan songs . . . ": Horton, 1963, n.p.

Chapter 2
"curve in an arc . . . ": Bernbaum, 1997, 120.
"triadic melodies . . . ": Schepping, 1998, 651.
"more suave . . . " Witzig, 1949, 15.
"calls, yells, recitatives . . . ": Hoffman and Delorenzi-Schenkel, 1998, 683.
"Thousands of Swiss folksongs . . . ": Witzig, 1949, 15–16.
But with the Reformation . . . : Meylan 2001, Sadie (ed.) 1995, 417–422.
History suggests . . . : Baumann, *New Grove*, Internet.
"Cantilena Helvetica": Ibid.
"searched for the famous . . . ": Myers, 1993, n.p.
"national folk identity": Baumann, *New Grove*, 1995, 417–21.
As yodels began to be documented . . . : Ibid, 419.
"The [EJV] treats Switzerland": Seiler, 1993: Seiler, 1998, 37.
"In Switzerland . . . the Schweizerische . . .": Schmid, September 2002 email.
"The notating of these songs": Leuthold, 1985, 88.
"descending melodic patterns . . . ": Hoffman and Delorenzi-Schenkel, 1998, 692.
This process allowed them . . . ": Baumann, *New Grove*, 1995, 422.
Their vocal songs . . . ": Hoffmann and Delorenzi-Schenkel, 1998, 694.
"sustained block harmony": Baumann, *New Grove,* 1995, 422.
"independent part-movement": Ibid., 419.
In Luzern, singers gather in a circle . . . : Hoffmann and Delorenzi-Schenkel, 1998, 691.
"ugly yelling and screaming": Ibid., 692.
"harmony with the mountain echo.": Boulton, 1953, liner notes.

Chapter 3
" . . . opening with its horn yodel": Hoffman and Delorenzi-Schenkel, 1998, 690.
"did not have widespread popularity,": Russell, 2001, 161.
"purposes of triumphalist nationalism": Will, Wilfried van der, "The Functions of 'Volkskultur', Mass Culture and Alternative Culture," in Kolinsky, 1998, 162–63.
"discovered new folklore and folksongs . . . ": König, 2002, internet.
"has her home": Koch, 1975, 31.
"unfruitful patriotism": Ibid.
"The growth of the . . .": Potter, 1998, 192.
"certain national traits . . . ": Apel and Daniel, 1960, 108.
"German folk music . . . ": Potter, 1998, 191.
"Several people told me . . . ": Toelken, 1982, 201.
"Maidla, mach's Ladele Züa": Kiehl, from Quedlinburg, is a folk music researcher. 2002, 161.
Every yodeler is free . . . : Ibid., 168.
Unlike the EJV in Switzerland . . . : Ibid., 181.
"although records exist . . . ": Ibid., 247.
Although herding occupations . . . : Ibid., 251–56.

"Improvisation is rare . . .": Mantner quoted in Glanz, et al., 1999. n.p.
"The bygone folk . . . ": Goertzen and Larkey, 1998, 671.
"played by brass- or accordion-based ensembles . . . ": Ibid.
"find their way into the world": Glanz et al., 1999, 11.
"with parallel thirds and triads": Roberts 1978, liner notes.
"a mixture of Anglo-American . . . ": Glanz et al., 24–25.
"three- and four-part homophonic yodels . . . ": Goertzen and Larkey, 1998, 673.
The influential *Schottisch* . . . : Breuer, 1950, 10–13.
"it is difficult to distinguish . . . ": Goertzen and Larkey, 1998, 672.
"and the struggle . . . ": Glanz et al., 1999, 9.
"fascinated by the strong . . .": Johnson 1984, 43.

Chapter 4
"a mountain cry . . . ": Witzig, 1949, 15–16.
"songs interspersed with yodels . . . ": Koskoff, "Gender," 1998, 194.
"distorted falsetto, distorted jaw": Jordania, 1998, 828.
Doine often include dramatic flamboyant vocals . . . : Apan, 1998, 872–73.
Any yodeling in pop songs . . . : Toni Smith, May 2000 email.
"legendary singer and performer . . . ": Belgian Pop & Rock Archives, Internet.
" . . . to communicate with the herd . . . .": Wallin, 1991, 428.
it is "significantly different . . . ": Megan Lynch, May 1999 email.
"The governing principle . . . ": Wallin, 1991, 428.
"goat calls [*geitlokkar*] . . . ": Hopkins, 1998, 412–13.
Kulokkar is the general term . . . ": Ibid., 412.
"performed with a type . . . ": Ransten, 1987, 102–103.
A Norwegian "*Gjeite-lok*" . . . : Luchner-Löscher, 1982, 27.
These *lockruf*-like: Ibid., 23.
The Norwegian *rop*: Ibid., 24.
"can be heard . . . ": Johnson, 1984, 43.
"a very high and penetrating sound": Ransten, 1987, 102.
"fascinated by the strong . . . ": Johnson, 1984, 43.
"*kuln*'s falsetto . . . ": Ibid., 44.
"While the kulning articulation . . . ": Ibid., 58.
"content and happy": Linnaeus, quoted in Koerner, 1999, 75.
Reindeer herders: Stockmann, Doris, "Synthesis in the Culture of Scholarship," in Kartomi
    and Blum, 1994, 1–9.
"Where melody": Ibid.
"To sing *yoik*": Ibid.
"To sing *yoik* . . . ": Sami culture Web site.
"improvised non-strophic type . . . ": Stockmann, in Kartomi and Blum, 1994, 2.
"church looked on . . . ": Sami culture Website.
"recalling to the performer's . . . ": Stockmann, in Kartomi and Blum, 1994, 9.
"an upper or lower . . . ": Ibid., 8.
"He would often sing . . . ": Paul Hazell, who helped put the British Isles on the yodeling
    map, November 2002 email.
"I started off . . . ": Grundy, Internet.
"from his grandparents . . . ": Hazell, November 2002 email.
"Columbia executive Norman . . .": Ibid.
"None of us suspected . . . ": Lomax, Back cover notes, *Italian Treasury*.
with its ancient application of the alphorn-fa: Luchner-Löscher, 1982, 43
"cattle calls survive . . . ": Hoffmann and Delorenzi-Schenkel, 1998, 697.
"In Italy, Spain . . . ": Rice, "Traditional Performance Contexts," 1998, 142.
"probably influenced by African . . . ": Ibid.

Chapter 5
"Modern Indian . . . ": Manuel, 1990, 184.
"Indian ornamentation . . . ": Ibid.
"virtuoso coloratura improvisations . . . ": Ibid., 181.
"can incorporate . . . ": Miller and Williams, 1998, 93.
"falsetto songs . . . ": Tatar, 1982, 91.
"the Western scale . . . ": Ken Sitz, interviewed in Vale and Juno, 1994, 100.
Chanters effortlessly . . . : Tatar, 1982, 86.
"*paniolo*, or Spanish-Indian . . . ": Ibid., 87.
Tatar offers concrete evidence . . . : Ibid., 88.
"perched in a mango tree singing.": Ibid., 236.
"Executed only on . . .": Ibid.
"Another characteristic . . . ": Ibid.
"Though partial yodels . . . ": Ibid., 89.
"a gift from God": Ibid., 197.
"the grooves . . . ": Ibid., 198.
In New Guinea: Love, 1998, 297.
The Huli of the . . .: Pugh-Kitingan, 1998, 538.
"Yodeling is an important . . . ": Ibid., 298.
"collective yodeling . . . ": Ibid., 299.
"Women have solo . . . ": Ibid.
"Huli say thoughts . . . ": Ibid., 298.
"guitar songs . . . ": Webb, 1998, 151.
"'Carry Me Back . . . ": Ibid.
"Komasa [of Papua] . . . ": Kunst, 1931, 7.
"yodeling . . . occurs . . . ": Love, 1998, 297.
"walking in the forest . . . ": Lindstrom, 1998, 706.
"Singing with these bands . . . ": Ibid., 709.
"falsetto, flexible-sliding . . . ": Luchner-Löscher, 1982, 45.
"The songs of Guadalcanal . . . ": Zemp, *Garland: Australia*, 1998, 665.
"with a break . . . ": Stillman, *Garland:* Australia, 916.
"in a lashing . . . ": Sachs, 1962, 87.
such as Dougie Young . . . : Wild, 1998, 413.
"cowboys become boundary riders": Smith, 1994, 300.
"contained more . . . ": Ibid., 305.
Author Graeme Smith . . . : Ibid., 297–311.
Buddy Williams's forlorn style . . . : Ibid., 306.
Smith further notes . . . : Ibid., 301.
"habitual and optional decoration . . . ": Ibid., 298.

Chapter 6
"The yodeling and . . . ": Kisluik, 1998, 688.
even *eaten* by: "Congolese Rebels are Eating Pygmies" *de Volkskrant*, Jan. 9, 2003, 5a.
"'people pertaining to the pygmé . . . " Kisluik, 1998, 688.
"men a cubit high": Shoumatoff, 1984, n.p.
"about a hundred . . . ": Ibid.
"Pygmies may have originally . . . ": Ibid.
"Their vocal polyphonies . . . ": Sallée, liner notes.
"almost supernatural . . . ": Ibid.
"Egalitarianism permeates . . . ": Kent, 1996, 263.
"Pygmy musical style and practice . . . ": Turino, Thomas. "The Music of Sub-Saharan Africa," in Nettl, 1992, 174.
"African music . . . is common property": Bebey, 1975, 116.

"the objective of African music . . . ": Ibid., 115.
"any individual who . . . ": Ibid.
"Pygmies are classified . . . ": Kebede, 1995, 42.
"polyphonic shouting . . . " Bebey, 1975, 130.
"Since the 1960s . . . ": Kisluik, 1998, 688.
"interlocked and yodeled sections": Ibid., 689.
The Mbuti, for example, trade . . . : Adinoyi-Ojo, 1996, 45.
"naturally good": Kebede, 1995, 42
"associate divinity . . . ": Turino in Nettl, 1992, n.p.
"Song . . . is believed . . . ": Turnbull, 1965, 254.
"some of their performance . . . ": Kebede, 1995, 43.
"glottal attacks . . . ": Ibid.
"sung melismatically with trills . . . ": Ibid.
"erupts in broken vocalizing . . . ": Sallée, liner notes.
"African singer . . . ": Bebey, 1975, 132.
"Rites performed . . . ": Joiris, in Kent, 1996, 263.
"the *yeli* spirits . . . ": Ibid.
"rapid opening and closing . . . ": Carlin, 1986, 94.
"Both Khoikhoi and San . . . ": Kubik, 1998, 307.
"elements such as polyphonic vocal . . . ": Kavyu, Paul in Stone (ed.) *Garland Africa*, 1998, 635.
"the Shona practice . . . ": Kaemmer, 1998, 744.
"She heard sounds . . . ": Burroughs, 1963, 92.
"vivid train of imaginings . . . ": Ibid., 103.
"When I was a kid . . . ": Weissmuller, quoted in Fury, 1994, 69.
"hyena's yowl played . . . ": Fury, 1994, 69.
This belief was transmitted . . . : Moses, Internet.
"You may be amazed . . . ": A Cappella Online.
"African singers often use falsetto . . . ": Courlander, 1963, 25. Courlander also compiled music for *Negro Folk Music of Africa & America*, Folkways.
"African and Spanish cultures . . . ": Landeck, 1969, n.p.

Chapter 7
"vocal pulsations . . . ": Frisbie, in Kolinsky, 1997, 97.
"the Apache act . . . ": Sachs, 1962, 74.
ethnomusicologist George Herzog, who notes that "Africans . . . ": Courlander, 1963, 10.
The first Africans . . . : Flanders 1998, 49.
"In Negro tradition . . . ": Courlander, 1963, 25.
" . . . Negro influence again . . . ": Malone, 1993, 96.
"The blue yodel": Ibid.
"a cry from a distant hill": Courlander, 1963, 81.
"often ornamented and employ . . . ": Kebede, 1995, 130.
"sometimes sung with . . . : Courlander, 1963, 87.
"the tremendous enthusiasm . . . ": in Bluestein, 1994, 58.
"despite the fact that the United States . . . ": Ibid.
"Carolina yell.": Olmsted, quoted in Wish, 1959, 114–15.
"Sounds of this general type . . . ": White and White, 2001, n.p.
"originated with the rainforest . . . ": Ibid.
as "O—e-e-e.": Parrish, 1992, 216.
"the trick of dropping": Ibid., xxxiii.
" . . . come now, echo! . . . ": Olmsted in Wish, 1959, 114–15.
"Frederick Douglass . . . observed . . . ": White and White, 2001, n.p.
"very similar—[hollers have] . . . ": Leonard Emanuel, in introduction to *Hollerin'*.

"ornamentations and free . . . ": Courlander, 1963, 88.
"are deeply rooted in tradition": Ibid., 89
"many African vocal devices . . . ": Kebede, quoted in White and White, 2001, n.p.
"an unlimited number of possible . . . ": Bluestein, 1994, 57.
killed the workday's monotony with . . . : Garson, 1980, 92–93.
with the "trance-like repetition": Mellers, 1978, 266.
"hollered to themselves . . . ": Ibid.
"to employ calls . . . ": White and White, 2001, n.p.
"the Old Chisholm Trail . . . ": Lomax, liner notes.
"yodel-like larnyx technique": Baumann, Internet.
"the tremendous enthusiasm . . .": Lomax quoted in Bluestein 1994, 58.
"When a cotton-picker . . . ": Dorham, 1970, n.p.
"extra musical devices": Lomax, liner notes.
"field-holler-style whoops.": Ibid.
"seedbed": Malone, 1993, 12.
"first man to explore . . . ": Ephrata Cloister.
"the Asylum of the distressed . . . ": Quoting the journals of Mittleberger, Workers of the
    Writers' Program, 1940, 183.
" . . . there was little prejudice against . . . ": Buck and Buck, 1939, 364.
"newcomers brought their folk . . . ": Korson, 1949, n.p.
"the Germans of Pennsylvania . . . ": Parsons, 1976, n.p.
"The Germans, push[ed] past the English . . . ": Workers, 1940, 117.
"strong local folk tradition . . . ": Schroeder, 1996, n.p.
"yodler of note": Wagner, *Folk Roots*, 1998, 31.
"were yet another curiosity . . . ": Ibid.
"singing, yodeling, accordion solos,": Leary, 1991, 29.
"They have no direct connection . . . ": Milnes, May 2002 email.
"'learned to play clarinet while . . . ": Leary, 1991, 10.
"rang out in 19th-century Wisconsin": Ibid, 12.
"'in praise of the cowherd . . . '": Meylan, quoted in Ibid., 22.
"a few pseudo-Afro-American . . . :" Ibid., 17.
"the Upper Midwest's foremost . . . ": Ibid., 36.
"live and recorded musical . . . ": Ibid., 34.
"Happy led the orchestra . . . ": Grimm, 1937, 52.
"was Betty on accordion and yodeling.": Leary, 1991, 30.
"persists because it serves . . . ": Thompson, 1996, n.p.
"In the community . . . ": Ibid.
"are typically either in Bernese . . . ": Ibid.
and the *jodellied* "Niena Gates.": Bachmann-Geiser, 1988, 156.
"*Lily of Laguna* has a yodelled chorus.": Russell, 2001 [1970], 193.
"new meanings when . . . ": Smith, 1994, 304.

Chapter 8
"illiterate white whose creed . . . ": *Variety,* quoted in Peterson, 1997, 8–9.
Musician Al Hopkins: Actually first used in 1900 in the *New York Journal,* a daily newspa-
    per.
"music that had been entirely . . . ": Ibid., 4.
"In the process . . . ": Ibid.
"minstrel show yodel . . . ": Tosches and Wagner, among others, refer to this earliest *docu-
    mentable* reference to country yodeling.
"yodeling became almost . . . ": Charles Wolfe, quoted in Wagner, 1998, liner notes.
"1920 [Victor] catalog . . .": Porterfield, 1979, 86.
"yodelers and balladeers . . . ": Dawidoff, 1997, 12–13.

"infamous blue yodel . . . ": Bob Dylan, liner notes *The Songs of Jimmie Rodgers,* 1997.
"curlicues I can make . . . ": Jimmy Rodgers, quoted in Tosches, *Country,* 1998, 114.
"His message is all . . . ": Dylan, *The Songs of Jimmie Rodgers*, 1997.
"[Rodgers] couldn't read a note . . . ": Porterfield, 1979, 5.
"brought up in a series of foster homes . . . ": Lilly, 1992, n.p.
"all sorts of odd jobs, unofficially . . . ": John Lilly, November 2002 email.
Here he learned his licks: Malone, 1988, 84.
"made [their] way . . . ": Lilly, November 2002 email.
"because its falsetto delivery . . . ": Dawidoff, 1997, 12–13.
"'the identifying characteristics of the 'blue yodel'": John Greenway, in Russell 2001 [1970], 191.
"effortless informality." Malone *Country Music* 1988, 94.
"A hybrid music . . .": Wagner, *Folk Roots* 1998, 31.
"Kenny was renowned . . ." Hazell, Internet.
"treated me like a dog." Hank Snow quoted in Russell, 1999, 18.
"quasi-yodeling in 'Lovesick Blues.'": Tosches, in Kingsbury and Axelrod, 1988, 245.
"He could break his voice . . . ": Quoted in Ibid., 244.
"a deep, rich baritone . . .": Boyd, 1998, 234.

Chapter 9
"[He] conquers his chosen bit of wilderness . . . ": Miles, 1975 [1905], 68–69.
"the fabric of usable symbols, which surrounded him.": Malone, 1988, 139.
"In 1951, Gene Autry published: Wortham, 306–321, n.d.
"Anything with a musical": *Los Angeles Times*, 2002, Internet.
"sympathy went out to cattle everywhere . . . ": John Wheat, The Texas State Historical Association, 1997–2002.
who welded country to western: Koster, 1998, 6.

Chapter 10
"We should never let this sound . . . ": Charles quoted in Flippo, 1998, n.p.
"freeform scream: the Ooooohhoooohh! Aaaaaaaaoooooow . . . ": Rose, 1990, 127.
"Whites don't realize what that scream is . . . ": Thompson, quoted in Ibid.
"worked with a hillbilly band . . . ": Charles, 1978, 87.
In New Orleans, humid incubator: Bluestein, 1994, 57.
As Giles Oakley points out, Handy: Oakley, 1976, n.p.
At some point, "jazz emerged out of the amalgam.": Ibid., 34.
"the light airy music: Ibid., 34.
"Jimmie . . . reminded me more'": Quoted in Russell, 2001, 193.
"the deep though often confused nature of our ethnic interactions": Bluestein, 1994, 58.
"one of the strangest . . .": Tosches, 2001, 47.
"a white man in blackface . . .": Ibid., 3.
"loopy jazz singer stuff": Erwin, 2001 email.
"wry, bizarre phrasing . . . ": Tosches, 2001, 63.
"that wild rushing flight of swarming inflections . . . ": Ibid., 70.
"a near marriage of blues fiddling . . . ": Russell, 2001, 187.
Lewis borrowed lines: Ibid., 191.
Lewis covered "Waiting for a Train": Ibid., 192.
Rodgers "proved to be . . . influential on black styles . . . ": Guralnick, 1992, 20.
"Jackson-based singers like Ishman Bracey . . . ": Evans, quoted in Russell, 2001, 194.
"the basis for Howlin' Wolf's patented howl": Guralnick, 1992, 20.
"They had a similar device, however, in the falsetto . . . ": Russell, 2001, 193.
Skip James' "Yola My Blues Away" . . . ": Evans, quoted in Russell, 2001, 194.
"the bluest of the white blues": Russell, 2001, 196.

The colorful white blues singer: Ibid., 206.
Novelty blues songs arose in the 1930s: Ibid., 218.
"Talking" with a musical instrument: Mellers, 1978, 269.
Or as Nathaniel Mackey put it: *Sulfur*, 205.
"His demeanor was jovial . . .": Horst, Internet.
"I was one place and my body was another . . . ": Lazarus, 1995.
"I could hardly open my mouth . . . ": Ibid.
They may have had their "Leon Thomas-like moments,": Horst, March 2002 email.
"A lots of fans . . .": Lewis, Internet.
"I like "Hocus Pocus," . . . ": Tim Gane, Interview "Yesterday's Tomorrow" by Adam
    Gollner, Internet.
Rapper Ice T, *after* an interview on Dutch TV: Interview with TV-interviewer Jan Douwe
    Kroeske, by Pieter Webeling in *Het Volkskrant Magazine* 2002, 8.

Chapter 11
"electronic digital recording system . . . ": Cutler, Internet. See also his excellent *File
    Under Popular*, NY: Autonomedia, 1992.
in both cases recordings of ethnic music: Ibid.
"deeper exploration of national musics.": Hernandez, 1992, 360.
"The hype surrounding the new global economy . . . ": Taylor, 2001, 120.
"that the future evolution of electronic music . . . ": Mellers, 1997, xiii.
"the uneasy silence,": Reynolds, 1995, 62.
"most sounds are intermittent and ephemeral . . . " Maconie, 1997, 3.
" . . . expansion into bigger and bigger spaces . . . ": Godwin, Joscelyn, "Speculative Music,"
    in Paytner 1992, 263.
"dematerializing and eroding the integrity of singers and song.": Davis, 1997, 14.
"the glossalalian disruption of the irreducible . . . ": Fred Moten, quoted in "Voices/Forces"
    Writing Aloud 2002, 56.
"emancipation from meaningful words.": Sachs, 1962, 69.
"art of making an experience more vividly real by adding an unexpected ingredient on the
    spur of the moment.": Maconie, 1997, 123.
be "any cry resembling this musical mode,": *Grolier's Academic American Encyclopedia*,
    Internet, 1995.
"has at least two . . .": Bangs, 1987, 88.
"begins with a Tarzan. . .": Ibid.

Appendix A
"everything seemed even more beautiful . . . ": Spyri, 1976, 132.
"His voice had yet to change . . . ": Gavin, 2002, 17.

Appendix B
"Alpine blue note,": Baumann, *New Grove Music Dictionary*, Internet.
"fourth step of the scale . . . ": Zemp, Hugo. *Switzerland: Zäurli*, liner notes.
"The . . . vocalization is assisted by such syllables . . . ": Roberts, liner notes.
Herma van den Elsen argues that: Elsen, 1988, 66–69.
"But for the people of Appenzell it seems to make little difference . . . ": Zemp,
    Switzerland: Zäuerli, liner notes.

Bibliography

Books

Abrahams, Roger. *Singing the Master*. New York: Pantheon, 1992.

Adinoyi-Ojo, Onukaba. *Mbuti*. New York: Rosen, 1996.

Andreotti, Libero, and Xavier Costa, eds. *Theory of the Dérive and other situationist writings on the city*. Barcelona, Spain: MACBA, 1996.

Apan, Valeria. "Romania." In Rice, Porter, and Goertzen, 1998, 868–89.

Apel, Willi, and Ralph T. Daniel. *The Harvard Brief Dictionary of Music*. New York: Pocket Books, 1960.

Applegate, Celia. *A Nation of Provincials: The German Idea of Heimat*. Berkeley: University of California Press, 1990.

Arnold, Alison, ed. *The Garland Encyclopedia of World Music: South Asia: The Indian Subcontinent*. New York: Garland, 1998.

Bachelard, Gaston. *The Poetics of Reverie*. Boston: Beacon Press, 1969.

Bachmann-Geiser, Barbara. *Amische: Die Lebenweise der Amsichen in Berne, Indiana*, Bern, Switzerland: Benteli Verlag, 1988.

Bangs, Lester. *Psychotic Reactions and Carburator Dung*. New York: Vintage Books, 1988.

Baumann, Max Pieter. *Kuhreihen, Jodel unde Jodellied Nach den Gedrukten Quellen*. This serves as an appendix to his groundbreakng work *Musikfolklorismus*. Bern, Switzerland: 1974.

———. *Musikfolklore und Musikfolklorismus: eine ethnomusikologische Untersuchung zum Funktionswandel des Jodels*. Winterthur, Switzerland: Amadeus-Verlag, 1976.

Bebey, Francis. *African Music: A People's Art*. Translated by Josephine Bennett. Westport, CT.: Lawrence Hill, 1975.

Bernbaum, Edwin. *Sacred Mountains of the World*. Berkeley: University of California Press, 1997.

Berry, Mary Francis, and John Blassingame. *Long Memory: The Black Experience in America*. New York: Oxford University Press, 1982.

Bickerton, Derek. *Language and Species*. Chicago: University of Chicago Press, 1990.

Bluestein, Gene. *Poplore: Folk and Pop in American Culture*. Amherst: University of Massachussetts Press, 1994.

Boyd, Jean. *The Jazz of the Southwest: An Oral History of Western Swing*. Austin: University of Texas Press, 1998.

Breuer, Katherine. *Dances of Austria*. London: Max Parrish, 1950.

Brodersen, Momme. *Walter Benjamin: A Biography*. Translated by Malcolm R. Green. London: Verso, 1998.

Brothers Grimm. *Snow White and the Seven Dwarfs*. Chicago, IL: Rand McNally, 1937.

Buck, Solon J. and Elizabeth H. Buck. *The Planting of Civilization in Western Pennsylvania*. Pittsburgh: University of Pittsburgh Press, 1939.

Burroughs, Edgar Rice. *Tarzan the Untamed*, New York: Ballantine Books, 1963.

Carlin, Richard. *Man's Earliest Music*, New York: Facts on File, Inc. 1987.

Chambers, Theodore. *The Early Germans of New Jersey, Their History, Churches and Genealogies*, Dover, NJ: Dover, 1895.

Charles, Ray, with David Ritz. *Brother Ray: Ray Charles' Own Story*. New York: Dial Press, 1978.

Collier's Encyclopedia. New York: Crowell-Collier, 1967.

Cone, Edward T., ed. *Berlioz: Fantastic Symphony*. New York: Norton, 1971.

Courlander, Harold. *Negro Folk Music USA*. New York: Columbia University Press, 1963.

Critchley, MacDonald, and R.A. Henson. *Studies in the Neurology of Music*. Springfield, IL: Thomas, 1977.

Dawidoff, Nicholas. *In the Country of Country: People and Places in American Music*. New York: Pantheon, 1997.

Deutsch, Didier, ed. *Videohound's Soundtracks: Music from the Movies, Broadway and Television*. Detroit: Visible Ink, 1998.

Dixon, Robert, John Goodrich, and Howard Rye. *Blues and Gospel Records 1890–1943*. Oxford, U.K.: Oxford University Press, 1997.

Emery, Ralph. *The View from Nashville*. New York: William Morrow and Co., 1998.

Encyclopedia Brittanica, 15th edition. Chicago: Encyclopedia Britanica, Inc., 1974.

Essoe, Gabe. *Tarzan of the Movies*. New York: Citadel Press, 1968.

Flanders, Stephen. *Atlas of American Migration*. New York: Facts on File, Inc., 1998.

Floros, Constantin. *G. Mahler: The Symphonies*. Aldershot, U.K.: Sclora Press, 1993.

Fury, David. *Kings of the Jungle: An Illustrated Reference to Tarzan on Screen and Television*. Jefferson, NC: McFarland, 1994.

Garson, Barbara. *All the Livelong Day: The Meaning and Demeaning of Routine Work*. New York: Penguin, 1980.

Gassmann, A. L. *Zur Tonpsychologie des Schweizer Volksliedes* (Regarding the Psychology of Sound among Swiss Folksongs). Zurich, 1936.

Gavin, James. *Deep in a Dream: The Long Night of Chet Baker*. New York: Knopf, 2002.

Glanz, Christian, Gertraud Pressler, Ernst Weber, and Herbert Zotti. *Music from Austria, Vol. 3: Folk Music*. Vienna, Austria: Mica, 1999.

Godwin, Joscelyn, ed. *Music, Mysticism, and Magic*. New York: Arkana, 1986.

Goertzen, Chris, and Edward Larkey. "Austria." In Rice, Porter, and Goertzen, 1998, 670–81.

Grange, Louis de la. *Gustav Mahler: Vienna—Triumph and Disillusion*. Oxford, UK: Oxford University Press, 1999.

Green, Douglas B. *Singing in the Saddle: The History of the Singing Cowboy*. Nashville, TN: Country Music Foundation, 2002.

Grolier's Academic American Encyclopedia, Grolier, Internet, 1995.

Guralnick, Peter. *Lost Highway: Journeys and Arrivals of American Musicians*. New York: Penguin, 1992.

Henetek, Ûrsula. *Echoes of Diversity*. Vienna: Bölau Verlag, 1996.

Hesse, Herman. *Peter Camenzind*. New York: Farrar, Strauss & Giroux, 1973. (London: Peter Owen/Vision Press, 1961, 1st English edition).

Hoffman, Johanna, and Silvia Delorenzi-Schenkel. "Switzerland." In Rice, Porter, and Goertzen, 1998, 682–700.

Hoffmannsthal, Hugo von. *Arabella*. London: Boosey & Hawkes, n.d.

Holm-Hudson, Kevin, ed. *Progressive Rock Reconsidered*. New York: Routledge, 2002.

Honan, Mark. *Switzerland*. Victoria, Australia: Lonely Planet, 2000.

Hopkins, Anthony. *The Nine Symphonies of Beethoven*. Aldershot, U.K.: Scolar Press, 1996.

Hopkins, Pandora. "Norway." In Rice, Porter, and Goertzen, 1998, 411–33.

Hopkins Porter, Cecilia. *The Rhine as Musical Metaphor: Cultural Identity in German Romantic Music*. Boston: Northeastern University Press, 1996.

Horton, John. *Scandinavian Music: A Short History*. New York: Norton, 1963.

Hutchinson, J. J., G. G. Clark, E. M. Jope, and R. Riley, eds. *The Early History of Agriculture*. Oxford, U.K.: Oxford University Press, 1975.

Jarrett, Michael. *Soundtracks: A Musical ABC*. Philadelphia: Temple University Press, 1998.

Johnson, Anna. "Voice Physiology and Ethnomusicology: Physiological and Acoustical Studies of the Swedish Herding Song." In *Yearbook of Traditional Music, vol. 16*. New York: UNESCO and Columbia University, 1984.

Jordan, Terry, and Matti Kaups. *The American Backwoods Frontier: An Ethnic and Ecological Interpretation*. Baltimore: Johns Hopkins University Press, 1989.

Jordania, Joseph. "North Caucasia." In Rice, Porter, and Goertzen, 1998, 850–66.

Kaemmer, John E. "Music of the Shona of Zimbabwe." In Stone, 1998, 744–58.

Kaeppler, Adrienne, and J. W. Love, eds. *The Garland Encyclopedia of World Music: Australia and the Pacific Islands*. New York: Garland, 1998.

Kartomi, Margaret J., and Stephen Blum, eds. *Music-Cultures in Contact: Convergences and Collisions*. London: Gordon and Breach, 1994.

Kebede, Ashenafi. *Roots of Black Music: The Vocal, Instrumental, and Dance Heritage of Africa and Black America*. Trenton, NJ: Africa World Press, 1995.

Kent, Susan, ed. *Cultural Diversity among 20th Century Foragers*. Cambridge, U.K.: Cambridge University Press, 1996.

Kerouac, Jack. *Dharma Bums*. New York: Penguin, 1991 (reissue).

Kiehl, Ernst, et al. *Auf den Spuren der Musikalischhen Volkskultur im Harz*. Munich: Bezirk Oberbayern, 2002.

Kingsbury, Paul, and Alan Axelrod, eds. *Country: The Music and the Musicians*. New York: Country Music Foundation/Abbeville Press, 1988.

Kisliuk, Michelle. "Musical Life in the Central African Republic." In Stone, 1998, pp. 681–98.

Koch, H. W. *The Hitler Youth: Origins and Development*. London: MacDonald & Jane's, 1975.

Koerner, Lisbet. *Linnaeus: Nature and Nation*. Cambridge, MA: Harvard University Press, 1999.

Kolinsky, Eva, and Wilfried van der Will, eds. *The Cambridge Companion to Modern German Culture*. Cambridge, U.K.: Cambridge University Press, 1998.

Korson, George, ed. *Introduction to Pennsylvania Songs and Legends*. Philadelphia: University of Pennsylvania Press, 1949.

Koskoff, Ellen. "Gender." In Rice, Porter, and Goertzen, 1998, 191–203.

——— (ed.). *The Garland Encyclopedia of World Music: The United States and Canada*. New York: Garland, 2001.

Koster, Rick. *Texas Music*. New York: St. Martin's Press, 1998.

Kotek, Georg. *Volkslieder und Jodler aus der Waldheimat: für gemischten Chor gesetzt von Hans Täubl*. Graz, Austria: Doblinger, 1987.

Kubik, Gerhard. "Intra-African Streams of Influence." In Stone, 1998, 293–326.

Kunst, Jaap. *A Study of Papuan Music*. New York: AMS Press, 1931.

———. *Indonesian Music and Dance*. Amsterdam: Royal Tropical Institute, 1994.

Labelle, Brandon, and Christof Migone, eds. *Writing Aloud: The Sonics of Language*. Los Angeles: Errant Bodies, 2001.

Landeck, Beatrice. *Echoes of Africa*. New York: McKay, 1969.

Leary, James P. *Yodeling in Dairyland: A History of Swiss Music in Wisconsin*. Mount Horeb, WI: Wisconsin Folk Museum, 1991.

Leuthold, Heinrich. In *Volksmusik in der Schweiz*. edited by Mario Müller. Zurich: Ringier, 1985.

Leuthold, Heinrich J. *Der Naturjodel in der Schweiz*. Altdorf, Switzerland: Robert-Fellmann-Liederverlag, 1981.

Lindstrom, Lamont. "Vanuta: Southern Area." In Kaeppler and Love, 1998, 702–709.

Love, J. W. "Timbre." In Kaeppler and Love, 1998, 296–97.

Luchner-Löscher, Claudia. *Der Jodler: Wesen, Entstehung, Verbreitung und Gestalt*. München-Salzburg: Musikverlag Emil Katzbichler, 1982.

Lucretius. *On the Nature of Things*. Book V. Translated by H.A.J. Munro. New York: Random House, 1940.

McCue, George, ed. *Music in American Society 1776–1976*. New Brunswick, NJ: Transaction Books, 1997.

McNeil, W. K. *Traditional Songs from the Appalachians and the Ozarks*. Little Rock, AR: August House, 1993.

Maconie, Robin. *The Science of Music*. Oxford, U.K.: Oxford University Press, 1997.

Mallet, Robert. *Les Signes de l'Addition*. Quoted in Bachelard, Gaston. *The Poetics of Reverie*. Boston: Beacon Press, 1969, 156.

Malone, Bill. *Country Music U.S.A.* Austin: University of Texas Press, 1988.

———. *Singing Cowboys and Musical Mountaineers*. Athens: University of Georgia Press, 1993.

Manuel, Peter. *Cassette Culture: Popular Music and Technology in North India*. New York: Oxford University Press, 2001.

———. *Popular Music of the Non-Western World*. New York: Oxford University Press, 1990.

Marek, George. *Beethoven: Biography of a Genius*, New York: Funk & Wagnalls, 1969.

Mellers, Wilfrid. *Music in a New Found Land*. London: Faber & Faber, 1978.

Melly, George. *Revolt into Style*. London: Penguin, 1970.

Merriam, Alan. *The Anthropology of Music*. Bloomington, IL: Northwestern University Press, 1964.

Miles, Emma. B. *Spirit of the Mountains* (1905). Knoxville: University of Tennessee Press, 1975.

Miller, Terry E. and Sean Williams, "Culture, Politics, and War." In Miller and Williams, eds. *The Garland Encyclopedia of World Music: Southeast Asia*. New York/London: Garland, 1998, 87–94.

Moravetz, Bruno, ed. *The Big Book of Mountaineering*. Woodbury, New York: Barron's Educational Series, 1980.

Morris, Desmond. *The Illustrated Naked Ape*. London: Jonathan Cape, 1986.

Myers, Helen, ed. *Ethnomusicology: Historical and Regional Studies*. London: MacMillan, 1993.

Nettl, Bruno, et al., eds. *Excursions in World Music*. Englewood Cliffs, NJ: Prentice-Hall, 1992.

Oakley, Giles. *The Devil's Music: A History of the Blues*. London: BBC, 1976.

Oliver, Paul. "Yonder Come the Blues" in *Yonder Come the Blues*. Cambridge, U.K.: Cambridge University Press, 2001 [1970].

Olmstead, Frederick Law. *The Slave States*. Edited by Harvey Wish. New York: Capricorn Books, 1959 [1856].

Olsen, Dale, and Daniel Sheeley, eds. *The Garland Encyclopedia of World Music: South America, Mexico, Central America, and the Caribbean*. New York: Garland, 1998.

Parrish, Lydia. *Slave Songs of the Georgia Sea Islands*. Athens: University of Georgia Press, 1992.

Parsons, William. *The Pennsylvania Dutch: A Persistent Minority*. Boston: Twayne, 1976.

Paytner, J., et al., eds. *Companion to Contemporary Music*. London: Routledge, 1992.

Peterson, Richard. *Creating Country Music: Fabricating Authenticity*. Chicago: University of Chicago Press, 1997.

Peterson, Roger. *A Field Guide to the Birds East of the Rockies*. Boston: Houghton Mifflin, 1980.

Porterfield, Nolan. *Jimmie Rodgers: The Life and Times of America's Blue Yodeler*. Urbana: University of Illinois Press, 1979.

Potter, Pamela. *Most German of the Arts*. New Haven, CT: Yale University Press, 1998.

Pugh, Ronnie. *Ernest Tubb: The Texas Troubadour*. Durham, NC: Duke University Press, 1996.

Pugh-Kitingan, Jacqueline. "Huli." In Kaeppler and Love, 1998, 536–43.

———. "Huli Yodeling." In Kaeppler and Love 1998, 298–99.

Random House Webster's College Dictionary. New York: Random House, 1995.

Ransten, Marta. "Folk Music." In Lena Roth, ed. *Musical Life in Sweden*. Stockholm: Swedish Institute, 1987.

Reese, Gustave. *Music in the Middle Ages*. New York: Norton, 1940.

Rhaw, Georg. *Bicinia gallica, latina germanica* (1545). Wihelmshaven, Germany: Heinrichshofen's Verlag, 1968.

Rice, Timothy. "Traditional Performance Contexts." In Rice, Porter, and Goertzen, 1998, 139–48.

Rice, Timothy, James Porter, and Chris Goertzen, eds. *The Garland Encyclopedia of World Music: Europe*. New York: Garland, 1998.

Richard Strauss: Ein Alpen Symfonie. Introduction by Adolf Alber. Munich: Verlag von F.E.C. Leudkart, n.d.

Rolland, Romain. *Beethoven*. London: Kegan Paul, 1918.

Rose, Cynthia. *Living in America: The Soul Saga of James Brown*. London: Serpent's Tail, 1990.

Rozelle, Robert V., et al., eds. *Black Art Ancestral Legacy: The African Impulse in African-American Art*. New York: Harry N. Abrams, 1989.

Russell, Tony. "Black, Whites and Blues." In *Yonder Come the Blues*. Cambridge, U.K.: Cambridge University Press, 2001 [1970].

Sachs, Curt. *The Wellsprings of Music*. The Hague: Martijnus Nijhoff, 1962.

Sadie, Stanley, and John Tyrell, eds. *The New Grove Dictionary of Music and Musicians*, 2d ed. London: MacMillan, 1995.

Schauffler, Robert. *Beethoven: The Man Who Freed Music*. New York: Doubleday, 1937.

Schepping, Willhelm. "Germany." In Rice, Porter, and Goertzen 1998, 682–700.

Schiller, Friedrich von. *Wilhelm Tell*. Project Gutenberg-Etext, Internet, 2003.

Schroeder, Adolf. "German Americans." In *American Folklore: An Encyclopedia*. Jan Harold Brunvand, ed. New York: Garland, 1996.

Sichardt, Wolfgang. *Der Alpenländische Jodler und der Ursprung des Jodelns*. Berlin: Bernard Hahnefeld Verlag, 1939.

Spyri, Johanna. *Heidi*. New York: Moby Books, 1976. (Boston: Cupples, Upham & Co., 1885. first U.S. ed.).

Stillman, Amy K. "Hawaii" in *Garland Encyclopedia of World Music: Australia and The Pacific Islands*. New York: Garland, 1998.

Stone, Ruth H. ed. *Garland Encyclopedia of World Music: Africa*. New York: Garland, 1998.

Talbot, Daniel, ed. *A Treasury of Mountaineering Stories*. London: Peter Davies, 1955.

Tatar, Elizabeth. *Nineteenth Century Hawaiian Chant*. Honolulu: Bernice P. Bishop Museum, 1982.

Taylor, Timothy. *Strange Sounds: Music, Technology and Culture*. New York: Routledge, 2001.

Thoreau, Henry David. *Journal vol. 4*. Boston: Houghton-Mifflin, 1906.

Toop, David. *Ocean of Sound: Aether Talk, Ambient Sound and Imaginary Worlds.* London: Serpent's Tail, 1996.

Tosches, Nick. *Country: The Twisted Roots of Rock 'n' Roll.* New York: Da Capo Press, 1996 (1977).

———. *Where Dead Voices Gather.* Boston: Little, Brown and Company, 2001.

Townsend, Charles R. *San Antonio Rose: The Life and Music of Bob Wills.* Urbana: University of Illinois Press, 1976.

Toye, Francis. *Rossini: A Study in Tragi-Comedy.* New York: Alfred A. Knopf, 1934.

Tunger, Albrecht. "Erst Seine Triller Hersprudeln: Auf den Spuren des Appenzellischen Kureihengesangs." No other information.

Turnbull, Colin. *Wayward Servants: The Two Worlds of the African Pygmies.* London: Eyre & Spottiswood, 1965.

Twain, Mark. *A Tramp Abroad.* New York: Hippocrene Books, 1982. (Hartford, CT: American Publishing Co., 1906 first edition).

Vale, V. and Andrea Juno, eds. *Incredibly Strange Music vol. II.* Re/Search, 1994.

Wallin, Nils. *Biomusicology.* Stuyvesant, New York: Pendragon Press, 1991.

Webb, Michael. "Popular Music: Papua New Guinea." In Kaeppler and Love, 1998, 146–55.

Wild, Stephen A. "The Music of Australia." In Kaeppler and Love 1998, 408–15.

Witzig, Louise. *Dances of Switzerland.* London: Max Parrish & Co., 1949.

Work Projects Administration. *Pennsylvania: A Guide to the Keystone State.* Compiled by Workers of the Writers' Program. New York: Oxford University Press, 1940.

Articles / Internet / Liner Notes / Theses / Other

A Cappella Online <http://www.singers.com/>.

Appenzellerland Tourismus <www.appenzell.ch>.

Baumann, Max-Peter, *The New Grove Dictionary of Music and Musicians*, Internet entry: <http://yas.cc.columbia.edu:2176/data/articles/music/5/525/.xml?section=music.5255.1>

Berman, Louis. "What It Was Like before Ozma," in *Cosmic Search* vol. 1 no. 4, <http://bigear.org/vol1no4/ozma.htm>.

Boulton, Laura. *Songs and Dances of Switzerland,* liner notes. Washington, DC: Folkways, 1953.

Brown, Oren. *Journal of Singing,* 53, no. 2: 25–26. Nov.–Dec., 1996.

Cairns, David. "The Symphony as Drama," liner notes to *Rèvolutionnaire et Romantique*, Philips, 1993.

Campagnoli, Mauro.<info@maurocampognoli.com>.

Canby, Peter. "The Forest Primeval." *Harper's Magazine,* July 2002: 41–56.

Clarke, Donald. *The Rise and Fall of Popular Music,* Chapter One: The Origins of Popular Music, Internet.

Commanday, Robert. "Caballe Spins Out Her Own Special Evening of Song," *San Francisco Chronicle*, October 12, 1987, n.p.

———. *San Francisco Chronicle*, March 2, 1992, n.p.

Corey, Elena. "Yodel-AA-EE-EEE." *Bluegrass Breakdown*, August 1998.

Cutler, Chris. "A History of Plunderphonics." Internet.

Davis, Erik. "Roots & Wires." *Fringecore* 2 (Dec. 1997): 14.

Dixon, Gail. November 2001. <www.worldchristians.org>.

Dorham, Kenny. "Fragments of an Autobiography." *Down Beat Music '70*, 1970.

Dylan, Bob. *The Songs of Jimmie Roders*, Egyptian Records, 1997. Liner Notes.

Dyson, Frances. "Circuits of the Voice: From Cosmology to Telephony." Internet.

Elsen, Herma van den. "The Sound of Music: Een Tekstuele Analyse Volgens het Model van Raymond Bellour." Doctoral Thesis, Kunst Universiteit at Nijmegen, 1988.

Emanuel, Leonard. *Hollerin'*, recorded in Spivey, North Carolina, in the 1970s, Rounder Records. Vocal introduction.

Encyclopedia.com <www.encyclopedia.com>.

Ephrata Cloister. <www.phmc.state.pa.us>.

Euaawll, Tony. "Hank Snow Country music tales of trains and travel," Manchester, U.K.: *The Guardian*, December 22, 1999, pp. 1 and 18.

Fuqua, Sam. "Musica Mundi." A weekly music show on KGNU in Boulder, Colorado.

Fink, Cathy. *Grandma Slid Down The Mountain*. Rounder 8010, 1984.

Flippo, Chet. "Ralph Emery Pays Tribute to Ray Charles in New Book." *Billboard*. November 14, 1998.

Gollner, Adam. "Yesterday's Tomorrow" Internet.

Grundy, Ray. Interview with Frank Ifield, February 1, 2002, Internet.

Haymes, Max. "The Birds and the Blues." Internet.

Hazell, Paul. "Kenny Roberts: An Englishman's Perspective." Internet.

Hernandez, Deborah Pacini. "Bachat: From the Margins of the Mainstream." *Popular Music*, 11, no. 3, 1992, n.p.

Historical Committee of the Mennonite Church.

Horst, Ian Scott, <http://members.aol.com/ishort/ian.html>.

Ibold, Hans. "Was Ist Das Jodeln," *Inside*, 1, no. 4, 1998, n.p.

König, Helmut. "Der Zupfgeigenhansl und seine Nachfolger." April 2002 conference notes of *100 Jahre Wandervogel*. published in Kopchen, Dorweiler: Burg Waldeck, Germany <www.burg-waldeck.de>.

Lazarus, Damian. Interview with Leon Thomas. *Straight No Chaser*, no. 33, Autumn 1995.

Leukerbad Feel It <www.leukerbad.ch>, tourism site.

Lewis, Alan. New England Music Scrapbook News. <www.geocities.com.nemsnewz.news.0015.htm>

Lilly, John. "Jimmie Rodgers." *The Old-Time Herald*. Spring 1992, n.p.

Los Angeles Times. "Yodeler Drops Lawsuit Against Yahoo." vol. 122, no. 20, August 23, 2002. Internet.

Lomax, Alan, *Black Texians*, liner notes. Washington, DC: Folkways, 1998.

———. *Italian Treasury: Folk Music & Song of Italy* (1953), back cover notes. Rounder, 1999.

Lucas, Eric. "Yodel-Ay-Hee-Who?" in *Alaska Airlines Magazine*. October 2001, n.p.

Mackey, Nathaniel. "Sun Poem by Edward Kamau Brathwaite" (book review). *Sulfur*, 4, no. 2, Fall 1984: 205.

Moses, Wayne. "Bacoo with Bananas." Internet.

Moten, Fred. "Voice/Forces," in Labelle, Brandon, and Christof Migone, eds. *Writing Aloud*: The Sonics of Language, Los Angeles: Errant Bodies, 2001.

Musica Helvetica: *Swiss Folk Music: Yodeling*, programme no. 7, 1975. Production/narration: Lance Tschannen and Nicolas Lombard.

The Music of Sound. <http://whyfiles.org/114music/3.html>.

Musik und Volk. Berlin: Georg Kollmeyer Verlag, 1930s.

Nash, James. *Houston Chronicle*. May 17, 1998. n.p.

Ol' Boppin' Styles. <http://wildcat53.tripod.com>.

Reichmann, Ruth. Max Kade German-American Center at Indiana University. 2002 email.

Reynolds, Simon. "The New Ambient: Muzak of the Fears." *Art Forum,* January 1995: 62.

Roberts, David. *Folk Music of the Magic Salzburg Mountains: The Original Wolfgangseer Musikanten*, liner notes. New York: CMS Records, 1978.

Rucker, James. "Robert Johnson and the Roots of the Delta Blues." Internet, 1999.

Sallée, Pierre. *Gabon: Musique des Pygmées Bibayak*, liner notes. OCORA, 1984.

Sami culture website: <www.sametinget.se>.

Seiler, Christian. "Spiel mir den Blues vom Muotathal," in *Die Weltwoche*, no. 31 August 5, 1993, n.p.

Shoumatoff, Alex. "Reporter at Large: The Ituri Forest." *The New Yorker*. February 6, 1984. n.p.

Schweizer Annalen. April 1936.

Smith, Graeme. "Australian Country Music and the Hillbilly Yodel." *Popular Music* 13, no. 3: 297–311.

Thompson, Chad L. "Yodeling of the Indiana Swiss Amish," *Anthropological Linguistics* 38, no. 3 (Fall 1996), n.p.

Toelken, Barre in *Jahrbuch für Volksliedforschung*, Brednich, Rolf, and Jürgan Dittonar eds., Berlin: Erish Schmidt Verlag, 1982.

Vaughn, Michael. "Riders in the Sky Keep a Singing Cowboy Tradition Alive," *MetroActive Music*. March 28, 1996, <www.metroactive.com>.

de Volkskrant. "Congolese Rebels are Eating Pygmies," January 9, 2003, 5a.

Wagner, Christoph. "T for Tyrol." *Folk Roots* 179 (vol. 19, no. 11) May, 1998.

———. "Yodeling in America." *American Yodeling: 1911–1946*, liner notes. Munich: Trikont, 1998.

Webeling, Pieter. *De Volkskrant Magazine*, 2002, 8.

Wheat, John. The Texas State Historical Association, 1997–2002. <comments.tsha@lib.utexas.edu>.

White, Shane, and Graham White. "Hearing Slavery: Recovering the Role of Sound in African American Slave Culture." *Commonplace* 1, no. 4, July 2001, n.p.

Wortham, Anne. "Behind the Walls of Segregation: Playing Cowboys." *The World & I*, 14, no. 11, n.d. 306–321.

Zemp, Hugo. *Switzerland: Zäurli, Yodel of Appenzell*, Auvidis-UNESCO, 1979, liner notes.

Index

[**bold** indicates profile or focus, *italic* indicates illustration]